Cultural Theory

Cultural Theory

An Introduction

Second Edition

Philip Smith and Alexander Riley

Blackwell
Publishing

BLACKWELL PUBLISHING
350 Main Street, Malden, MA 02148-5020, USA
9600 Garsington Road, Oxford OX4 2DQ, UK

First published 2001
Second edition published 2009 by Blackwell Publishing Ltd

1   2009

Library of Congress Cataloging-in-Publication Data

Smith, Philip (Philip Daniel), 1964–
Cultural theory : an introduction / Philip Smith and Alexander Riley. – 2nd ed.
p.   cm.
Includes bibliographical references and index.
ISBN 978-1-4051-6908-0 (hardcover : alk. paper) – ISBN 978-1-4051-6907-3 (pbk. : alk. paper)
1. Culture.   I. Riley, Alexander.   II. Title.

HM621.S57 2009
306.01–dc22
2007052261

A catalogue record for this title is available from the British Library.

Set in 10 on 12.5 pt Photina
by SNP Best-set Typesetter Ltd., Hong Kong
Printed and bound in Singapore
by Fabulous Printers Pte Ltd

For further information on
Blackwell Publishing, visit our website at
www.blackwellpublishing.com

Contents

Preface to the First Edition: About this Book   vi
Preface to the Second Edition   ix
Acknowledgments   x

Introduction: What is Culture? What is Cultural Theory?   1
1   Culture in Classical Social Theory   6
2   Culture and Social Integration in the Work of Talcott Parsons   26
3   Culture as Ideology in Western Marxism   34
4   Culture as Action in Symbolic Interactionism, Phenomenology, and
        Ethnomethodology   54
5   The Durkheimians: Ritual, Classification, and the Sacred   69
6   Structuralism and the Semiotic Analysis of Culture   92
7   The Poststructural Turn   111
8   Culture, Structure, and Agency: Three Attempts at Synthesis   128
9   British Cultural Studies   144
10 The Production and Reception of Culture   158
11 Culture as Text: Narrative and Hermeneutics   176
12 Psychoanalytic Approaches to Culture and the Self   195
13 The Cultural Analysis of Postmodernism and Postmodernity   207
14 Postmodern and Poststructural Critical Theory   228
15 Cultural Theories of Race and Gender   241
16 The Body in Cultural Theory   262

References   280
Index   296

Preface to the First Edition: About this Book

As we enter a new millennium, "culture" seems to be one of the things that everybody is talking about, both within and outside of the academy. It is widely held that that we are living in a world where signs, symbols, and the media are becoming central to the economy, that our identities are increasingly structured by the pursuit of an image, and that inequality and civic participation are defined by discourses of inclusion and exclusion. Anecdotal evidence would seem to support this view. The trial of O. J. Simpson, for example, was not just a judicial event, but also a cultural one where symbolism, narrative, and belief intersected with race politics. Conflict in the Balkans during the 1990s and afterward was driven by deeply-seated nationalisms, each grounded in complex historical memories. The growing power of corporations like Sony and Nike is linked to the iconography and mythology surrounding their products as well as to their functional efficiency. Today the political challenges raised by feminists, gay/lesbian activists, indigenous peoples, and racial minorities are as much about identity and cultural recognition as about economic inequality and legal rights. If we reflect on our own everyday lives, we will find that here too, culture is ubiquitous. It shapes our purchasing decisions in the mall, the television programs we choose to watch (and how we watch them), our responses to global events, our face-to-face interactions with other people, and even our sense of who we are.

In such a context the ability to understand culture becomes a vital component of competent and active citizenship. Cultural theory provides one important resource for this task. It offers paradigms, models, and concepts that can be applied in the diverse settings that we encounter in our personal, public, and intellectual lives. It is not merely an arcane academic literature, but rather a resource through which we can reflect intelligently on the world around us and, perhaps, make informed choices and assume a greater level of control. This book provides a brief introduction to the field. It is, of course, already possible to find many works on library and bookstore shelves introduction *social* theory. Yet these tend to marginalize *cultural* theory, allocating it little room and discussing key theorists from a point of view that is not directly relevant to those working in the cultural field. Such texts are typically concerned with other issues, such as divergent models of class or the state, distinctions between various network theories, and so on. These themes are not usually of central interest to those exploring meaning as a component of human experience. There are also books about specific cultural theories, theorists or theoretical issues – postmodernism, Marxism, Foucault, and so on. These tend to be narrow in focus and to assume specialized knowledge. Often the author will have an axe to grind, leading to a one-sided commentary on issues and debates.

This book is different. It provides what I hope will be seen as a balanced and wide-ranging introduction and overview of contemporary cultural theory. It assumes no specialist knowledge whatsoever, but at the same time will deal with some of the most sophisticated and complex issues in contemporary social thought. The book will be of primary interest to those working in sociology, and of substantial use to students in the fields of anthropology and cultural studies. It will also contain material relevant to cultural geography, urban studies, and history. In short, anybody with a stake in undertaking the theoretically informed investigation of culture and society will find this book a worthwhile resource.

As there is a lot of ground to cover the book moves very quickly. The style is direct rather than discursive. The intention is to provide the maximum amount of essential information and the greatest number of conceptual tools in the minimum amount of space. With an aim to helping readers acquire a basic familiarity with the area, the book contains a number of features.

- Priority has been given to introducing major thinkers, perspectives, and concepts. Many key terms are highlighted in **bold** when they are first introduced. These will build up the reader's theoretical vocabulary. There is an emphasis on scholars and themes that everybody working in the area knows and talks about, regardless of their own personal research orientation. In many cases original publication dates and titles of classic books are also included in the text, as well as standard bibliographic information. This will help readers understand the chronology of the field. In some cases, however, I have referred to studies that are representative rather than definitive. This is particularly the case when giving a feel for the kind of work that goes on in a given field where there are no dominant figures or foundational texts (e.g., chapter 10). I have also mentioned some of my own research in one or two places. This is not because I consider myself a leading thinker worthy of extended discussion, but rather to give the reader an idea of my interests and, by implication, biases. One of the lessons we have learnt from poststructuralism is that a neutral, omniscient text is an impossibility. Hence my intention is to offer food for readerly reflexivity about possible limitations of this book.
- Material is organized according to theoretical traditions rather than empirical topics. In this way the conceptual connections and lines of influence between diverse scholars can be highlighted. Using this perspective, more contemporary research can be understood as the product of an intellectual lineage.
- As can be seen in the material you are now reading, bullet points are used from time to time to condense certain bodies of information down to essentials, summarize main points, and cut out laborious digressions.
- Throughout the book critical comments and evaluations will enable the reader to consider the limitations of each theory and provide balance.

- Notes on selected major scholars help provide a broader biographical, intellectual, and geographical context for understanding the theories discussed in the body of the text.
- Suggestions for further reading are provided which will help direct those with an interest in any particular area. Where possible, original texts have been suggested to encourage immediate reader familiarity with the style and thinking of leading figures.
- Chapters in the book are self-contained, each dealing with a theoretical perspective or field. The book has been written so it can be read in any order. Cross-referencing assists in this task. This will allow it to be instantly adapted to any course of study or research need.
- Where possible, emphasis has been given to theories and theorists that are influencing current debates and inquiry. I have tried to avoid lengthy discussions of figures who are today, for the most part, only of historical or scholastic interest (e.g., Comte, Spencer, Ruskin). By contrast, greater attention has been accorded to concepts and thinkers which seem to crop up time and time again in contemporary publications, theses, and project work.

Philip Smith
Brisbane, Australia, 2001

Preface to the Second Edition

The first edition of this book received considerable critical and popular acclaim. Known as "the magic book" in some student circles because of the clarity and breadth of its coverage of a sometimes difficult and wide-ranging field, it has been translated into several languages and used for reference and teaching by scholars around the globe. This is a gratifying result.

In this fully revised and expanded second edition, we have aimed for the same delicate balance of accessibility and sophistication. It will be up to our readers to decide whether or not we have attained this objective. Eight years have passed since the publication of the first edition. The field of cultural theory has continued to grow and change during that time, the stock of specific thinkers and theories has risen or fallen, new conceptual terms and arguments have emerged. In addition to attending to these shifts in the field, we have listened closely to the readers of the first edition and added sections and chapters on a number of themes and topics that they suggested were important in such a volume.

The most obvious of the changes are the two entirely new chapters at the end of the book. The two fields of cultural theory treated in those chapters (race and gender in chapter 15 and the body in chapter 16) have been the intellectual equivalent of growth stocks in recent years, with much creative work being produced and audiences both scholarly and popular expanding rapidly. Other new material focuses on late nineteenth- or early twentieth-century cultural theorists whose importance to the field has recently become more widely recognized and whose ideas help shed light on more recent theoretical developments – e.g., Friedrich Nietzsche and W. E. B. DuBois. Contemporary thinkers working in or close to traditions discussed in the first edition whose influence has risen in the new millennium have been added to the relevant chapters – e.g., Roy Bhaskar in chapter 3, Randall Collins in chapter 5, and Manuel Castells in chapter 13. Finally, many of our revisions are devoted to discussion of themes and concepts that were present at the time of the first edition but which have grown considerably in their importance in the field – e.g., computer-mediated communication and virtual reality, cosmopolitanism and globalization, narrative and performance theory.

Although a good deal of the material here is new, the overall framework outlined in the preface to the first edition remains unchanged.

Philip Smith, New Haven, USA
Alexander Riley, Lewisburg, USA
2008

Acknowledgments

We deeply thank the editorial team at Blackwell, and especially Justin Vaughan, for supporting the new edition with such enthusiasm. Sarah Dancy moved the project through the production stage with efficiency and expertise. Smith's Yale colleagues Jeffrey Alexander and Ron Eyerman and the graduate students in the Center for Cultural Sociology provided a constant stimulus in thinking about culture. Riley's Bucknell undergraduates road-tested the first edition as well as some of the new material in this second edition and gave the book a collective "thumbs up." Thanks are due also to our many scholarly colleagues around the world who have provided feedback on the book and to the team of anonymous reviewers who examined our prospectus for the revised volume. The broader communities of scholars and cultural theorists in the ASA Culture Section and elsewhere, with whom we have interacted over the years, certainly have earned a mention in this section as well. A tip of the virtual hat goes to "daughterofdadust," the amazon.com user who gave the original edition of the book a five-star rating. Finally, a special note of thanks is reserved for our families, Philippa Smith and Esmeralda and Valeria Riley, for all their support and understanding.

We dedicate this second edition to four towering and unique figures in cultural theory who have passed away since the first edition was published, in recognition of their contributions to the field: Jean Baudrillard, Pierre Bourdieu, Mary Douglas, and Clifford Geertz.

Introduction: What is Culture?
What is Cultural Theory?

At the start of any text it can be useful to define the central concept. In the case of "culture" this has proven to be surprisingly, even notoriously, difficult. According to one expert, Raymond Williams, "culture is one of the two or three most complicated words in the English language . . . because it has now come to be used for important concepts in several distinct intellectual disciplines and in several distinct systems of thought" (1976: 76–7). An illustration of this diversity is the fact that, writing way back in the 1950s, Alfred Kroeber and Clyde Kluckhohn (1952) were already able to assemble an astonishing number of definitions of culture from popular and academic sources. We begin, then, with a brief but necessary examination of some of the history of this complicated concept in order to move toward a usable definition for this book.

In its early uses in English, culture was associated with the "cultivation" of animals and crops and with religious worship (hence the word "cult"). From the sixteenth century until the nineteenth, the term began to be widely applied to the improvement of the individual human mind and personal manners through learning. This was a metaphorical extension of the idea of improving land and farming practices. For this reason we can still speak of someone as being "cultured" or, if they are uncouth, as "having no culture." During this period, the term began to refer also to the improvement of society as a whole, with culture being used as a value-laden synonym for "civilization." A typical usage of the time might compare the nations of Europe that had "culture" with the "barbarism" of Africa. Such an expression would have included technological differences as well as those of morals and manners. However, with the rise of Romanticism in the Industrial Revolution, culture began to be used to designate spiritual development alone and to contrast this with material and infrastructural change. Along with Romantic nationalism in the late nineteenth century, there came inflections which accented tradition and everyday life as dimensions of culture. These were captured in the ideas of "folk culture" and "national culture" which emerged around this time.

According to Williams (1976: 80), these various historical shifts are dimly reflected in the three current uses of the term "culture":

- to refer to the intellectual, spiritual, and aesthetic development of an individual, group, or society;
- to capture a range of intellectual and artistic activities and their products – film, art, theatre (in this usage culture is more or less synonymous with "the Arts," hence we can speak of a "Minister for Culture");
- to designate the entire way of life, activities, beliefs, and customs of a people, group, or society.

Until very recently, the first and second of these uses were the most common, and were often synthesized in intellectual work. Aesthetes and literary critics like Matthew Arnold, John Ruskin, and F. R. Leavis used the term to refer to works of high art which could educate, edify, and improve those who came into contact with them. Arnold, for example, wrote that culture was "a pursuit of total perfection by means of getting to know . . . the best which has been thought and said in the world . . . culture is, or ought to be, the study or pursuit of perfection . . . sweetness and light . . . an inward condition of mind and spirit" (quoted in Kroeber and Kluckhohn 1952: 29). The German concept of **Kultur** also taps into this theme by broadly equating culture with civilization and with individual or collective moral progress. Such uses are often highly value-laden and elitist, seeking to validate artistic products that experts and dominant social groups consider as important or interesting.

The third usage of culture was championed by many anthropologists in the first part of the century and remains central to that discipline today. It is an interpretation that is more value-neutral and analytic. It asserts that "culture" is to be found everywhere and not just in the high arts or in Western "civilization." It is of course this third usage of the term with which we are working in the contemporary social sciences. Yet even delimiting the concept in this way allows for a fairly wide range of social scientific definitions. Insofar as it is possible to isolate a core usage for the social sciences today, it revolves around the following themes:

- *Culture tends to be opposed to the material, technological, and social structural.* While it is recognized there may be complex empirical relations between them, it is also argued that we need to understand culture as something distinctive from, and more abstract than, an entire "way of life."
- *Culture is seen as the realm of the ideal, the spiritual, and the non-material.* It is understood as a patterned sphere of beliefs, values, symbols, signs, and discourses.
- *Culture is recognized as having a powerful and complex relationship to practices and performances as well.* Much cultural study today is engaged in exploring the influence of cultural codes, narratives, and discourses on the specific activities of groups and individuals.
- *Emphasis is placed on the "autonomy of culture."* This is the fact that it cannot be explained away as a mere reflection of underlying economic forces, distributions of power, or social structural needs.
- *Efforts are made to remain value-neutral.* The study of culture is not restricted to the Arts, but rather is understood to pervade all aspects and levels of social life. Ideas of

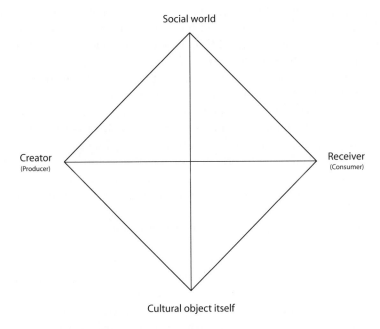

Adapted from Griswold 2003:17

Figure 0.1   Wendy Griswold's cultural diamond

cultural superiority and inferiority play almost no place in contemporary academic study.

Looking back at Williams's discussion, this prevailing understanding combines the anti-elitism, value-neutrality, and relativism of the anthropological approach to culture, with perspectives on culture as the non-material that are derived from nineteenth-century idealist and Romantic philosophy. It can also be seen as an emergent product of developments in cultural theory itself, especially the work of Parsons and subsequent innovations from structuralism, poststructuralism, and hermeneutics (we come to these later on in this text), which emphasized the autonomy of culture from other aspects of social life. Broadly speaking, the theories of culture dealt with in this book can be fit into one of two categories: (1) those that see culture as something produced by society in various ways, and (2) those that see culture as an autonomous force steering society. The trend in cultural theory seems to point in the direction of the second of these options, but debates between the two perspectives remain vivid and important and we do our best to attend to that fact throughout the chapters that follow.

Navigation through the undeniable complexity of varying definitions and conceptual boundaries applied to the term "culture" is aided by the use of heuristic devices like Wendy Griswold's **cultural diamond** (see figure 0.1). This is a figure that attempts to lay out the four elements involved in the production and reception of any piece of culture (the cultural object itself, its creator/s, its receiver/s, and the social world/ context in which it comes into existence and takes meaning) and the six relations between these four elements (Griswold 2003). Though Griswold is clear that this "accounting device" does not specify the nature of those relationships, it does provide a helpful visual representation of the elements and relations the cultural analyst must account for in the effort to describe or explain the meaning of a particular cultural object, whether it be a GAP t-shirt, a national memorial, or a rap CD. We should note that while the cultural diamond is quite readily applicable to material cultural objects, its utility for examining non-material culture (e.g., a pattern of belief such as racism, or a diffuse societal ethos and worldview such as the "culture of democracy") is somewhat less clear. This is perhaps still more testimony to the complexity of the term and the difficulty involved in trying to find a single analytical lens through which to examine it.

"Theory" is a word that is perhaps as difficult to define as "culture." We can defer to the dictionary here and define theory as "[a] supposition or system of ideas explaining something, especially one based on general principles independent of facts" (Concise Oxford English Dictionary 1980: 1201). Theory, then, is more than a description of, or generalization about, the empirical world. Rather, it consists of abstract and systematically ordered understandings and models that can be used to account for what actually goes on in the world. "Cultural theory," the topic of this book, can be thought of as a literature aiming to develop such tools in a specific domain – explaining the nature of culture and its implications for social life. As we shall see, there is a broad and astonishingly diverse literature. Nevertheless, it is possible to identify three core issues that are absolutely pivotal to debates in the field and which provide an underlying thematic continuity:

1   *Content.* Theories provide tools for understanding the make-up of culture. As we shall see, divergent traditions have understood culture as values, codes, narratives, ideologies, pathologies, discourses, and common sense, as well as in many other ways. Each of these understandings has its own repercussions for interpreting the ways that culture works and how we should study it. One of the central themes to emerge in the examination of much of the theory examined in this book is a split between theories of culture as essentially a code or text and theories of culture as action or ways of doing.

2   *Social implications.* Here, theory is concerned with offering models of the influence that culture exerts on social structure and social life. Theorists attempt to explain the role of culture in providing stability, solidarity, and opportunity or in sustaining conflict, power, and inequality. Cultural theory also suggests divergent mechanisms through which this influence is channeled, ranging from individual-level socialization through to macro-level institutions and social systems.

3   *Action, agency, self.* The connection between culture and the individual is what is at stake here. The most critical issue concerns the ways in which culture shapes human action. Some thinkers stress the constraining nature of culture, while others point to its ability to enable action. Issues relating to the cultural construction of the self, motivation, and identity are fundamental to both sets of arguments.

Throughout this text, we will find these overlapping but analytically distinct themes taking a central role as theories are described and evaluated. Chapter 1 begins this exploration with a brief survey of the role of culture in what has come to be known as classical social theory.

CHAPTER ONE

Culture in Classical Social Theory

In a letter of 1675, the scientist Isaac Newton wrote: "If I have seen further it is by standing on the shoulders of giants." The point he was making was that his own contribution to knowledge would not have been possible without those of his intellectual predecessors. Likewise, contemporary cultural theory has been made possible by significant earlier work. Coming to an understanding of this foundation is therefore a step of great importance. While we could begin this process with a discussion of thinkers extending back through the Enlightenment and on to Ancient Greece, perhaps the most useful place to start is in the body of literature generally thought of as classical social theory. More particularly, we begin with the work of four founding figures in sociology, Marx, Durkheim, Weber, and Simmel, and two other thinkers from roughly the same period, Friedrich Nietzsche and W. E. B. DuBois. While these last two have not traditionally been classified among the founding figures in the emergence of the discipline of sociology, they nonetheless made contributions to the sociological study of culture that have been widely and increasingly recognized in the past few decades. Many current debates are shot through with foundational themes, problems, and perspectives that originate in the works of these six scholars. As thinkers with powerful minds, they provided a set of core concepts and tools that are still serviceable 100 years or more after they were developed. When they are not drawing directly upon them, current authors as likely as not are revising, refining, or critiquing lines of thinking that originated around a century or so ago. We forget history at our peril, and so knowledge of these resources provides an essential starting point and common ground for all cultural theorists.

Karl Marx

One of the greatest minds of the Victorian era, Karl Marx is generally thought of as an anticultural theorist. This is certainly the case when we focus on his **historical materialism**. Such a position is most clearly advocated in his late masterwork *Das Kapital* (*Capital*), the first volume of which was published in 1867 (Marx 1956). Here, he proposed what has become known as the **base/superstructure** model of society. According to this perspective, the real motor in capitalist society was the **mode of production** (very roughly, the economy) that was concerned with providing for material needs. He identified as key aspects of this sphere the private ownership of the **means of production** (e.g., factories, machine technology) and a system of **relations of production** that pivoted around the exploitation of productive labor. Arising from these was a broader social structure organized around a class system. This divided society into owners and workers. Under this materialist understanding of industrial society, culture (along with politics and the law) was seen as an epiphenomenal superstructure built upon a determinant economic base. For Marx, culture in industrial society operates as a **dominant ideology**. This has several characteristics:

- It reflects the views and interests of the **bourgeoisie** (the ruling, capitalist class of owners) and serves to legitimate their authority.
- It arises from and expresses underlying relations of production. As Marx and Engels wrote in the *Communist Manifesto*: "Your very ideas are but the outgrowth of the conditions of your bourgeois production and bourgeois property" (1978 [1848]: 487).
- It makes that which is conventional and socially constructed (e.g., wage labor, the commodity form) seem natural and inevitable. It transformed into "eternal laws of nature and of reason, the social forms springing from [the] . . . present mode of production and form of property" (1978: 487).
- It engenders a mistaken or distorted view of reality. This condition, sometimes known as **false consciousness**, allows people to feel happy with their miserable lot. Religion, for example, was an "opium," which prevented the formation of **class consciousness** (awareness of a common class identity and interests) among the **proletariat** (workers).

The broad perspective marked out in *Kapital* and Marx's other writing remains foundational for writers in the tradition of critical cultural studies, whether or not they are specifically Marxist in orientation. To this day, scholars writing from such a position suggest that we should read cultural forms as reflections of hidden interests and social forces. As a counter to the insidious power of ideology, the duty of the analyst is to expose distortions and reveal a more rational and true picture of the world – a process known as **demystification**.

The materialist Marx of "scientific socialism" that we find in *Das Kapital* is perhaps the best known. However, in his earliest writings that were more strongly influenced by the thinking of the German idealist philosopher G. W. F. Hegel (1770–1831), Marx provided indications of a more culturally sensitive vision of social life. Writing in *The Economic and Philosophical Manuscripts* of 1844 (also known as the Paris manuscripts), Marx (1978a) developed a more humanistic vision with an emphasis on the mental life of the subject. He spoke of **species being** as a form of solidarity toward which people aspire. He also wrote about **alienation**. This complex term had multiple meanings. Some were economic, referring to the objective exploitation of labor power (e.g., not being paid a fair wage) and the rise of the commodity. In other contexts it refers to separation from fellow humans, sentiments of isolation, and an inability to live in a fulfilling community. Marx drew contrasts between the authentic life possible in organic and craft settings and the subjective alienation that was experienced under industrial capitalism. He suggested that with the arrival of communism and the end of private property, there would once again be an end to alienation. While the ideas of the *Economic and Philosophical Manuscripts* are often rather metaphysical and difficult to apply in empirical research, they have exerted a major influence on critical cultural theory (see chapter 3).

KARL MARX (1818–83)

Marx was born in Prussia and studied philosophy, languages, law, and history at university. He then worked as a journalist and was a member of a circle of Young Hegelians – a group of idealist intellectuals influenced by the ideas of the philosopher Hegel. His radical opinions attracted disapproval from the Prussian authorities, and he was accused of treason and exiled. During the 1840s he shifted from Hegelian idealism to a materialist position. He began to publish his major works and developed a lifelong friendship with Friedrich Engels, who was later to support him financially. Marx lived in Paris, Brussels, and eventually London. Here he spent much of his time reading in the library of the British Museum and writing in the area of history and political philosophy. When not engaged in his academic work, he assisted in the formation of the Communist movement. He died in March 1883.

Reference: Tucker 1978

The great strength of Marx's thinking has been his ability to connect culture to power and economic life in systematic ways. The price of this, it is generally agreed, has been an inability to theorize the autonomy of culture and a tendency, especially in his later work, to view human action in a deterministic framework. Under the Marxist vision, the economy seems to drive both collective ideology and individual behavior with a clockwork precision. Marxist thought in the twentieth century massively elaborated upon the agendas initiated by Marx, while also attempting to move beyond a narrow mechanistic determinism. Efforts have been made to explore further the links between culture, class, and domination, but in ways that emphasize the centrality of the ideal as well as the material in maintaining capitalism. As we will see in chapters 3 and 16, the concepts of alienation and commodification have proven useful tools in this quest to think through the reciprocities between capitalism, human subjectivity, and ideological forces. More recently, post-Marxist critical theory has challenged the class-driven focus of traditional Marxism and argued that social divisions centered on gender, sexuality, and race are equally important. We explore such alternatives in chapters 7, 9, 14, and 15.

Emile Durkheim

For much of the twentieth century, Emile Durkheim was best known as an advocate of functionalism and positivism. This is the Durkheim who advocates "social facts," the systemic integration of society, and the need for objective data that tests laws and hypotheses. Yet an increasingly prominent way of thinking about him is as an advocate of cultural analysis. Central to this reading is Durkheim's insistence that society was very much a moral phenomenon held together by sentiments of **solidarity**. These played their part in ensuring the survival of a smoothly functioning, well-integrated society in which every piece had its place.

In his doctoral thesis, *The Division of Labor in Society*, Durkheim (1984 [1893]) argued that simple and industrial societies were characterized by different kinds of solidarity. In the former, people were more alike and performed the same tasks. The result was **mechanical solidarity**. In industrial societies, by contrast, there was a division of labor and **organic solidarity**. Durkheim suggested that under mechanical solidarity people tend to think alike, as they all do the same work. There is little tolerance for deviance, and conformity is the norm. Within organic solidarity there is more tolerance for difference thanks to the role diversity that comes from the increased division of labor. Durkheim used the term **collective conscience** when talking about the shared moral awareness and emotional life in a society. According to Durkheim, the collective conscience could be seen very clearly during the punishment of deviants. Such episodes documented collective outrage and were expressive as much as practical in orientation. He argued that in societies with mechanical solidarity, punishments tended to be harsh and violent, while organic solidarity saw punishment aimed at the reintegration of the individual into the group.

Looking at the sweep of history, Durkheim suggested that although the increasing division of labor had opened up the potential for greater individual freedom and

---

EMILE DURKHEIM (1858–1917)

Durkheim was born into the tight-knit Jewish community of north-eastern France. He was the son of a rabbi and he studied Hebrew and scripture alongside his regular schooling. While this background was repudiated by his embrace of secular modernity and civic morality, it may have influenced his later religious sociology. Early in his academic career, Durkheim taught philosophy and obtained a position at the University of Bordeaux. The publication of *The Division of Labour in Society*, *The Rules of Sociological Method*, and *Suicide* in the 1890s moved him to the front of the French intellectual stage and established sociology as an academic discipline in France. He moved to Paris in 1902 and founded a school around the journal *L'Année sociologique*. During World War One, Durkheim's son and many of his promising students died. His health suffered as a consequence of these losses and he died in 1917.

Reference: Coser 1971

happiness, we have not managed this transition very well. He argued that **anomie** had resulted. This is a situation of social dislocation where customary and cultural controls on action are not very strong. In his study of *Suicide*, Durkheim (1966 [1897]) looked at suicide data in order to document the social conditions under which an individual will experience anomie. He suggested that lack of social integration and rapid social change could be key factors in this process.

The Division of Labour in Society and *Suicide* are similar in their approach in that Durkheim argues for the centrality of **social facts** over individual volition. These are collective or "social" in nature and are external and constraining on the individual. Durkheim suggested that sentiments, moralities, and behaviors could be explained away as social facts that were linked to other objective features of society like social organization, societal differentiation, and social change. There is a tendency toward reductionism here which undercuts his emphasis on the moral and normative aspects of social life. That is to say, sentiments and beliefs, like other dimensions of the social, are accounted for as a response to social structural forms and needs. In particular, they tend to work to generate social order and social integration. This vision of a stable society made up of mutually reinforcing institutions, sentiments, and roles is known as **functionalism**.

In *The Elementary Forms of Religious Life*, Durkheim (1968 [1915]) turned to the study of religion in order to explain processes of social integration. Some scholars have argued that this later book is less reductionist than his earlier work. Durkheim sees religion more as a *sui generis* phenomenon that needs to be explained on its own terms. Consequently, he produces a picture of culture as a dynamic and motivating force in society rather than as simply a response to social needs for organization and harmony.

Durkheim claimed that all religions revolved around a distinction between the **sacred** and the **profane**. The sacred involves feelings of awe, fear, and reverence and is set apart from the everyday or profane. The sacred is potentially dangerous as well as beneficent, and is often separated from the profane by special taboos, while its power is regulated by special rites (e.g., ritual, prayer, sacrifice). Durkheim suggested that "a society can neither create nor re-create itself without at the same time creating an ideal" (1968: 422). The point is that the sets of symbols and beliefs in religious systems provided societies with a way of thinking about and concentrating their diffuse moral sentiments and feelings of common identity.

According to Durkheim, the purely ideal power of symbol systems is complemented by concrete acts of observance. He pointed out that societies periodically come together in **ritual** in order to fulfill the need to worship the sacred. These events involve the use of bodies and symbols and further help to integrate society in that they bring people into proximity with each other. With the aid of music, chants, and incantations, they generate collective emotional excitement or **collective effervescence**. This provides a strong sense of group belonging. Durkheim, to conclude, argued that the reconstruction of social bonds was the real reason for the existence of religion and ritual – not the worship of gods. He writes: "There can be no society which does not feel the need of upholding and reaffirming at regular intervals the collective sentiments and the collective ideas which make its unity and its personality. Now this moral remaking cannot be achieved except by the means of reunions, assemblies and meetings where the individuals . . . reaffirm in common their common sentiments" (1968: 427).

Durkheim's study was largely based upon ethnographic data collected from Aboriginal Australia. However, he was eager to argue that it had wider applicability to contemporary settings. These might be more complex than those of a small-scale society, but the fundamental role of religion was the same. He asserted that even the seemingly secular had a moral basis that was essentially religious in nature. He asks: "What essential difference is there between an assembly of Christians celebrating the principal dates of the life of Christ, or of Jews remembering the exodus from Egypt or promulgating the decalogue, and a reunion of citizens commemorating the promulgation of a new moral or legal system or some great event in national life?" (1968: 427). For Durkheim, of course, there was very little difference. Certainly he believed that the religious vision of society he had developed was one with universal relevance.

Major criticisms of Durkheim's cultural sociology usually elaborate on one or another of the following points:

- He assumes culture brings social consensus or social integration and therefore cannot account for its role in generating conflict or sustaining social exclusion. As David Lockwood (1996: 23) puts it, his "interest in consensus does not extend to include the question of whether strength of commitment to collective beliefs is related to inequalities of power and status."
- His perspective is one-sided in an idealist direction. It privileges the role of culture in generating social stability and patterns of social interaction. He has little to say about the role of force, power, interest, or necessity as key variables influencing social life (see Tilly 1981).
- His evolutionary perspective is often empirically wrong and denies the complexity of traditional societies and their beliefs by assuming that they are somehow more "basic" or "elementary" than those of industrial settings.
- There is a mechanistic tendency in his works thanks to the influence of functionalism. This sees patterns of action, belief, and sentiment (culture) arising from the needs and organization of the social structure rather than from the agent's choice or interpretation of the social world. As we have seen, Durkheim speaks of social facts as external and constraining on individuals rather than as enabling creativity and agency.

On the positive side, Durkheim's advocates suggest that his later thinking provides a key resource for linking culture with social structure in a way that resists materialist reductionism. Society for Durkheim was an idea or belief as much as a concrete collection of individuals and actions. Writing about religion, for example, he insisted that it "is not merely a system of practices, but also a system of ideas whose object is to explain the world" (1968: 428). By placing the study of such idea systems at the center of his analysis, in addition to the study of practices, Durkheim's work marks an important early call for a more culturally sensitive form of social inquiry.

Durkheimian cultural work in the twentieth century listened to this call and expanded on a number of themes in his work while, in many cases, also trying to compensate for the perceived errors in his thinking. We return to look at this literature in later chapters and demonstrate the continuing vitality of the Durkheimian tradition. In chapter 2, we examine the work of Talcott Parsons, which elaborated Durkheim's functionalist understandings of the reciprocal relationship of culture and society. Chapter 5, by contrast, has at its center explorations of ritual, classification, morality, and symbolism that have built mostly on the legacy of *The Elementary Forms of Religious Life*.

Max Weber

Max Weber is a complex author whose work covered a vast historical and theoretical territory. It is arguably the case that Weber's *oeuvre* does not amount to a systematic social theory, but rather consists of scattered, brilliant insights. Much of his work is quite materialist, pointing to the role of power, military force, and organizational forms in maintaining social order. However, there is also a strong idealist streak in some of his writings and we will focus on this here.

At the center of Weber's relevance for cultural theory is his understanding of human action. Weber's thinking on this topic, like his religious sociology (see below), was decisively influenced by the German hermeneutic tradition (see Coser 1971: 244ff.). This, in turn, was a specification of the German idealist legacy of Kant and Hegel. Kant had argued that we needed to make a radical distinction between the mind and the body. While the latter was constrained, the former was free from determination. Consequently, human life was very much about freedom. This emphasis on the power of the ideal had influenced thinkers like Hegel, who saw the development of history as the spontaneous unfolding of *Geist*, or "spirit." As a young man, Marx had shared this view. As we have seen, he later reacted against idealism of this kind by developing a rigorous materialist explanation of cultural and mental life. Weber, by contrast, tried to learn from idealist philosophy at the same time as acknowledging realities of power, economic development, and so on. In thinking through this issue, he was influenced by the writings of Wilhelm Dilthey (1833–1911), who was a powerful figure in the German hermeneutic tradition of the nineteenth century. Dilthey argued that knowledge concerning humans had to take account of the meaningful nature of action. What was required was **Verstehen**, or understanding. This requires the observer to try to reconstruct the subjective meanings that influenced a particular line of action – an activity that could involve recreating shared cultural values as well as empathizing with individual psychologies and life histories. Dilthey argued that the study of human life belonged to the **Geisteswissenschaften** (literally: "sciences of the spirit") rather than the natural sciences (see also pp. 188–9).

Drawing upon Dilthey, Weber also advocated a *Verstehen* approach to social analysis and suggested that human agents be thought of as active and meaning-driven. He expressed these ideas most clearly in his monumental *Economy and Society* (1968 [1922]). Weber insists that it is the job of the analyst to try to uncover the motive or subjective intent behind an action: "for a science which is concerned with the subjective meaning of action, explanation requires a grasp of the complex of meaning in which an actual course of understandable action thus interpreted belongs" (1968: 9).

As a start in this direction, Weber drew attention to two contrasting modes of action. **Wertrational**, or value-rational action, was driven by cultural beliefs and goals, such as the search for religious salvation. Here, there is a "conscious belief in the value for its own sake of some ethical, aesthetic, religious or other form of behavior" (1968: 25). By contrast, **Zweckrational**, or goal-oriented action (also known in cultural theory as purposive rationality, means–ends rationality, and instrumental action), was driven by norms of efficiency. These emphasized the need to calculate precise means of attaining specified ends, but lacked the ability to identify overarching moral directions and culturally specified goals. Weber suggested that as we entered modernity, *zweckrational* action was becoming more common (see below). His discussions on *Verstehen* and on the forms of social action have provided significant philosophical support for advocates of interpretative sociology. While many of these have been "micro" in orientation, the broader community of cultural sociologists has also built upon Weber's conceptual edifice and argued that we need to interpret the social world rather than subject it to positivist, "scientific" scrutiny.

In cultural circles, Weber is probably best known for his work, *The Protestant Ethic and the Spirit of Capitalism* (1958 [1904]). In this, he argues against materialist views of the origins of capitalism, asserting that religious beliefs also played a part. He looked at the role of the doctrine of predestination held by early Protestants. This argued that fate with respect to heaven and hell was determined before birth. **Salvation** could not be bought or sold nor earned by good deeds. According to Weber, this led to feelings of unease. Protestants looked for signs that they had been chosen to be saved by God. Economic success was one such sign. The unintended consequence of the doctrine of predestination was a rational and planned acquisition of wealth with an associated **Protestant ethic** about the need for methodical and disciplined hard work. Over time, the religious foundations of capitalist accumulation dropped from view, leaving a field characterized by a shallow, unfulfilling, and constraining *zweckrational* mode of action and an economic order of "pure utilitarianism" organized around thrift, profit, and constraint. Weber writes: "The Puritan wanted to work in a calling; we are forced to do so . . . [The modern economic order] is now bound to the technical and economic conditions of machine production which today determine the lives of all the individuals who are born into this mechanism" (1958: 181).

The Protestant ethic book has often been misunderstood as an idealist argument. In point of fact, Weber was an admirer of Marx as much as of German idealism. When we look at Weber's total *oeuvre*, we find an account of the rise of capitalism that is complex and multidimensional. Weber argued for the importance of economic and organizational factors as well as religious motivations and opposed one-sided explanations, whether material or ideal in nature (see Weber 1958: 183). Seen in this light, *The Protestant Ethic and the Spirit of Capitalism* is part of a larger jigsaw of explanation.

Although the Protestant ethic thesis is perhaps Weber's best-known work, it is perhaps misleadingly so. Other texts in his study of the great religions of the world are arguably better researched and more comprehensive. Certainly, Weber himself saw his study of the Protestant ethic as only a small component of a much wider and more systematic research agenda. In his monumental comparative inquiry, he emphasized the universality of the problem of salvation in all known religions. He suggested that the Judeo-Christian tradition was characterized by a "this-worldly asceticism" which promoted evangelical activism and world-transforming activity. By contrast, the religions of the Orient, such as Confucianism, Taoism, and Hinduism, suggested that salvation could come from withdrawal from the world, conformity to tradition, and contemplation. Weber saw these differences as contributing to the rise of industrial modernity in the West. Even though China had been technologically advanced in the Middle Ages, its religious values had prevented the emergence of the entrepreneurial innovation and social dynamism to be found in Europe at the same time.

Clear affinities exist between Weber and Durkheim in that both point to the centrality of religion as a core dimension of culture. However, Weber's approach places a greater emphasis on the intellectual content of abstract belief systems, while Durkheim foregrounds visceral, embodied emotions. A more significant difference is in their attitude toward the role of religion in contemporary societies. As we have seen, Durkheim was very clear that moral ties and sacred goals were of vital importance in today's world. Weber, by contrast, advanced a thesis of **disenchantment**. This asserted that with the onset of modernity, meaning was being emptied out of the world. We are living in an age of bureaucracy, where the focus is placed on efficiency and rationality rather than on attaining some kind of transcendence or pursuing ultimate meanings. In Weber's terms, the *Zweckrational* was coming to replace the *Wertrational*. Life had lost its sense of purpose, and people had become trapped in what he called an **iron cage** of meaningless bureaucracy and rationalism.

Two other themes remain to be addressed in this all-too-brief review of Weber's contribution to cultural theory. The first is the discussion of the forms of **authority** or **legitimate domination** (*Herrschaft*). Weber (1968: 215ff.) insisted that rule was justified by reference to broader structures of meaning, and suggested three **ideal types** (models or simplified versions of reality) to understand this process. **Traditional authority** was based on the idea that things should be as they always had been. Weber had little to say about this, but suggested it was prominent in small-scale and preindustrial societies. A problem here is for the ruler to introduce change. **Charismatic authority** is organized around the belief that a ruler possesses exceptional powers or some kind of divine gift. Weber argues that this form of authority is linked to social dislocation and social change and is antithetical to economic considerations. A key feature of charismatic authority is its instability. According to Weber, the charismatic leader is under constant pressure to produce signs of their power. If they fail to produce results, their charismatic power can evaporate. Further problems revolve around the issue of succession. Once the charismatic figure dies, a power vacuum can arise. For these reasons Weber suggested that over the long term charisma was inevitably routinized and replaced by a bureaucratic mode of domination. While charisma has generally been treated as a psychological or interpersonal phenomenon, it can also be understood in more cultural terms. Weber's writings discuss religion, prophecy, salvation, and redemption as much as group psychology, and so the concept has much to offer those interested in the role of symbolic patterns in political life (for further discussion, see Smith 2000). **Legal-rational authority** characterizes highly bureaucratized contemporary societies. It emphasizes the role of law, procedure, and efficiency as standards against which administrative acts are judged. According to Weber, disenchantment arises as this form of authority replaces the more religiously and symbolically meaning-ful forms associated with tradition and charisma.

MAX WEBER (1864–1920)

Weber grew up in an affluent but rather repressive Protestant family. He attended Heidelberg University as an undergraduate and participated in its masculine culture of drinking and dueling. He later studied at the University of Berlin. Here he adopted a more ascetic lifestyle and studied obsessively. His interests and reading were diverse, and included history, law, and philosophy. Unlike Simmel (see below), his talent was recognized early and he obtained a prestigious chair at Heidelberg at a young age. Weber's mental and personal life was very complex. He never consum-mated his marriage and in 1897 had a mental breakdown after an argument with his authoritarian father. Restored to health in 1903, he began writing again and also speaking out on public issues. Weber was highly critical of Germany's conserva-tive elites, yet he never fully embraced radical politics. By the time of his death in 1920, he was recognized as a leading intellectual in his country.

Reference: Coser 1971

The final concept from Weber to be considered is that of status. In contrast to Marx's class-driven model of social organization, Weber distinguished between **class** and **status**. Class refers to position in the economic order. Weber provides examples such as entrepreneurs, laborers, and *rentiers*. Status, which is of most interest here, refers to groups with a common "style of life" and a shared level of social prestige. Weber pointed to the ways that the authority of elites often depended upon their distinctive culture and value system. They might share customs, conventions, and educational training. These could be used as the basis of obtaining deference or other kinds of special privi-leges such as monopolies and sinecures. Weber argued that class and status could interact in complex ways. He claimed there was no necessary reason why a group with economic power would also enjoy the other forms of power, as Marx had argued. He notes that a student, a civil servant, and an army officer might have very different class locations and yet share a common status, "since upbringing and education create a common style of life" (1968: 306).

Weber's work has a number of attractive features. He provides a compelling argu-ment for the centrality of human agency to sociological explanation. In highlighting the pivotal and near-universal significance of religious beliefs in human life, he creates space for the autonomy of culture. His theories also foreground questions of power and domination and link these in definite ways to culture. These attractive features, however, are perhaps undercut by an insistence on the disenchantment of the modern world and on the routinized and rationalized qualities of contemporary life with a cor-responding instrumental (rather than normative) regulation of human sociality. It is almost as if Weber is arguing that culture was once important, but now needs to be excluded from social analysis. Perhaps for this reason, it is rather difficult to identify a

Weberian school or camp in contemporary cultural theory. To follow Weber to the letter is to insist on the weakness of meaning in contemporary society, and the decline of religious and normative motivations for action.

Unlike Durkheim and Marx, both of whom founded self-defining and comparatively bounded traditions, Weber's work has had a diffuse impact in a number of fields. This reflects his own scholarly diversity. Work influenced by Weber has taken some of the following paths:

- Research has taken place on the social implications of religious beliefs, including those relating to political legitimation and political culture. Durkheimians like Edward Shils, for example, have made use of Weber's ideas in this area (see chapter 5).
- Weber's writing on *Verstehen* and the forms of social action have provided an extremely useful charter for qualitative inquiry, especially where issues of social action are being considered. They also influenced Parsons's discussions of the bases of agency in *The Structure of Social Action* (see chapter 2).
- Studies of stratification which wish to escape from the straitjacket of class theory have often turned to Weber for help. Many investigations of cultural capital and social status count Weber as an important intellectual heir. Discussions of "fields" and *habitus* in Bourdieu, for example, have distinct Weberian parallels (see chapter 8).
- Explorations of societal rationalization as a component of modernity and modern culture take Weber as a keystone. Many scholars working in this area are Marxists who use Weber to think further through the impacts of alienation and bureaucratic control on modern life. We review some of these theories in chapter 3.

Georg Simmel

According to his core of enthusiastic devotees, Georg Simmel deserves to be ranked alongside Marx, Weber, and Durkheim in the pantheon of founding fathers. Efforts to elevate his status have been hampered by Simmel's tendency to avoid systematic theory. He wrote in an essayistic style on a bewildering variety of topics. Although his writings are universally acknowledged to be brilliant and insightful, they have also been considered to be lacking in the persistent intellectual focus that was required of a really major figure. Since the 1980s, this perception has slowly been changing and Simmel is now widely understood as a thinker whose work needs to be taken very seriously.

Simmel's model of society differs radically from the more collectivistic one proposed by Durkheim. For Simmel, society was essentially the product of the ceaseless interactions of individuals. He argued that the task of sociology was to describe the ways that people came together, the ways they formed groups, and how these related to each other. His overall position was to favor empirical observation over the construction of a priori models and elaborate conceptual categories. According to Simmel, we should be looking at patterns of concrete interaction rather than developing abstract theories of society. Aside from this distinctive vision, Simmel's interest for cultural theory lies in a number of studies providing diverse views on modern life. In various ways, these foreground the importance of interaction patterns and modernity for the self and for sociality. Simmel argued that the self had become more free thanks to the removal of customary constraints upon action in the course of societal modernization. Yet at the same time, our relationships have become more anonymous, and our lives mediated by science, technology, commodities, and other social phenomena that appear alien to us.

GEORG SIMMEL (1858–1918)

Simmel was born in Berlin in 1858, and was to spend much of his life in that city. He had a prodigious output of some 25 books, in fields ranging from sociology to psychology, to philosophy and aesthetics. Despite this scholarship, he found it difficult to obtain academic advancement. This seems to have been due to anti-Semitism, disapproval of his socialist sympathies, and jealousy at the large numbers attending his lectures. It probably did not help that he championed the cause of women and other minority students in the university system. After failing to obtain senior positions in Berlin and Heidelberg, Simmel eventually obtained a chair at the provincial University of Strasbourg.

Reference: Frisby 1984

These themes are taken up in *The Philosophy of Money* (1978 [1900]), perhaps Simmel's most important work. Here he explores the ways that money has transformed human interactions by making it possible for them to be impersonal. He argued that the economy was really about interactions focused on exchange rather than production, thus providing a distinctive alternative to Marxian understandings. Yet, at the same time, he agrees that contemporary life is characterized by something like alienation. He notes that money makes our interactions more instrumental and calculable in character, and that acquiring money can become an end in itself. The result has been a subtle transformation of human sociality. Individuality and care are removed from interactions, to be replaced by hardness, a matter-of-fact attitude, and a "calculative exactness of practical life" (Simmel 1997: 177).

This idea that contemporary life had become more impersonal was extended in a famous essay, *The Metropolis and Mental Life*, first published in 1903. Here, Simmel asserts that in the contemporary city (he was drawing on his experience of Berlin *circa* 1900) we are constantly bombarded by information and there is an "intensification of nervous stimulation" (1997: 175). Everything is new, rapid, and ephemeral, and citizens are surrounded by strangers and advertisements, traffic signs, and other such messages, as in the photograph of Manhattan's Times Square, shown in figure 1.1 overleaf. Simmel sees these various aspects of urban life as threatening to our sense of self and our ability to operate as autonomous subjects in the metropolitan environment. He

Figure 1.1   Times Square, Manhattan, New York

writes: "The deepest problems of modern life derive from the claim of the individual to preserve the autonomy and individuality of his existence in the face of overwhelming social forces" (1997: 174–5).

In order to cope with this situation, we have to shut down some of our emotional responses and develop what Simmel calls a blasé attitude. This involves remaining cool, aloof, and distant from other people and from the streetscape around us. There is a tendency to respond to everything in the same way and not to take an interest in any one thing in the urban environment. According to Simmel, we face a tension between our need to remain inconspicuous in such settings and the need to assert our identity (if only to ourselves) or to be noticed.

In his writing *Philosophy of Fashion*, dating from 1905, Simmel maintained a similar line of analysis that revolved around issues of modernity and identity. He suggests that the codes of fashion are arbitrary and respond to cultural needs rather than practical ones. Hemlines and colors make little difference to our survival chances – their primary function is social, not material. He argues that fashion is a response to our desire to modulate the tension between the expression of the individual self and belonging to a larger collectivity. The success of fashion as an institution arises from its unique ability to fulfill both simultaneously. On the one hand, people can imitate others and thus have the psychological security of being members of a collectivity. On the other, they can use it to express their individuality, perhaps by only subtle adjustments to a given style.

Simmel also notes that fashion plays a role in the stratification system and tends to exist only in societies that are highly stratified. "Fashion is . . . a product of class division and operates . . . the double function of holding a given circle together and at the same time closing it off from others" (1997: 189). It responds to the needs of high-status groups to symbolize their difference from those of lower status, and allows those of lower-status groups to make claims to higher status. The result is a never-ending game of catch-up. Once fashions trickle down to the lower groups, those of higher status will abandon them in favor of new styles. The image he presents here is of con-sumer goods and cultural tastes being used as a marker of distinction – a theme that anticipates the later work of Bourdieu (see chapter 8).

Simmel's impact on subsequent cultural theory has been diverse. His work on money deeply impressed Weber and influenced his thinking about the Protestant ethic (see above). For a period of time, Georg Lukács was a student of Simmel's, and it is no sur-prise that there are parallels between Simmel's work and Lukács's studies of the ratio-nalization of modern life (see pp. 34–5). As he rejected reified, grandiose visions of society and centered attention on concrete interactions, Simmel has been an important influence on interactionist approaches to culture. Early translations of his essays in the *American Journal of Sociology* helped to shape the Chicago School approach to spatial and community studies in urban settings. His attention to the characteristics of life in the metropolis was to also influence more critical theorists, such as Walter Benjamin (see pp. 39–41). More recently, Simmel's interest in exchange, consumption, and the self has seen him marked out as a pioneer in this area. He is being increasingly reread not so much as the founding father of interactionism (as was the case in the 1960s and 1970s) or as a critical theorist of modernity, but rather as a pioneer in the cultural analysis of consumerism.

Friedrich Nietzsche

Nietzsche has traditionally not been understood as a thinker concerned with culture in a social scientific sense, but nevertheless a grasp of the basic elements of his thought is crucial to understanding some of the most important contemporary cultural theory, especially some of the developments in poststructuralist and postmodernist thought and theory about the body (see chapters 7, 13, 14, and 16). Even some of the theorists discussed above were profoundly marked by their encounters with Nietzsche's work. Weber's work on religion and rationality clearly bears the traces of that encounter, while Simmel (1986 [1907]) dedicated an entire book to a discussion of the relationship of Nietzsche's thought to the ideas of one of Nietzsche's own influences, the philosopher Arthur Schopenhauer.

While Nietzsche is perhaps best known for his proclamation that "God is dead," which he immediately complicated by asking "Is not the greatness of this deed too great for us?" (1974 [1887]: 181), the core of Nietzsche's contribution to cultural theory is found in his project for the "**revaluation of all values**." This sought to challenge existing modern morality by showing that "the so-called goodness of modern man is not virtuous, that his so-called religion is not religious, and that his so-called truths are not truthful" (Kaufmann 1959 [1950]: 97). The central source of modern morality, in Nietzsche's account, is Judeo-Christian culture, and so he mounts a profound critique of its methods for assigning moral value. Judeo-Christian culture is based in a framework for the construction of identity and the understanding of history that is quite different from the Greek culture which it superseded. In the latter, Nietzsche argues, the self is **active**, seeking through rigorous self-examination and a spiritualized, aestheticized experience of pleasure to make itself into a higher type of human being, something that is culturally produced but still in tune with the basic natural drive that orients human beings, the **will to power**. This is an important concept that has been defined in many ways since Nietzsche's death, some of them directly contradictory to others. It can be understood as the basic drive of an organism or a force to perpetuate itself, to enhance and expand its purview and its frame of existence. As Nietzsche put it in *The Gay Science*: "The great and small struggle always revolves around superiority, around growth and expansion, around power – in accordance with the will to power which is the will to life" (1974: 292). This may in some cases involve conquering other forces, but it also requires formidable control of self-destructive instincts within the organism or entity itself. It is the drive in a force or entity to distinguish itself and to resist being reduced to likeness with other forces and entities, thereby expressing its **difference**. Entities with high quanta of the will to power are active rather than **reactive**, motivated by and at peace with internal drives and values rather than directed outward to the values of others.

In Judaism and, later, in a still more distorted form in Christianity, a different kind of self emerges, according to Nietzsche. Instead of seeking its meaning via the will to power and the effort to transform and direct itself, the self engages in what Nietzsche famously labeled with the French term ***ressentiment***. A culture of *ressentiment* is based in an outward-directed, reactive morality that starts with an assumption of suffering on the part of the subject that is seen as caused by some external agent. For Jewish and Christian culture, Nietzsche contends in *On the Genealogy of Morals* that there is the need for a "hostile external world . . . [and] external stimuli in order to act at all" (1967 [1887]: 37). And there are always external enemies, the Godless who have not accepted the one true God, who seek to enslave them, or who have already done so, e.g., in the Old Testament narrative of Pharaoh and the Exodus. Members of Judeo-Christian culture do not see themselves as morally good and proceed from there, as is the case with the Greeks, in Nietzsche's account. They see their purported tormentors as evil, understand themselves then as the victims of that evil, and build a moral culture on this basis.

The outcome for Nietzsche is a culture in which superior examples of human being, those who assert their difference and are uninterested in the values of the masses, are attacked and destroyed as evil victimizers. Culture becomes a repressive weapon for fighting the purported evil opponent instead of a training program for the creation of higher human beings. The self is thoroughly domesticated and leveled, and the differences between selves are denied and attacked. This Christian culture becomes, even in a secular form (socialism is for Nietzsche the secular political form where Christian cultural influence is the most direct, but we see it in any humanitarianism that emphasizes identification and allegiance with the weak), the basis of modern democratic culture, and the depletion of creative activity that follows its establishment in modernity is inevitable.

If to this point Nietzsche's perspective on culture might seem to resonate with some of the elitist and pre-social scientific definitions we discussed in the introduction, other elements of his thought make clear close connections to some very contemporary perspectives and concerns in cultural theory. His first book, *The Birth of Tragedy out of the Spirit of Music* (1967 [1872]), is an investigation of the relationship of tragic art forms to ritual. The cultural genius of Greek civilization, according to his argument, was rooted in a recognition of the falsehood of the "*principium individuationis*," or the idea that the human condition is fundamentally determined by individualization. Instead, Nietzsche shows how the cultural practice of primitive ritual festival and frenzy reveals the true collective and pre-rational nature of human experience and then traces the evolution of ritual through the development of the dramatic form of tragedy. Greek tragic culture is superior to the Judeo-Christian culture that will follow it in Nietzsche's view because it embraces the idea that "all that comes into being must be ready for a sorrowful end" with no possibility of redemption in a supernatural world (1967 [1872]: 104). Ritual, and later tragedy, are the cultural practices by which humans can affirm a joyful acceptance of life in all its many facets, including the fact of its own inevitable end. This interest in ritual and dramatic performance in social life would be taken up by many later cultural theorists (see chapters 5 and 11). In another early work (1873), this one much less well known than the book on tragedy, Nietzsche made an argument about the relationship between language and reality that would serve, a century or so later, as a fundamental claim of poststructuralist theory. Language, he contended, does not simply reflect an objective reality beyond itself. It actually obscures the reality of the irreducibility of any one thing to another by providing us with general concepts that hide that difference. The word "leaf," for example, refers to a vast number of objects that are not identical, but the very existence of the word leads us to believe in that non-existing identity. This theory of language leads one to the epistemological observation that "truth" as expressed in language is never anything more than a "mobile army of metaphors, metonyms, and anthropomorphisms" (Nietzsche 1954 [1873]). Many linguists and anthropologists of language have followed Nietzsche's position here in arguing that the categories of a given language powerfully affect the ways in which subjects who speak that language can conceive of the world around them.

Finally, Nietzsche contributed important insights to the cultural sociology of the body in his examination of the relationship between *ressentiment* and a certain attitude to the body and its drives. He argues that a particular form of physically sickly asceticism that rejects the body as evil has come to dominate in the West with the triumph of Judeo-Christian culture, and its effects have been extensive. In the place of this self-destructively ascetic approach to the body, Nietzsche proposed that truly cultivated individuals would embrace embodiment and pursue physical desires and pleasures as part of the expression of their will to power. In remarks written in the last productive year of his life, he noted the profound importance of nutrition for the intellectual, linking philosophical profundity to particular climates and cuisines (Germany fared badly here, while north-western Italy rated first place). However sketchy and anecdotal these notes might seem, they certainly demonstrate a clear appreciation for the embodiment of even the most traditionally ideal of human practices that has been tapped into in much contemporary cultural theory (see chapters 7, 8, and 16).

We can summarize the contributions Nietzsche makes to cultural theory as follows:

- an emphasis on the notion of difference that would become so important in later cultural work;
- an attachment to the kind of cultural relativist perspective in his critique of Judeo-Christian tradition that would later become *de rigueur* in the social scientific perspective on culture;
- a positioning of drama and narrative as fundamental to the social;
- a significant interest in embodiment and an early sociology of the body;
- a focus on the role of irrational motivations and emotional drivers of action.

Criticisms of Nietzsche's understanding of morality and culture have frequently relied on distortions of his work by the Nazi regime, which explicitly set out to make him into a philosopher of fascism despite the many explicit examples in his writing of his hatred of the "anti-cultural sickness" of racist nationalism (1967 [1888]: 321). More reasoned criticisms touch on the fact that his critical perspective can seem to fall into relativism when pushed sufficiently. Nonetheless, his work has been invoked and adapted by some very influential contemporary cultural thinkers on the political left. Michel Foucault, Gilles Deleuze, and other poststructuralist thinkers, for example, have very deliberately used Nietzschean concepts to launch a systematic critique of what they saw as the static culture of European social democracy.

FRIEDRICH WILHELM NIETZSCHE (1844–1900)

Nietzsche was born in Röcken, Germany (then Prussia) into a family of Lutheran ministers – his father and both grandfathers were members of the clergy. Even before he had received his doctorate in philology from the University at Leipzig, he was appointed to a post at the University of Basel, where he taught from 1869 to 1879. He was not yet 30 when he published *The Birth of Tragedy* in 1872. The book attracted attention outside the university among artists and musicians such as the composer Richard Wagner, but was attacked by traditional philologists. Health problems and his dissatisfaction with the conservative nature of academic scholarship led to Nietzsche's departure from university life. From 1879 until his nervous breakdown (likely caused by syphilis) in January 1889, he lived the nomadic life of the isolated philosopher, moving from one boarding house to another in Germany, Switzerland, and Italy as the seasons changed. He produced a vast amount of work in this 10-year period, including *The Gay Science, Beyond Good and Evil*, and *On the Genealogy of Morals*. He lived another decade after falling ill, finally dying in 1900 in the care of his sister Elisabeth. She assumed sole rights over his work, including unpublished notes, and later turned it over to the Nazi regime, where it was selectively edited, thereby posthumously turning Nietzsche into the intellectual spokesman for an anti-Semitic movement he had denounced during his lifetime.

Reference: Kaufmann 1959

W. E. B. DuBois

DuBois focused most of his intellectual attention during his long life on the element of culture that so profoundly affected his own life and career: the question of **race and racial identity**. Despite a Harvard PhD (his was the first doctoral degree ever awarded by the institution to an African-American) and experience studying in Germany with Max Weber and other prestigious German social scientists of the late nineteenth century, DuBois was not offered an academic position at any leading university and had to settle for teaching Latin, Greek, German, and English at a small African-American college in Ohio. In 1896, however, he was invited to Philadelphia to carry out a study of the African-American community there. The result was a classic and enduring treatment of race in America: *The Philadelphia Negro* (1996 [1899]).

In the 1890s, the reigning paradigm for understanding race was squarely biological in orientation. Although there was considerable disagreement as to how many basic human racial types existed, it was broadly accepted that race was fundamentally a phenomenon rooted in objective physical differences with concomitant behavioral characteristics that emerged from those biological facts. DuBois radically challenged this paradigm by pointing to the cultural factors that drove and differentiated the African-American population of Philadelphia. African-American criminal activity and the formulation of a political response to it formed one of the central motivations for the study on the part of those who funded it, who likely shared at least some of the notions of the nature of African-Americans presented by the biological racist theories of the time (Lewis 1993: 188–9). DuBois immediately complicated the analysis of this phenomenon by showing that the vast bulk of that crime was committed by a very small minority of this larger population, and that it was driven by non-biological factors. He argued that African-Americans could be divided into four distinct sub-groups, based in part on occupational and economic considerations but also on cultural factors. In a narrative that presages more recent social scientific formulations of the **black underclass**, DuBois showed how biological arguments about racial identity and character fell apart in the face of evidence that the upper class, the laborers, and the morally respectable poor of the African-American population did not engage in criminal activity in any greater propensity than did European-Americans, and "a distinct class of habitual criminals" that he called "the submerged tenth" were in fact responsible for the great bulk of African-American crime (DuBois 1996: 259, 311). Structural facts such as poverty, racial discrimination in the job market, and competition for jobs from European immigrants were strong factors in the production of the criminality of this group, but their cultural values, which distinguished them from other poor African-Americans in precisely the way Elijah Anderson has famously formulated as the difference between the "decent" and the "street" (see chapter 15), also played a significant role. A central legacy of slavery, in DuBois's analysis, had to do with the emergence of African-American familial practices that prevented full integration into American culture. The strongly monogamous familial culture of early America had been only partially adopted by African-Americans, who, at the time DuBois was writing, were only a few generations removed from the polygamous family structures of their African origins. Plantation slavery created a powerful barrier to the adoption of monogamy and led to "practically unregulated polygamy and polyandry" (1996: 192). In the wake of liberation, then, the poorest African-Americans largely experienced sexual couplings in two forms: unmarried and temporary cohabitation, and "the keeping of men," where young men from the criminal underclass used machismo and sexual prowess to control and exploit numerous young women at the same time. DuBois recognized that efforts to aid the poorest African-Americans would have to focus on these familial issues.

DuBois also described the profound importance of the African-American churches in Philadelphia. These institutions had taken on a particular significance as a result of the dual character of their African cultural heritage. The African-American church was, in DuBois's reading, both a preserve of tribal organization and a surrogate family. Ultimately, though, it had proven incapable of effectively diverting poor African-American youth from the amusements of the gambling and dance halls. DuBois believed that a reinforcement of the African-American family would necessarily mean a decrease in the influence of the African-American church. Insofar as the church's role as a social meeting place was at least as significant as its role as a religious institution in the African-American community, it served as a setting for some of the status ranking competition that DuBois saw as harmful to the economic advance of African-Americans. Much money was, in his view, frivolously wasted on, e.g., showy clothing for church attendance and decoration of the churches themselves when it should have been directed toward education, the buying of homes, and the possibility of the arrival of "a rainy day" (1996: 392).

In later work, DuBois continued his investigation of racial identity, albeit with a political focus that transitioned gradually from reformism based on the ideas of Booker T. Washington to support for the international communist movement and especially for Third World communism. Perhaps his most well-known theoretical contribution is the notion of the **double consciousness**, which is found in his *The Souls of Black Folk* (1961 [1903]). African-Americans, according to DuBois, experience identity in a complex, even contradictory manner, quite different from that experienced by European-Americans. They are constantly aware of being both American and of African descent, and they constantly see themselves not only from their own situated perspective but also from the perspective of the broader, European-American-dominated society which so cruelly dominates them. The end result is that African-American self-awareness is at once richer and more fragile than European-American identity. African-Americans can see more (and in chapter 15 we will examine how standpoint theorists of race have expanded on this point), but they are also constantly in danger of losing their hold on their own self-conception and succumbing to the racist gaze to which they are subjected by those around them, essentially internalizing racist hatred as a form of self-disgust.

It is widely recognized that DuBois did not fully reject the role of the biological in racial identity and in this sense he did not go as far as contemporary cultural theorists of race would go to present race as a constructed category (see chapter 15). Nonetheless, he is almost certainly the central figure in the initiation of the intellectual movement to see race as a cultural category that has dominated much social science in the late twentieth and early twenty-first centuries

W(illiam) E(dward) B(urghardt) DuBois (1868–1963)

DuBois was born and spent his early life in Great Barrington, Massachusetts, a small New England town of 5,000 inhabitants. As a youth there, he later wrote, he perceived almost no racial discrimination and what he did find he tended to attribute to social class distinctions. As his family lacked resources, others in the community helped raise money to send DuBois to Fisk University (an African-American college) in Tennessee in 1884. There, in the American South, he saw racism at its most vicious, in the form of the hundreds of African-Americans lynched throughout the South each year during this period. He later studied at Harvard and then at the University of Berlin, where he met Max Weber, Heinrich von Treitschke, and other celebrated figures of the German intellectual world. His Harvard dissertation focused on the suppression of the African slave trade. His subsequent teaching career at African-American colleges further brought home to him the intransigence of the American racial problem and he began to direct his attention more fully to political activism. In 1905, he formed the Niagara Movement, which soon transformed itself into the NAACP (National Association for the Advancement of Colored People). DuBois dedicated much of his energy to this organization through the mid-1930s. He grew steadily more politically radical and eventually became sympathetic to the global communist movement, visiting with Mao Zedong during the Chinese Great Leap Forward and expressing admiration for Stalin. His long and eventful life came to an end in Ghana the day before Martin Luther King Jr. delivered his famous "I Have a Dream" speech at the civil rights march on Washington of August 1963.

Reference: DeMarco 1983

Suggested Further Reading

More than 35 years after its initial publication, Lewis Coser's *Masters of Sociological Thought* (1971) still provides an unsurpassed brief introduction to the lives and works of Marx, Durkheim, Weber, and Simmel. After reading Coser, those wishing to gain further knowledge should have no difficulty in locating specialist volumes dedicated to each of these scholars. Among the more accessible original works by each of these authors are Weber's study of the Protestant ethic, Simmel's essay on the city and mental life, and *The Communist Manifesto* of Marx and Engels. Dipping into *The Elementary Forms of Religious Life* offers perhaps the best opportunity to glimpse Durkheim's distinctive vision of the spiritual dimensions of society. The Nietzschean concepts discussed in this chapter are laid out most clearly in his *On the Genealogy of Morals*. DuBois's *The Philadelphia Negro* is accessible and rich in detail, even if much of that detail is now historically dated. Elijah Anderson's essay, "Drugs and Violence in the Inner City" in the edited volume *W. E. B. DuBois, Race, and the City*, shows clearly how DuBois's perspective on race and culture prefigured much of the more complex study of race today, including Anderson's own recent work on the "code of the streets."

CHAPTER TWO

Culture and Social Integration in the Work of Talcott Parsons

Talcott Parsons is widely recognized as a key figure in twentieth-century sociological theory. Less often acknowledged is his specific contribution to cultural theory. His work is important for several reasons:

- More than any other theorist of the previous century, Parsons made efforts systematically to theorize the relationship between culture, personality, and social structure by developing abstract and universally applicable models.
- Parsons was an important advocate of Durkheimian and Weberian cultural sociology. He was the first major thinker to take on board and synthesize their ideas.
- He was the figurehead for functionalism as an intellectual paradigm.
- Critical responses to his work have provided the basis for equally important innovations in thinking about culture. Knowing Parsons's work is therefore an important platform for understanding more contemporary cultural theory.

As a thinker Parsons was in many ways closer to philosophy than sociology. He was not drawn to empirical research, and when he wrote about empirical issues, he often did so with the aid of co-authors or by drawing on the established literature in a field. Parsons tends to think through a problem or issue in abstract ways, making logical deductions about what had to be going on in order for something to happen or exist. For example, he observed that society was relatively orderly and that social behavior was patterned rather than random. How could this come about? Parsons reasoned that a host of forces had to be at work to achieve this end: norms about behavior, socialization into roles, sanctions for deviance, and so on. These provided for predictable behavior and stable institutions.

Parsons's work can be conveniently divided into phases, each of them epitomized by a pivotal text. The following makes use of this chronology as an organizing tool.

Early Work on Social Action

With the publication *of The Structure of Social Action* in 1937, Parsons became a leading figure in American sociology. The book is of central importance for cultural sociology because it makes a sustained attack on **rational actor models** of human agency, which have had a number of guises over time:

- *Behaviorist models in psychology emphasizing stimulus and reward.* These models are most associated with research on animals by people like Pavlov and Skinner.
- *The sociological exchange theory of Homans and Blau that was developed in the 1950s and 1960s.* This argued that people seek to maximize certain things (e.g., social approval) and will engage in interactions when there is a net benefit to so doing.
- *Game theory, which was very popular in sociology during the 1970s and 1980s.* This argues that social life is a game with strategies, rewards, and penalties.
- *The model of "economic man" advanced by neoclassical economics going back to the time of the Enlightenment.* This suggested that humans make rational calculations of their interests and act upon them. Social life is analogous to a market in which people calculate profit and loss.

Varied as these approaches may be, they all share the assumption that humans are rational, calculating, selfish, and individualistic. In an argument that is still remarkably overlooked, Parsons demonstrated that this utilitarian model of human action is deeply problematic. It proclaims the importance of human freedom, but is ultimately caught in the **utilitarian dilemma** (1968 [1937]: 64). If humans are really free, then the ends of action will be random (and social life impossibly chaotic). As an alternative, utilitarian theorists can acknowledge the existence of external constraints on action (e.g., heredity, environment, pre-social needs for power or sex). These provide non-random ends, but come at the cost of a deterministic model of action. Action is now explained away in terms of "the conditions of the situation, that is to elements analyzable in terms of non-subjective categories" (1968: 64). Parsons argued that freedom and non-randomness could be brought together only by acknowledging the role of culture.

TALCOTT PARSONS (1902–79)

Parsons was born in the US Midwest in 1902 and grew up in a strongly Protestant family. He studied at Amherst and later at the London School of Economics, where he encountered the functionalist thinking of Malinowski. Later he moved to Heidelberg in Germany, where he became familiar with Max Weber's work. Returning to the United States, he obtained a position at Harvard. In his early Harvard years he synthesized his European learning in *The Structure of Social Action* and undertook some important translations of Weber. These achievements helped to establish his reputation. He went on to train a number of talented and important graduate students and to develop his systems theory. By 1950, Parsons had become the most influential sociologist in the United States. While his functionalist theory was to remain significant for the rest of his life, it was also to come under increasing attack. By the time of his death in Germany in 1979, many viewed Parsons as a figure of the past, even though he continued to be a prolific author.

Reference: Hamilton 1983: 31–55

Parsons claimed that human action always has normative and non-rational dimensions. Because these are internal to the individual and provide motivation, they afford the basis for a **voluntaristic model of action** rather than a deterministic one. In creating this argument, Parsons made a detailed synthesis of four previous theorists: Marshall, Pareto, Durkheim, and Weber. Of these four figures, Durkheim and Weber are of greatest interest for our purposes. Parsons drew on Durkheim's theory of religion and on ideas about the collective conscience shaping individual behavior. From Weber, he took particular note of the religious sociology and the concept of value-rational activity (we discussed these ideas in chapter 1). For Parsons, these more cultural understandings allow us to theorize how freedom and constraint could be reconciled in the explanation of human action and subjectivity. Motivation is internal and patterned, leading people to voluntarily work toward particular shared ends.

The Middle-Period Systems Theory

As Parsons switched his interest toward the analysis of social systems, his work began to make more extensive use of functionalist logic. From the late 1930s onwards, Parsons and his colleagues collaborated on an attempt to develop an all-embracing model of action and society. This is something that his admirers call a **general theory** and his detractors a **grand theory** (the unspoken subtext to this label being "grandiose theory").

In *The Social System* (1970 [1951]) and *Toward a General Theory of Action* (Parsons and Shils 1962 [1951]), the key components of this model are spelled out. Parsons sees the central problem of society as one of **integration** and **allocation**, both of which are necessary for an efficiently functioning world. Allocation refers to the distribution of scarce rewards among people and the distribution of people to particular positions in society. Integration is concerned with managing the tensions that this causes. In exploring these issues, Parsons and his colleagues developed a model of society as comprising three systems.

The social system is made up of interactions between people. It is an area where there is potential for conflict between actors over scarce resources and goals. Parsons stresses the need for the social system to deal with potential sources of strain and to provide stability and predictability. It does this by means of roles. These define legitimate action patterns and inform the operation of institutions that embody particular value patterns. Importantly, roles carry with them complementary expectations which help to stabilize concrete interaction patterns. So, for example, doctors and patients interact in a context of shared role content and expectations that makes their interaction efficient.

Drawing on Freud, Parsons suggested that the personality system is made up of "need dispositions." These are preferences, desires, and wants. Parsons emphasized the way that these, and ideas about suitable ways to attain them, are shaped by means of the socialization process and the value system of society.

It is the **cultural system** that is of most concern to us in this book. Parsons insisted that this allowed people to communicate with each other and to coordinate their actions, in part by establishing role expectations. He asserted that there are three major domains to the cultural system:

1   The realm of cognitive symbols (e.g., mathematical equations, financial reports) is concerned with ideas and beliefs about the world. These are usually evaluated according to normative standards linked to truth and are associated mostly with instrumental activity.
2   Expressive symbols (e.g., art, music) usually communicate emotion. Their evaluation involves aesthetic criteria. They are linked to creative activities and pleasure.
3   Moral standards and norms are concerned with whether or not something is right or wrong. Here values play a major role. Concrete actions are assessed according to their fit with abstract ideals.

Parsons placed an emphasis on the last domain in dealing with the problem of integration because values helped to define roles and expectations about the allocation of scarce resources. He suggested that agreement about common values was at the heart of social order. By internalizing norms about, say, fairness and inequality, and by subscribing to common goals (e.g., achievement), people align their actions with those of others. Moreover, they are able to agree on common standards with which to evaluate concrete behaviors and patterns of resource allocation.

It is important to note that although Parsons specifies the analytic separation and independence of the social, cultural, and personality systems, they do not all seem to have equal power in his model. In practice, the cultural system looks to be the more important. It invades the personality by shaping need dispositions and is institutionalized in the social system via roles. There seems to be no space in the model for a reciprocal influence of the personality and social systems on the cultural system. In part this appears to be because of the way that the cultural system is conceptualized in *Toward a General Theory of Action*. It is treated in very abstract ways and looks to be rather free-floating from social determination.

Late Systems Theory: The AGIL Model

The **AGIL Model** represents an even more complex refinement of the systems theory developed in *The Social System* and *Toward a General Theory of Action*. The finished model was first published in *Economy and Society* (Parsons and Smelser 1966 [1956]). It is so general and abstract that Parsons and Smelser believed it could be applied not only to every known society, but also to any subsystem within that society. They insisted that society is made up of four differentiated subsystems, each of which has its own function with regard to solving a particular problem. These subsystems might take the form of discrete institutions, or they might be more amorphous activities and procedures.

In textbooks we often find the model specified diagrammatically, as shown in figure 2.1.

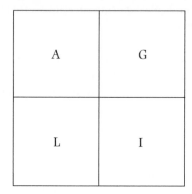

Figure 2.1   The AGIL model

- A stands for "adaptation" and refers to the way the system adapts to the outside world and fulfills material needs for survival (e.g., food, shelter). The economy is particularly important here.
- G stands for "goal attainment." This subsystem is concerned with ensuring there are system outputs and leadership. Politics is central to this arena.
- I represents "integration" and is concerned with the maintenance of order. The legal system and community institutions which promote social order are associated with this.
- L stands for "latent pattern maintenance and tension management" and refers to the need for the society to have guiding directions and ends of action. Institutions concerned with the production of cultural values, the maintenance of solidarity, and with socialization are found here. These include the church, schools, and the family.

An important feature of the model is that it can be applied at varying levels of analysis. For example, insofar as society as a whole is concerned, the church is situated in the L subsystem. It provides moral and symbolic goals that normatively regulate social action. However, if we take the church as a unit of analysis we will find that it too has AGIL subsystems. For example, there might be theological committees and prayer groups (L), disciplinary boards (I), policy steering committees (G), and entities concerned with building maintenance, fundraising, and collecting rents (A). The overall picture is of a society as a series of nested "boxes," each with four cells, that fit inside one another rather like Russian dolls.

Parsons and Smelser emphasized the significance of active interchanges between the cells as well as their differentiation. They saw the subsystems swapping things they needed with each other. Each had its own **generalized medium of exchange** that facilitated these transactions. These were money (A), power (G), influence (I), and value commitment (L). A church, for example, might provide moral leadership on an issue in return for political decisions that enable it to survive.

Worthy of special comment here are Parsons's views on the medium of power in particular. For Parsons, power was not a property of individuals, nor was it linked to domination. Rather, it was a property of systems, and was a good thing in that it enabled society to get various tasks done. This view contrasts with those of critical theory and has a curious resemblance to that of Foucault, which also sees power as diffused throughout society and as productive rather than just repressive (see chapter 7). It is also important to notice how the AGIL model, like Parsons's earlier work, combines a concern with both material and cultural needs and can be thought of as multi-dimensional. Yet, once again, a primary emphasis is given to culture (the L subsystem) in that it sets the ultimate goals toward which society works and ensures system stability. Parsons thought about this in terms of his **cybernetic model** of system regulation – an understanding borrowed from the field of biology. The idea here is that culture operates as a system of control. Just as a small output from the brain can direct the movements of the human body, Parsons suggested that small symbolic and informational inputs from culture could have a large input on the overall direction of a social system.

The Triumph of Modernity

Aside from his writings on systems theory, much of Parsons's work during the 1950s and 1960s was concerned with social change and the role of culture in that change. In *The Social System* and *Toward a General Theory of Action*, he had already developed a model of "**pattern variables**" (e.g., Parsons and Shils 1962: 77) and used them to explore roles and their associated interaction norms. In thinking through this issue, he drew on the work of Toennies and Durkheim. Writing around the turn of the century, Toennies had drawn analytical distinctions between traditional societies (***Gemein-schaft***) and complex, modern societies (***Gesellschaft***). Durkheim, as we have already seen, developed an important series of contrasts between mechanical and organic solidarity. Also central was Weber's work on the shift toward an impartial bureaucratic society from those characterized by traditional authority. Building on this literature, Parsons argued that we are able to distinguish between societies on the basis of their commitment to certain key opposed value patterns.

- *Particularism v. universalism.* Do we relate to people according to abstract general principles (fairness, justice) or according to their relationship to us (friend, kin, etc.)?
- *Affectivity v. affective neutrality.* Should we be influenced by feelings and emotions, or should we interact in a cooler, more rational, and calculated way?
- *Collectivism v. individualism.* Is the society and individual action organized around group needs and group belonging, or does it prioritize the rights and opportunities of the individual?
- *Diffuseness v. specificity.* Are issues and people evaluated according to an all-embracing logic or are they examined in detail on a case-by-case basis?
- *Ascription v. achievement.* Do individuals obtain their positions at birth or according to merit?

Parsons suggested that in the course of modernization societies have tended to move from the first term in each pair toward the second one. He broadly sums up this process with his idea of **value generalization** and suggests that it is an adaptive response to social evolution. As societies become more complex and differentiated, cultural systems need to become more abstract, flexible, and universalistic in order to bring about social integration and allow for maximum efficiency of social organization. Parsons also notes that in modern societies there has been a growing commitment to **institutionalized individualism** as a component of value generalization. This sees people evaluated equally according to their achievements and merit, rather than their caste, class, or clan. Parsons sees these developments as a good thing, believing that justice, fairness, and peaceful coexistence are better served by these more inclusive values. Whilst acknowledging general shifts, Parsons also stressed that we might find differing applications of these patterns in different aspects of our lives. In the family, for example, we might find the "pre-modern" values to be dominant. Similarly, Parsons suggested that we can distinguish between contemporary societies in terms of their differential commitment to modern value patterns. A distinctive feature of the United States, for example, is that it has a stronger attachment than several other developed nations to individualism.

In his works of the 1960s and 1970s, such as *Societies: Evolutionary and Comparative Perspectives* (1966) and *The System of Modern Societies* (1971 [1966]), Parsons was to continue his interest in the characteristics of modernity. In contrast to Weber, Marx (see previous chapter), and critical theory (see the next chapter), Parsons saw modernity in a favorable light and claimed that the process of differentiation brought greater affluence and freedom. He detected benefits such as greater respect for the individual, greater inclusiveness, and more democracy. The broad canvas that he paints is of modern society (and the United States in particular) becoming better and better, "more decentralized and associational" and with "a far broader range of freedoms than . . . any previous society" (1971 [1966]: 114–16).

Parsons: An Evaluation

The major criticisms of the Parsonian understanding of culture and its role in social life can be summarized as follows:

- Parsons assumes rather than demonstrates commitment throughout society to common value patterns. As critics like Alvin Gouldner (1970) and C. Wright Mills (1959) have pointed out, this leaves his theory vulnerable to accusations that it is excessively conservative and that it is unable to explain the dynamics of competition and conflict between groups.
- The Parsonian model of culture is very abstract, and consequently it might be suggested that it lacks the flesh and blood of a genuine explanation.
- Several critics claim that Parsons's theory denies human creativity and agency. Culture is implicated in the construction of an "oversocialized" human actor or a

"judgmental dope" who has internalized values and norms and who performs their social role in a robotic way.

- From the perspective of postmodern and critical cultural theory, Parsons's enthusiastic embrace of modernity is also problematic.

Yet, while it has been fashionable for some time to critique Parsons, it is also important to recognize that his treatment of culture has a number of positive features:

- It is informed by a reading of the classics.
- It is systematic and is integrated into a general theory of society.
- He provides the most vigorous arguments against the view that modernity has eroded meaning.
- Parsons's attempts to arrive at a multidimensional theory mark a significant effort at overcoming the idealist biases that can often handicap cultural analysis.
- By insisting on the centrality of cultural inputs to human action, Parsonian theory provides a robust model of the link between agency and culture and a well thought-out alternative to behaviorist and rationalist models of human action.

In the 1980s a brief effort was made under the banner of neo-functionalism to revive Parsons by recovering his belief in multidimensional explanation and taking on board the issues raised by his critics, such as the need for more sensitivity toward power and interests (Alexander and Colomy 1990). This did not seem to have any lasting impact. But another response to Parsons, and one chosen by several of his students (Clifford Geertz, Robert Bellah, and Edward Shils among them), has yielded more dividends. This perspective rethinks the Parsonian emphasis on culture by exploring actual symbolic structures and practices in more detail and texture than Parsons himself did. This makes possible an understanding of culture and society that maintains a central role for culture, but at the same time is more realistic and convincing. We look at some of this work in chapters 5 and 11.

Suggested Further Reading

Parsons himself can be very difficult to read. Some of the essays in *The Social System*, and in particular the discussion of the sick role, are sufficiently empirical to be accessible. The opening statement of *Toward a General Theory of Action* provides an elegant and time-efficient way to become familiar with his middle-period systems theory. For a remarkably clear and broadly sympathetic reading of Parsons, see chapters 2 through 6 in Jeffrey Alexander's *Twenty Lectures*. Still the most cutting critique of Parsons is the denunciation of "Grand Theory" in C. Wright Mills's *The Sociological Imagination*. For an accessible and brief description of the response of cultural theory to the Parsonian model of value analysis, see the opening few pages of Alexander and Smith (1993).

CHAPTER THREE

Culture as Ideology in Western Marxism

As we saw in chapter 1, Marx's thinking was characterized by a materialist bias. The result was a treatment of culture as generally unimportant and as the dependent product of an underlying economic base. A substantial proportion of twentieth-century Marxian thought reacted against this dimension of his work. In looking at what is sometimes thought of as the **Western Marxist** tradition we can detect several common features.

- *There has been an attempt to assimilate cultural explanation within a Marxian framework.* The aim has been to provide culture with an active and autonomous role in the regulation of social life and the maintenance of the capitalist economic order.
- *A major concern is to explain the non-arrival of the revolution that Marx predicted was inevitable.* Whilst other Marxian theorists developed elaborate theories of colonialism and the state to account for this, the writers we are interested in here pointed to the centrality of ideology in preventing the emergence of working-class radicalism.
- *There is a strong humanistic element to work in this tradition.* Drawing on Marx's *Economic and Philosophical Manuscripts*, there has been an interest in human experiences, consciousness, freedom, collective association, alienation, creativity, and subjective wellbeing. This orientation contrasts with the harsher, more structural Marxism that is inspired by *Das Kapital* with its "science" of historical materialism, structural models of society, and visions of "iron laws" of social development.

Georg Lukács

Born in Hungary, Georg Lukács (1885–1971) was a brilliant student who studied with Simmel and Weber, among others. He had wide-ranging intellectual interests, writing both within and outside of Marxian frameworks. Lukács's own spin on Marxism was developed in the first decades of the twentieth century. It draws heavily on Marx's discussions of commodity fetishism and alienation as well as upon readings of Weber, Simmel,

Hegel, and Dilthey, and embraces most of the themes that were to become central to Western Marxism later on. Most important of all, Lukács played a major role in the "rediscovery" and promulgation of the almost forgotten *Economic and Philosophical Manuscripts* (Marx 1978a [1844]), thereby providing a legitimating charter for a more cultural Marxism. For this reason he is often seen as a pivotal figure in the tradition.

Lukács's major work, *History and Class Consciousness* (1971), is a collection of essays written between 1918 and 1930. Here he describes the ways that capitalism was colonizing more and more dimensions of social life. He claims that commodity relations have impoverished the world and denuded it of authentic meaning. According to Lukács, social relationships, activities and human worth are increasingly defined in terms of an alienating and objectifying monetary exchange value – a process known as **commodification**. Drawing on Marx's analysis of wage labor, Lukács paints a bleak picture of contemporary life: "[The worker's fate] is typical of society as whole in that this self-objectification, this transformation of a human function into a commodity reveals in all its starkness the dehumanized and dehumanizing function of the commodity relation" (1971: 92).

Operating in parallel, and driven by the logic of industrial capitalist production, were processes of rationalization and standardization of the kind that Weber wrote about in his analysis of bureaucracy. As a result, "the principle of rational mechanization and calculability must embrace every aspect of life" (1971: 91). According to Lukács, the commodification of the social world is linked to a process of **reification**. This leads to a false perception of the social world as driven by objective forces that are beyond human control, and as denuded of inputs of human agency and creativity. An associated process of **commodity fetishism** helps build an economy structured around market exchange and to an uncritical stance toward the sale of goods and labor power. As a consequence of reification and commodity fetishism people are unable to grasp the **totality** of the capitalist system and its effects upon them (something they could only do, Lukács tells us, if they came to embrace Marxism). Consequently, their understanding of social life was **fragmented** or incomplete. Reacting against deterministic Marxism, Lukács (like many Western Marxists after him) emphasized the importance of human agency, writing that: "History is at its least automatic when it is the consciousness of the proletariat that is at issue" (1971: 208). He argued that a sense of class identity and political activism, or **class consciousness**, was needed among the proletariat. This could only come about through critical self-awareness and reflexivity about the ideological effects of capitalism.

Antonio Gramsci

Writing slightly later than Lukács, Antonio Gramsci also perceived the need for greater interpretative sensitivity in Marxian analysis. His own work simultaneously addressed two lacunae in Marx's own thinking – the neglect of politics and the neglect of culture. With the exception of essayistic works like *The Eighteenth Brumaire of Louis Bonaparte*, Marx (1978b [1852]) never really came to terms with the need for political strategy in advancing the cause of communism. Nor did he think about the role of the state in regulating social life and maintaining the necessary conditions for the perpetuation of capitalism. His deterministic framework seemed to proclaim that revolution was inevitable – all that was needed was to wait until the right economic conditions were in place. It was not until the twentieth century that Marxian political strategists like Lenin and Gramsci began to ask how culture and politics might promote or hold back an "inevitable" revolutionary change.

Gramsci's work is important precisely because it points to the links between politics, culture, and socialist strategy. In his *Prison Notebooks* (1992 [1929–33]), he argued that domination was not simply rooted in the economic sphere, but also had a major political and cultural component. He claimed that in Italy the objective conditions for revolution had been present for some years – an advanced capitalist economy in crisis, a large proletariat, and so on – and yet it had not come to pass. In seeking to explain this paradox he pointed to the role of the state, the role of intellectuals, and the role of ideas. According to Gramsci, the state was growing rapidly in power and invading civil society. He saw institutions like the church and trade unions, which had previously been independent, being taken over and regulated by governmental agencies. In Gramsci's view the state was not a disinterested, all-consuming bureaucracy (*à la* Weber), but rather an instrument of class domination. In particular, it represented the interests of capital and the bourgeoisie.

Culture comes into the picture when it is realized that a major component of state power was the control of ideas, as well as the use of physical force (e.g., by the police). The key concept here is **hegemony**. This is the ability of the state and the ruling class to regulate beliefs within civil society. Hegemonic beliefs are dominant cultural motifs which reinforce inequality and which short-circuit attempts at critical thinking. They allow dominant groups to rule more efficiently as they permit a reduction in the level of force required to maintain social order.

Gramsci claimed that the activities of **organic intellectuals** were central to the propagation of hegemonic beliefs. These are people like priests and journalists who translate complex philosophical and political issues into everyday language and who offer guidance to the masses on how to act. Intellectuals also played a role in making

---

ANTONIO GRAMSCI (1891–1937)

Gramsci was born in Sardinia, Italy, into a middle-class family. Although he did well at university he quit before graduating, and became involved in left-wing journalism. Aside from being an intellectual, Gramsci was also an activist. His role as a leading figure in the Italian Communist Party saw him targeted by Mussolini's Fascists. In June 1928, Gramsci was sentenced to 20 years in prison after a show trial. While in prison he studied and wrote his famous *Prison Notebooks* (sometimes known by their Italian title, the *Quaderni del carcere*). These consist of handwritten entries on diverse themes, and range in length from single sentences to complex essays. He died of a cerebral hemorrhage after years of ill health exacerbated by prison conditions.

Reference: Gramsci 1992: 65–94

possible the establishment of a **hegemonic bloc**. This was an alliance of dominant forces in society (e.g., industrialists, the aristocracy, the petty bourgeoisie). Typically, he asserted, these groups were held together by a hegemonic ideology that incorporated aspects of nationalist and common-sense thinking and used this to paper over divergent interests and class locations.

Gramsci argues that breaking down hegemony is a fundamental precondition for mobilizing latent socialist tendencies and initiating a revolutionary consciousness. Converting organic intellectuals or providing socialist ones was a step in this task. Other important tasks involved establishing alliances within subordinate classes (e.g., between peasants and industrial workers) and also between classes (e.g., between intellectuals and the proletariat). His hope was that in this way a **solidaristic bloc** could emerge in contradistinction to the dominant one. Rebuilding the autonomy of institutions in civil society would also contribute to the formation of an effective resistance movement. According to Gramsci, it was the church which provided the major hegemonic force in the Italy of his time, thanks to its moral authority among the proletariat. He believed that a significant political gain could be made if the church and its teachings could be changed so that it could provide moral and intellectual leadership for subaltern classes, rather than operating as a tool of the bourgeoisie. The overall picture of political life Gramsci painted was of a **war of position** in which the Left should try to outmaneuver hegemonic forces on cultural and political fronts, rather than engaging in an immediate full-on revolutionary attack.

Gramsci: an evaluation

Many of Gramsci's ideas bear the hallmark of his life experiences. He was an eyewitness to the rise of Italian Fascism, a political force whose corporatist ideas attacked distinctions between state and civil society, and whose success rested to a large extent on the populist appeal of its ideologies. Yet his thinking has a wider applicability than just early twentieth-century Italy. Gramsci's major contribution is arguably in the area of Marxist political praxis. In pointing to the importance of strategic alliances and the state in maintaining and challenging the capitalist system, he contributed to a major shift away from deterministic materialist thinking. His work suggests that we need to move away from a cookie-cutter model of class relations and revolutionary process to explore the contingent, historically, and nationally specific ways in which alliances are constructed and broken down in various settings. His thinking also provides a major role for creative political activists who are able to seize opportunities and construct innovative political strategies. In so doing, he offers a refreshing antidote to Marxist fatalism.

Gramsci's views on culture are equally important to critical thinkers and probably of more interest to readers of this text. His central achievement is in thinking about the role and operation of culture rather than its content. The emphasis on the flexible and actively constructed nature of political ideologies, captured by the concept of hegemony, provides an alternative to visions of monolithic dominant ideologies which automatically fall into place and which will automatically be replaced by those of socialism. His work also calls for detailed and situated, comparative and historical analyses of particular settings and ideological constellations rather than global denunciations of capitalist ideologies. Gramsci's attention to the state, civil society, intellectuals, and institutional life is also significant in that it suggests that hegemonic ideals cannot exist without organizational and infrastructural support. This helps to anchor culture in concrete structures and in the work of concrete actors.

These manifold virtues were to see Gramsci elevated to the pantheon of major Marxian thinkers as the twentieth century wore on. The New Left intellectuals of the 1960s found in him a prototype and justification for the kind of political and cultural activity in which they saw themselves as engaged. During the 1970s, Gramsci's ideas of hegemony were combined with more powerful interpretative tools by the British cultural studies movement and underpinned their efforts to understand the mass media and everyday life (see chapter 9). It was only during the 1990s, perhaps, that Gramsci's star began to wane as the critical mass among left-wing cultural theorists began to shift from Marxist to poststructural understandings of culture and society.

The Frankfurt School

"The Frankfurt School" is a name given to a group of German-speaking intellectuals who had an association with the Institute for Social Research in Frankfurt – an establishment founded in the early 1920s. However, the group was so diverse in terms of research interests that it is not immediately clear what benefits are to be had from thinking of them as a "school." Moreover, they were dispersed with the rise of Nazi Germany, many ending up in the United States. So the name is of very little geographical use either. When we look closely, however, we can detect a common theme in their methodological stance toward rationality and their critique of capitalist modernity. Drawing (like Lukács) on Weber's writings as well as upon Marx's cultural critiques, they suggested that formal rationality (*Zweckrationalität*) was an insidious force in society. It focused on means rather than ultimate goals or ends. Consequently what was required was an intellectual approach grounded in human values such as freedom, and which evaluated society in terms of its ability to further or to frustrate that end. Members of the School vigorously attacked the idea of value-free social research, and denounced positivistic analyses as purposeless exercises lacking in "critical reason." This attack on *Zweckrationalität* was to also inform their critiques of the bureaucratic enterprise, consumerism, and the culture industries, which are discussed below. Aside from the assault on formal rationality, we can discern various other dimensions of a family resemblance within the Frankfurt School:

- a concern with the impact of technology on social life, especially in the reproduction of popular culture;
- a concern with the impact of popular culture upon the mass populace;
- an interest in human sexuality and personality formation that was strongly informed by Freud (this work is discussed in chapter 12);

- a concern with identifying conditions under which human consciousness was either "fragmented" or able to comprehend "totality" (i.e., able to attain a neo-Marxian understanding of the world and with it true freedom).

There are many figures associated with the Frankfurt School, including Adorno, Benjamin, Fromm, Horkheimer, Lowenthal, Mannheim, and Marcuse. Their respective reputations have varied widely during their careers. At the time of writing, Theodor Adorno, Max Horkheimer, and Walter Benjamin seem to stand out as the most accomplished and creative intellects within the group. In the discussion that follows, we focus on their work before going on to explore the important work of Jürgen Habermas, the current heir to the Frankfurt legacy. Fromm and Marcuse are reviewed in chapter 12.

Walter Benjamin

Walter Benjamin is highly respected as a cultural critic and aesthete as well as for his contributions to social theory. His reputation lies mainly in a series of essays that, arguably, do not amount to a systematic vision of culture and society. Rather, they provide points of insight into diverse topics. The great appeal of Benjamin's work is that it exhibits a "musicality" or sensitivity to culture that far surpasses the best efforts of his Frankfurt School colleagues. He is a fine interpreter and writer and his essays provide an entertaining aesthetic experience as much as an intellectual one.

Perhaps Benjamin's most influential essay was his seminal study on "The Work of Art in the Age of Mechanical Reproduction." In this text Benjamin (1973 [1936]) is clearly influenced by Marx's writing on alienation and also his praxis theory. This understood human creativity to be embodied in the products of human labor. Benjamin argues that with the rise of industrial capitalism, cultural products – and especially artistic ones – undergo a radical transformation. In pre-capitalist societies their production is shot through with rich textures of meaning. They are organic products of social relationships and are invested with a sacred and spiritual character. They might be the object of a cult (as in a medieval religious icon) or be understood as in some ways connected with genius, authenticity, and creativity. According to Benjamin, while handcrafted artistic products are genuine and embody an **aura**, reproductions are somehow debased. He writes: "The presence of the original is the prerequisite to the concept of authenticity. . . . That which withers in the age of mechanical reproduction is the aura of the work of art" (1973: 214–15).

Technology, then, has removed the auratic quality from contemporary cultural products. They lose their unique value and spirituality, becoming routinized and standardized (there are strong affinities here with Weber's disenchantment thesis). Benjamin asserted that unified audience responses tended to be evoked by the artistic products of the machine age. The contemplation of an original painting used to be a private and individual activity. By contrast, with a product such as a movie, "individual reactions are predetermined by the mass audience response" (1973: 227–8) thanks to the simultaneous collective experience of its consumption. The result was a general deadening of critical and intellectual faculties. "The public," he writes, "is an examiner, but an absent-minded one" (1973: 234).

WALTER BENJAMIN (1892–1940)

Benjamin was born into an affluent Jewish family in Berlin. In his early life he appears to have been a gambler and *bon vivant* with a passion for books and fine *objets d'art*. He faked illness to avoid conscription in World War One and to continue his university studies. After failing to obtain a university post in the 1920s he started writing high-quality essays and journalism. He continued in a Bohemian existence, living and traveling off the proceeds of his writings and becoming a core member of the German left-wing avant-garde. He fled the country after the Nazi rise to power and drifted around Europe, supported in part with funds from the Institute for Social Research (Frankfurt School), arranged by his friend Theodor Adorno. Following the German invasion of France, Benjamin attempted to flee to Spain. As a Jewish, left-wing intellectual, his life chances in Nazi-occupied Europe were not very good. Finding the border closed, he committed suicide. Shocked by this experience, the Spanish border guards let his companions pass through.

Reference: Roberts 1982

A further and increasingly important aspect of Benjamin's work was what has subsequently been reconstructed as a study of consumer sites, consumer behavior, and urban form. Benjamin (1997 [1935–8]) had a great interest in the ideas of the French poet Charles Baudelaire, whose texts he translated and championed. He uses Baudelaire's poems as a window through which to capture the cultural milieu of nineteenth-century Paris. Perhaps the closest equivalent to this endeavor is Bakhtin's use of Rabelais to reconstruct the aesthetics of the medieval carnival (see chapter 11).

Benjamin shows how many of Baudelaire's poems reflected a new urban experience of fleeting interpersonal contacts, decadent sensuality, shady underworlds of conspiracy and poverty, flashy commodities and their display, and the tidal movements of crowds and people through streets and arcades. Benjamin's central contention is that the world of the capitalist city is one where strangers, goods, and appearances become central to human activity and subjectivity in new and surprising ways. A pivotal concept in this vision is that of the *flâneur*. This person is a wandering urban spectator who engages with urban spaces, crowds, and shop windows as a disinterested, strolling voyeur. As Benjamin (1997: 36) puts it, he "goes botanizing on the asphalt." The *flâneur* actively seeks out the life of the streets and wanders around the city, joining in with the crowd and moving through consumption spaces with a gaze that is at once ironic and appreciative. In this process the *flâneur* surrenders to the "intoxication of the commodity around which surges the stream of customers" (1997: 55). The image Benjamin presents here is a complex one. On the one hand, the *flâneur* is an active agent, behaving rather like a detective and engaging in the nonchalant study of human nature. On the other, he or she is an alienated individual seeking superficial solace in the anonymous crowd, the fetish of the commodity, and the relentless quest for novelty.

Benjamin emphasized the close links between *flâneurie* and the built forms of capitalism. His unfinished "arcades project" was intended to explore the ways that ideology and urban fabric of nineteenth-century Paris were interconnected. While this work was to remain uncompleted, the suggestive sketches that survive remain influential for those studying consumerism and urban form. Benjamin suggests that the seductive powers of commodity fetishism were enhanced by new architectural forms. The arcade emerged during the 1820s and 1830s. These were enclosed spaces constructed of glass and iron, lit by gas, and used to display luxury goods. Unlike the bustling street, they provided a safe place for the strolling *flâneur*, whose gaze was stimulated by the display of commodities. According to Benjamin, this relationship between subjectivity, space, and the commodity was to continue with the department store, which "made use of *flâneurie* in order to sell goods" (1997: 170). These sorts of ideas have subsequently exerted a considerable influence on research in the area of leisure and consumption, most notably in the burgeoning literature on the shopping mall.

Theodor Adorno and Max Horkheimer

Like Benjamin, Theodor Adorno was a diverse author who was highly respected by the German cultural elite. He was a noted music critic and friend of leading modernist composers like Alban Berg. Outside philosophical circles, Adorno is best remembered for his discussion of the "culture industries" and for his critique of mass culture. The pivotal text here, *Dialectic of the Enlightenment*, was written in conjunction with fellow Frankfurt School member Max Horkheimer (Horkheimer and Adorno 1972 [1947]). This text provides a damming indictment of the mass entertainment culture of consumer capitalism. It is widely noted that Adorno's exile in Los Angeles (home of Hollywood) during the 1940s may well have influenced his perspective on these issues. Probably equally important was an awareness of the populist mass culture produced in Germany during the Nazi era under the watchful eye of Goebbels's propaganda ministry. For the most part, this output was aimed not so much at political indoctrination as at superficial entertainment.

In *Dialectic of the Enlightenment*, Adorno and Horkheimer argue that the project of the Enlightenment has reached a dead end. It was supposed to bring human freedom and encourage critical thinking. Yet rationality, reason, and scientific knowledge have brought with them the instrumental control of social life. Instead of leading to an intelligent and caring society, the Enlightenment has resulted in a world that is shaped by a narrow, pragmatic form of rationality. Bureaucratic, technological, and ideological forces have limited human freedom and created a **mass society** of passive, uniform consumers. Social elites, by contrast, have consolidated their power thanks to these shifts.

Horkheimer and Adorno claim that a Weberian *Zweckrationalität* has combined with capitalism in the **culture industry**. These are major entertainment and media corporations. In the United States at the time he was writing, these would have been organizations like Metro-Goldwyn-Mayer (MGM), Twentieth-Century Fox, and the Radio Corporation of America (RCA). Were he alive today, Adorno would probably point to companies like Disney, Sony Pictures, Time-Warner, and Rupert Murdoch's News Corporation with interests in the production and distribution of entertainment products. According to Adorno and Horkheimer, such organizations produce goods with the intention of maximizing profit rather than enhancing critical thinking and human freedom. In doing this, they are guided by a narrow means–end rationality and take on the characteristics of bureaucratic and industrial combines rather than allowing for true artistic creativity. There has been "a regression of enlightenment to ideology which finds its typical expression in cinema and radio. Here enlightenment consists above all in the calculation of effectiveness and of the techniques of production and distribution" (1972: xvi).

The result of this process has been a production line approach to culture. Movies, music, and so on are assembled like any other manufactured product with standardized tasks divided up between workers. Accountants and balance sheets play a major role in determining what and how culture is produced. The final product is stereotyped and formulaic and is ultimately empty of authentic meaning. It will involve simplistic plot lines and cardboard characters and is designed to appeal to the lowest common denominator.

According to Adorno and Horkheimer, the culture industry plays a major role in the reproduction of capitalism. It produces stultified and content consumers without any critical faculties. As they put it: "No independent thinking must be expected from the audience" (1972: 137). Central to this process is the manufacture of superficial amusement and fun, something that Horkheimer and Adorno claim allows the audience "a flight from a wretched reality" (1972: 144) and prevents resistance.

THEODOR ADORNO (1903–69)

Adorno came from a wealthy Jewish-Catholic background. As a child, he showed musical and intellectual gifts. When he entered university he had already published two articles, and he attained his Doctor of Philosophy degree at the age of twenty-one. During the 1920s he studied with the composer Arnold Schoenberg and began an association with Institute of Social Research in Frankfurt. Following the Nazi rise to power he fled to Paris, Oxford, and then the United States, returning to Germany after the war. Always aloof from practical politics, he continued to write extensively on culture, sociology, and aesthetics from a left-wing perspective until his death in 1969.

Reference: Jay 1984

Aside from creating a zombie-like and relentlessly amused mass society, the culture industries also actively propagate pro-capitalist ideologies. Messages about the need to conform, to consume, to work hard, and to achieve individually are a typical feature of culture industry products. These help to motivate the workforce and prevent collective action.

Taken as a whole, Adorno's orientation to popular culture is dismissive. He sees it as superficial, trivial, manipulative, and pernicious. Jazz music and popular film in particular are condemned. By contrast, his orientation toward "high art," especially avant-garde modernism, is for the most part appreciative. He believed that it was superior in terms of its intellectual values, and could encourage reflexivity and critical thinking. This orientation has since become unfashionable. The school of British cultural studies, for example, has championed the political validity of the popular. Empirical research into audience reception of mass culture also suggests that ordinary people are more critical and discerning than Adorno imagined (for discussion of these points, see chapters 9 and 10). For the most part, Adorno's thinking in this area belongs more properly to aesthetic theory than to the kind of cultural theory that is current today. More useful is his general insistence that business and money are centrally involved in much cultural production, and we need to be alert to the consequences of this fact.

Jürgen Habermas

Jürgen Habermas is often considered to be the last member of the Frankfurt School. A generation younger than the others, Habermas was in his youth a student of the leading figures in the circle. Consequently their ideas have exerted a decisive influence on his thinking. While his work has undergone many phases and transformations, a common thread is the critique of capitalism and instrumental reason. Like his teachers such as Horkheimer and Adorno, he sees these as corrosive forces which prevent liberating, ethical, and democratic forms of human association. As we have seen, Horkheimer and Adorno saw the Enlightenment as having led to a dead end of control and oppression. Habermas has continued this critique, but has also attempted to salvage the Enlightenment project by defining "reason" in new ways.

The public sphere

These sorts of themes are apparent even in his early work. Habermas's doctoral thesis, on *The Structural Transformation of the Public Sphere* (1989), was written during the 1960s. It was a largely forgotten text during the 1970s and 1980s, but was rediscovered by a substantial intellectual audience in the 1990s. An impetus for this new interest came from the velvet revolutions in Eastern Europe. These saw popular demonstrations against communist regimes leading to the collapse of authoritarian state power and the rise of democracy. Social scientists read this as a sign that **civil society** (the citizenry and non-state sphere of social life) could stand up to the state through the active construction of a **public sphere** of debate and civic activism.

Habermas argues that during the eighteenth century there had been an active public sphere consisting of debate and the intelligent exchange of ideas about fundamental questions concerning philosophy, economics, politics, and social organization. This activity had the potential to impact upon formal politics. He singles out the coffeehouse as a core location for public-sphere engagement. People would meet here and discuss topical issues with friends and strangers alike. Also important was the rise of print media. Through early newspapers and affordable pamphlets, ordinary members of the community were able to publicize and share their views.

Habermas sees things going wrong with the rise of industrial capitalism in the nineteenth century. He suggests that the public sphere was replaced by a *bürgerliche Gesellschaft*. This term, which had also been used by Marx, is a pejorative one that refers, roughly speaking, to a "bourgeois association." The implication is that the public sphere was hijacked by a particular class interest. He goes on to suggest that with the shift to the contemporary era the public sphere has disappeared altogether, thanks to the impact of the mass media and the institutional differentiation of politics from broader social life. People became talked to, rather than being talkers actively creating the society in which they lived.

The concept of the public sphere is an important one. It has refocused a good deal of social research on the role of discourse in arenas that are outside of formal political life. Critics acknowledge these benefits while pointing to problems with Habermas's argument (for an overview see Calhoun 1992). Perhaps the most important of these is a kind of idealization of the public sphere (something that also influences his concept of "lifeworld," below). Habermas tends to eulogize the nineteenth-century public sphere but is relatively inattentive to the forms of exclusion that took place. In reality, coffee houses were chiefly frequented by educated and affluent men. By formal or informal means, the working class, women, and minorities were largely excluded from participation. A related problem is that Habermas tends to depict a single, unified public sphere. In complex and differentiated societies, it may be more useful to think about multiple public spheres organized around communities defined by race, gender, sexuality, and religion. These are sometimes overlapping, sometimes separate.

Knowledge and human interests

In his middle-period work on *Knowledge and Human Interests*, Habermas (1978) expanded on the familiar Frankfurt School attack of positivism and natural science. He argued that they allow only for the solution of narrow technical problems and fail to ask the more important questions that would allow for a radical rethinking of social relations and ideas about the nature of the good society. The interpretive discourses of the arts are deemed equally inadequate in that their major concern is increasing mutual understanding rather than discovering the conditions for human emancipation. Only critical social sciences, Habermas claims, are able to combine the quest for knowledge with a profound understanding that human interests lie in maximizing freedom through the implementation or fundamental social change.

The theory of communicative action

Whilst *Knowledge and Human Interests* tours over familiar Frankfurt School territory, Habermas was to take a more innovative approach in his later work. He returns in detail to themes nascent in his study of the public sphere, looking in particular at the potential for human communication to enhance human freedom. His major publication of the 1980s, *The Theory of Communicative Action*, is a long and densely argued work that is difficult to summarize without risking triviality. Habermas (1984) draws on authors as diverse as Marx, Weber, Durkheim, Parsons, and Mead in constructing his position. Perhaps the best starting point, however, is to realize that Habermas is working in the Frankfurt School tradition and is building on the legacy of Horkheimer and Adorno's *Dialectic of Enlightenment* (see McCarthy 1984). As we have seen, in that work they had argued that reason had reached a dead end in the bureaucratic rationalization of society. A fatalistic pessimism pervaded their thinking to the point where they could not see how reason could provide the foundation for emancipation.

Habermas suggests that the Enlightenment project (which saw reason as leading to emancipation) could be saved if reason was redefined in a novel way. He asserts that we need to work with a concept of **communicative reason**, consisting of the undistorted activities of people attempting in a genuine way to attain clear mutual understanding. The problem, as he sees it, is that the rise of modernity took a wrong turn. On the one hand, it allowed for the possibility of clearer communication as the conventional restraints of tradition were removed. Central to this was the process of differentiation as described by Durkheim and Parsons. This entailed value generalization, an increasing autonomy for various spheres of social life and a potential ability for them to reflexively self-regulate. On the other hand, processes of bureaucratization and commodification became too powerful. They cut off institutional life from community inputs – especially those relating to substantive values (e.g., equality, democracy, human solidarity). The result was a society driven by impersonal and alienating forces, especially those of capital and Weberian *Zweckrationalität*. These obeyed their own logic and no longer required value-inputs from human agents.

Habermas's analysis is in many ways similar to that of Lukács, who had written on the subject some 60 years before (see pp. 34–5). An important conceptual elaboration that allows him to move beyond such previous approaches is his extensive use of systems theory, and in particular the concepts of **system world** and **lifeworld**. These serve as a conceptual shorthand in his theoretical model. The system world consists of the state, capitalism, and large bureaucratic or capitalist organizations. The lifeworld consists of solidarity, face-to-face contact, family, community, and substantive value commitments. Habermas paints a picture in which the system world has been progressively "invading" or "colonizing" the lifeworld as modernity has unfolded. He draws loosely on Parsons's AGIL model (see chapter 2) to understand this process, but suggests that it presents "too harmonious a picture, because it does not have the wherewithal to provide a plausible explanation of pathological patterns of development" (McCarthy 1984: 203). Parsons, as we have seen, argued that society involved more or less equal inputs from its various subsystems. Habermas, by contrast, claims that the "media of exchange" of the system world – money and power – have become dominant and have prevented true communicative rationality. They now trespass where they do not belong and are replacing ethical, emotional, and value commitments as key players in the organization of the lifeworld. This process has involved the extinction of the public sphere at the hands of a capitalist mass media, the growth of meaningless Kafkaesque bureaucracies, the subversion of democracy by big business, continuing inequality, and the substitution of passive workers, taxpayers, and consumers for active debaters and communicators. Habermas seeks a way of revitalizing the lifeworld and allowing it to fight back against the colonizing forces of commodification and bureaucratic rationalization. The answer lies in his theory of communicative rationality. This consists of open, honest, and informed debate between individuals which is free from the distorting constraints of ideology and power.

Critiques of the theory of communicative action

Habermas's argument has been criticized on various fronts. Poststructural critics like Foucault question whether the Enlightenment project can, or indeed should, be salvaged. Others have pointed to the utopian aspects of Habermas's work. Feminists comment that he idealizes the lifeworld of the domestic sphere rather than seeing it as a fundamental locus of patriarchal oppression. For many feminists increased state intervention in the family and private life (e.g., domestic violence legislation, child-support payments) has been a positive rather than negative dimension of social change. Utopian thinking is also evident in the way that Habermas's diagnosis of the ills of modern society is more convincing than his cure. He has relatively little to say about concrete ways to build a better world, seemingly believing that his task has been to identify the possibility of communicative rationality, thus making it possible for people to freely choose it. From a realist perspective this is not enough – it is also necessary to think about plausible institutional forms that can support this kind of activity. These might include a diverse mass media, grass-roots social movements, civic activism, and so on.

Louis Althusser

Like other cultural Marxists, the French philosopher Louis Althusser attempted to incorporate a more nuanced understanding of culture and human subjectivity into the legacy of Marxian thinking. Where he differs from writers like Lukács and the Frankfurt School is that he did not embrace the humanistic younger Marx in order to attain this end. Indeed, Althusser equated humanism with individualism, and considered both of them to be sins of bourgeois thinking. Althusser is unusual in that he wished to accommodate a cultural perspective within the framework of the "scientific" later Marx. In this respect his work has a strong resemblance to the structuralist project of Lévi-Strauss (see chapter 6), which also saw itself as scientific. It is no accident that in many discussions of "structuralism," Althusser's work is often placed alongside that of the great cultural anthropologist. Both scholars explore parts in relations to wholes, both see themselves as objective analysts, and both have a penchant for theorizing about systems. There are, however, significant differences. Thanks to a rejection of Marxism, the models of culture produced by Lévi-Strauss provide a strong basis for theorizing the autonomy of culture. Althusser's model, by contrast, was unable to unambiguously accomplish this task. Those favorable to critical cultural analysis, however, may find Althusser's understanding of the close ties between social structure, power, and culture to offer advantages over Lévi-Strauss's rather reified conceptualization of the cultural sphere.

Althusser argued that Marx had undergone an **epistemological break** during his life. According to Althusser, Marx's early writings were humanistic and subjectivist and were still infected with Hegelian idealism. By contrast, in his later work, such as *Capital*, Marx advocated an objective and "scientific" approach. Althusser believes this later, more materialist vision is the superior one. He sees it as broadly structural in orientation and, therefore, as more intellectually powerful. In a sense this was a fateful and unusual step. It cut Althusser off from reference to Marx's *Economic and Philosophical Manuscripts* (1978a [1844]). By abandoning this resource as an inferior and immature dimension of Marx's *oeuvre*, Althusser left himself with the difficult task of developing a cultural theory from the later works constructed from within the tradition of dialectical materialism. In order to do so he turned toward structuralism for a solution.

LOUIS ALTHUSSER (1918–1990)

Like so many other French intellectuals, Louis Althusser was born in Algeria (for much of the century Algeria was a province of France). His educational profile fits the template for a dominant French thinker, involving study at the leading Parisian institutions and a thorough grounding in philosophy. For much of his life he was a leading intellectual figure in the French Communist Party as well as a key Parisian academic. His influence reached a peak during the late 1960s, when radical students and active trade unions were on the center stage of French politics. For all his intelligence, Althusser was not only prone to fits of depression, but also mentally unstable. He killed his wife in 1980, but was found innocent by reason of temporary insanity; he subsequently spent several years in a mental hospital. His autobiography, published posthumously, reveals that he was insecure and that he was worried that his work would be "found out" as shallow and he would be dismissed as an intellectual fraud.

Reference: Benton 1984: ix

Althusser (1971) read Marx's later works very carefully and claimed to derive from them the basis for a structural model of society which gave culture and politics an independent role. He asserted that there was an economic base (the mode of production, means of production, etc.) and a superstructure, consisting of a political and legal structure (the state and legal system) and an ideological structure (the church, political beliefs, etc.). According to Althusser, the superstructure worked to help generate the conditions necessary for the survival of capitalism – its major function, then, was to allow for the **reproduction** of capitalism. The state and legal system are a "machine of repression which enables the ruling classes . . . to ensure their domination over the working class" (1971: 137). They are concerned with regulating the supply of labor, dealing with social discontent, and ensuring that the economy ran in ways that facilitated the accumulation of capital by the dominant class. The ideological system (we return to this later) provided legitimation for capitalism and offered people identities and roles that were necessary for the reproduction of the capitalist system. Taking a structuralist position, Althusser stressed the ways that these systems were interlinked, each one performing a vital social function and each one meshing with the others to form a seamless, smoothly functioning, industrial capitalist society.

So far this seems like orthodox, materialist Marxism with its base-superstructure model of social life, albeit with a twist of left-wing functionalism (see pp. 7, 10). Althusser, however, wished to give more power to the superstructure than was traditional in what his supporters termed "vulgar materialism." In order to do this he developed some significant (and controversial) concepts. He argued that the superstructure had a "**relative autonomy**" (1971: 135) from the base. This is a complex and much debated term and Althusser was never really clear what he meant by it. He implies that the superstructure could have an impact of its own upon social life and that the economic base provided only broad limits and guidelines for the forms of institutions and ideologies that could emerge within it. Another term that Althusser used to explain his thinking was that of "determination in the **last instance**" (1971: 135). This, again, is generally taken to mean that there are complex, reciprocal relationships between the base and superstructure and that only at the end of such complex webs and chains of causation we will find an economic cause.

The ideological state apparatus and subject positions

Althusser's efforts to escape from the iron clutches of simplistic economic determinism whilst working within a structural model of social relations denote one key feature of his work. Another was his attention to the role of the state in cultural life. In his collection entitled *Lenin and Philosophy and Other Essays*, Althusser (1971) argued that in working to reproduce capitalism the state made use of two kinds of systems. The **repressive state apparatus (RSA)** consisted of institutions which made use of coercive force. Examples include the police, the military, and prisons. These might by used to crush protest and dissent on the streets, to break strikes, and to suppress left-wing military insurgencies. The **ideological state apparatus (ISA)** consisted of institutions that promulgated illusions about the nature and organization of society. These included the media, the church, and above all the school. All of these have links to the state via regulation, funding, or administration. While the church was the most important ISA in pre-capitalist societies, today this role is played by the educational system. It provided the trained, passive, and compliant workforce required by capitalist enterprise.

By linking concepts of ideological reproduction to the operation of the state in this way, Althusser's work points to specific loci of ideological production. In this respect his work (like Gramsci's) is important in adding specificity to Marxian ideas which often tend to posit somewhat free-floating dominant ideologies. The concept of the ISA helps us to tie these ideologies to concrete agencies and processes – or at least to look for ties in specific locations.

Althusser argued that the role of the ISA was to provide agents with false concepts about society and their place in it. Rather than understanding their true role in society and the nature of the capitalist system, Althusser sees actors living their lives in a false subjective world. As he puts it: "Ideology represents the imaginary relationship of individuals to their real conditions of existence" (1971: 162). So, as people go about their daily business, they have illusory relations to others and to the capitalist system, rather than having a complete and scientific understanding of what is really going on. Thanks to the influence of Jacques Lacan on his thinking (see chapter 12), Althusser sees self-identity as playing a crucial role in this process. According to Althusser, the needs of the economic base determine the kinds of "functions" that individuals must fulfill – as workers, administrators, and so on. People, however, are generally unaware of their objective identities as functionaries within a capitalist system. Instead, they inhabit illusory **subject positions** and identities which are propagated and allocated by the ISAs. As he puts it: "all ideology has the function . . . of constituting concrete individuals as subjects" (1971: 171). Althusser stresses the ways that people voluntarily subscribe to particular identities such as these and the ways that they mesh with the objective needs of the system to for reproduction. The subjectivities that people occupy seem "natural," and so ideology is not recognized as such.

Critiques of Althusser

Althusser should be praised for the systematic nature of much of his thought and for attempting to assimilate an understanding of culture and cultural autonomy within a structural Marxian framework. This is arguably a task of much greater difficulty than the more common humanist Marxist approach. It is no surprise, therefore, that critics generally argue that Althusser's work fails to reconcile historical materialism with an understanding of the autonomy of culture and subjectivity. Perhaps the most compelling argument along these lines is a famous essay entitled "The Poverty of Theory" by the British neo-Marxian historian E. P. Thompson (1978), which launches a sustained and vitriolic attack on Althusser's work. The agenda behind this attack was a desire to defend the tradition of humanist, empirical Marxism and to prevent theoretical structuralist thought from hijacking the Marxian legacy. Thompson's critique has several strands. He argued that:

- Althusser's work was too abstract and failed to engage with concrete data about the real struggles of real people.
- Althusser was a master of complex word games, but failed to deliver genuine theoretical innovation.
- Althusser's vision of social process was too deterministic. His concepts, such as "relative autonomy," merely substituted a complex deterministic mechanism for a simple one. Drawing a pointed analogy, Thompson suggests that Althusser has replaced the clock-like determinism of vulgar materialism with a theoretical orrery. An orrery is an elaborate mechanical device that tracks not only time but also the movements of the sun, moon, stars, and planets. Thompson's point is that even though the model may be more complex, the underlying mechanism is still one of clockwork determinism.

- In the final analysis, Althusser's vision of social life was one which denied the potential for human freedom and creativity – specifically, the potential for people to make their own history.

Gramscian writers during the 1980s also attacked Althusser. While they were somewhat sympathetic to his political orientation, they often used his thinking as a foil with which to distinguish their approach. Stuart Hall (1980a: 32–5), for example, pointed to the superior capacity of Gramscian models to acknowledge contingency, flexibility, agency, and cultural autonomy. Viewed in this light, Althusser begins to look like a rigid and doctrinaire systems theorist, whose abstract models are unable to come to terms with the complexities of the real world.

Althusser's work reached its peak of influence in the late 1960s and 1970s among left-wing academics, before being replaced by the rising stars of Gramsci, Foucault, and Bourdieu during the 1980s. However, it was still possible to find large numbers of enthusiastic graduate student and faculty devotees up to the late 1980s. The reasons for Althusser's fall from grace are manifold. Some relate to the general decline of structuralist thinking and the need to incorporate agency into cultural explanation. Others relate to growing academic interest in the autonomy of culture and the inability of his approach to unambiguously acknowledge this possibility. Still more reasons reflect changes in the organization of society, such as the apparent decline of class as an organizing principle in post-industrial society. In the last instance, Althusser's theory was deemed less able to deal with each of these shifts than those of his major competitors within the camp of critical social science.

The Decline and Future of Western Marxism

Western Marxism today is not the force it once was. For much of the twentieth century it was a magnet for critical thinkers, its reputation enhanced by the plethora of great minds who worked in the tradition. Today its energy seems to have been largely dissipated. The collapse of communism in Eastern Europe in 1989 and the mainstreaming of West European socialist parties during the 1980s and 1990s took the wind out of the Western Marxist sails. Nobody else seemed to believe in the socialist alternative they were advocating. During the 1970s and 1980s, a smorgasbord of critical paradigms (e.g., feminism, poststructuralism, and postmodernism) came into common currency and compounded this isolation. These provided critical thinkers with ways to talk about power, culture, and inequality without carrying the Marxist baggage of class analysis, materialism, omniscience, and socialism. As a result, many cultural theorists on the left abandoned Marxism for pastures new. Finally, Western Marxism has become routinized into an academic trade. The era of charismatic leaders, intellectual giants, and world-historical struggles has passed. Its appeal now is prosaic rather than messianic, leaving ideas to compete on their own merits for an audience in what is an increasingly competitive marketplace of ideas. The future of Western Marxism will depend on its ability to adapt to this changed environment while retaining a minimally Marxian identity.

One intriguing strategy for the survival of the Western Marxist tradition can be observed in the work of two important contemporary theorists, the philosopher Roy Bhaskar and the literary critic Terry Eagleton. It involves an entrance into a dialogue with one of Marxism's longtime cultural enemies: religion.

Like Althusser (who deeply influenced him), Bhaskar has concentrated much attention on the philosophy of science and specifically the question of whether human society can or should be studied in the same way that we study the natural world. His response to this question involves an attempt to overcome the disputes between positivism and hermeneutics with a series of very Marxist-like moves. Positivism is rejected for trying to map crudely mechanistic frameworks taken from the natural sciences to the social sciences and failing correctly to understand the role played by the critical consciousness of humans in the production and transformation of the objectively given structures of social life. Hermeneutics (see chapter 11) is equally insufficient, however, because it gives human consciousness too much power to create the world and fails properly to recognize the trans-individual and real structures that constrain us. Bhaskar calls his approach **critical realism** – it is "realist" in its rigorous refusal of "mere" interpretative social science and "critical" in its commitment to a Hegelian and Marxist understanding of human consciousness as capable of directing us to emancipatory subjectivity.

So far, this sounds quite consonant with the earlier Marxist tradition. More recently, however, Bhaskar has, to the dismay of many of those attracted to his earlier work, turned to an attempt to reconcile "the New Left and the New Age" (Bhaskar 2000: 6). Here, he argues for the need of a rapprochement between Western and Eastern ways of thinking about emancipation. The former (Marxism can be taken as a representative) start with basic dualisms (free/non-free) and emphasize action (class struggle); the latter (we can take Buddhism as an example) embrace monism (all are one) and inaction (retreat from the world as the way to enlightenment). Bhaskar claims that a full understanding of the emancipatory human project to which Marxism dedicates itself requires an incorporation of the mystical ideas of the East. The scope of this recent work is monumental, and the language he adopts often almost prophetic: "To change the world, man has only to realise himself . . . The time for unconditional love has struck" (2000: 152).

Eagleton's early work was also heavily influenced by Althusser. He advocated a method for literary analysis bursting with straightforward Marxist theoretical categories adapted for use in the literary field. Texts (or works, which he preferred because of its invocation of the notion of labor) have to be situated not only with respect to a general mode of production and dominant ideology, but also with respect to a **literary mode of production** (relations between the various participants in the making of literary works) and **aesthetic and authorial ideology** (the former concerns the specific literary practices considered legitimate; the latter is the version of the general ideology accepted by a particular author as a result of his or her specific social position). For this straightforwardly Marxist Eagleton, literary works bear the imprint of the class situation in which they are written and should be read as reflections of those conditions of class relations and conflict.

More recently, however, he has expanded his theoretical vision to include a significant interest in theological and religious concepts, even while still adhering to a revolutionary socialist politics. Several of his recent books have witheringly criticized both the orthodox Marxist left and its primary theoretical rival, postmodernism (see chapter 13) while staking out a position somewhere between the two. He believes the Marxists have failed to understand how some key conceptual categories from religion, notably sacrifice and the tragic, can be utilized from a critical materialist position. Tragedy is not simply an elitist and pessimistic narrative, as conservative cultural thinkers would have it, because we find affirmative tragedy in Hegel's account of "Spirit, once pitched into contention with itself, restor[ing] its own unity through nega-tion" (Eagleton 2003: 42). Even Christianity and Marxism can be read as affirmative tragic forms, wherein the evils of sin and exploitation are confronted with a hope (eternal life or social revolution) that may or may not prove triumphant. Sacrifice can also be recuperated by the cultural left insofar as it can be read as ethical and not merely cultic – i.e., as representing a radical and destructive rupture with an existing social order and the establishment of a new community rather than as the sign of a covenant with gods. Eagleton mines the theological narratives of ritual sacrifice in order to con-struct a left materialist reading in which the sacrificial scapegoat becomes the global underclass dispossessed by capitalism and suicide bombers are a culturally complex sacrificial response to this dispossession in which the same individual acts as both sov-ereign and victim (Eagleton 2003). If the Marxists have missed this, postmodernists have missed something of even greater import, and this is the collection of universal properties that unite all humans and defeat the radical cultural relativism they assert. Simple truths – sexual desire, ageing, fear of our own death, and sorrow at the death of others – connect all of us in purely material ways. Culture, for Eagleton, is "put . . . back in its place" by the remembrance that, however many different ways we have of understanding death, we all die (2000: 131).

It is of note that these recent trajectories taken by two of the more visible theorists to spring from the Western Marxist tradition have turned to the cultural object most absent in the traditional Marxist corpus: religion. Furthermore, perhaps the single most visible living descendant of the Frankfurt School, Habermas, recently acknowledged in a dialogue with Pope Benedict XVI that the Western secular liberal state should acknowl-edge the Judeo-Christian religious tradition as an ally in the struggle against contempo-rary global forces of alienation (Ratzinger and Habermas 2007). While orthodox adherents to the Western Marxist tradition have been critical of these recent develop-ments, one can only wait to see precisely what theoretical dividends this new work will yield and how much it will change the Marxist framework for thinking about culture.

Suggested Further Reading

The discourse of the Western Marxists is often dense, abstract, and philosophical. It can also be quite incestuous, with authors debating the finer points of Marxism among themselves in an "enciphered language" (Anderson 1979: 32, 53–4). While these debates might be important for insiders, they can be rather off-putting for outsiders looking for an accessible, empirically driven point of entry. Perry Anderson's *Consider-ations on Western Marxism* offers an efficient and sympathetic introduction to the area by a leading proponent.

The philosopher Richard Rorty said that when he could not understand Habermas he read interpretations of his work by Thomas McCarthy. I recommend the same strategy. McCarthy's introduction to his translation of Habermas's *Theory of Communicative Action* covers the main points of a monumental work in only 32 pages and will prepare the reader for the hundreds of pages that are to follow. Ted Benton's (1984) book on structural Marxism provides a fair summary of Althusser's distinctive approach. The well-known writings by Benjamin, Althusser, and Adorno discussed here are also just about within the scope of novice readers. Eagleton's recent work is reader-friendly, if drenched in literary references. An edited volume, *Critical Realism and Marxism* (Brown et al. 2002), provides insights into the core of Bhaskar's thought and its relationship to the thought of Althusser and other Marxists. A hard-to-find book by Roger Scruton entitled *Thinkers of the New Left*, will amuse those who dislike critical theory and enrage those who are devotees. Scruton is a conservative philosopher who argues, in a somewhat flippant way, not only that much cultural Marxism is hopelessly confused and simplistic, but also that it is merely old Marxism in drag. We hesitate to recommend this book, but even if it is sometimes inaccurate and rather acid, at least it is lively and provocative.

CHAPTER FOUR

Culture as Action in Symbolic Interactionism, Phenomenology, and Ethnomethodology

This chapter is about the so-called micro theories of symbolic interactionism, phenomenology, and ethnomethodology. We use the words "so-called," as many scholars within and outside the area reject the term "micro." They see it as part of a divisive discourse which marks out certain intellectual questions and approaches as being separate from, and antithetical to, mainstream social and cultural theory. While contestation between "micro" and "macro" theory was a hallmark of polemics during the 1960s and 1970s, most theorists today are interested in working toward a rapprochement. The general mood within cultural theory has changed, and there is a feeling that micro and macro levels and styles of analysis are complementary rather than incommensurable. We review some of these efforts at synthesis in chapter 8. Here, we look at traditional micro perspectives and see what they have to offer the broader field of cultural theory.

Micro perspectives are diverse and sometimes in competition with each other. There are, however, a number of family resemblances within this diverse tradition. These can be summarized as follows:

- face-to-face encounters between actors are a central feature of social life;
- people are creative, intelligent, and knowledgeable;
- social order arises as an accomplishment of actors who are able to manage encounters and make them predictable, successful, and mutually understandable;
- in order to study how society works, we need interpretative methodologies which try to capture the actor's definitions of the situation.

This intellectual position has two points of origin, one positive and the other negative. The positive origin lies in a series of ancestral influences. Weber's advocacy of *Verstehen* (see pp. 12–13) provides an important charter in that it highlights the centrality of meanings to social action. Pragmatism in American philosophy during the first quarter of the twentieth century was still more important for the emergence of this perspective. There were significant differences among the leading figures associated with pragmatism (William James, Charles Sanders Peirce, and John Dewey), but the core that is useful for cultural theory has to do with an argument about how meaning is generated in human interaction. For the pragmatists, knowledge and meaning are dependent on context, with this often shaped by the practical task at hand or by the intent of the persons in a particular setting. The model is of culture as something produced and used in interaction. For example, by the 1870s Peirce had already developed a theory of meaning and truth that presented reality as something only knowable through a system of signs or representations, which are always, in practice, the achievement of a community of knowers. Objective knowledge or truth, insofar as by that term we mean knowledge not presented in the particular symbolic representations of a particular human group, is impossible (Thayer 1973). Meaning is produced as a process of interaction between three elements:

1   The **sign** (e.g., the word "dog" in English).
2   The **object** in the world referred to by the sign (a certain furry creature with four legs and a tail).
3   The **interpretant** (the thought or understanding produced in an interlocutor when he or she reads or hears the word "dog").

With this innovation, Peirce essentially invented the field of **semiotics**, the study of signs. While some thinkers would take semiotics in a direction that removed it from the interactive context in which Peirce placed it (see chapter 6), others built on this work in a distinctly micro-sociological fashion. The work of George Herbert Mead and Charles Cooley was key here. Both developed triadic theories of interaction and identity based on this pragmatist theory of signs and meaning. The constituent elements of Cooley's idea of the **looking-glass self** are an individual's imagination of another's perception of him/her, followed by the imagination of that other's evaluation of the person he or she is seeing, followed in turn by the emergence in the first person of some kind of evaluation of him/herself. The self is, in other words, an interactive production from the very first, since we only apprehend ourselves and come to think of ourselves in a particular way (attractive, unattractive, witty, boring) by putting ourselves into the imagined perspective of another perceiving us. Our understanding of, and even our very development of, a self is dependent on an already-existing community that shares a symbolic universe. Mead's notion of **taking the role of the other** is very similar. We develop selves through the practice of pretending to be others; first, those who are generally close to us (mother, father), or the **significant other**, then later a more abstract collective other that Mead calls the **generalized other**. It is interesting to note that these early theoretical moves have received support from a surprising direction: experimental studies on the medical problem of autism. People with this condition often lack the capacity for appropriate and smooth social interaction and can seem insensitive. They are apparently unable to intuit the moods and perspectives of those around them and act accordingly. The argument has been made that autistic persons do not have a "theory of mind," that they cannot make the imaginative leap that is required to guess or second guess the thoughts of others. Early Chicago School ethnographies (the University of Chicago had become a focal point for American pragmatism in the early 1900s, with both Dewey and Mead on the faculty there) were also a key impetus for the micro perspective. They suggested that social research should take a humanist form and explore the worldviews, cultures, and life experiences of particular groups. Finally, the European tradition of phenomenology, about which we will say more shortly, has emphasized the role of human perception and provided some theoretical heavy artillery in support of an agency-focused research orientation.

On the other hand, the negative origin of micro theory lay in a hostile reaction to Parsonian functionalism (Alexander 1987; Heritage 1984). As we saw in chapter 2, Parsons proposed a mode of analysis emphasizing that the maintenance of social order was an achievement of systems rather than actors. From the mid-1950s onward, the various micro theories progressively detached themselves from the Parsonian agenda as they attempted to explain how order could arise as a product of concrete interactions. This involved empowering the actor in their theoretical models and recognizing possibilities for reflexivity, creativity, and responsible agency. So far so good, one might think. Unfortunately, this step also involved an ambivalent relationship toward cultural explanation. Thanks to a grounding in the *Verstehen* tradition, micro theory recognized that meaning was central to action and its explanation. Yet it could not be fully acknowledged that action was organized by an overarching cultural order or by collective symbols. To do so would be to reproduce the sins of Parsonian systems theory. The consequence was a body of literature that talks about meanings and actions, but largely sees the former arising from the latter.

Such a position was nicely summarized by Herbert Blumer in one of his numerous polemical manifestos for symbolic interactionism. Blumer (1969: 2) insists that people relate to each other and to objects on the basis of shared meanings. This is a position with which few cultural theorists would disagree. However, Blumer goes on to argue that "the meaning of such things is derived from, or arises out of, the social interaction that one has with one's fellows" (1969: 2). In other words, the focus in understanding action is on how people create and use meanings, rather than on how "cultural prescriptions, norms and values . . . provide such explanations" (1969: 3). The result is an overwhelming emphasis on explaining how actors can be creative, rather than on telling how culture can inform action patterns and be analytically distinct from them. This theme of prioritizing action over the exegesis of culture is well illustrated in the work of Erving Goffman.

Erving Goffman

Erving Goffman is widely recognized as a uniquely talented observer of social life, and would be a strong candidate in any poll to name the twentieth century's most influential symbolic interactionist. Perhaps the best way to get an overview of Goffman's broad take on social life is to quickly run through the contents of some of his major books.

The Presentation of Self in Everyday Life

In this, his first and arguably most influential work, Goffman (1959 [1956]) suggested that social action could be studied using an elaborate **dramaturgical metaphor** (social life is like a staged drama). The aim was to show how "the individual in ordinary work situations presents himself and his activity to others, the ways in which he guides and controls the impression they form of him, and the kinds of things he may and may not do while sustaining his performance" (1959: xi). So while Parsons saw actors as inhabiting an internalized role, Goffman sees the actors as "performing a role" and emphasizes what he calls **role distance**. The distinction is important, as it highlights the reflexivity and active crafting of social life. Goffman argues that people have to make an acceptable show of whatever they are supposed to be doing. This is called **impression management**. In acting out their role, they may well make use of objects as **props**. There is also an audience watching them and perhaps a team supporting them. When people are in interaction each will have to be both an audience and an actor. Goffman also suggests that spatial regions have an implication for interaction. There is often a **backstage** area where they carry out tasks that are hidden from the audience, but which are essential for a smooth **frontstage** performance. Goffman provides numerous examples to support this vision, perhaps the most compelling of which is that of a restaurant. The skillful waiter will act out his role before an audience of customers supported by a backstage team in the kitchen. He will use props like corkscrews and menus, and try to give off an impression of professional solicitude.

Dramas in the theatre are usually scripted, rehearsed, and polished. Getting through social life, however, is a chancy business. Goffman discusses the ways that people have to be able to maintain their self-confidence, risk making mistakes, and deal with disruptions to their performance. The overall impression we get from *The Presentation of Self in Everyday Life* is of people being ingenious and talented. They are constantly giving off signals to each other. These say who they are and what they are doing and assist actors to maintain a mutually agreed definition of the situation. A danger with this perspective, however, is that the logic of the dramaturgical metaphor leads us perilously close to a simplistic vision of people as fakes and frauds, acting strategically to

---

Erving Goffman (1922–82)

Goffman was born in Canada, but spent most of his professional life in the United States after training at Chicago with some of the original Chicago School scholars. His work is of interest to researchers in a number of fields, including ethology, anthropology, and psychology, as well as sociology and cultural studies. This is hardly surprising, as he was well read and dipped into diverse literatures in search of ideas that could be applied to the study of human behavior. He rose to prominence with the publication of *The Presentation of Self in Everyday Life*, a book which drew on his fieldwork in the Shetland Islands of Scotland. Here he looked at face-to-face behavior in detail and its relationship to the self. Other works throughout his career also focused on the self and covered a bewildering number of topic areas, from mental hospitals to advertising, from eye contact to behavior in elevators. Goffman was a brilliant writer and much of the appeal of his work lies in his beautifully crafted and accessible essays.

Source: Burns 1992

manipulate impressions in order to control other people. This rather instrumental understanding of action sees people standing outside of culture and using it, rather than culture being internalized into the self as a deep, motivating force for action.

Asylums

With his book *Asylums*, Goffman (1968 [1961]) looked once again at the self in interaction settings. His focus here was on the ways that the self of the mental hospital inmate interacted with the institutional regime. Goffman begins by defining the **total institution**. This is a place that is closed off from the world and where every aspect of daily life is controlled. Other examples include monasteries, the army, prisons, and orphanages. Goffman points to the ways that such places attempt to transform the selves of those who enter them. They do this through a **rite of passage**. This concept is borrowed from Arnold van Gennep (1960 [1908]), a figure who also influenced Victor Turner (see pp. 76–7).

In his book, *The Rite of Passage*, Van Gennep noted that major life transitions in all cultures involve ritual processes. These mark out the movement from one status to another. Examples include birth, baptism, initiation into manhood/womanhood, marriage, and death. He also noted that in many such episodes there is a period of separation from the group (e.g., the honeymoon) before people return to society with a new status. The concept is of great value, in part because it draws our attention to the wide variety of contexts where the self is ritually transformed. In the case of the asylum, Goffman observed this universal process at work. When a new inmate entered such an institution, a series of activities took place that stripped away a civilian identity and replaced it with an institutional one. These included interviews, photographs, the removal of clothes, disinfecting the body, putting on a prison uniform, being told the rules, and being assigned to quarters (you have probably seen these stages in action at the start of stereotyped movies set in prison). The sum total of this process was a mortification of the old self and the emergence of a new identity that suited the needs of the institution. Goffman writes: "Admission procedures might better be called 'trimming' and 'programming' because in thus being squared away the new arrival allows himself to be shaped and coded into an object that can be fed into the administrative machinery of the establishment, to be worked on smoothly by routine operations" (1968: 26).

Once they were in the institution, Goffman claimed that a punishment/reward system offered inducements to the inmate to become a conformist and retain a passive demeanor. Inducements included visiting rights, a private room, day release, and so on, while negative sanctions were things like solitary confinement and electric-shock therapy.

This bleak picture of an all-powerful institution crushing the human spirit is moderated by an alternate theme in the book. Goffman's subtext documents the various tricks and ruses that inmates get up to in order to maintain their sense of autonomy and dignity. These include: just pretending to go along with the rules of the game in order to win privileges, taking part in an activity for the wrong reasons (e.g., joining a therapy group in order to meet members of the opposite sex), withdrawal into a world of television and books, the use of official objects for illegal purposes (e.g., drying clothes on the radiator), and the identification of secret places for illicit activities like sex and gambling. The overall picture in *Asylums* is one of a struggle between the institution and the inmate. It is not surprising, then, that during the 1960s it struck a chord with prevailing anti-authoritarian sentiments and became something of a bestseller.

Some other influential books by Goffman

In a collection of essays entitled *Interaction Ritual* (1967), Goffman pointed to the ways that everyday face-to-face encounters were structured by a desire to maintain face, avoid anxiety, and head off embarrassment. He suggests that much everyday social life consists of small ritual exchanges (e.g., greetings) in which people reaffirm their identities as competent human beings. The argument here is broadly Durkheimian. Goffman draws on Durkheim's discussion of the soul in *The Elementary Forms of Religious Life* and asserts that "the person in our urban secular world is allotted a kind of sacredness that is displayed and confirmed by symbolic acts" (1967: 47). For Goffman, displays of **deference** and **demeanor** play a crucial role in this process, as actors work to dramatize mutual respect and status recognition. What Goffman called **face work** is central here, with persons attempting to maintain face in their interactions by performing in ways that correspond to social expectations. So important are these micro rituals of interaction that people will frequently show deference even to those whose demeanor marks them as persons who have opted out of at least some parts of the interactional ritual game – e.g., they will refuse to stare at or otherwise bring attention to someone sleeping in the street (see figure 4.1).

In *Gender Advertisements* (1979), Goffman looked at the ways in which men and women were portrayed in advertisements. He argued that women tended to be shown as passive, supportive (of men), and childlike. The exact nature of his claims is unclear. Some have taken his book to be about representations of gender in advertising. Others suggest he is merely using advertisements as a convenient (and arguably rather poor) data source to explore wider social attitudes and embodied behaviors. The book has become important, however, as an influence on more contemporary cultural studies analyses of images in the mass media, especially those involving the body. *Frame Analysis* (1974), another of Goffman's later books, explores the ways that contexts give meanings to actions. An example would be a frame such as "play." We read a "pretend" fight in a different way from a "real" fight. A focus of the book is on the ways that people identify and maintain particular frames in ordinary social life. In many respects, these two books from the 1970s are more "macro" in orientation than his other work. There is less attention given to face-to-face interaction itself and more to the collective representations and symbol systems through which action is interpreted.

Goffman: an evaluation

From the perspective of cultural studies, Goffman's work has much to offer. Positive aspects of his work include:

Figure 4.1   Civil inattention towards the homeless – an interaction ritual

- *An attention to the ways that humans use culture in interactions.* He shows that people use cultural resources to maintain common definitions of the situation and offer situationally appropriate behavior.
- *His focus on links between action, meaning, and the self.* In some ways this foreshadows concerns with "identity" in more recent cultural studies work.
- *His understanding that semiotic activity was fundamental to social interaction.* Goffman shows that we live in a world where meanings are constantly exchanged. In a sense this is a profoundly cultural model of social life.
- *His focus on the ritual aspects of social life in institutions and in face-to-face encounters.* This marks an important elaboration within the Durkheimian tradition.
- *A recognition of the embodiment of culture.* Goffman's work demonstrates how important the body is as a carrier and conveyor of cultural codes and information.

There are, however, some problematic dimensions to Goffman's *oeuvre*. The most important of these, we have intimated, is that his emphasis on role distance and performance can create the impression of cynical and strategic actors. There is nothing wrong with this per se. However, it does lead to a culturally denuded understanding of action. Motivations can appear shallow and material rather than complex and ideal. To get an idea of what is at stake here, think for a minute about Weber's Protestant ethic thesis (see pp. 13–14). It emphasized transcendental needs for salvation, fear of damnation, reverence for Holy Scripture, a hatred of sin, and desire to do God's bidding. Now imagine how Goffman – at least in his early guise – might have analyzed everyday life in the sixteenth century. He would point to the Bible and somber clothing as props that allow people to pass as devout Protestants. He would emphasize the need for the preacher to work on his technique so that he gave a charismatic impression. He would see the church as a stage or setting, and so on. Clearly something is missing here. This is an understanding of the power of culture to motivate actors and to establish passionate structures of internalized emotion and commitment.

This critique brings us to a related point, which is that Goffman actually has very little to say about the content of culture. His account makes extensive uses of words like "understandings," "conventions," and "norms," but there is no extensive discussion suggesting that he tried hard to think beyond these concepts. While he may have gone beyond Parsons in unpacking agency, his approach to culture itself did not constitute an advance. By itself, the Goffmanian approach is inadequate for getting at the stuff of meaning. A multitude of other criticisms have also been raised. These should be noted briefly before we move on.

- Goffman's perspective is one which tends to falsely universalize from the perspective of a white, middle-class male in 1950s America. Real problems exist in deciding to what extent his observations are applicable to other contexts, most notably the experiences of women, minorities, and so on.
- In terms of methodology, Goffman tends to rely on anecdotes rather than systematic data collection. This is not really a concern if all we are interested in generating exciting ideas. Many (perhaps most) great cultural theorists have been terrible empirical researchers. A problem does emerge, however, once claims are made about the generalizability of theoretical models to the real world.
- Notwithstanding the institution-level analysis of *Asylums*, and the media-based study of *Gender Advertisements*, a big question-mark hangs over the ability of his approach to inform more "macro" issues about culture. These might include, to pick examples at random, long-term historical trends like disenchantment (Weber), systems-level analyses of culture and society (Parsons, Habermas), or explorations of culture as a commodity form (Marxism).
- Issues of power are neglected. While Goffman is able to deal with this question in some of his work (e.g., *Asylums*), it is generally the case that he overlooks the ways that power might influence the course of face-to-face interactions. People bring to encounters statuses (e.g., race, gender) and inhabit roles (e.g., police officer) which are to some extent non-negotiable in face-to-face interaction. Even more importantly, Goffman needs to pay more attention to the ways that external structures of power or culture (rather than "mutual expectations") might influence the definition of the situation within a given interaction. Foucault's work (discussed in chapter 7), for example, shows how discourses can frame events and identities in particular ways and thereby exert a determining force on human actions.

Labeling Theory

Labeling theory, which was developed mainly in the fields of criminological and health research during the 1960s, marks an important extension of symbolic interactionism that in many ways deals with some of the major problems we encountered with Goffman. It is most associated with Edwin Lemert and Howard Becker. Labeling theory retains the idea that meanings about selves play a key role in social life. Yet its general orientation is compatible with more macro understandings of how culture works. At the core of the theory was the idea that there was no such thing as deviance per se. Rather, there were certain types of person and activities that were classified – or labeled – as deviant. Becker focused on the way that lawmaking institutions created deviance by making certain things illegal (e.g., drugs). Once the law was in place, the persons violating the law could be considered as deviant. As Becker (1973 [1963]: 9) famously wrote: "The deviant is one to whom that label has successfully been applied; deviant behavior is behavior that people so label." Becker's work stresses the importance of dominant groups and institutions (e.g., the Federal Bureau of Narcotics) in establishing these laws. He argued that they would often do so to protect their own interests.

The general thrust of such analyses is to shift our gaze away from the individual deviant toward a study of the social forces that are behind the labeling process. In particular, power and interests are highlighted as determinants of identities. This perspective contrasts sharply with Goffman's interest in the mutually reinforcing, cooperative display of deference and demeanor in the maintenance of legitimate identities. Indeed, labeling theorists have focused almost exclusively on labeling as a form of social control directed against vulnerable classes of persons. Studies of mental illness, for example, suggest that the label of "mentally ill" has been used to control and imprison people who are really against the system or even just unconventional. With this shift away from the face-to-face and toward discourse and institutions, labeling theory is important as a point of contact between symbolic interactionism and several other trends in more mainstream cultural research. There are clear affinities, for example, with studies of classification, power/knowledge, and moral panics (these are discussed elsewhere in this book: see pp. 87–9, 116, 152).

Phenomenology

Phenomenology has its roots in philosophy. Major figures in the field include Descartes, Heidegger, Husserl, and Merleau-Ponty. Within the field of philosophy, the main focus of analysis in phenomenology is the exploration of conscious experience. Researchers in the area ask questions like: How is color experienced? Why can we attribute the color brown to the table? How are our senses of touch and sight aligned so that we believe we are touching and feeling the same table rather than two different ones? What is a sense of self? What does it mean to have a thought? These are the kinds of questions that people never ask themselves in everyday life, and exploring them requires the phenomenologist to suspend their everyday ways of thinking and develop new methods for interrogating conscious experience.

Perhaps the best known of these techniques is Edmund Husserl's methodology of "bracketing." This involves stripping away the taken-for-granted from our experience of the world. The idea is to parse an experience and to work out what its constituent elements might be so as to reveal a pure perception untainted by common sense. The operation is rather like peeling an onion from the outside in. Suppose that we see a table. Husserl would argue that this involves numerous elements – a sense of being a self so that we can be conscious of our perceptions, a mental image of something large and wooden, and allocation of meaning to that image as a coherent object ("it's a table"), and so on. In his works Husserl uses his method of bracketing to remove and account for each of these stages of perception in intricate detail.

The bridge between this tradition of phenomenology and mainstream sociology came from the work of Alfred Schutz, who argued vigorously for the need to study the **Lebenswelt** (**lifeworld**) of the ordinary person. Schutz was a student of Husserl and sought to make his teacher's findings more relevant to explaining everyday life than to abstruse philosophical controversies. In order to do this, Schutz had to take Husserl and stand him on his head (metaphorically speaking, of course!). Husserl's intellectual approach, as we have seen, involved taking experience apart and eliminating common sense. Schutz argued that much of social life is able to go ahead precisely because people do not do this. Rather than asking difficult questions, we inhabit a *Lebenswelt* made up of the **taken-for-granted**. We also draw on stocks of **common-sense knowledge** to get through life. Schutz suggested that **typification** was central to this activity. This is the way that we group things we experience into classes. He writes: "the outer world is not experienced as an arrangement of individual unique objects . . . but as 'mountains', 'trees', 'animals', 'fellow men'" (Schutz 1973: 7–8). Thanks to this classifying activity, we can behave toward them in similar ways, until practical experience dictates that we should modify our generalizing categories. Such activity obviates the need to treat each object we encounter as puzzling and unique.

Schutz also maintained that our interactions with others are guided by the assumption that, for the most part, they see the world the same way that we do. We assume that they share our common-sense knowledge and experience the phenomenal world in similar ways and that "both of us have selected and interpreted the actually or potentially common objects and their features in an identical manner or at least . . . one sufficient for all practical purposes" (1973: 12). He calls this belief the **reciprocity of perspectives**. Schutz argues that **intersubjectivity** (mutual understanding) and practical action can be established because of this assumption. If we relentlessly questioned everything other people said or did, or went about our lives presuming that other people could not understand us, we would never accomplish anything. As Garfinkel's breaching experiments showed (see below, p. 64), social life would rapidly become bogged down in a morass of explanations, instructions, and crippling uncertainty.

Ethnomethodology

The founder of **ethnomethodology**, Harold Garfinkel, was influenced by Schutz's work. In his early career, Garfinkel studied with Parsons at Harvard. This gave him a lifelong interest in the problem of social order (Heritage 1984). At the same time, Garfinkel became dissatisfied with the kinds of solutions Parsons had developed in *The Structure of Social Action* and *Toward a General Theory of Action* (see chapter 2, pp. 26–9). Garfinkel wanted a theory that would recognize the centrality of social action and intelligent actors to the maintenance of social order. Building upon Schutz, and in a less direct way on the American pragmatist tradition with its focus on practical action, Garfinkel developed an account of social order that was not dependent on explanation at the level of the system. In his seminal work, *Studies in Ethnomethodology* (1967), Garfinkel rejected the Parsonian emphasis on values and norms as the major source of integration, insisting that they reduced the actor to the status of a **judgmental dope**. He also rejected the idea of a single abstract theory being able to account for the diversity of human action, and called instead for concentrated empirical investigations of concrete contexts and settings. By contrast to Parsons, Garfinkel claimed social order emerged in specific settings as an accomplishment of actors. He saw them working to make their own context-specific actions understandable to others, as well as constantly striving to understand what others were doing. The model of the actor he developed was a rather cognitive one. According to Garfinkel, people have to keep making sense of the world and each other and perform activities that are designed to make sense to each other. Ethnomethodology was to be the study of the "ethno" "methods" (folk methods) through which ordinary people did this in diverse situations and organizational environments. In his inimitable fashion, he writes that ethnomethodology is all about: "learning how members' actual, ordinary activities consist of methods to make practical actions, practical circumstances, common sense knowledge of social structures and practical sociological reasoning analyzable and of discovering the formal properties of commonplace, practical common sense actions, 'from within' actual settings, as ongoing accomplishments of those settings" (1967: vii–viii).

Drawing on Schutz, Garfinkel insisted on the centrality of common sense in allowing this sense-making activity to happen. One way in which he did this was through a series of innovative **breaching experiments** that set out to violate, and thereby highlight, the significance of the taken-for-granted. For example, he had students ask relentless questions in everyday conversation (e.g., "I had a flat tire." "What do you mean, you had a flat tire?"), or had them pretend they were boarders in their own family homes. The result was often hostility and anger. This suggested to Garfinkel that the taken-for-granted had some of the characteristics of a moral order and that we all expect each other to play our part in its maintenance.

Much of Garfinkel's work revolves around a series of innovative concepts which capture the features of common-sense, everyday reasoning. The most significant of these are listed below:

- *Accounts/accountability/accounting.* This refers to the ways that people attempt to develop frames and explanations for understanding what is going on. Garfinkel insists that social order emerges because people organize their own behavior so it will be accountable to others. He sees this as providing an alternative to the Parsonian view of social order emerging from internalized norms.

- *The etc. clause.* Garfinkel (like Wittgenstein and Bourdieu) attacked the idea that society could be governed by "rules." Instead he pointed out that no rule could ever be specific enough to cover all possible circumstances. If rules did exist, they could only do so because "**members**" (the ethnomethodologist's favorite word for "social actors") applied their common sense to work out the various other contexts (etceteras) in which they either applied or didn't.
- *The documentary method.* Garfinkel borrowed this concept from the Frankfurt School sociologist, Karl Mannheim. It refers to the ways that members build up coherent frames from small clues. A case in point would be the work of a coroner, who has to decide whether a violent death was an accident, suicide, or misadventure by looking at the various circumstances, before arriving at a big picture that can incorporate all the clues.
- *Indexicality.* This is the way that things only make sense within a specific context. "This chair" will mean different things according to when and where it is said, and who says it. Garfinkel suggests that because meaning is so context-bound, we have to study it as something that emerges in specific sequences of action in specific places.
- *Ad hocing.* This is a device that people use to apply knowledge from one context to another. The concept captures the creative and improvisatory way that people transpose common-sense knowledge across domains.

The other leading early advocate of ethnomethodology was Harvey Sacks (see, e.g., 1992 [1964–8]). Sacks placed a major emphasis on the role of language in everyday life. He demonstrated that many of the features of social life that Garfinkel had documented were present in ordinary conversation. Conversations, he maintains, are inherently indexical in that they only make sense in particular contexts. If we do not know the context it can be difficult to figure out what is going on. Moreover, conversations work only because people themselves work to ensure the reciprocity of perspectives. With each competent utterance they demonstrate that they have understood the one that went just before it. For this reason, Sacks argued that the reproduction of social order in conversation inevitably had a sequential organization.

Sacks also pointed to the role of common-sense knowledge with his concept of the **membership categorization device** (MCD). He argued that particular labels (MCDs) operate as a kind of shorthand. They carry with them sets of assumptions about behavior, motivation, moral worth, and so on. Moreover, particular MCDs seem to go together in sets. When we hear one of these MCDs invoked our common sense comes into play to fill in the gaps. Consider the sentence: "The baby cried. The mommy picked it up." Sacks (1992: 243ff.) suggests that we tend automatically to read this something like: "The baby cried because it wanted something. The mother was the mother of the baby. The mother picked up the baby because it was crying and because she wanted to look after it." While none of this is explicitly stated, our common sense makes use of the MCDs to construct a coherent picture or "account" of what is going on. The idea of the MCD remains one of the most useful contributions of ethonomethodology to unpacking the organization of common sense as a constituent part of culture.

Ethnomethodology after Garfinkel and Sacks

Since the publication of *Studies in Ethnomethodology* in 1967, Garfinkel has written nothing that has had the same impact as his early masterwork. Sacks, Garfinkel's heir-apparent, was tragically killed in a car accident, leaving a scattered literature behind him. The agenda for ethnomethodology has subsequently taken a number of turns. An important line of influence has been in the social studies of science. These have argued that scientific activity isn't really "scientific" at all. Rather, it depends heavily on the same kind of common-sense thought as everyday life. A substantial emphasis is placed on relativizing scientific knowledge and showing that it is an accomplishment of a scientific community with a particular set of ideas about what is "truth" and a "research finding" (e.g., Latour and Woolgar 1979). Another significant area of study has emerged from Harvey Sacks's interest in language (Heritage 1984). This field of **conversation analysis (CA)** has taken on a curiously positivist and empiricist feel, with a strong emphasis being placed on the rigorous collection of data. A major accomplishment has been the creation of a cumulative body of knowledge about features of everyday language use. Some ethnomethodologists feel unhappy about this, suggesting that the originating focus on the *Lebenswelt* of the actor has been replaced by a technology-driven activity which accords epistemological privilege to the analyst (Lynch and Bogen 1994). Still others suggest that the radical edge of ethnomethodology has been betrayed thanks to the mainstreaming activity of CA. According to Pollner (1991), ethnomethodology was once an area that promised fundamentally to reshape social science by generating "radical reflexivity." Its findings could potentially have been turned inward and used to relativize social science research as a series of locally produced accounts, ethnomethods, and so on. Pollner asserts this would have produced a more thoughtful and rigorous discipline. Finally, there have emerged in the ethnomethodological tradition a number of studies of "work." These involve the use of CA to study settings like doctor's consultations, telephone helplines, and school classrooms. The idea here is to detect how the kinds of devices identified by Garfinkel and Sacks allow people to get their job done. A major focus is on the ways that the "setting" for the interaction is something to which members reflexively organize their behavior, providing both a resource for intersubjectivity and an outcome of their activities.

Ethnomethodology and Phenomenology: An Evaluation

Ethnomethodology and phenomenology have made a contribution to mainstream cultural theory that has been indirect rather than direct. More so than any other approaches, they have argued forcefully for the role of the actor in maintaining social order. This challenge has been so forceful that recent cultural theories have had to react. The structuration theory of Giddens (see pp. 136–8) and the agenda of neofunctionalism (above, p. 33), for example, both tried to incorporate improved understandings of agency into general models. Ethnomethodology and phenomenology have also done a great deal to introduce everyday life as a key area of cultural research and to document the centrality of meaning to even the most commonplace and seemingly trivial activities. In so doing, they suggest that culture is an inescapable aspect of our lives.

On the negative side, the model of culture provided by these perspectives shares many of the disadvantages of symbolic interactionism. Ideas of power are weakly developed or non-existent. The persistent micro focus makes the theory difficult to apply to areas that interest many other cultural researchers – such as the study of discourses and ideologies in historical and comparative contexts. Moreover, there is an ambivalent relationship to culture itself within the field. Ethnomethodologists are reluctant to see culture as something "out there" which exists beyond concrete actions. They see culture as somehow immanent in activity, or as emerging from it, rather than as a separate and autonomous system. This raises a serious question-mark over the ability of such approaches to understand "culture" as an independent, *sui generis* influence of social life. Some commentators (e.g., Alexander 1987) have even suggested that ethnomethodology is actually anti-cultural because it rejects normative explanation. Certainly, when we read texts by ethnomethodologists, there is little sense of the symbolic, semiotic, and textual dimensions of social life which contemporary cultural theory places at the foreground. Indeed, in this respect ethnomethdological understandings are less "cultural" than those of symbolic interactionism. This neglect arises, perhaps, from the cognitive turn and the influence of phenomenology – an approach which tends to understand mental life as a kind of dispassionate problem-solving exercise. Yet if one is prepared to accept a broader definition of culture as being about the role of meaning in social life, then ethnomethodological perspectives have much to offer. Certainly, it provides the most extensive exploration of the routine, everyday, sense-making activities of people operating as active constructors and maintainers of meaning.

Micro Theories: A General Evaluation

Looking at micro theories of culture as a whole, we can detect three master characteristics. We can use these to evaluate the contribution of the literature considered in this chapter.

- The first of these is that significant advances have taken place in thinking through how agency can be related to meaning. The focus on humans as active creators and manipulators of meaning provides a refreshing antidote not only to Parsonian ideas of role-internalization, but also to Marxian ideas about dominant ideologies, and so on. Anyone interested in exploring how action and culture go together should become familiar with this literature.
- Secondly, there is frequently an impoverished and stunted understanding of culture. In comparison to other paradigms (e.g., semiotics, hermeneutics), symbolic interactionism is long on interaction, but short on the symbolic. Much the same can be said for ethnomethodology. If you are looking for a model that will help you unpack the deeply meaningful symbolic and hermeneutic aspects of cultural systems and texts, you will probably need to look elsewhere.

- Thirdly, problems arise in explaining how micro levels relate to the macro level. While other approaches to culture typically have an ancillary model of social structure, this is often lacking in more micro understandings. The result is a series of studies of what goes on in particular locations (e.g., the medical examination), but these are rarely connected to a generic explanation or model of the social and cultural orders (e.g., ideas about medical dominance). Ideas about action-chains (Collins 1975, 2004) and systems as the emergent properties of encounters go some way toward this goal, but (from the perspective of macro theory at least) fail to really take seriously the constraining effects of structure upon agency or the idea of an autonomous cultural system. Some recent theoretical work borrows from pragmatism in order to develop a notion of culture as a set of resources that actors strategically utilize to act in different situations. It endeavors to make of these "strategies of action" the link between the micro level and the level of social structure, but, in doing so, it moves away from the more purely micro-interactional legacy of pragmatism (Joas 1996; Swidler 2001). Rather than reducing all social life to an expression of micro forces, many suggest a better approach is perhaps to think of social life as being made up of discrete but interacting layers of activity which can be approached at different levels of analysis (see Alexander 1987; Layder 1994).

Suggested Further Reading

Goffman's works are easy and enjoyable to read. Many readers will find they have an intuitive appeal and find themselves seduced into becoming a symbolic interactionist. Start by dipping into *The Presentation of Self in Everyday Life* and then browse around Goffman's other works at will. Herbert Blumer's (1969) theoretical essays provide a more tub-thumping, evangelical attempt at conversion. He argues relentlessly and passionately against objectivist, positivist, and quantitative efforts to understand meaningful human activity. Works in the field of phenomenology and ethnomethodology are not for the fainthearted. Practitioners in the area have elaborate specialist vocabularies and write in a dense and highly technical style. Begin with a user-friendly guide like John Heritage's *Garfinkel and Ethnomethodology*, before moving on to sample the exciting, but difficult, works of Garfinkel and Schutz themselves.

CHAPTER FIVE

The Durkheimians: Ritual, Classification, and the Sacred

We tend to hear a lot about Western Marxism and the development of Marxist cultural thought in the twentieth century. Until recently, a good deal less attention was given to the legacy of Durkheim for researching culture. Books on Durkheim used to point to his role as an ancestor of the structural functionalism of Parsons and Radcliffe-Brown, or as the father of positivist, quantitative sociology rather than as a cultural theorist. This situation is now changing and recent years have seen a significant revival of interest in his approach to society and culture. As we suggested in a previous chapter, Durkheim's ideas about solidarity, ritual, religion, and symbolism mark him out as an important point of origin for contemporary cultural theory. Here we study the ways that these ideas have been taken up and used by his students and those who came after him. In the later part of the twentieth century much of this work was concerned with elaborating on the themes provided by Durkheim while, at the same time, making his theories more relevant to issues of conflict, power, and pluralism. We begin, however, with a study of those closest to Durkheim in terms of time and approach before moving onto these more contemporary applications within the Durkheimian tradition.

The First Half of the Twentieth Century

Before World War One, Durkheim built up around him a coterie of talented researchers. The group was closely associated with the *Année sociologique*, the journal that they established in order to publish their work. The school was all but wiped out during World War One, and, following Durkheim's death in 1917, the Durkheimian legacy was threatened. Its survival depended to a great extent on the work of Durkheim's nephew, Marcel Mauss.

Marcel Mauss

In his *Essai sur le don, forme archaïque de l'échange*, a work first published in 1925 and translated into English as *The Gift*, Mauss (1974) drew upon ethnographic and historical data from around the world to consider the centrality of **gift exchange** in primitive society. This could include the giving of presents, the preparation of feasts for others, and even sacrificial activities. Taking a broadly Durkheimian approach, Mauss argued that gift exchange was a social fact. It had to be explained in terms of its role in the social organization as a whole, in relation to systems of morality, and in terms of hidden social forces. Mauss understood gift exchange as driven by a series of normative expectations which participants took for granted. He pointed out that gifts carry with them a kind of magical force and a strong sense of obligation – a feature that differentiates them from mere commodities. The normative expectations are:

- the obligation to give;
- the obligation to receive;
- the obligation to repay gifts received;
- the return gift has to be different from the original gift;
- the return gift has to be delayed.

Mauss noted that gift exchange often served no obviously useful function. People in gift-exchanging situations were usually able to fulfill their own material needs and did not need to swap things in order to stay alive. Exchanges were often purely ceremonial and involved objects of great symbolic value, but little material wealth or practical utility. In other situations, such as the Native American potlatch, there was even the deliberate destruction and donation of property in extravagant ceremonies.

While Mauss did not talk extensively about industrial societies, the continuing relevance of these norms is obvious if we think about situations like Christmas, birthdays, and even buying a round of drinks in a bar. He suggested that such gift giving was evidence that a corrosive mercantile spirit had not yet fully invaded social life. He wrote: "Much of our everyday morality is concerned with the question of obligation and spontaneity in the gift. It is our good fortune that all is not yet couched in terms of purchase and sale . . . Our morality is not solely commercial" (1974: 63). This analysis shares the vision of critical theory about the negative impact of commodity relations and the cash nexus. Where Mauss differs from neo-Marxism and Weberianism is in suggesting that the process is incomplete and that islands of symbolic and meaningful behavior persist.

In accounting for the prevalence of gift exchange, Mauss indicated two chief mechanisms. One was the pursuit of prestige by leaders and political entrepreneurs. When analyzing the potlatch system, for example, he suggested that ritual exchanges were part of a game in which powerful figures sought to build up networks of clients beholden to them by ties of obligation. The second mechanism was more indirect and operated at the level of the social system. The exchange of gifts was a mechanism for avoiding war, allowing for stability, and generating solidarity and peaceful coexistence. Mauss suggested that, "in order to trade, man must first lay down his spear" (1974: 80). Consequently, gift giving had an important role for cementing peace and prosperity.

MARCEL MAUSS (1872–1950)

Mauss was Durkheim's nephew and arguably the most gifted and important of his students. He was a person of wide learning, with a particular interest in the history of religions. For the first half of the twentieth century, Mauss was a key figure in French sociology. He fought in World War One and, unlike many of Durkheim's students, survived. He spent much of his life editing and publishing the unfinished works of his dead colleagues as well as those of Durkheim himself. He is chiefly known for his thoughts on gift exchange, but also wrote on many other topics, including sacrifice, magic, prayer, the nation, the body, and human ecology.

Reference: Evans-Pritchard 1954

Mauss's *Essai sur le don* is important for several reasons. These can be outlined as follows:

- It highlights the importance of gift relations in social life and theorizes these in a cultural way as exchanges marked with special symbolic force. This provides an important resource and point of analytic contrast to the more numerous studies of the commodity form (see the discussions in chapter 3).
- Mauss introduces ideas about exchange into cultural theory. The concept would later be adopted by other theorists, most notably Lévi-Strauss in his study of kinship.
- The book remains central to studies of voluntary work, voluntary associations, and charity.

Aside from *The Gift*, Mauss's other most influential work has been *Primitive Classification*. In this book, Durkheim and Mauss (1963 [1903]) attempted to explain the ways that societies classified phenomena as diverse as time, space, types of person, and animal species. Their argument was resolutely sociological and reflected the mechanistic logic of the middle-period Durkheim, in which social forms and social structure determined just about everything else in a society. In this case they argued that the organization of a society influenced the way that its people saw and classified the world around them. A society with two clans, for example, might divide the year into two seasons. Not surprisingly, such a simple model does not work too well when we look at data. As Rodney Needham (1963) pointed out, *Primitive Classification* is a book in which few of the examples fit the predicting theory. Nevertheless it did much to put classification on the map as a topic for cultural enquiry – a topic so important that Needham (1963: viii) designated it "the prime and fundamental concern of social anthropology." Less often noted, but perhaps more important, is the fact that Durkheim and Mauss insisted on the moral and emotional nature of classifications. Rather than seeing classificatory systems as simply an intellectual exercise, they stressed their normative and religious dimensions. They write: "Things are above all sacred and profane, pure or impure, friends or enemies, favorable or unfavorable. . . . And it is this emotional value . . . which plays the preponderant part in the manner in which ideas are connected or separated. It is the dominant characteristic in classification" (1963: 86).

In drawing attention to this dimension of symbol systems their work provides an important foundation not only for *The Elementary Forms of Religious Life*, but also more recent Durkheimian efforts – such as those of Mary Douglas – which explore issues of purity and pollution as they relate to classificatory systems. This emphasis on the emotionally "hot" and value-laden characteristics of culture is a central element of the Durkheimian approach. We return to this theme later in the chapter.

Maurice Halbwachs

Like Mauss, Maurice Halbwachs was a diverse and gifted scholar. Despite a wide-ranging scholarly output, he is best known today for his thinking on the topic of **collective memory** (Halbwachs 1992 [1925]). While the originality and importance of this work was not fully recognized at the time, it has since come to be seen as a path-breaking analysis. Halbwachs is concerned with the ways that people recount and mythologize the past. While we have direct mental access to previous events in our own lives, those in the historical past can only be made relevant to us by means of social institutions. Collective actions of commemoration, festivals, storytelling, and writing record these events and pass them on. There is nothing automatic, then, about the process of remembering. Halbwachs also argues that our collective memory of the past is far from comprehensive. Some events are forgotten and others remembered. More-over, those we do remember are recorded in selective ways. A particular spin is put onto past events by the groups, institutions, and rituals which are responsible for keeping them alive in the collective memory.

MAURICE HALBWACHS (1877–1945)

Halbwachs was born in France and in his student years in Paris came under the influence of both Durkheim and the idealist philosopher Henri Bergson. As a young man, he was attracted to socialism and had a strong sense of social justice. In 1911, for example, he was expelled from Germany after publishing an article that was critical of police brutality. While he was initially attracted to Bergsonian individual-ism, he later became more strongly committed to a collectivistic, Durkheimian vision of social life. Many of his most productive years were spent in Strasbourg, but later in life he received the call to Paris, took up a chair at the Sorbonne and became rec-ognized as a major intellectual figure. Following the German occupation of France, some of his relatives were murdered. At great personal risk to himself Halbwachs inquired into their deaths. He was arrested, transported to Germany, and died in a concentration camp.

Reference: Coser 1992

Halbwachs saw his theory of collective memory as compatible with Durkheim's work. He suggested that the collective memory operates to hold society together. Stories about heroes, epic events, and group origins provide people with a source of emotional

Figure 5.1   Memorial to UA flight 93, Pennsylvania

and intellectual solidarity. A powerful example in contemporary American society can be seen in the efforts to construct heroic narratives around the crash of United Airlines flight 93 in Shanksville, Pennsylvania on September 11, 2001 (Riley 2008). Here, significant energy has gone into the production of a collective memory of the bringing down of that plane (apparently intended to be flown into the Capitol Building or the White House) by passengers as a heroic first strike in the war against terrorism officially declared later by the administration of George Bush. The actions of individual passengers in the assault on the hijackers have been enshrined in film and other media as almost superhuman efforts to defend the country. At the site of the crash, a temporary memorial represents each passenger as an American patriot Christian angel/martyr (see figure 5.1). Consistent with Durkheim's functionalist approach, Halbwachs argued that it was the needs, problems, and beliefs of the present that determined the memory of the past. The collective memory, then, was constantly being renewed and reshaped with each passing generation. He also emphasized that religion itself was a form of collective memory, asserting: "We can say of every religion that it reproduces in more or less symbolic forms the history of migrations and fusions of races and tribes, or great events, wars, establishments, discoveries and reforms that we can find at the origin of the societies that practice them" (1992: 84).

Halbwachs's understanding of the synergies between history, religion, politics, and mythology has proven increasingly influential for cultural theory during recent decades, even if his functionalist tendencies have been abandoned. We briefly mention some representative studies later in this chapter.

Other early Durkheimians

Constraints of space prevent a detailed discussion of the work of all the Durkheimians in the first part of the century. It is, however, necessary to be aware of some other important figures and texts. Henri Hubert, a specialist in the religions and cultures of pre-Christian Europe and Mauss's closest friend, co-wrote a number of important works with Mauss for which the latter is sometimes incorrectly given sole credit (e.g., the studies of magic and sacrifice). He also was the sole author of two important pieces in the classical Durkheimian contribution to the study of culture: an essay on the experience of time in religious festival that showed how collective representations and thus the social unit to which individuals belong structure that experience (2005 [1905]), and a lengthy introduction to his student Stefan Czarnowski's book on the cult of St Patrick. This turns out, on close examination, to be a Durkheimian treatise on the sociology of national heroes and their associated cults and mythologies. Robert Hertz, who studied with Durkheim, Mauss, and Hubert, wrote important analyses of the symbolism of left and right and the cultural play of sacred and profane in ceremonies surrounding death (1960), which were published in *L'Année sociologique*. In the latter work, he studies death as a "collective representation," that is, as something that derives from the social and symbolic life of the community, and he uses this notion to criticize the misunderstanding of death as a wholly biological phenomenon existing outside the symbolic. The newly dead actually occupy, for a period of time and under conditions that vary from society to society, a liminal space between the living and the dead. This period of liminality (see pp. 76–7) precisely demonstrates the construction and operation of this collective representation – i.e., the complex social ways in which the dangerous pollution of the social body (via the death of one of its members) is recognized and then corrected, or purified, through ritual acts and interdictions. In the study of left and right, he claimed there were cultural universals (symbolic patterns to be found in all known societies) linked to their symbolism. The right hand was tied to "life, truth, beauty, virtue, the rising sun, the male sex" (1960: 103), and the left hand to their opposites.

Hertz asked: "How is it that the sacred side should invariably be the right and the profane the left?" (1960: 110). He was unable to provide a complete or convincing answer to this question, but this is of little importance. The study remains a pioneering demonstration of the universal importance of dualism to classification systems – a principle that would later be elaborated upon by Lévi-Straussian structuralism (see chapter 6). Celestin Bouglé's *Essays on the Caste System* (1971 [1899]) provided an equally important cultural analysis, in this case of the Indian stratification system. Bouglé insisted on its religious character and pointed to the ways in which distinctions between the pure and the impure were fundamental to Hindu ritual activity and social organization. Like Hertz, he suggested that the pattern he identified was universal. He maintained that all societies have caste-like features, and that these are highlighted and present in a strong form in the Indian case. What his work provides is an understanding of stratification as a reflection of cultural logic rather than economic forces. It therefore offers a distinctive alternative to Marxian understandings of class.

During the 1930s, Durkheim's authority in French sociology waned. The most important torchbearer of the Durkheimian tradition was a librarian – Georges Bataille.

Also influenced by Nietzsche, de Sade, surrealism, and Marxism, Bataille was a complex figure whose writing combined interests in theology, philosophy, eroticism, and aesthetics, as well as sociology and politics. A unifying feature of these diverse concerns was an interest in the sacred and mystical qualities of human experience. Bataille drew particular attention to the links between that which is conventionally seen as filthy, disgusting, excessive, and lewd (which he called **heterology**), and the sacred and transcendent. Writing about an encounter in a brothel, for example, Bataille (1997a [1941]) pointed to the awe-inspiring qualities of lust and female sexuality. By the same token, the economy was a domain of energy, desire, waste, and excess that could not be understood using the narrow prism of rationality. Bataille wrote that "an immense industrial network cannot be managed in the same way that one changes a tyre . . . it expresses a circuit of cosmic energy on which it depends, which it cannot limit, and whose laws it cannot ignore without consequences" (1997b [1949]: 184–5).

In the later 1930s Bataille established a research and discussion group in Paris known as the Collège de Sociologie. The group was devoted to the study of the sacred in social life and to the possibility of constructing a utopian sense of community – a project which clearly built on the intellectual foundations provided by Durkheim's *Elementary Forms of Religious Life* (see pp. 10–11). One of his associates in this project was Roger Caillois, who studied with Mauss and Georges Dumézil (see chapter 6) and wrote a good deal on the same topics that were of interest to Mauss, Hertz, and Hubert: myth and the sacred, the latter especially in its transgressive forms. The sacred, as Durkheim himself noted, is not only one of the terms in the binary sacred/profane, but is itself a dual term. Alongside the pure or right sacred, which preserves moral order by means of taboos, there is an impure or left sacred, which deliberately transgresses against that order through the debauchery of festival. An example in the Christian calendar is the complementary pair of Lent and Carnival. Caillois provided an elaborated theory of the festival to balance Durkheim's emphasis on the pure sacred. The ritual transgression of festival is given meaning by myths describing how the moral order must be created anew each year from the violent chaos that pre-existed it. Caillois considered myth to be an aesthetic and political key to the understanding of ancient and modern societies. In "Paris, a Modern Myth," he called for a kind of "literary sociology" capable of mapping the visionary efforts of novelists and poets such as Charles Baudelaire and Honoré de Balzac. These writers do not simply describe the urban modern, but in fact prescribe ways to exist in it that may themselves be taken up as modern myths. Caillois argues that a much more nuanced cultural sociology will be necessary for studying this work of modern literary mythologization (2003: 177). Today, however, the work of Bataille and Caillois has been largely forgotten by Durkheimians and is most appreciated by poststructuralists and postmodernists. Bataille's interest, especially in sexuality, the body, and the excessive – as well as his vivid, hallucinatory style – has been appreciated by writers such as Barthes, Kristeva, and Derrida, thus ensuring his position as an important twentieth-century thinker.

During the 1930s and 1940s Durkheim's influence became international. Talcott Parsons imported it to the United States and drew upon Durkheim's normative understandings in developing his structural functionalist models of society and multidimensional understandings of human action (see chapter 2). In British anthropology, the influential figure of Radcliffe-Brown drew upon *The Division of Labor* in insisting on the correlation between sentiments and social organization. Much of his work is taken up with ideas about social equilibrium and the stability of the social system. More attuned to the later Durkheim's emphasis on the autonomy of the religious and symbolic was the slightly younger E. E. Evans-Pritchard, who by the 1950s had begun to move away from the orthodox structural functionalism of British social anthropology. In *Nuer Religion*, for example, he claimed that it was important to study and interpret religion on its own terms (Evans-Pritchard 1956). The task of the anthropologist, he suggested, should be to try to understand the logic and meanings of the belief system, rather than attempting to explain it away as a reflection of an underlying social structure. Here Evans-Pritchard presages the hermeneutic and cultural turn in anthropology that was to flower in the work of Clifford Geertz (see pp. 189–91).

The Second Half of the Twentieth Century

During the second half of the twentieth century we can identify four broad trends within the Durkheimian tradition:

1   The process of internationalization continued and reached a point where the center of gravity for Durkheimian scholarship was overseas, especially in Britain and the United States.
2   It was increasingly recognized that Durkheim's *Elementary Forms of Religious Life* was a key resource for cultural theory, as well as his middle-period works like *The Division of Labour*.
3   A fruitful union was formed between French structuralism, and especially the work of Lévi-Strauss, and Durkheimian theory in the areas of ritual, symbolism, mythology, and classification.
4   Attempts were made to address some of the major criticisms of Durkheimian cultural perspectives. This resulted in efforts to theorize power, inequality, and struggle, using Durkheimian tools.

Ritual, classification, and cosmology

Victor Turner
Writing in the late 1960s, the anthropologist Victor Turner pointed out that "the research and theoretical concerns of many anthropologists have once again been directed toward the role of symbols – religious, mythic, aesthetic, political, and even economic – in social and cultural processes" (1977 [1969]: v). His own work was very much situated in this field. Whilst much of it was concerned with the application of Lévi-Straussian ideas to the analysis of symbolism and ritual, he is perhaps best known for his ideas about **liminality** and **communitas**.

Turner suggests that anthropology has been too concerned with the study of "structure" and has paid too little attention to spontaneous and loosely organized situations. In order to understand these less structured moments, he looked to the work of Arnold van Gennep (1960 [1908]), who had identified a liminal phase in rites of passage (see also pp. 58). During this period the person involved in a status transition was outside of society and had an ambiguous status. The term "liminal" comes from *limen*, the Latin word for "threshold," and nicely captures this quality of being in a boundary position. The threshold itself is neither inside nor outside. The liminal person is "betwixt and between the positions assigned and arrayed by law, custom, convention and ceremonial" (Turner 1977: 95).

Turner builds on van Gennep and highlights the collective aspects of liminality as well as its links to the individual life-course. During liminal periods the collectivity will experience the breakdown of established social classifications and cultural codes. Hierarchies will tend to be replaced by a community of equals characterized by a sense of solidarity, which Turner designated as "communitas." According to Turner, societies, or groups in society, tend to oscillate between periods of order and periods of disorder. He drew particular attention to carnivals and rituals as key liminal events, and identified common features of liminality such as the absence of status, humility, creativity, unselfishness, foolishness, and the inversion or minimization of sex distinctions. Central to his vision was the idea that communitas involved contact with the sacred, generated intense emotional experience, and was responsible for renewing social bonds and energies. In this respect there is a very direct connection between Turner's work and Durkheim's *Elementary Forms of Religious Life*. Even though Turner (incredibly) makes no direct reference to Durkheim's great work in *The Ritual Process*, it is evident that Durkheimian thinking about collective effervescence is at the core of his argument. For example, Turner writes: "Spontaneous communitas is richly charged with affects, mainly pleasurable ones. Life in "structure" is filled with objective difficulties. . . . Spontaneous communitas has something magical about it. Subjectively there is in it the feeling of endless power. . . . Structural action swiftly becomes arid and mechanical if those involved in it are not periodically immersed in the regenerative abyss of communitas" (1977: 139). While Turner's discussion is dominated by an understanding of temporal movement into and out of liminality, he also noted the existence of relatively stable social settings and roles which embodied the spirit of liminality. According to Turner, monasteries, court jesters, and even hippie countercultures could be seen as efforts to institutionalize the liminal as an enduring feature of social life.

The concept of the liminal has been an extraordinarily fruitful one. It has been applied not only to things that are obviously "ritual," but also more widely to phenomena as diverse as political demonstrations, seaside resorts, youth subcultures, and illness experiences. Herein lies a possible problem with the concept. Because it can be applied to anything that is not "business as usual" (characterized by rules, hierarchies, regulations, and tightly-bounded classifications), liminality can be detected just about everywhere. While these broader uses offer an important demonstration of the power of the concept, there is also a risk that they dilute its precision and focus. Another problematic issue in many applications of the concept relates to the matter of value neutrality. For many writers in the field of cultural studies the liminal is hailed as an antidote to rationalization, power, and control. The result can be a kind of simplistic dualism in theory between a "good" liminality and a "bad" structure. Turner himself tries to avoid this kind of thinking, insisting that a balance between periods of structure and periods of "antistructure" is required in social life. Notwithstanding these matters, the concept of liminality is here to stay and is proving to be a powerful tool in contemporary cultural theory. Particularly important are the links that have been forged between Turner's ideas about the liminal and Bakhtin's aesthetics of the carnivalesque (see pp. 187–8). Studies have also built on Turner's important efforts to theorize the role of drama and narrative in social life. We consider these works in chapter 11.

Mary Douglas

Mary Douglas stands alongside Victor Turner as a key figure in Durkheimian anthropology. An abiding interest in her work has been the link between classification systems and the dangerous or risky. This theme builds on the tradition established by Durkheim's concept of the profane from *The Elementary Forms of Religious Life* and the earlier ideas sketched out in *Primitive Classification*. In *Purity and Danger*, Douglas (1966) argued in a relentless and sustained way that ideas of purity and pollution were central to cultural life. In particular she claimed that "uncleanness is matter out of place" (1966: 40). For Douglas, things that did not fit into orthodox classification systems and which violated or crossed symbolic borders tended to be seen as polluted. A familiar example from Western culture would be bodily fluids (phlegm, semen, blood) and other bodily characteristics (hair, nail clippings) which transgress the routine boundaries of the body. These require special technologies for their control (e.g., the condom, the tampon), and are seen as unpleasant, disgusting, or inappropriate if they are found in the wrong symbolic or spatial location.

Douglas draws particular attention to the systemic, non-random nature of cultural beliefs about pollution, claiming that they can only be understood within the context of a wider classification. She writes: "Defilement is never an isolated event. It cannot occur except in view of a systematic ordering of ideas . . . the only way in which pollution ideas make sense is in reference to a total structure of thought whose key-stone, boundaries, margins and internal lines are held in relation by rituals of separation" (1966: 41).

In perhaps the most famous demonstration of this theory, Douglas looked at the Jewish dietary prohibitions as set out in the biblical Book of Leviticus. She showed that the apparently haphazard list of foods the Jews could not eat (including the camel, hare, chameleon, and pig) was not random at all. Rather, the foods did not fit in with a few simple rules that were used for classifying the edible and the inedible. Animals that could not be eaten violated a wider scheme for classifying nature. They were "imperfect members of their class" (1966: 55). The pig, for example, did not fully fit in with the wider category of cloven-hoofed animals. Unlike the (edible) antelope, goat, and sheep, it did not chew the cud (eat grass). As an anomaly it was seen as impure and therefore as inedible.

Like Durkheim and Mauss, Douglas argues that social morphology has a good deal to do with systems of classification, cosmology, and social values. The best-known example of this is her so-called **grid/group** model, which is explicated in her works *Natural Symbols* (1970) and *Cultural Bias* (1978) (see figure 5.2). Group refers to the strength of the boundary around a social group, while grid is concerned with the level

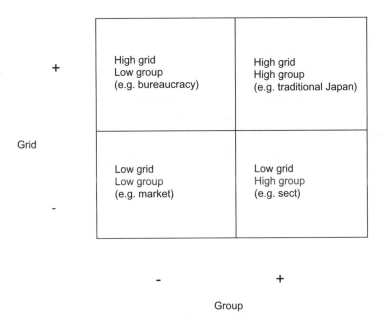

Figure 5.2   The grid/group model

of hierarchy and social differentiation within it. Using this typology, we can construct a four-cell typology of groups or types of social organization.

Douglas argues that each location on the grid/group model has its own form of **cultural bias**. This means it will tend to have a particular worldview and set of values, and a particular means of settling disputes. For example, those societies or spheres of social life that are low on both dimensions tend to be individualistic and governed by relations of exchange. An example of this would be entrepreneurial capitalists, who have little sense of collective identity and who think that the market can solve social problems. Sects and cults, by contrast, tend to have high group but low grid. They have a strong sense of collective identity, and are idealistic and highly egalitarian. They value consensus and cooperation as ways to deal with problems, but tend to demonize outsiders and perceive evil to be afoot. Groups that are high-group and high-grid, such as the army, give a preference to formal rules and power. They have little tolerance for disobedience.

During the 1980s the model was somewhat redefined as a "center and periphery model" (Douglas and Wildavsky 1982). The aim here was to explore relationships between powerful groups with wealth and influence (bureaucracies, professions, governments) and those on the fringes of society (cults, lobby groups, voluntary associations). Along with Aaron Wildavsky, Mary Douglas applied the model to explore environmentalism in the United States. She charted the way that the extremist worldview of the environmentalists corresponded to their sectarian organization. Their tightly-knit organization led them toward idealism. They tended to see money and power as polluting and dangerous, were suspicious of the center, and were unwilling to compromise their values. Nature was idealized as a realm of purity, and so the environmentalists were hypersensitive to threats and risks posed by developers and industrial pollution. They tended to see environmental disputes in quasi-religious ways. It was a battle of good against evil rather than something that could be fixed with a legal statute or financial compensation.

Douglas's work on classification provides an exemplary demonstration of the autonomy of semiotic systems. However, her work on cultural bias arguably leaves little room for the autonomy of culture by tending to read off cultural beliefs from social organization. Nevertheless, the model deserves applause as a major effort to develop a systematic and generalizable Durkheimian model of culture and society. In recent years Douglas's work on environment and risk has attracted renewed interest thanks to the rise of research about "risk society" (see p. 139).

The religious dimensions of contemporary societies

Robert Bellah

Following Durkheim, and his own convictions, much of Robert Bellah's work points to the centrality of religion in contemporary social life. Like Clifford Geertz, who we discuss in a later chapter, during his career Bellah came to see the need for an approach that better captured the autonomous force of culture than orthodox Parsonian functionalism. The essays collected in *Beyond Belief* (1970) trace out this movement. The earlier ones tend to be concerned with religious evolution and the interactions between growing social complexity and religious change. These essays echo the concerns of Parsonian systems and developmental theory. By the end of the 1960s, however, Bellah had moved beyond functionalism in a decisive way. He was writing about faith, religious experience, and transcendence rather than system integration and functional equilibrium and suggesting that "social science may soon play the role that traditionally philosophy filled: that is, to provide the intellectual tools for religious self-reflection" (1970: 191).

Somewhere in the middle of this transition he wrote perhaps his most important essay on "Civil Religion in America." Here, Bellah argues that the prevailing concept of religion is too narrow and that we need to think about "the Durkheimian notion that every group has a religious dimension" (1970: 187). He suggests that contemporary American religion is not just located in churches, but that there is also a non-denominational **civil religion**. By looking at various Presidential statements, he is able to show how references to God are a central feature of public discourse. Although there has been a separation of church and state, politics and civil life is still themed in religious ways. Dimensions of this civil religion include:

- the obligation to carry out God's will on earth;
- the idea that God supports law, order, and authority;
- the notion that God is actively involved in history and sits in judgment on the nation;
- a belief that the American people have been chosen by God.

In public speeches, these themes are supported with rhetorical references to the biblical narratives of the Exodus, the Chosen People, and so on. Yet at the same time American civil religion is not identical with either Judaism or Christianity. Bellah writes that "it has its own prophets and its own martyrs, its own sacred events and sacred places, its own solemn rituals and symbols" (1970: 186). These include figures like Washington, Lincoln, and Kennedy, events such as Gettysburg, and rituals like Memorial Day. Bellah sees this civil religion functioning in a Durkheimian way. It generates national solidarity and encourages people to make personal sacrifices for collective goals. It has inspired democratic reforms, the end of slavery, and the civil rights movement. Yet it has also had a darker side. The notion that America was a vehicle for God's work was linked to the idea of manifest destiny and colonialism, both within and outside national borders.

Edward Shils

Like Bellah, Edward Shils looked to Durkheim in order to theorize the religious qualities of apparently secular states. In so doing he too moved away from Parsonian systems theory toward a more hermeneutic and empirically driven approach. During the 1950s, Shils had collaborated with Parsons on *Toward a General Theory of Action* (Parsons and Shils 1962 [1951]). However, he soon became aware of the limitations of its dry, abstract, over-elaborate approach, later suggesting that the model he had helped to create was "cumbersome." Of particular concern was the way that culture was treated in formal systems theory. Shils's own interest in primordial ties, group bonding, and psychology suggested that people were united by incredibly strong moral and emotional forces. He considered the theory he had helped to create to be inadequate in capturing these kinds of visceral cultural dynamics and the ways that they actively created social structures.

In thinking through this issue Shils turned to Weber and especially Durkheim as he came "to appreciate the place of the sacred in society" (1975a: xxviii; see also Greenfeld 1996). In a comparatively early paper, Shils and his collaborator Michael Young looked at the coronation of England's Queen Elizabeth II in 1952. Building on Durkheim's theory of ritual, they claimed that it was "an affirmation of the moral values by which the society lives. It was an act of national communion" (Shils and Young 1975 [1956]: 139). Drawing attention to the street parties and television audiences, Shils and Young suggested that the ritual was not confined to Westminster Abbey, but rather was diffused throughout the community. The point of the essay was to suggest that "the sacred" and "ritual" can exist outside of the context of religion as conventionally defined – they were also linked to civic, political, and popular life. The essay stands alongside Lloyd Warner's study of "Yankeetown" as a pioneering application of ritual analysis to complex societies. Lloyd Warner (1975 [1959]) looked at Memorial Day activities in a small Massachusetts town and argued that they amounted to a cult of the dead through which the nation could be worshipped. Although such analyses have been criticized as simplistic (see below), they mark an important milestone for *The Elementary Forms of Religious Life* as a key influence in cultural theory.

Perhaps more sophisticated than his analysis of ritual was Shils's discussion of the dynamics of **center and periphery.** During the 1950s and early 1960s, Shils wrote a number of key essays including "Primordial, Personal, Sacred and Civil Ties," "The Concentration and Dispersion of Charisma," and "Center and Periphery," which explored this theme. Of particular concern was the question of how people of diverse religious, racial, and class backgrounds were able to live together in a broadly inclusive wider society (Shils 1975a: vii). Shils developed an answer which claimed that every society had a "sacred center" that operated as the focus of its collective identity. This was not so much geographical, but rather was about the core symbols, values, and beliefs in a society. These are considered to be "ultimate and irreducible" and to "partake of the nature of the sacred" (1975b: 3). The center, then, was the realm of what Shils called a "central value system" which linked a society and its members to something which "transcends and transfigures their concrete individual existence" (1975b: 7). Whilst Shils worked hard to emphasize the cultural qualities of the center, he observed that it was also linked to certain dimensions of the social structure. Elites, governmental authority, and important administrative and intellectual institutions were often tied to the center and basked in the aura of the sacred thanks to this association.

These sorts of theses also inform Shils's writings on charisma. According to Shils, Weber's original theory placed too much emphasis on the peripheral social location of charismatic authority and its role in revolutionary, destabilizing, and transformative activity. Shils claimed, by contrast, that charisma could also be associated with the center. It was "imputed to persons, actions, roles, institutions, symbols and material objects because of the presumed connection with 'ultimate', 'fundamental', 'vital' order-determining powers" (1975c [1968]: 127). He saw charisma as something that was potentially associated with high office and the exercise of mundane political power. Charisma, in other words, could be linked to social stability and to dominant authority locations. Shils also emphasized the difference between intense, concentrated charisma and dispersed, attenuated charisma. According to Shils, Weber's writings focus on the

---

EDWARD SHILS (1910–95)

During the 1930s Shils was an undergraduate at the University of Chicago. He studied with leading figures of the time, such as Robert Park and Harold Lasswell, and also read widely in classical sociological theory – especially the works of Durkheim, Weber, Simmel, and Mannheim. In the wake of World War Two he became known for psychological studies of small group cohesion in the German army, but soon developed more macro-sociological research agendas. A spell in India consolidated interests in intellectuals, development, and problems of social integration. After a period of collaboration with Parsons working on systems theory, Shils developed his own distinctive center and periphery model during the 1950s and 1960s. Although he has often been considered a conservative theorist, it is noteworthy that he courageously spoke out against McCarthyism in a book published in 1955 entitled *The Torment of Secrecy*. Shils's death in 1995 led to a renewed interest in his ideas, although the full significance of his intellectual legacy has yet to be determined.

Reference: Shils 1975a

former, which is spectacular, transformative, and located in a specific individual. However, most charisma is of the latter, more low-key type and supports and legitimates routine political activity. This "normal charisma" is associated with deference to authority, law, and systems of stratification rather than their overthrow. For Shils, charisma and the sacred were interwoven dimensions of the religious as it influenced seemingly secular social life. While his approach might be criticized for diluting or redefining the concept of charisma away from its Weberian core (see Smith 2000), it provides perhaps the most important synthesis of Weberian and Durkheimian themes in twentieth-century cultural theory.

Critiques and revisions of Durkheimian approaches to civic ritual

As critical sociology gained in strength during the 1960s and 1970s, the approach to political life that was advocated by the Durkheimians came under attack. The single most important of these assaults was by Steven Lukes (1975). Lukes pointed out that Lloyd Warner and Shils often had no evidence for their claims about integrative effects of civic rituals, and suggested that we might expect to find uneven or weak impacts to ritual events. Looking at the coronation, for example, Lukes asserted that many people (ignored by Shils and Young) were either apathetic or hostile. He also thought many of the causal mechanisms invoked by the Durkheimians (e.g., the social need for stability) to be vague and unsatisfactory. For Lukes, rituals should be seen as events staged by particular groups with particular interests. We should understand them less as a spontaneous collective celebration, and more as a political maneuver by motivated actors aiming to build alliances and public support for their position.

Another important critique of Durkheimian idealism has been offered by David Kertzer (1989). He suggests that rituals have integrative effects because people do things together, rather than because people believe in the same values or sacred symbols. The logic behind this argument comes from Durkheim himself. In some of his writings he takes a rather mechanistic view of ritual, suggesting that physical association and coactivity were important components of the ritual experience. This line of thinking has also influenced micro-sociologists such as Goffman (see p. 59), who deemphasize the centrality of sacred symbols as indicators of a ritual event, and focus more on conventionalized bodily and linguistic behaviors. Kertzer's main point is that ritual coactivity enables people to coexist in the absence of common beliefs and values. In a sense it papers over social and cultural divisions.

Those who remain sympathetic to an approach broadly informed by *The Elementary Forms of Religious Life* have responded to these critiques in various ways (see Smith and Alexander 1996):

- claims about solidarity inducing ritual effects are subject to greater empirical scrutiny;
- issues of conflict and resistance have begun to be theorized through studies of events like wars, riots, and revolutions;
- causal agency and responsibility tend to be situated in active agents and concrete institutions rather than in the workings of an abstract social system.

A further and less often noticed development in the Durkheimian analysis of ritual has been to rethink and expand the idea of the "ritual." Common sense tells us rituals involve people coming together in one place to participate in peaceful celebrations that last for a definite period. In recent work this conventional understanding has been augmented by new ones. These de-emphasize time – space boundedness and give even greater weight to the role of symbolism and discourse as the defining feature of open-ended ritual episodes. To pick a couple of examples at random: Smith (1991) has argued that the British experience of the 1982 Falklands/Malvinas war can be understood in ritual terms. What made it a ritual was a concerted period of public discourse that involved the relentless invocation of sacred and profane themes rather than the business-as-usual, cost-benefit language of realpolitik. In a similar vein, Edward Tiryakian (1995) asserts that the velvet revolutions of 1989 in Eastern Europe had ritual qualities. He shows that they were marked by a constant collective effervescence, a sense that events were of extraordinary, epochal importance, and a feeling of popular empowerment.

Perhaps the most systematic recent attempt to develop Durkheimian thinking about ritual as a theoretical concept for understanding elements of social life beyond the religious comes from Randall Collins. He calls on Goffman's mechanics of the interaction ritual (which we discussed in chapter 4) to augment Durkheim's theory. Ritual can be formal, stereotyped, and formulaic (thereby potentially more powerful in its effects, but also subject to the danger of mere empty ceremonialism), or natural, situational, and non-scripted (though not therefore merely spontaneous). In both cases, however, it consists of four main ingredients:

1 physical co-presence of participants;
2 exclusion of outsiders;
3 a collective focus on the same object or activity;
4 a shared emotional mood (Collins 2004: 48).

Once this is understood, rituals can then be evaluated according to the amount and variety of **emotional energy (EE)** they generate. Those that are successful at building up high levels of rhythmic entrainment generate high EE, a long-term emotional mood of attachment to the group involved with the ritual and the associated symbols. Those that are not successful create low EE, which manifests itself as long-term emotional alienation from the group and its symbols. EE, Collins suggests, can be empirically observed and measured, and, at least theoretically, an individual's pathway through various interaction rituals and the outcomes it has produced in him or her in terms of EE can be reconstructed as an **interaction ritual chain**, which permits a thoroughly sociological approach to the psychological categories of personality and identity (2004: 118–19, 131–3).

Collins also offers some intriguing reflections on stratification, which critics have frequently claimed is a realm generally underappreciated in Durkheimian theory. He argues that categorical identities (e.g., white, black, male, female, upper-class, lower-class) are in fact of variable value in micro-situational encounters. It may be that in **formal rituals**, which rely on scripted and ceremonial forms of interaction, those categorical identities are of central importance. But in **natural rituals**, this is not necessarily the case. How otherwise to explain, e.g., the often largely female administrative assistants and clerical staff who defer in the abstract to their generally male bosses, but who in fact exercise vast amounts of power over the actual operation of many bureaucratic organizations and can frustrate many of the designs of those bosses when they choose to do so (2004: 286)? For Collins, stratification is ultimately about micro rituals that include some and exclude others, rather than macro-level qualities such as class or racial position.

This suggestion that our understanding of stratification might be significantly enhanced by a more Durkheimian emphasis on micro ritual is echoed in the work of class analysts like David Grusky, who has suggested Durkheim's argument in *The Division of Labour* that "big classes" at the macro level were a transitory phenomenon, and that class action and identity in modernity will be increasingly about the local occupational level, captures much of the contemporary reality of social class structure (Grusky and Galescu 2005). The identities of workers and the processes that contribute to their collective action come largely not from the macro-level social classes but rather from occupational groupings. This makes much sense in light of Collins's case for interaction rituals as members of a shared professional group are much more likely to ritually interact than are members of a big class who can never physically be in the same place at the same time.

Critics of Collins question some of the foundations of the theory. Finding and measuring the emotional energy levels of individuals is much more difficult than Collins claims. Moreover, the picture we can get from reading Collins is all too easily of individuals coordinating and mirroring their activities so as to generate a mutual high. Collins needs to do some deft theoretical footwork to explain activities like solitary reading or the influence of non-material symbolic forms, like the media, myth, and fantasy, on generating human activity. His focus on physical co-present activity can potentially be seen as a kind of biological reductionism by the unsympathetic.

An equally important development has been thinking about the role of the media and long-distance participation in the ritual activities of contemporary society. Daniel Dayan and Elihu Katz (1992) have made the most notable efforts in this direction. They develop the idea of the **media event** in their quest to "bring the anthropology of ceremony to bear on the process of mass communication" (1992: 1–2). Examples of such events include Queen Elizabeth's coronation, the funeral of President Kennedy, and the first moon landing. These were experienced by most people in their living-rooms, not in the streets. According to Dayan and Katz, the defining features of the media event are that they are live, preplanned, interrupt routine, are remote from the viewer, and are watched by huge audiences. In terms of their semantic content, such events tend to involve reverence and ceremony, they proclaim themselves as "historic," they are about great leaders, and they make use of themes of reconciliation and celebration. Dayan and Katz point out that such events are broadly hegemonic or conservative, in that they are organized by powerful groups and tend to celebrate mainstream values and structures of authority. Drawing on Durkheim and Turner, they suggest that the successful media event often "creates an upsurge of fellow feeling, an epidemic of communitas" (1992: 196) and can serve to "integrate nations" (1992: 204). They do this

not only by manipulating symbols on the day, but also by generating a sense of anticipation, by bringing people together into the living room for "festive viewing," and by
providing a common focus for conversation and emotion (see also p. 173).

Commemoration

Closely linked to the literature on ritual is a growing body of work on commemoration.
Halbwachs's theme of collective memory has proven to be of central significance here,
with clear empirical applications in the study of phenomena as diverse as monuments,
memorials, historical texts, rituals, and celebrations. Perhaps the most ambitious
empirical agenda to be inspired by the idea is Pierre Nora's (1996 [1984]) *Les Lieux de
mémoire* project. This is a large-scale collaborative work in which a team of French
historians collected materials on the various ways in which "France" has been represented and celebrated. These range from official representations in state ceremonial and
iconography (Bastille Day, the flag) to those of everyday life, such as the bicycle. The
interpretations made of these sites of Frenchness verge on those of cultural studies
rather than orthodox history, with a continual interest in the association between
social representations and political interests.

Nora makes the claim that we should distinguish "memory" from "history." The
former is rich in meaning and symbolism but possibly distorted, while the latter is
analytic, abstract, and objective. He paints a picture of history taking over from memory
– a thesis that is broadly consistent with Weberian ideas of disenchantment. Recent
developments in historical theory, however, make such arguments problematic. It is
now being realized that, far from being objective, academic historical writing is partial,
selective, and mythological. Indeed, historians today often analyze the writings of
other, earlier, historians, taking them as a data source for exploring the process of collective memory formation.

For the most part, Halbwachs's work emphasized the importance of positive events
in the past associated with heroic acts. It neglected issues such as social division and
the possibility of weak or incomplete commemorative effects. These kinds of errors and
omissions are typical of Durkheimian work in the first part of the twentieth century.
An important trend in more recent work on collective memory has been the exploration
of these themes. Controversial events are now being included in the academic agenda.
Robin Wagner-Pacifici and Barry Schwartz (1992) suggest that the ways that such
episodes are memorialized reflects enduring ambiguities. They show that the Vietnam
Veterans Memorial in Washington, DC has both heroic and tragic, public and personal
meanings built into its form and fabric (see also pp. 173–4). A variant on this new
theme in Durkheimian research is to take an event that could have been successfully
coded as a sacred part of national history, and explore the ways that this potential
might be unrealized. Smith (1999), for example, addresses the possibility of a disjunc-
tion between a heroic mythology and its commemorative institutionalization. The fall
of the Bastille is universally perceived in France as a pivotal and heroic moment in the
national narrative. It has been commemorated in time thanks to a public holiday
(July 14), but attempts at a spatial commemoration have never been fully successful.
The history of the place de la Bastille is one of many botched and bungled attempts at

creating a worthy sacred space. It is also a record of struggle with contending national sites such as the Eiffel Tower. The general trend in contemporary studies, then, is to understand collective memory as a puzzle, contest, and achievement rather than as an automatic and unproblematic product of social needs and circumstances.

A final theme in contemporary research has been to look at forgetting and the blasé attitude, as well as esteem and reverence. For example, in exploring Abraham Lincoln's contemporary reputation, Barry Schwartz (1998) detects growing popular indifference coexisting alongside more traditional heroic narratives and beliefs. He suggests that this reflects the growth of postmodern suspicion toward metanarratives as well as residual elements of a prior national mythology. In a similar vein, a central aspect of Lyn Spillman's (1997) exploration of centennials and bicentennials in Australia and the United States is the effort of elites to construct events that would overcome potential mass apathy and have widespread appeal.

The analysis of deviance

If contemporary Durkheimian studies now exhibit greater realism, with concurrent attention to conflict and causality, some credit for this must be given to prior work in the area of deviance. This literature pioneered the application of Durkheimian themes to the explanation of social conflict and violence. Although such work has generally drawn on *The Division of Labour* rather than *The Elementary Forms of Religious Life*, it nevertheless taps into issues related to symbolism and ritual. The most important study in this tradition was written during the 1960s – Kai Erikson's *Wayward Puritans*.

In *Wayward Puritans*, Erikson (1966) sets out to explain three "crime waves" in the town of Salem in seventeenth-century Massachusetts. Each of these involved the identification of deviant groups and their punishment. The first episode, the Antinomian Controversy, involved a sect which preached Christian beliefs that differed from those of Salem's Puritan leaders. Next was the persecution of the Quakers. Finally came the famous witch crisis of 1692. Looking back on these events from the perspective of the present, it is notable that in each of the "crime waves" there was little evidence that those persecuted had done anything wrong. Deviants were identified on the basis of flimsy evidence (such as "confessions" by children in the case of witches), and disputes were often over trivial details (such as long hair in the case of the Quakers, or minor points of doctrine with the Antinomians).

Erikson suggests that we can explain these episodes in terms of a **boundary maintenance** process. The idea here comes from Durkheim's insistence in *The Division of Labour* that deviance was functional for a community. By identifying and punishing the wrongdoer, the community could unite itself and reaffirm its core moral values. Following Durkheim, Erikson suggests: "deviance makes people more alert to the interests they share in common and draws attention to those values which constitute the 'collective conscience' of the community. Unless the rhythm of group life is punctuated by occasional moments of deviant behavior, presumably, social organization would be impossible" (1966: 4).

In the case of Salem, Erikson suggests that the crime waves took place when there were threats to the sense of mission and purpose that had defined the strict Protestant community. These included the entry of less religious migrants into the area, a loss of political autonomy, the conquest of the surrounding wilderness, and infighting within the community over land. According to Erikson, acts of symbolism and punishment served to mark out the boundaries of the community and reestablish a sense of moral direction. From this perspective, the persecutions have more to do with social and cultural needs for integration than with the control of an objective danger to society.

Wayward Puritans is an important book, which does much to demonstrate how morality, ritual, and symbolism work together in defining good and evil and in generating violence and conflict. Nevertheless, it exhibits some typical Durkheimian flaws of the kind that Lukes (see above) identified. The most important of these is that causal agency is hard to establish. It seems as if abstract social needs are dictating both the identification of deviants and wider community beliefs about their deviant status. In this regard, Stanley Cohen's work marks an important step forward.

In *Folk Devils and Moral Panics*, Stanley Cohen (1973) looked at reactions to riots and fighting in British seaside resorts during the 1960s. Cohen does not cite Durkheim and prefers to draw on literature from labeling theory and social psychology. Nevertheless, he cites Kai Erikson's work in an approving way, and his general approach is sufficiently consistent with a Durkheimian perspective to merit inclusion here rather than elsewhere in this book (he might have sat equally uncomfortably in chapter 9). The riots Cohen explored involved groups of youths riding motorcycles and scooters, throwing rocks at each other, drinking, and so on. Cohen's particular focus was on the role of the media in reporting these events, although he was also interested in broader public concern. According to Cohen, media and public reactions were disproportionate to the real harm caused by the riots, and were marked by exaggeration and distortion. He developed the term **moral panic** to capture this response in which "A condition, episode, person or group of persons emerges to become defined as a threat to societal values and interests" (Cohen 1973: 9). The term is arguably superior to Erikson's "crime wave." Whilst the idea of a crime wave suggests that crime really was happening, the idea of a moral panic suggests an emotive social response to a minor episode. Cohen's major conclusions about the cultural processes central to the moral panic included the following:

- Media reporting constructed a **folk devil**. This was a stereotyped image of evil, such as the long-haired biker.
- A process of **sensitization** took place in which the media reported even trivial events that could be connected to the panic.
- A process of **deviance amplification** led to media reports becoming a self-fulfilling prophecy. In periods before public holidays, they would often run features about expectations and fears of forthcoming violence. These would attract the potential troublemakers and create a climate of tension that was conducive to conflict.

Cohen's study has since proven highly influential in a number of fields, ranging from Durkheimian studies of deviance, to British cultural studies, to critical media theory. Its great attraction lies in its detail and realism. In contrast to Erikson's rather abstract analysis of causal forces, Cohen points to the role of specific institutions (e.g., the media, courts, the police) in generating false pictures of deviance. He also flags the way that relations of power play a role in shaping both an originating deviant act and the societal reaction to it.

The future of moral panics

The concept of the moral panic has proven to be one of the most important in cultural sociology, especially for those with an interest in the media. The idea has been applied widely to understand public, political, and media reactions to issues such as youth subcultures, drugs, Satanism, crime, AIDS, public health, and so on. Notwithstanding this popularity, it has been suggested that the days of the concept are numbered. Writing from within the British cultural studies tradition, Sarah Thornton and Angela McRobbie (1995) list several reasons why we should treat the idea with caution. Most of these relate to changes that have taken place since Cohen's study of 1960s England:

- The public is now more media-savvy and is aware of tendencies in the media toward sensationalism. Niche media are replacing national media suggesting that multiple narratives will emerge about any given potential panic.
- Minority groups who might have been demonized as folk devils in the past are now more articulate and organized. Single mothers, for example, have an association, with its own spokesperson.
- Cohen's theory suggests a tightly knit and cozy relationship between the media and those in authority. Today the media is less respectful of authority and seems to delight in cutting down tall poppies.
- Behind the idea of panic is the idea of misrepresentation of reality. Thanks to shifts toward the postmodern (see chapters 13 and 14), these ideas become problematic – the real is to some extent created by the media.
- Minority groups might actively seek to generate a panic in order to obtain publicity and kudos. The punk rock band, the Sex Pistols, for example, tried to manufacture scandal and shock whenever they appeared on television or before photographers in the mid-1970s.

Effervescence, the sacred, and popular and youth culture

Youth and popular culture are topics that have been the object of attention for some time from perspectives informed by the Marxist tradition, and especially those deriving from British Cultural Studies (we discuss some of this work in chapters 3 and 9), but they have gotten little attention from Durkheimian theory. In recent years, however, this situation seems to be changing. Caillois's study of play and games (2001 [1958]) has dug some of the foundations for recent work in which Durkheimian tools are applied to the interpretation of these realms. He compares human play and games to religious interaction with the sacred. Both involve a transcendence of ordinary, mundane existence, where actors motivated by both ecstatic abandon and serious attention to rules participate in ritualized acts that represent deep symbolic truths in a space and time carefully separated and protected from the everyday, profane world. He also distinguishes four basic types of play/game: *agon*, or those oriented to aggressive competition between two players or teams; *alea*, or games of chance; *mimicry*, or play involving masks and dissimulation; and *ilinx*, or play/games where vertigo and disorientation is sought by participants. Much popular and youth culture can be demonstrated to belong to one or more of these play forms. Sport is the most obvious example, but others are not hard to find. Rock, pop, and rap concerts and videos display characteristics of hybrid *mimicry/ilinx* forms of play, while much video gaming can be understood as a hybrid of *agon* and *mimicry*.

A contemporary French thinker, Michel Maffesoli, has built on some of the insights of Caillois and Georges Bataille to argue for what he calls the orgiastic and effervescent nature of contemporary Western society and the "return of the tragic" in the affirmation of intense, spontaneous experience in youth subcultural situations (Maffesoli 1996 [1988]; 1993 [1982]). Alexander Riley has explored hip-hop culture and rap music from this perspective, arguing that gangsta rap culture can be understood as a cultural narrative immersed in the transgressive violence and pleasure of the left sacred. The culture of mourning and vengeance, the embrace of intoxication and sexual license, and the avid interest in the "battles" of rappers in the genre (which sometimes go beyond the lyrical and entail actual physical violence) are likely read by middle-class consumers of that genre of youth music as a variety of agonistic tragedy wherein they can construct identities for themselves that mimic their mistaken impressions of what actual ghetto life is about (Riley 2005).

Durkheimian perspectives: an evaluation

For much of the 1960s and 1970s, Durkheim suffered from a negative press within the area of cultural theory. He was variously perceived as a positivist, a determinist, and as an advocate of quantitative sociology. On top of this, his theories were seen as conservative and as functionalist. Critics like David Lockwood (1996), Charles Tilly (1981), and Steven Lukes (1975) claimed that too much importance was given to cultural systems as an integrating social force, and not enough to:

- the ways that cultural systems reflect social and material interests or work ideologically to favor some groups above others;
- the ways that agents create, manipulate, or use symbols and discourses;
- the ways that culture is implicated in change, struggle, and historical process.

One problem with these now well-known arguments is that they tend to be based upon critical readings of an older literature, such as the work of Shils and Smelser, and to be centered on the critique of what Lockwood calls "normative functionalism." This is the idea that culture exists in order to contribute to social stability.

Yet, as we have already seen, a different kind of Durkheimian work has been gaining momentum since the 1980s. Much of this has been dedicated to breaking free of functionalism, responding to critique, and developing more flexible applications of Durkheim that are informed by other contemporary cultural theories (for an overview, see Smith and Alexander 1996; Alexander and Smith 2005). At the time of writing, Durkheimian cultural studies would appear to be a growth area. According to its advocates, the appeal of the tradition rests upon several pillars:

- a powerful vision of the autonomy of culture, grounded in the idea of binary oppositions between the sacred and profane;
- key concepts like ritual, symbolism, classification, morality, the sacred and profane, which can be applied in diverse empirical settings;
- an understanding of the religious basis of social life which confronts ideas of disenchantment in the strongest possible terms;
- possibilities for creative synthesis with structuralist and poststructural theory, thanks to a shared interest in the symbolic and in classification.

For these reasons, supporters affirm that the promise of a cultural sociology contained in *The Elementary Forms of Religious Life* is slowly being realized. The historical sociologist Charles Tilly cautions that "sociologists always have one more version of Durkheim to offer when the last one has failed" (1981: 107). This time around, they have abandoned his functionalist freight while retaining some of his key concepts. They have also adopted a more Weberian approach, exploring in detail how culture works to bring change or stability, consensus, or conflict in particular settings and historical sequences. The jury is still out on this newer literature. Whatever its adequacy, it is clear that the future challenge for Durkheimian cultural theory is to continue to address the concerns of its critics without compromising its existing strengths and diluting its distinctive intellectual agenda.

Suggested Further Reading

Empirical works in the Durkheimian tradition tend to be relatively accessible when compared to those influenced by many other styles of cultural theory. The studies discussed in this chapter should not present too many difficulties to most readers. For a sample of more current empirical work inspired by Durkheim, see Alexander (1988), the references in Smith and Alexander (1996), the individual chapters of Alexander and Smith (2005), and some of the other recent material we have looked at here.

CHAPTER SIX

Structuralism and the Semiotic Analysis of Culture

It is often remarked that the structuralist movement arrived like a tidal wave in the 1950s, radically transforming the way we think about culture. In truth, however, subtle groundwork had been laid during the first half of the twentieth century. We begin this chapter by highlighting the characteristics of structuralism as a compelling and powerful intellectual approach. We then track back in time to look at that ground-work, before exploring the work of several key structuralist theorists, including a detailed consideration of Lévi-Strauss and Barthes – arguably the two most important structuralist influences on contemporary cultural theory.

The Characteristics of Structuralism

Although it is a diverse field, there are a number of core features to structuralist approaches to culture. Identifying these commonalities provides a useful starting point for our investigation of this theoretical movement of pivotal importance.

- *Depth explains surface.* A central belief of structuralists is that social life is only super-ficially chaotic, unpredictable, and diverse. Beneath the level of perplexing and unique events are hidden generative mechanisms. In order to understand what appears on the surface, therefore, we have to look at this deeper level.
- *This depth is structured.* Not surprisingly, ideas of "structure" are fundamental to structuralism. Deeper generating mechanisms are not merely present and potent (as we remarked in the previous point), they are also organized and patterned. Structuralists tend to see these deep structures as being made up of a limited pool of elements. These are combined and recombined into ways that explain surface diversity.
- *The analyst is objective.* Structuralists tend to see themselves as detached and scien-tific observers who are discovering some kind of truth that is not apparent to actual social actors. This self-understanding differs radically from those advocated by some other positions, most notably postmodernism.

- *Culture is like language.* Structuralism is heavily influenced by work in the area of structural linguistics. This points to the ways that language can be understood as a system made up of words and even micro-elements like sounds. Relationships between these enable language to work to transmit information – to signify. Structuralist approaches to culture focus on identifying analogous elements (signs, concepts) and exploring the way that they are organized to carry messages. This process is sometimes thought of as one involving the "decoding" of semiotic processes.
- *Beyond humanism.* Structural approaches tend to diminish, ignore, or even negate the role of the human subject. The major focus is on the role and workings of the cultural system, rather than on the consciousness and genius of the individual human agent. Structuralists often see themselves as opponents of existentialism and phenomenology – perspectives which they denounce as individualistic and unscientific. In the final chapter of *La Pensée sauvage* (*The Savage Mind*), for example, the structuralist anthropologist Claude Lévi-Strauss launched a polemical attack on his rival, the existentialist philosopher Jean-Paul Sartre. According to Lévi-Strauss, his opponent's position failed to appreciate the constraining role of society and culture in shaping individuals, their thinking, and their actions. He saw it leading to a kind of self-indulgent and introspective thinking which elsewhere he termed "shop-girl metaphysics" (1973 [1955]: 58). Contrasting with the efforts of existentialists and phenomenologists was a structuralist analysis. This took as its point of departure the "scientific" exploration of objectively available systems of ideas and signs rather than the interior thoughts and experiences of individuals. As Lévi-Strauss put it: "I believe the ultimate goal of the human sciences to be not to constitute, but to dissolve man" (1966 [1962]: 247). In other words, his aim is to displace the conscious human subject from the center of analysis. This idea has subsequently become known in poststructuralist circles as **decentering the subject**.

For the most part, these diverse characteristics can be traced back to a point of origin in the work of the founder of structural linguistics, Ferdinand de Saussure.

Ferdinand de Saussure

During his lifetime the French linguist Ferdinand de Saussure was regarded as an intelligent person. Yet it was only after his death that he became recognized as one of the leading thinkers of the twentieth century. Saussure's lectures were published posthumously as the *Course in General Linguistics*. In this work Saussure (1986 [1916]) laid the foundations not only for a structuralist approach to language, but also for structural approaches to culture more generally. According to Saussure, language consisted of an acoustic image (words, sounds) linked to concepts (things or ideas). The relationship between these was purely a matter of convention. There was no necessary reason why the word "tree" should represent the concept of the tree – as he famously put it, "the linguistic sign is arbitrary" (1986: 67). Saussure claimed that language was essentially a system of signs involved in a complex process of signification. In order to understand it we have to uncover the structure and functioning of this sign system. But how does language work? In looking at this question Saussure suggested that language operates by means of contrasts. The word "dog," for example, has a distinctive meaning because we can differentiate it from others like cat, tree, and so on. Words exist, then, as part of a network of signs that are tied together by a structure of differences.

Rather than tracing the history of the word "dog" and its changes over time (a **diachronic** approach), Saussure advocated a **synchronic** analysis of language. This involved mapping out a language system at a given moment in time, instead of accounting for it as a historical product. He also insisted on the need to differentiate *langue* (language) from *parole* (speech). According to Saussure, the latter term referred to actual empirical instances of language use – things that people actually say in particular times and places. *Langue*, by contrast, was a deep structure – the entire sign system that underpinned parole. Saussure's approach, as we might expect, was more concerned with langue than parole. He was less interested in what people said, than in the underlying linguistic system that made it possible for them to say anything at all.

Saussure's accomplishment is universally acknowledged as formidable. By emphasizing the arbitrary nature of language and its internal structure and logic, he showed that it was a *sui generis* phenomenon which could not be explained away as a mere reflection of reality itself nor as an ideology. This is because meaning is generated within the linguistic system via a system of differences. Aside from demonstrating the autonomy of language, this point can be applied more widely to underpin the autonomy of any conventional signifying system and marks an important resource for cultural theory. The autonomy of culture under any approach informed by semiotics can usually be guaranteed by such an insistence on the arbitrary nature of the sign system. In his *Course in General Linguistics* Saussure raised the possibility of such wider applications. He suggested that it was possible to "conceive of a science which studies the role of signs as a part of social life. . . . We shall call it semiology. It would investigate the nature of signs and the laws governing them . . . linguistics is only one branch of this general science" (1986: 16).

Saussure's words were prophetic. His perspective was to provide an intellectual seed that was to flower in later decades as structuralism became a major approach to the analysis of culture. While linguistics has remained the keystone of the structuralist movement, developments in anthropology, psychoanalysis, and cultural studies have established semiology (or what is now generally known as **semiotics**) as an innovative and powerful tradition that covers diverse disciplinary fields.

Claude Lévi-Strauss

Claude Lévi-Strauss is generally regarded as the leading structuralist theorist of culture, and so we need to look at his work in some detail. In the autobiographical *Tristes Tropiques*, Lévi-Strauss (1973 [1955]) provides some examples of fields with similar properties to structuralism which informed his early intellectual development. These were Marx, Freud, and geology. In each, he suggests, there lay the germ of his own intellectual approach.

For Marx, the diverse surface details of economic and political life (such as strikes, revolutions, poverty, exploitation, consciousness, ideology, and so on) could be traced back to a deeper causal nexus. This revolved around the ownership of capital, the means of production, and the class structures and class interests that emerged from them. Taken in its scientific form (see discussion of Althusser on pp. 46–9), structural Marxism is very much about the reduction of complexity. Its analytic power comes from an ability to account for detail in terms of a limited set of relationships between defined structuring social forces. Before moving on, we should add that although Lévi-Strauss was impressed by the power and consistency of Marxist thought, he never really embraced Marxism or Marxist modes of cultural analysis. To the contrary, his work provides one of the most significant anti-materialist approaches to culture.

Freud's work on the interpretation of dreams, mythologies, and neuroses also impressed Lévi-Strauss. Freud's patients typically presented to him with baffling and bizarre symptoms. These might be weird nightmares, strange fetishes and phobias, inexplicable fears, and embarrassing sexual problems. Freud's genius lay in his ability to explain these diverse phenomena in terms of a limited repertoire of generating mechanisms. There was the psyche, with its id, ego, and super-ego in systematic relationship with each other. And there were also series of defined processes like transference, denial, wish-fulfillment, and repression. Although every patient, every personality and life history, and every condition was unique, each problem could be accounted for in terms of common, hidden, psychic mechanisms (see also pp. 195–7). While Lévi-Strauss admits to the influence of Freud's intellectual approach, he takes little else from Freud. He does not make significant use of Freudian concepts, and would contest the individual-centered nature of much of Freud's inquiry. Nevertheless, he shares with Freud an interest in the structure of the human mind and the idea of the unconscious. A more subtle input from Freud, which is worth discussing here, relates to questions of intellectual style. Both Freud and Lévi-Strauss draw upon their formidable erudition in making explanations and forming intellectual connections between ideas – especially when considering minute points of detail. Moreover, both enjoy setting up a research puzzle in their essays. Freud often starts his writings by first describing a patient and their symptoms – rather like Sherlock Holmes introducing a new arrival at 221b Baker Street. Lévi-Strauss, too, will begin with a baffling myth, ritual, or custom and go on to explain it in virtuoso style. His methodology is often rather like that of a detective assembling clues to build up a picture and solve a complex mystery.

Geology is the study of landscape. Lévi-Strauss writes of his childhood in France and the ways that he grew to appreciate the fact that hidden structures in the bedrock could be used to account for patterns in the landscape – hills, river valleys, vegetation, and so on. His approach to culture also has something of this quality. Like the geologist, he sees himself as a scientist uncovering deep, causative patterns that lie under the visible landscape. His primary concern is not with explaining detail, but rather with using detail to reconstruct larger, and more important, underlying forms.

Lévi-Strauss sums up what he learnt from Marx, Freud, and geology as follows: "All three demonstrate that understanding consists in reducing one type of reality to another; that the true reality is never the most obvious; and that the nature of truth is already indicated by the care it takes to remain elusive" (1973: 57–8).

Beyond these early influences, there are two more direct ancestors informing the work of Lévi-Strauss. The first of these is structural linguistics. The work of Saussure, which we discussed above, provided a set of concepts that Lévi-Strauss adopted with enthusiasm. It also influenced his general intellectual approach. Just as Saussure had argued that we needed to explore *langue* and not *parole*, Lévi-Strauss saw a need to go beyond the study of surface contingency (e.g., a particular myth) to locate a deeper, generative logic within the cultural system (e.g., the structure of mythical thought).

CLAUDE LÉVI-STRAUSS (1908–)

Lévi-Strauss was born in Belgium and had a typical intellectual training in the leading institutions of Paris. After a trip to Brazil in the 1930s he began to become more and more interested in anthropology. He escaped Nazi Europe and World War Two by moving to New York. Here he encountered Roman Jakobson and became interested in linguistics. Lévi-Strauss established himself as a major intellectual figure with his work *The Elementary Structures of Kinship*. This book attempted to explain all known kinship systems as expressions of a simple underlying cultural logic. His later studies centered on the analysis of myth, ritual, and classification systems. In contrast to many other leading anthropologists of his generation, he is not particularly known for his fieldwork. His great talent lies in a keen theoretical mind and an encyclopedic grasp of abstruse ethnographic data from around the world.

Reference: Leach (1974), Lévi-Strauss (1973)

The second major influence on Lévi-Strauss is almost never discussed. He only occasionally cites Durkheim's work, and most notably provides a fulsome dedication at the front of *Structural Anthropology* (1963 [1958]). There are, however, an astonishing number of parallels in their thinking. Although Durkheim sees society as a moral force and Lévi-Strauss sees it as an intellectual force, both understand society as a realm of the abstract, ideal, and "mental." Durkheim's idea of the collective conscience that is expressed in ritual and religion has strong parallels with Lévi-Strauss's understanding of a collective unconscious that reveals itself through myth. Lévi-Strauss's ideas on binary opposition are prefigured in Durkheim's ideas about the contrastive relationship between the sacred and the profane. Both Durkheim and Lévi-Strauss are interested in distinguishing "primitive" (mechanical solidarity, the savage mind, the *bricoleur*) and "modern" forms of mental life (organic solidarity, the scientist), while at the same time highlighting common properties. Both are interested in the detection of cultural universals and their ability to explain the particular. Durkheim wrote a book called *The Elementary Forms of Religious Life*. Lévi-Strauss wrote a book called *The Elementary Structures of Kinship*. He even explicitly positioned the thought of Durkheim's premier disciple, Marcel Mauss (see pp. 69–72) as proto-structuralist in a long introduction to a collection of Mauss's works. The list could go on, but the point has been established. The exact nature of Durkheim's influence on Lévi-Strauss's thinking must remain debatable. It is not certain, for example, whether it was exerted largely through conscious or unconscious mechanisms. What is clear, however, is that there is a strong affinity of style and approach between the two scholars. These profound, but largely unacknowledged, ties have facilitated the rise of a structuralist Durkheimian cultural sociology in the later decades of the twentieth century (see pp. 78–80). A more negative repercussion, however, has been that many of the problems with Durkheim's cultural theorizing (viz. the lack of attention to agency and power, and the use of simplistic evolutionary dichotomies) are reproduced in that of Lévi-Strauss. We discuss these questions later. First we review some of his major works and theoretical innovations.

The structural analysis of kinship

Kinship theory is a highly specialized, quasi-mathematical area that is often inaccessible to those without a robust anthropological training. It is concerned with phenomena as diverse as family structure, patterns of marriage, the organization of kin-based clan groups, the names given to various relatives, the characteristics of family relationships, patterns of residence, the ownership of property, and so on. In non-Western societies, kinship often provides the backbone of social organization.

In the late 1940s, Lévi-Strauss (1969 [1949]) produced *The Elementary Structures of Kinship* – his first work of major international importance. It is a book that displays a typically structuralist move. Lévi-Strauss assembled a vast array of disparate ethnographic material and argued that beneath the chaos of seemingly unique cultural detail from hundreds of cultures around the world there was a deeper order. Essentially, kinship systems could be reduced to a limited pool of types. These in turn were underpinned by an equally limited set of "superficially complicated and arbitrary rules [that] may be reduced to a small number" (1969: 493). The most important of these concerned issues of descent (e.g. who could belong to a given clan) and marriage (e.g., who was allowed to marry whom). Even more fundamental than kinship rules was the incest taboo, a universal prohibition which Lévi-Strauss saw as being the point of origin for cultural life. Thanks to the incest taboo, he claimed, people were forced to become sociable in the search for mates.

Lévi-Strauss argued that his understanding of kinship systems was made possible by applying lessons from linguistics to the analysis of social phenomena. He suggested that "linguists and sociologists do not merely apply the same methods but are studying the same thing" (1969: 493). In his view, kinship systems were like language in that both involved exchange (of women and words, respectively), and were a form of communication that reflected the higher intellectual faculties of the human mind. The job of the analyst was to decode the abstract rules governing these systems of human communication. The overall effect of these transactions was to engender human sociality and provide for the construction of complex cultural systems. Hence he writes that "The emergence of symbolic thought must have required that women, like words, should be things that were exchanged" (1969: 496).

The Elementary Structures of Kinship stands as a cornerstone in the application of structuralist thinking and linguistic analogies to the study of cultural phenomena.

During the 1950s and 1960s Lévi-Strauss was to continue his theoretical progress in this direction, but he switched the focus of his powerful analytic mind away from kinship systems toward the study of myth and classification.

The structural analysis of myth and classification

The years following *The Elementary Structures of Kinship* saw Lévi-Strauss work on a series of essays that would revolutionize his discipline. These were collected in *Structural Anthropology* (1963 [1958]). Here Lévi-Strauss argued for a "Copernican revolution ... which will consist of interpreting society as a whole in terms of a theory of communication" (1963: 83). The aim was to excavate the underlying language-like characteristics of culture and the formal properties of its generative grammar. Lévi-Strauss believed that through this method he would be able to reach "a significant knowledge of the unconscious attitudes of the society or societies under consideration" (1963: 87). In other words, he thought his structural method would teach us something about the human mind – a task which is in the tradition of Durkheim's exploration of the collective conscience.

The most spectacular demonstration of this approach can be found in Lévi-Strauss's analysis of myth. Lamenting the unscientific qualities of previous efforts to understand mythology, Lévi-Strauss proposes that "myth is language" and insists that "the past experience of linguists" (1963: 211) may help us develop an improved method for understanding them. Just as speech consists of elements like phonemes that are built up into more complex patterns of meaning, he suggests that myths are constructed from smaller units known as **mythemes**. The meaning of a given myth is derived from these, and reflects the way they are combined in larger patterns. In his famous exploration of the Oedipus myth, Lévi-Strauss applies this principle. The Oedipus myth is a legend from Ancient Greece that on first inspection appears to be as bizarre, surreal, and dreamlike as any other myth. Lévi-Strauss first reduces the story to its most simple form and identifies mythemes such as "Oedipus kills his father" and "Oedipus marries his mother." He goes on to look for common features and contrasts between these mythemes. In this case, "Oedipus kills his father" belongs to a class of incidents in the myth which involve the "underrating of blood relations," whilst "Oedipus marries his mother" is concerned, like many other events, with the "overrating of blood relations." According to Lévi-Strauss, **binary oppositions** of this kind (underrating/overrating) are a fundamental property of myth and endow it with a deeper, structural meaning that we might miss if we only looked at the plot. He goes on to explore other binary oppositions in the Oedipus myth and claims that it is a meditation on dilemmas posed by social and cultural life in the spheres of kinship, myth, and reproduction. Impressed by the coherence and profundity of this deep structure, he takes these hidden meanings to be evidence that "the kind of logic of mythical thought is as rigorous as that of modern science" (1963: 230).

Such an attempt to redeem "primitive" thought was a central feature of *The Savage Mind* (1966 [1962]) – arguably Lévi-Strauss's most important work. Drawing on data sources as diverse as kinship systems, mythology, art, and literature, he argued that cultural systems operate primarily to classify the world and suggested that "[the] thought we call primitive is founded on this demand for order" (1966: 10). Much of the text is taken up with case studies documenting the various ways in which this activity takes place. Resisting attempts to portray primitive thought as inferior, he insisted that science and magic were two "parallel modes of acquiring knowledge" and required "the same sort of mental operations" (1966: 13). Having said this, Lévi-Strauss does not argue they are identical. He suggested that primitive thought operated by means of a **science of the concrete**. This built up classification systems and knowledge by locating difference and resemblance in things according to their superficial appearance and use value. An example of resemblance would be using a seed that looks like a tooth as a talisman against a snakebite. Relationships of difference were central to the construction of binary oppositions, such as those in totemic kinship systems. These divided people into separate clans named after diverse animals. In contrast to mythical thought, Lévi-Strauss maintains that scientific thought tends to hunt for deeper causes and relationships. It tries to go beyond appearance and use hidden properties of things as the basis for its classification systems.

Lévi-Strauss likened primitive thought to **bricolage**. In France the **bricoleur** is a kind of odd-job person. A *bricoleur* tends to be good at home improvements, at fixing things, and at improvising repairs from whatever is at hand (for this reason there is a hardware chain in France called "Mr. Bricolage"). According to Lévi-Strauss the primitive mind operates like that of the *bricoleur*. It put together systems of classification, mythologies, and rituals from whatever is available in the surrounding natural and social environments (animals, plants, landscape features, other myths, etc.), treating these as signs that could be assembled into more or less coherent cosmologies. Lévi-Strauss famously suggested, for example, that totemic animals were **bons à penser** (good to think with). That is to say, they served as arbitrary tokens through which more elaborate sign systems, binary oppositions, kinship systems, and mythologies could be constructed. This process of creating culture from nature frequently involved **systems of transformations**, in which the elements in a preexisting symbol set are taken up and recombined in new patterns. By use of "analogies and comparisons" mythical thought could be innovative. Working by means of a "new arrangement of elements" and "continual reconstruction from the same materials," the savage mind was able to build incredibly complex cultural systems (1966: 20–1), just as a talented *bricoleur* could manufacture ingenious contraptions using whatever could be found in the garden shed.

Lévi-Strauss: an evaluation

Lévi-Strauss is rightly understood as a giant in twentieth-century cultural theory. The major strength of his approach lies in its ability to map the autonomy of culture. Structuralist approaches like that of Lévi-Strauss point to the self-sustaining and self-supporting properties of cultural systems. He shows how complex meanings arise from the arbitrary conjunction of signifying elements in structured relationships with each other – hence cultural systems have their own rules and logic of operation, just like languages. A related dimension of his work is the way that he elaborated a conceptual toolkit for thinking about and decoding culture. The binary opposition is now a ubiquitous concept. Ideas about *bricolage* and systems of transformation are also widely applied to cultural creativity and change in both non-Western and Western contexts. Finally, Lévi-Strauss teaches us that we need to go beneath the obvious level of manifest meanings and personal experience so as to understand culture fully. Sometimes we need to step back and look for patterns that might not be immediately apparent to either analysts or social actors. Having said this, Lévi-Strauss has been subject to sustained criticism on a number of fronts. The most important of these are as follows:

- Ideas about power are curiously absent from his work. There is no understanding of the ways that mythologies might become institutionalized because they support certain interests (the work of Roland Barthes, considered below, suggests that this might often be the case). If there is a "society" behind his theory, it seems to be one that is framed in functionalist terms as an arena of sociality, exchange, and common humanity rather than conflict and domination.

- A related criticism is that Lévi-Strauss sees culture as an abstraction that is able to exist without active human intervention. Agency seems to be denied, with culture operating in a rather deterministic way to pattern action in areas like marriage and myth. He famously insists at one stage that "We do not claim . . . to show how men think in myths, but rather how myths think themselves through men, and without their knowing it" (1964: 20). The cultural system, it seems, dances to its own peculiar, mathematical logic. The savage mind appears to be disembodied, collective, and transcendental. In reacting against Sartrean individualism, Lévi-Strauss perhaps went too far in the other direction. As Bourdieu (1977) and others have suggested, there is little space for strategy, agency, or individual reflexivity in the Lévi-Straussian universe.

- Scholars looking at myth have suggested that plot is relentlessly downgraded in Lévi-Strauss's search for an underlying cultural grammar organized around the binary opposition. As we shall see in chapter 11, other thinkers suggest there is a payoff to exploring the sequential dimensions of stories.

- Lévi-Strauss does not always come across as a very politically correct writer. His discussion of the "savage mind" has been attacked as an oversimplification that (despite its universalistic motivation of praising mythical thought) essentializes and reproduces contrasts between the "primitive" and the "modern." Similarly, his argument that kinship systems involve the exchange of women by men have been condemned as sexist. Evaluating such criticisms is no easy task, depending as it does on our ability to clearly distinguish normative (what should be), analytic (how things work in the abstract world of ideas), and empirical (how things really happen) claims in Lévi-Strauss's thinking. Neither Lévi-Strauss nor his critics are very accomplished at this activity.

- Technical criticisms have also been leveled at Lévi-Strauss. It has been suggested that he has fundamentally misunderstood many core concepts in linguistics when applying them to cultural materials. In Lévi-Strauss's defense, we might suggest that his misreading was at least a creative one that enabled him to take his work in directions where nobody else had yet ventured.

Georges Dumézil and Algirdas-Julien (A. J.) Greimas

Neither of these two thinkers, both roughly contemporaries of Lévi-Strauss, is as widely recognized as the author of *Tristes Tropiques*, but their influence on structuralist thought in its French context in the 1950s and 1960s was considerable, and the frameworks they present for understanding culture continue to attract attention in contemporary work on culture. Dumézil (1898–1986) was a comparative mythologist who studied with Marcel Mauss and Henri Hubert (see pp. 69–72, 74). His key conceptual contribution, which diversified the prevailing structuralist preoccupation with binarism, was that of the **trifunctional hypothesis**. His study of the Indo-European peoples who controlled much of the European continent by the end of the third millennium BCE revealed their use of a basic tool of mental classification which consisted of a tripartite division of the social world: the functions of the priests/judges, those of the warriors, and those of the agricultural workers. Dumézil believed that basic structural division of domains directed to order, action, and sustenance had been preserved in the myths of all the peoples descended linguistically from the Indo-Europeans, as it was deeply embedded in the Indo-European vocabulary and grammar. Thus, many frameworks for thinking about the organization of society in the Western world are derived from these fundamental Indo-European mythic structures, e.g., the feudal categories of king, knight, and peasant. One can even think of the Christian notion of the trinity in Dumézilian terms: God the Father as provider of cosmic order, Christ the Son as the active redeemer, and the Holy Spirit as provider of ongoing spiritual sustenance. Michel Foucault considered Dumézil one of the most important sources of his own thinking about structures (although Dumézil was uncertain of the relationship of their work) and Lévi-Strauss called him the creator of the structural method.

Greimas (1917–92) was a linguist by training, but he envisioned a semiotic structuralism that proposed to encompass all fields in the human sciences. His key theoretical innovation was that of the **semiotic square**. This is a visual representation of the structure of relations of signification between units of meaning. It starts with a pair of opposed or "contrary" terms and then expands on that initial relationship to include two new terms, each of which has either a "contradictory" or a "complimentary" relationship to the original two terms. So, if we take figure 6.1, which is adapted from James Clifford's use of the semiotic square to explore the complex cultural meanings taken on by primitive tribal artifacts when they are placed into Western art museums, we have a first term, "art," which is defined by its originality and its creation by an individual marked as such, i.e., an artist. Placed in the square, this term generates not only the contrary term, "culture" (objects, like tribal artifacts in their native context, that are unoriginal, collectively produced, and generally intended for practical use, e.g., in the serving or storing of food), but two new terms, each of which is related to the original two terms in the ways just described. In this example, the third and fourth terms are "not-art" (commodities such as tourist art that are commercially reproduced) and "not-culture" (objects such as counterfeit or faked paintings that purport to be works by some famous artist, avant-garde objects in the vein of, e.g., Marcel Duchamp's signed urinal that explicitly attack the conventions of the art world and yet find their way into

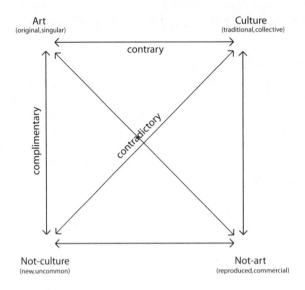

Adapted from Clifford 1988: 224

Figure 6.1   The semiotic square

museums, and commercial or technological objects that come to be displayed in museums of science and technology, e.g., the former sewage pumping system of the city of Cambridge that now makes up the Cambridge Museum of Technology). Greimas's intent was to demonstrate the limitations of purely binary oppositions (such as Durkheim's sacred and profane, p. 10) and posit a more complicated basic structure of signification. The logical functioning of meaning, he argued, calls into play all of the four terms of the square whenever any of the others is invoked.

Roland Barthes

The abstract formalism of the semiotic square made it less than easily accessible as a theoretical tool for some of Greimas's contemporaries, but his work made a significant impact on some other thinkers who would achieve much greater renown than the retiring linguist. One such thinker was the intellectual and philosopher Roland Barthes. Although Barthes moved toward an almost poststructural perspective later in his career (we discuss this in detail on pp. 107–8), in his early work he advocated a semiotic model of culture which drew heavily on Saussure and Greimas. The influence of the latter is most apparent in an early study he made of the fashion system, based on readings of women's fashion magazines, which fairly bristles with the formalism of Greimasian semiotics. In *Elements of Semiology*, Barthes (1984 [1964]) constructed a sort of base camp for his early structuralist work. He argued for a close convergence between linguistics and cultural inquiry and set out to elaborate some basic terminological and conceptual themes to inform semiotic inquiry. These are as follows:

- *Langue/parole.* This is the distinction made by Saussure that we have already discussed, which contrasts the abstract system of signs (language) and its particular use (speech). Barthes argues that it can be applied in all semiotic contexts, and not just to linguistic phenomena. In talking about "the food system," for example, he insists that there is a *langue* made up of alimentary taboos (things that can/cannot be eaten); "signifying oppositions of units" (e.g., sweet/savoury); rules of association (items of food that can/cannot go together), and rituals of use (e.g., table manners). This can be contrasted with alimentary *parole,* such as personal innovation or a given menu, which is "concocted with reference to a structure . . . but this structure is filled differently according to the days and the users, just as linguistic form is filled by the free variations and combinations which a speaker needs for a particular message" (1984: 94).

- *Signifier and signified.* Again, Barthes sees this fundamental Saussurian distinction between the thing or concept represented (signified) and the thing doing the work of representation (signifier) as essential to all sign systems. He reviews the various forms that this relationship can take in linguistic and visual spheres, before pointing out that things may be more complex than we imagine. It is not simply the case that signifiers denote signifieds which are already in existence. Rather, they help to construct them by dividing up reality and "cutting out" shapes from the amorphous mass of experience. Following Lévi-Strauss, Barthes sees the "future task of semiology" to be rather like that of taxonomy. We should "rediscover the articulations which men impose on reality" (1984: 120), that is to say, explore the often arbitrary ways that sign systems carve up and classify the world.

- *Syntagm and system.* The distinction here is very broadly similar to that between the longitudinal and the cross-sectional or the diachronic and the synchronic (see p. 94). **Syntagm** (or the **syntagmatic**) refers to the ways that signs are arranged in chains that extend over time in a sequence. Hence "each term here derives its value from its opposition to what precedes it and what follows" (1984: 121). System is about contrast with other (absent) units in the sign system with which it could be substituted. This is sometimes also thought of as the **paradigmatic** plane. Turning again to the food system, Barthes argues that the "horizontal" reading of all the entrées on a menu would involve the exploration of system, while a "vertical" reading through the sequence of dishes (starter, main course, dessert) involves syntagm. We can explore the semiotics of the menu using either or both of these approaches.

- *Denotation and connotation.* The issue here relates to orders of signification. Barthes argues that sign systems build upon themselves and so have many layers. **Denotation** refers to the lower-order processes and to the more or less literal meanings of signs. **Connotation**, by contrast, involves a kind of metalanguage. Connotations tend to be built up from a prior order of denotations. They are ideological and tend to "cap the denoted message" (1984: 151) with an overarching theme (see also p. 105).

This brings us to *Mythologies* (1973 [1957]). This earlier work consists of a collection of magazine articles written by Barthes which decode French everyday life and culture. It provides perhaps the best place to illustrate his approach to semiotics. According to Barthes, signs within culture are never innocent, but rather they are caught up in complex webs of ideological reproduction. In a series of virtuoso readings, he sets about interpreting a remarkable variety of phenomena and then relating them in a loose way to themes that are broadly characteristic of Western Marxist thought. These include authenticity, ideology, and commodity fetishism (see chapter 3). Here are some examples:

- The new Citroën automobile is understood as a kind of modern cathedral where people come to worship. Barthes draws attention to the fetishistic ways that people interact with this commodity.
- A magazine cover of a black man in French military uniform saluting the flag is read as an ideological statement supporting colonialism. It suggests that people in French colonies are happy to serve France.
- Wrestling is interpreted as a kind of theatre or spectacle for the working classes. As this staged quality is explicit, it is seen as more honest and authentic and less bourgeois than boxing.
- Manufactured children's toys are contrasted with artisanal ones. The latter are superior in that they are robust organic products that adapt over time and use to the hand of the child. Manufactured toys, by contrast, lack the auratic qualities of the artisanal product. They are cold and clinical products of alienated labor and technological systems.

In an essay entitled "Myth Today" at the end of *Mythologies*, Barthes attempted to draw some post-facto lessons from his assembled studies and place them within a politico-philosophical framework. He suggested that we needed to combine the abstract study of semiotics (how signs "work") with a more sociological account of their concrete form and function. This would allow us to "connect a mythical schema to a general history, to explain how it corresponds to the interests of a definite society" (1973: 128). In his case this "definite society" was a capitalist one. He insists that myth was always bourgeois and typically worked to justify or **naturalize** the existing social order. It did this through a variety of rhetorical figures that recurred in its discourses, objects, and images:

- *Inoculation* was the idea that by acknowledging some of the evils of class and inequality that existed in society, one could head off a more general criticism of the social order.
- *The privation of history* involves presenting objects but denuding them of all traces of their social origins. An example of this is the Blue Guide used by tourists. This enables them to visit places of tourist interest, but without meaningful awareness of ongoing social conditions and processes. Aesthetic experience is cut off from a wider social or historical consciousness.

- *Identification* refers to the processes through which we either identify with another or, by contrast, see them as ineluctably different from ourselves. If we identify with the black soldier saluting the flag, we are likely to feel more proud of our status as French citizens.
- *Tautology* involves defining things in terms of themselves. Barthes sees this as a kind of refuge from difficult questions and as a rejection of language. It might involve statements like "because that's how it is."
- *Neither-normism* involves balancing two alternatives and then rejecting them both (presumably in favor of the status quo).
- *The quantification of quality* concerns attempts to systematically measure and evaluate aesthetic realities or to make them predictable and amenable to market determination.
- *The statement of facts* concerns providing maxims about the world which are assimilated as common sense, thus preventing critical thinking.

A key aspect of *Mythologies* was the use of the distinction between denotation and connotation. Denotation, it will be remembered, refers to the literal meaning of an image, while connotation refers to the extra (mythological) meanings that are layered on top. The magazine cover showing a black person in military uniform saluting a piece of red, white and blue material, for example, can be taken to denote a colonial soldier in the French army saluting the flag. However, it has extra (ideological) connotations. According to Barthes, it shows "that France is a great Empire, that all her sons, without any color discrimination, faithfully serve under her flag, that there is no better answer to the detractors of an alleged colonialism that the zeal shown by this Negro in serving his so-called oppressors" (1973: 116). Barthes drew attention to the ways that such mythological connotations worked through common-sense reasoning. He suggested that we automatically and instantaneously read signs in a particular way and do not perceive an elaborate semiological system at work. The result is that "myth is experienced as innocent speech, not because its intentions are hidden . . . but because they are naturalized" (1973: 131). The power of myth lies precisely in this ability to make an arbitrary system of values appear as a system of facts.

The work of Roland Barthes in *Mythologies* is important for two main reasons. First, it opened up a new furrow by combining semiotics with critical theory. This provided a much-needed infusion of new conceptual blood into neo-Marxist cultural theory, much of which was still lumbering along under the impetus of concepts from Marx's century-old *Economic and Philosophical Manuscripts* (see pp. 7–8). Secondly, it legitimated the study of popular culture in academic circles. While other scholars of his era, such as Lévi-Strauss and Lacan, worked with esoteric materials, Barthes showed that even junk-culture activities like wrestling or mundane objects like the automobile were fair game for the withering irony of the analyst's pen. Barthes's intervention here was prescient. By the 1970s, his ideas were having a fundamental impact on the intellectual character of British cultural studies (see pp. 144–57), with their investigations of advertising, news programming, and the print media. By the 1980s, his work had become canonical for the area. It is important not to underestimate this contribution toward the construction of an empirical and semiotically rich form of critical cultural theory.

Perhaps the most important criticism that can be made of the text is that Barthes never really fully came to terms with the possibility of the Left having its own complex mythologies. This is a flaw he shared with many neo-Marxian thinkers of his generation. Leftist perspectives were generally seen as "realistic" and as objectively removing bias and distortion rather than as culturally informed and deeply symbolic modes of communication themselves. Barthes argued that: "The bourgeoisie hides the fact that it is the bourgeoisie and thereby produces myth, revolution announces itself openly as revolution and thereby abolishes myth" (1973: 146). When myth existed on the Left, Barthes thought it to be impoverished and handicapped by ties to reality that made it "stiff and literal." Barthes cites mythologies about Stalin, and decries them as "meagre" and as lacking in "inventiveness" when compared to bourgeois mythologies which are "rich, multiform, supple" (1973: 148, 149). By the later 1970s, he had increasingly come to believe (with a number of other French intellectuals on the Left who rejected the aggressive and often violent discourse of the revolutionaries of May '68 and their descendants) that it might be possible to talk of a rich and developed "mythology of the Left." He noted this only in a few interviews and never took it up systematically in his published work, at least partially, by his own admission, because of his own political affiliations. A further problem with Barthes, as with all studies which rely on purely semiotic readings, relates to the ways that the mythologies are read. Questions can be raised as to whether the meanings that he derives from the media are shared by other people. Subsequent developments in areas like reception studies and postmodern theories of reading argue that signs are open to multiple interpretations. Some lay interpretations might reproduce what Barthes thinks of as mythological thinking, but others could be divergent or critical (see pp. 147–9).

Finally, and relatedly, we have to think seriously about the possibility of reflexivity and irony among ordinary citizens. Barthes draws a distinction between the "mythologist" (e.g., himself) decoding texts and the "myth consumer." For Barthes, the latter group have been seduced and outmaneuvered by the mythologies of bourgeois society, but at the same time can participate in a full and active social life. Mythologists, by contrast, are somewhat lonely, if heroic, figures, excluded from society and history by virtue of their ironic stance. They can enjoy only a "theoretical sociality," and have a "connection with the world [that is] of the order of sarcasm" (1973: 157). These kinds of binary distinctions now appear rather dubious. In Barthes's description of soap and detergent advertisements, consumers are presented as uncritical dupes who buy fully into the advertisements' claims of purity and whiteness. Yet the contemporary advertising world is rich with "anti-ad ads" that deliberately poke fun at this kind of message and assume the consumer is a savvy reader of media who is in on the joke. The "Image is Nothing" Sprite soft drink ads, which depict a fictional soft drink, "Jooky," is one recent example of this kind of ironic "anti-ad ad." It flaunts the trite symbols of traditional soda advertising (big-breasted women, happy-go-lucky young people at the beach drinking Jooky) as a way of distancing Sprite from the conventional and banal. Another example can be seen in the Enzyte spots for their penis enlargement pill, which feature a comically dreary and impotent man who is magically transformed into a perpetually grinning lady killer (his name is Smiling Bob) by taking the pills. It is not clear how Barthes's notion of the myth consumer would make sense of these.

These issues draw our attention to the concept of **reading**. In the context of cultural theory this crucial concept refers to far more than the ways that people interpret books and other written texts. Rather, it captures the active processes through which they make sense of the range of symbols, myths, and ideologies in the world around them. Often the same item of culture (e.g., book, television program) or event (political scandal, sporting contest) will be read in different ways by different people. In his later works, to which we now turn, Barthes himself was to make a fundamental contribution to our understanding of this process.

Roland Barthes was continually shifting his position throughout his career and delighted in abandoning perspectives he had helped to establish (see Culler 1983: 12). Indeed, some scholars assert that in his later work Barthes goes beyond orthodox structuralism and prepares the ground for poststructuralism. The central themes at stake here concern the sensual pleasures of reading and the active power of the reader.

In *S/Z* (1975a [1970]) Barthes undertook the study of a novella, "Sarrasine," by Balzac. This text is often held to mark a decisive bridging point between his structuralism and poststructuralism. The book consists of an incredibly detailed, line-by-line analysis of the codes behind the story. Barthes fragments the story into chunks of text and refers these to codes that the reader draws upon in making sense of the narrative. Barthes argues that these codes exist in both specific literary conventions and our wider culture. Our ability to make a text "mean" anything depends upon our ability to mobilize these codes. This project is consistent with the "scientific" orientation of semiotics, which aims at disclosing the rules through which meanings become possible. Yet at the same time as engaging in an almost Lévi-Straussian enterprise, Barthes argues that there is no single definitive meaning to the story. He suggests that the complex codes in operation overlap with each other in wild and unpredictable ways. There is an excess of meaning. The codes open up possibilities for alternative interpretations, and so there is a role for the reader in making sense of texts. Barthes suggests that a simple example of this can be seen in the way that a book never means exactly the same thing the second time we read it. Rather, we notice different things and make different connections (both within the text, to outside events, and even to our own life experiences) each time we encounter it. In *S/Z*, then, Barthes made a call for the study of the **readerly** and well as the **writerly**. He argues that most literary texts are readerly in that they are open-ended. They invite and encourage diverse interpretations, the use of irony and reflexivity. Writerly texts, by contrast, tend to be dry and literal. Whatever the nature of the text, Barthes places great emphasis on the power of readerly activity to liberate the diverse meanings of any given book. He says: "To interpret a text is not to give it a . . . meaning, but on the contrary to appreciate what plurality constitutes it . . . the codes it mobilizes extend as far as the eye can reach, they are indeterminable" (1975a: 5–6). This vision of proliferating and multiple meanings that defy authorial intention and ideological fixity is more suggestive of Derrida's method of deconstruction (see chapter 7) than Barthes's own earlier *Mythologies*.

As the 1970s progressed Barthes came to advocate hedonism as a strategy for reading – a decisive move away from the cool scientific detachment of classical structuralism. Many argue that *The Pleasure of the Text* (1975b [1973]) is notably "poststructural" for the way that Barthes abandons the effort to construct a coherent theory or systematic

---

ROLAND BARTHES (1915–80)

Roland Barthes was born in 1915 into a middle-class background. For much of his early life he suffered from ill health and poverty and this held back his educational and career progress. He published his first major works in the mid-1950s and by the mid-1960s was recognized by his peers as a major figure on the French intellectual scene. Meanwhile Barthes had become famous among the general public during the 1950s for his incisive and readable analyses of popular culture which were published in the mainstream press and subsequently collected as *Mythologies*. Despite this public success, he subsequently obtained notoriety in France as a champion of abstruse avant-garde fiction and for the difficulty of his own writing. He was elected to the prestigious Collège de France in 1977. In February 1980, Barthes was run over on a Parisian street and he died four weeks later.

Reference: Culler 1983

---

reading. His approach is aphoristic, rather like that of Nietzsche, consisting of pointed observations and questions. Perhaps more importantly, Barthes emphasizes here the sensual and intellectual joy that can come from engaging with a text. He suggested that each reader derives their own embodied pleasures from the text, depending upon their psychological and sexual profile. This leads to diverse reading styles and strategies, as each reader looks, interprets, and takes away from the text whatever gives them pleasure. Fundamental to this argument was the concept of **jouissance** – a French word that encompasses sensations of ecstasy and sexual release. Barthes saw texts carrying with them a pleasure that was akin to sex. He writes, for instance: "The pleasure of the text is like that unbearable, impossible, purely fictional moment when the libertine, tasting the end of a *risqué* plot, cuts the rope by which he is hung at the moment of orgasm" (1973: 15). Barthes was at pains to stress the embodied nature of *jouissance*, as if to provide an alternative to the model of a rational inquiring mind and rational semiotic process that lies behind orthodox structuralism. With *The Pleasure of the Text*, then, Barthes draws our attention to the fusion of the intellectual, the physical, and the emotional – a theme that has since proven central to poststructural attempts to dethrone and question reason.

Considered somewhat puzzling at the time of its launch, thanks in part to its aphoristic structure, *The Pleasure of the Text* has since become recognized as a major influence on cultural theory. Within the field of critical cultural studies, ideas about multiple reading strategies and pleasure have proven influential in shaping studies of media reception (see p. 149). Barthes's ideas have also been combined with a range of theorists, from de Certeau (see pp. 154–5) to Kristeva and Irigaray (see pp. 201–2), in providing theoretical grounds for understanding pleasure and reading as acts of "resistance" to dominant ideologies. These ideas have been particularly influential in more recent work in the British cultural studies tradition. It has been argued, for example, that strategies of subversive reading (against the grain, between the lines, etc.) enable mainstream texts and media content to be appropriated and used for pleasure by disenfranchised groups. We discuss these ideas further in chapter 9.

Marshall Sahlins

The work of Marshall Sahlins constitutes perhaps the last gasp of orthodox structuralism. In his early work he was a rather materialist anthropologist. Later he turned toward a more cultural mode of theory that was heavily informed by cultural structuralism. *Culture and Practical Reason* (1976) is perhaps his most famous work in this genre. Here he sets out to confront rationalist ideas that claim that practical interests shape human action, especially in the economic arena. The sphere of production, Sahlins argues, is shot through with arbitrary cultural inputs that determine needs and wants. Cultural codes shape consumer preferences, which in turn shape economic production. Culture, then, is primary in shaping economic life, and not the converse, as claimed by Marxism. He writes: "the cultural order is realized also as an order of goods. The goods stand as an object code for the signification and valuation of persons and occasions, functions and situations. Operating on a specific logic of correspondence between material and social contrasts, production is the reproduction of the culture in a system of objects" (1976: 178). In other words, consumer items are *bons à penser* in the sense already laid out by Lévi-Strauss. They serve as signifiers within the cultural and social systems, and the economic system responds to this code by producing yet more signifiers.

Much of *Culture and Practical Reason* is taken up with a semiotic reading of *la pensée bourgeoise* (the reference to *La Pensée sauvage* is hardly oblique!) or the cultural codes of the Western middle classes. One of the clearest illustrations of this perspective is Sahlins's discussion of the American beef industry. He begins by noting that meat is coded by the sign system as embodying strength, virility, and so on. This cultural code establishes a basic demand. But why, he asks in an ingenious counterfactual turn, does the United States have a dominant industry producing beef rather than pig, horse, or dog meat – all of which are economically and nutritionally valid alternatives?

The answer, Sahlins suggests, lies in a cultural code (not, by contrast, in the institutional power of the cattle lobby) which he terms the "American meat system." The greatest taboo we have is toward cannibalism, and so a binary code sees animals as a preferred meat source to humans. Within the animal kingdom a series of further binary codes distinguishes animals that are more like us from those that are less like us. We allow dogs into our houses and establish emotional bonds with them. We also talk to, name, and love horses. According to Sahlins, a binary code marks off these "inedible" animals from "edible" ones (pigs and cows). Of these latter two, pigs are more contiguous with human society in that they scavenge in the farmyard and eat the remnants of human food. For this reason they are seen as in some ways connected to humans. Cows, by contrast, are closer to nature in that they are found out on the range. As the binary cultural codes of *la pensée bourgeoise* dictate that "edibility is inversely related to humanity" (1976: 175), cattle provide the meat of choice.

The Fate of Structuralism

The influence of Lévi-Straussian approaches to culture grew vigorously in the 1950s and reached a zenith in the mid-1960s with the publication of *The Savage Mind*. By the late 1960s, they were in trouble. Events like the Paris student uprising of 1968 and the Vietnam War dominated the headlines. Clashes between police and demonstrators throughout the West suggested that a different kind of theory might be required – one that paid greater attention to brute power and the role of the state. And so the late 1960s and early 1970s saw the structural Marxism of Althusser (see pp. 46–9) replace its more cultural rival in the academic fashion parade. During this period the approach spawned by Barthes fed into the development of contemporary critical cultural studies, as we have noted above. The work of Lévi-Strauss continued to be influential but became assimilated with other intellectual traditions, such as Durkheimian theory in the work of Mary Douglas (which we reviewed in an earlier chapter). The period since the 1960s has also seen some of its more radical claims watered down. In contrast to the Lévi-Straussian vision of a free-floating collective mind, greater attention has been paid to the role of agency, institutions, and history in the construction and propagation of semiotic systems. The work of Pierre Bourdieu (1977), for example, attempts to incorporate action, power, and change within a broadly structuralist understanding of cultural fields (see chapter 8).

Suggested Further Reading

Of the secondary texts on Lévi-Strauss the most time-efficient is probably Edmund Leach's (1974) slim paperback. If you are keen to read Lévi-Strauss in his own words, then we would suggest *The Savage Mind* and some of the key essays in *Structural Anthropology* (vol. 1). These are an exciting intellectual adventure and contain most of Lévi-Strauss's seminal discussions on the philosophy behind structuralist inquiry. *Tristes Tropiques* provides telling insights on his career and intellectual development. The pages dealing with his youthful experiences of French intellectual culture and higher education are priceless for anyone seeking to understand why French theorists turn out the way they do. His other works on myth and kinship are rather specialized and technical and are recommended to devotees only. The empirical studies in *Mythologies* by Roland Barthes are entertaining to read and should be compulsory for those in the cultural studies area. The introduction to *S/Z* provides a shortcut to his theory of reading and writing. *The Pleasure of the Text* is brief, but difficult and rather poorly translated into English. Still, a quick skim of the book (don't feel too guilty, this is a technique Barthes himself recommends!) will enable the reader to extract the gist of what he is saying. Jonathan Culler's (1983) short text on Barthes provides an outstanding, reader-friendly introduction to this major thinker. One can also profit from a look at *The Grain of the Voice*, a helpful collection of interviews ranging from the early 1960s until his death, in which, spurred by probing and informed interviewers, Barthes discusses many of his works and intellectual influences. *Structuralism in Myth: Lévi-Strauss, Barthes, Dumézil, and Propp* contains English translations of some key texts from a number of the authors discussed in this chapter, including a concise statement by Dumézil on the trifunctional hypothesis. Greimas makes for very difficult reading in the original French or in English translation, but *A. J. Greimas and the Nature of Meaning* (Schleifer 1987) provides an accessible summary of the semiotic square.

CHAPTER SEVEN

The Poststructural Turn

Notwithstanding the continuing and important work of Lévi-Strauss during the 1960s, and perhaps because of the theoretical innovations of Barthes, that decade saw structuralism slowly replaced by poststructuralism as the dominant paradigm in French cultural theory. The 1970s and 1980s saw this newer understanding of culture move into the Anglophone nations. While much is said about structuralism and poststructuralism, drawing boundary lines between them is a somewhat arbitrary task. This is because:

- Poststructuralism is best understood as a refinement and outgrowth of structuralism rather than as an opposing school of thought. Certainly it is the case that contemporary poststructuralist thought would not have been possible without the earlier innovations of structuralism. Some of the core thinkers involved (e.g., Michel Foucault, Jacques Derrida) were in fact first labeled structuralists before the developments in their thought that carried them outside that category. Although simplistic binary distinctions between structuralism and poststructuralism abound, it is far from clear how useful they are. It is perhaps more useful to think of them as types of theory with overlapping properties, and indeed some shared thinkers, rather than as empirical schools of thought that have clear boundaries and mutual antagonism.
- There is no single poststructuralism, but, rather, a plurality of approaches that are loosely collected under this title. So plural, in fact, are the styles of some of these thinkers frequently labeled "poststructuralist" that we have treated a number of their contributions to cultural theory not in this chapter, but in other chapters in the book that provide a somewhat clearer topical fit for them (e.g., Jacques Lacan, Gilles Deleuze, and Julia Kristeva are discussed in chapter 12, while Jean-François Lyotard and Jean Baudrillard are featured in chapter 13). For this reason, traits found in one poststructuralist author may not be found in another. Caution must be expressed about overgeneralizing from one or two scholars to the entire field.
- Published discussions of poststructuralism are almost invariably confounded by simultaneous efforts to define postmodernism and the postmodern (we look in more

detail at these other concepts in chapters 13 and 14). The result can be terminological chaos. The influence of poststructuralism has been wide and diverse and this
very success can make it difficult to categorize it neatly. Literary criticism, feminist
theory, and postcolonial and race theory have all been deeply marked by it, and
poststructuralism has made possible significant connections of sociology with
humanities and cultural studies.

Bearing these reservations in mind, the material presented below attempts to provide
a starting point for understanding the poststructural turn. We go on to look at the two
most important authors associated with this theoretical development: Foucault and
Derrida.

Structuralism and Poststructuralism: Two Commonalities . . .

In as far as one movement was made possible by the other, it is inevitable that we should
find strong traces of structuralism in poststructural thinking. The two most notable of
these are the conceptual resources used for understanding culture and the approach
to the human subject.

Vocabularies of culture

Like its predecessor, poststructuralism makes extensive use of linguistic and textual
models of culture. It builds in particular on the work of Lévi-Strauss, Barthes, and Lacan
(the latter is discussed on pp. 199–202), and so we find ideas about codes, myths, narratives, and symbolism taking a prominent position. The result is a rich and powerful
toolkit for reading and writing cultural life. Thanks to the adoption of semiotic models,
a major emphasis is also given to the autonomy of culture. This in turn has informed
a decisive rejection of Marxism in poststructural thinking. Ideas about ideology (which
imply social or economic determinism) have tended to be replaced by concepts of discourse (which we consider below). At the same time as using the structuralist toolkit,
poststructuralism has created a set of additional concepts, many of which are introduced in what follows. These provide researchers with even more grip in unpacking
the stuff of culture.

The death of the subject

Like structuralism, poststructural thinking has attacked the humanist idea that the
sovereign individual should be the major focus of analysis and advocated what is sometimes known as the **death of the subject**. The idea of the sovereign individual had its
origins in Renaissance thinking, and continued during the Enlightenment. It proclaims
the rational and motivated nature of human conduct. Under this humanist model,
society and culture are seen as the product of choices and contracts that are entered
into by autonomous human agents. By contrast, poststructuralists emphasize not only
the centrality of semiotic systems as targets of cultural analysis (rather than agents),

but also the ways that subjectivities and agency are constructed by arbitrary but power-ful cultural and historical forces. Here attention is given to the ways that individuals are constrained rather than free, continuing the attack on existentialism and phenom-enology that motivated Lévi-Strauss. Desires, motivations, and concepts of the human subject are shown to arise from particular discourses rather than free will and rational thought. Moreover, aspects of the self are considered to be often contradictory, frag-mentary, or incomplete. Such an understanding again attacks the idea of a unitary, sovereign actor. Taken in combination, this process of rethinking the self and situating it as a product of discourse is sometimes referred to as **decentering the subject** (see also p. 93). In chapter 12 we discuss the ways that psychoanalytic theory, and in par-ticular the work of Jacques Lacan, have contributed to these perspectives. Here, we look at approaches that are mostly inspired by philosophy and literary criticism – especially Foucault's ideas about the role of discourse and discipline in shaping the human subject, and Derrida's attack on the "metaphysics of presence."

. . . and Three Divergences

Saying that structuralism and poststructuralism have some common agendas is not the same as claiming they are identical. The latter movement introduced some decisive new ingredients to existing structuralist recipes. As we shall see in chapters 13 and 14, these have gone on to influence postmodern cultural theory.

Scientific knowledge, truth, and epistemology

Orthodox structuralism *à la* Lévi-Strauss operated with a model of the researcher as a detached observer. As we noted in chapter 6, Lévi-Strauss was inspired by Marx, Freud, and geology. From their writings it is clear that Marx and Freud took themselves to be engaged in scientific enterprises. As for geology, it is a natural science. Such a self-understanding promoted the view that the analyst was uncovering some single deep truth or could arrive at an objective, universally valid reading of culture with the appli-cation of "scientific" approaches. For the poststructuralist, such ideas are misleading. Their critique is founded on the following points.

- The social location and historical construction of the observer and their knowledge plays a role in shaping understandings and theories. Foucault's work suggests that all those involved in the human sciences are implicated in particular structures of power and knowledge, whose configuration has a decisive impact on the discourses they produce. Such arguments have some affinities with those in the sociology of knowledge tradition as well as with relativistic epistemologies. They question the attainability of a neutral, "true" reading of culture. In its place, they suggest it is better to turn our attention to exploring the social conditions of knowledge produc-tion and the impacts of knowledge and truth claims in defined social settings.
- Poststructuralists argue that cultures and texts can be interpreted in diverse ways and are capable of yielding multiple and endlessly proliferating, perhaps mutually

contradictory, readings. "Truth," therefore, may be more elusive than we think. Contrary to the structuralist position, there may be no single right or wrong understanding or definitive reading – something that is generally known as **closure**. Poststructuralists claim that the application of rigorous logic in our analyses does not help us resolve questions of meaning. To the contrary, writers like Derrida argue that it serves only to multiply readings and produce paradoxes and dead ends in interpretation.

• Structuralist theory emphasized the dry, mathematical qualities of cultural systems. In poststructural thinking desire, the body, and play are foregrounded as both observable dimensions of culture and as qualities of theoretical writing. The effort here is inspired by the nineteenth-century German philosopher Friedrich Nietzsche and his celebration of emotion and the will in place of the logical and rational. Contemporary poststructuralists have hunted out other early writers and theorists sympathetic to this position, the sexually deviant Marquis de Sade being perhaps the most notable (and notorious!) of these.

Power

The critique of the scientific stance is related to the issue of power. In its Lévi-Straussian guise at least, structuralism did not see cultural and social structures as products of power, but rather as outcomes of social ties, human needs, and a transcendental collective unconscious. In its Marxian incarnations, such as those advocated by Althusser and the Barthes of *Mythologies*, cultural structures could be understood as products of an objective and underlying capitalist system. Poststructuralists can be read as building on the Marxist understanding of culture as a product of power, but also as rejecting the metanarrative of Marxism as a plausible account of history and society. Instead of decoding unified, class-based ideological systems, as Althusser does, they point to the proliferation and mutual interpenetration of discourses and power/knowledge structures. These may have been informed by race and gender, by colonialism or by institutional struggles involving professionals and experts. Again, a key input here has come from Nietzsche and his belief that social life is driven by a "will to power" (see chapter 1).

History

The poststructural view of history is linked to its vision of power and truth. Structuralist thought tended to argue that history was knowable and linear. A defining aspect of poststructural thought is its rejection of metanarratives of emancipation and progress. For the poststructuralist a core feature of history is its chaotic nature rather than its ability to reveal plan and order. Ideas derived from Friedrich Nietzsche have come to replace deterministic ideas about movement through historical stages like feudalism and capitalism. An emphasis is consequently placed on discontinuity, rupture, contingency, and chance in shaping cultural and institutional dynamics. In addition, chaotic struggles for power are seen as the major dynamic force in explaining historical process. These ideas about history have been displaced onto the synchronic analysis of culture.

It is argued that we have to abandon presuppositions of culture as a coherent and ordered system. A better approach is to see it as a collection of ill-sorted fragments that collide and intersect with each other in context-specific struggles for power and domination.

Michel Foucault

Discussions of poststructuralism, at least in the social sciences, almost invariably revolve around the work of Michel Foucault. His work not only embodies many of the characteristics of poststructural thinking that we have outlined above, but in large part was responsible for constructing and institutionalizing the poststructural model. Whether or not they agree with him, commentators on Foucault concur that he has been one of the most influential thinkers in the contemporary field of cultural theory. This centrality reflects not only the power of his ideas, but also the uncanny ability of his work to resonate with the concerns of diverse disciplines: philosophy, history, psychology, sociology, and linguistics among them. Foucault saw himself as an authority on the "History of Systems of Thought," but, if pressed to offer a conventional label, would probably have seen himself as a philosopher. Although he rejected the tag of

---

MICHEL FOUCAULT (1926–84)

Foucault was the son of a wealthy provincial surgeon. Rejecting his father's wish that he should study medicine, he undertook academic training in philosophy and psychology in the elite institutions of Paris, where he developed a lifelong friendship with Louis Althusser. He and Derrida shared much of the same educational background and were also good friends until the latter viciously attacked an argument about Descartes in Foucault's first book and Foucault responded in an equally combative manner. In his younger days, he flirted with both Marxism (at one point he briefly joined the Communist Party) and phenomenology, but, after extensive reading of Nietzsche and his encounter with the revered philosopher and historian of science Georges Canguilhem, he eventually rejected both positions. During the 1950s, he worked briefly as a hospital psychologist before taking up junior teaching positions in provincial universities. During the 1960s, he began to publish prolifically and to develop his own distinctive intellectual style. After attaining a position at the Collège de France in Paris, he became recognized as a major figure in the French intellectual landscape and by the 1970s his writings were attracting significant interest in the Anglophone world. Aside from his academic work, Foucault was also a major participant in political debate in France and elsewhere, intervening frequently on issues including prisoners' rights and aid for refugees and dissidents from communist countries. His death in 1984 was of AIDS-related causes.

Reference: Eribon 1991

"structuralist," he did not endorse the tag of "poststructuralist" in describing himself. However, it is one that has been more widely applied to him than any other.

Foucault's work, which was mostly written during the 1960s and 1970s, is a complex *oeuvre* that shifted in orientation over time. This makes providing a summary rather dangerous in as far as it might suggest a false unity of approach rather than an evolving pattern of thought. Certainly Foucault scholars have spent a good deal of effort in detailing subtle shifts in his thinking. Nevertheless, perhaps the best way to introduce Foucault is through a study of the core themes that run throughout his work.

Discourse

Discourse is perhaps the central motif in Foucault's thinking. A discourse can be thought of as a way of describing, defining, classifying, and thinking about people, things, and even knowledge and abstract systems of thought. Foucault argued that discourses were never free of power relations. Nor should they be understood as the products of sovereign, creative human minds (as the humanist tradition maintained). To the contrary, they are implicated in and arise out of the power/knowledge relationships between the groups of people that the discourses themselves constitute and regulate. He writes that "power and knowledge directly imply one another . . . there is no power relation without the correlative constitution of a field of knowledge. . . . the subject who knows, the objects to be known and the modalities of knowledge must be regarded as so many effects of these fundamental implications of power/knowledge and their historical transformations" (1991a: 27–8).

The picture here is rather like that provided by Lévi-Strauss, insofar as human thought and action are shaped by cultural codes rather than individual will. The most obvious difference is that Foucault's approach emphasizes power and historical process. And so his studies explore the ways that knowledge operates to enmesh categories of person in relationships of power. In his empirical works such as *Madness and Civilization* (1967 [1961]), *The Birth of the Clinic* (1973 [1963]), and *Discipline and Punish* (1991a [1975]), he examined the ways that experts and professionals like doctors, psychiatrists, and criminologists had increased their authority thanks to the rise of new discourses. These discourses did more than just reinforce claims to professional expertise. They also constituted or invented deviant groups as objects worthy of study, containment, and reform and the experts who were entitled to control them. By emphasizing the arbitrary ways that such classifications have arisen and changed over the centuries, Foucault suggests that the claims to have discovered "truth" and "reason" that we find in professional discourses should be treated with skepticism. Rather than capturing an objective reality, such discourses create, reproduce, and mask relations of power and control.

Another key tool in attacking claims to reason were Foucault's theoretical works, *The Archaeology of Knowledge* (1972 [1969]) and *The Order of Things* (1970 [1966]). These made use of broadly structuralist thinking insofar as they demonstrated the ways that cultural systems tended to be self-referential and self-sustaining arbitrary efforts to classify and understand the world. According to Foucault, the task of analysis is to map discourse structures and their underpinning epistemic assumptions rather than evaluate their truth value by seeking a correspondence to an objective "reality." The process here is very broadly equivalent to Saussure's efforts to uncover the linguistic system behind speech. Foucault's parallel effort is in exploring the underlying cultural structures and orientations toward knowledge that make particular ideas and discourses possible, rather than investigating the merits of those ideas themselves. He uses the term episteme to refer to these deep epistemological foundations that may be behind a variety of specific discourses.

The concept of discourse is of great importance in that it provides a way of thinking about culture and power that is free of the intellectual baggage that comes with the concept of "ideology." It is difficult to use the term "ideology" without also invoking Marxian vocabularies of class, mode of production, false consciousness, historical materialism, and so on, with their associated tendency to relentlessly privilege the economic sphere. The idea of discourse, as elaborated by Foucault, can therefore offer greater potential autonomy to culture. Another advantage, according to Foucault's followers (variously termed Foucaultians or Foucauldians), is that we can move beyond the ideas of truth and falsity that are central to Marxian thinking about ideology. Marxists have traditionally argued that Marxism alone can provide an accurate reading of the world, and that other understandings are distorted, illusory, or dishonest. Drawing on Nietzsche, Foucault questions the capacity of any form of human knowledge to arrive at a complete and impartial understanding of the social world. Our task as analysts should be to be suspicious of all claims to truth. Instead of attempting to evaluate the accuracy of any given worldview or argument (as a positivist would do), we should instead consider it as dangerous. The job of the analyst is to map out the contours of a discourse and investigate its implications for relations of power.

Power

Foucault, like Nietzsche, suggested that power was a fundamental and inescapable dimension of social life. Using historical materials, Foucault argued that the forms of power that are at play have undergone a transformation over the past few centuries. During the eighteenth century, power was vested in the absolutist monarch. This is known as **sovereign power**. Foucault suggests that this kind of power had several defining characteristics:

- it tended to be brutal, involving torture and physical punishment;
- it operated intermittently, tending to be exercised only when rules had been broken;
- it was ritualized and full of symbolism;
- it took place in public.

To exemplify this argument, he points to the example of Damiens, who was tortured to death in 1757 for attempting to kill the French king. Damiens was attacked with red-hot pincers, had molten materials poured into his wounds and was eventually pulled apart by four horses. The whole ordeal lasted several hours. In his book *Discipline and*

Punish, Foucault (1991a) contrasts the case of Damiens with a prison timetable from some 80 years later. According to Foucault, the timetable is an indicator of **disciplinary power** – a form of power which has replaced sovereign power in the modern era. Foucault shows disciplinary power has a number of dimensions:

- it was associated with technologies of regulation, monitoring, and surveillance;
- it tended to operate continuously by changing patterns of thought and behavior through techniques of training that worked on the body;
- it was rational rather than ritual in orientation;
- it tended to take place within specific institutions like prisons, schools, and military barracks.

A pivotal and emblematic icon in the discussion of disciplinary power is Foucault's consideration of the **panopticon**. Advocated by the utilitarian philosopher Jeremy Bentham (among others), the panopticon was an architectural form in which a guard in a central tower could see into surrounding cells, but not be seen themselves. Prisoners would be subject to the gaze of the guard, but never really know if they were being watched. As a result, they would have constantly to monitor their actions and be on their best behavior. Foucault argued that such persistent self-monitoring and self-regulation would lead to the **normalization** of the deviant as they internalized the disciplinary regime to which they were subject. He argued that the form could be – and in fact was – exported to other social settings beyond the prison (e.g., the factory, the school) and his pessimistic conclusion was that the principle of the panopticon is in very broad application in our wider society. Commentators sympathetic to Foucault have suggested it can be found not only in visual devices like security cameras, but also in surveillance technologies like social security records, bank statements, and school reports.

It is this specific focus on technology that marks one of the major ways that Foucault goes beyond traditional critical theories of power. His concern is with the "how?" of power as much as with the "why?" Aside from the panopticon, Foucault's work also includes discussion of technologies such as the timetable, military drill schedules, and treadmills. Many of these technologies, he notes, work on reconstructing and normalizing the self by controlling and disciplining the body. The aim of this process is to create a **docile body** that is obedient to authority and amenable to social control. The general thrust of this work leads one to question the process of reform. What appears to be a progressive move away from barbarism and toward enlightened punishment turns out, on closer inspection, to involve the application of power in sustained, more subtle, and ultimately more effective and totalitarian ways.

The final form of power that Foucault investigated was **biopower** – a concept which he developed in his last major work, *The History of Sexuality* (1990 [1976]). The focus here is on the ways that modern states developed a concern with populations and with sexuality. His interest is in things like the census, epidemiological studies of health and illness, investigations into fertility rates, sexual deviance, and so on. Foucault suggests that discourses and technologies associated with this field boomed during the supposedly repressive Victorian era. The result was an explosion of expert fields such as psychoanalysis, sex therapy, social work, and statistics. The activities of experts defined normality and perversion and subjected individuals and populations to monitoring and control. Foucault writes: "Sex was a means of access both to the life of the body and the life of the species . . . becoming the theme of political operations, economic interventions . . . and ideological campaigns . . . a whole series of different tactics that combined in varying proportions the objective disciplining of the body and that of regulating populations" (1990: 146).

The novelty of this position is that Foucault suggests biopower worked in productive rather than repressive ways. It did this by mobilizing sexuality and desire, not just censoring them. Far from being opposed to or an escape from power (as common sense tells us), sex and sexuality are vehicles through which power operates. As Foucault (1990: 157) writes: "One must not think that by saying yes to sex, one says no to power."

Aside from identifying various forms of power, in his discussions on the topic Foucault introduced a number of other key ideas about how it works. These include:

- The **micro-physics of power**. This is the way that it influences everyday action and behavior at the level of the self and embodied practice.
- The **capillary nature of power**. This is the way that power permeates every aspect of social life, just as blood capillaries penetrate to the remotest and smallest reaches of the body. Foucault placed an emphasis on the workings of power at individual, local, and institutional levels rather than sweeping generalizations about the influence of hegemony, the state, and capital. An allied theme in Foucault's work was the stress on power "circulating" through a grid or net extending over a population. Actors were linked to each other by means of the power moving around this grid. From this perspective it is less useful to explore the domination one person has over another (e.g., the doctor over the patient) and more useful to look at the ways that both parties are positioned by a discourse (e.g., those of modern health science and administration).
- The *fragmentary and incomplete nature of power*. The agenda here is a critique of Marxist systems theory which understood power as part of a seamless, internally consistent, and coherently arranged system of domination linked to a mode of production. What Foucault is trying to do is to point to the multiple, contingent applications of power in diverse settings. These might be in conflict with each other rather than form part of a smoothly running unified system.
- The *constructive nature of power*. Weber's theory of power emphasized the domination one person had over another. Marx's theory pointed to the centrality of class dynamics. Such definitions stress the repressive and negative dimensions of power and the fact that it is held by particular parties in relation to others. Foucault, by contrast, suggested that power circulates within institutional and discursive contexts. Like Parsons, he tends to see power as something that resides in the system (not individuals) and enables it to produce certain outcomes. Foucault's emphasis is on the productive ways that power works by shaping positive ideas about selves, desires, and institutional goals rather than on the ways that it works, by blocking or repressing a "true" self or utopian vision.

- *The concept of governmentality* emerges from Foucault's work and has come to be widely used in investigations of the ways that administrative organizations are able to control and regulate populations. Following Foucault's lead, considerations of governmentality often play close attention to the role of discourses, technologies, and surveillance as tools of power in modern bureaucratic contexts. The work of Nikolas Rose has been exemplary in this vein. He has extended the Foucaultian critique of the psychological sciences as a machinery for producing knowledge about, and power over, subjects in his examination of the governing technologies those "psy" disciplines have put in place in factories and other work sites, in the military, and in the family (Rose 1998). His most recent work (2006) expands the analysis to recent biomedical technological innovations.

History

Like his views of power and truth, Foucault's discussions on history were also influenced by the work of Nietzsche. As we saw in chapter 1, an important dimension of Nietzsche's work was his confrontation with the modern belief that "God is dead" and that therefore there are no transcendental roots for values and morality. Nietzsche claimed that history had no broader meaning and was nothing more than a series of struggles for power. Such ideas had found support in the work of existentialist philosophers like Sartre, with their suggestion that human existence had no moral purpose other than that given to it by specific individuals through their action in the world. This bleak vision contrasts radically with that of Marx. Marxian theory places an emphasis on the evolution of society through distinct stages of development. From this perspective, history had a meaning or a grand narrative. Within this framework, events could be interpreted as part of an unfolding movement toward the eventual arrival of a communist utopia. Launching a subtle attack on his Marxist contemporaries, Foucault suggested that history was an arena of local, discontinuous struggles and discourses. Rather than identifying processes of evolution and continuity that might allow us to detect meaning, progress, and reason, his historical studies point to disjunctions (e.g., radical and rapid shifts between epistemes) and the arbitrary (e.g., fads and fashions in medical treatment). The upshot of this exercise is to question our confidence in the truth and morality of our own conceptual models.

A final aspect of Foucault's orientation toward history is that it brings to light the forgotten stories of marginal people like the insane and the criminal. The point here is again Nietzschean, foregrounding the ways that processes of inclusion, exclusion, and power are central to historical process, and questioning the possibility of a universal, true history that can transcend perspective and encompass all human experiences.

Foucault's analysis of the Iranian revolution in 1978 offers insight into the later development of his thought on this topic of unpredictable revolt and untenable grand narratives of history. The situation in Iran in 1978–9 fascinated him because of the fact that the Iranian movement that toppled the Shah's secular regime and brought radical Islamist cleric Ayatollah Khomeini to power seemed to have neither of the two elements that he claimed Westerners tend to recognize as constituting a "revolutionary situation": a class struggle or a revolutionary vanguard party (Foucault 1988: 213). The most common way Western academics tried to make sense of the Iranian situation was to label it a modernization crisis in which a clumsy leader tries to pull a traditional country into the modern world too quickly and the traditional elements of the society react in revolt against him. But Foucault rejected the implicit teleology of such arguments. Instead, he posited that, because of its populist and non-hierarchical spiritual structure, Shi'ia Islam might make possible the emergence of a "spiritual politics." He even believed that what was happening in Iran might be the "first great insurrection against . . . the weight of the entire world order" (Afary and Anderson 2005: 222). However misled he might have been about the ultimate nature of the Khomeini regime and of Islamist radicalism more generally, Foucault here is grappling with the possibilities presented by new, historically unprecedented cultural formations and revolts that might challenge the existing world order. We are very far away from the caricatures of Foucault as a functionalist who sees the human world as characterized by profound stasis.

Ethics

In his later work, Foucault shifted to the discussion of ethics. Some commentators see this as marking a radical break from his previous thinking. In his earlier writings, he tended to offer a picture of the individual as an entity shaped by discourses and power. Toward the end of his life, he wrote about the ways that the self is cultivated and how this is linked to internalized norms and ethical codes. The emphasis here is on an active and reflexive agent seeking some kind of self-mastery. The entirety of the last two volumes of his *History of Sexuality* and his last lecture courses at the Collège de France (which are now being translated into English) can be understood as something of a historical ethnography of cultural practices (in Greek, *askesis*) regarding the care of the self in the ancient Greek, Latin, and Christian worlds. The entirety of Christian modernity in the West has, for Foucault, been based on a misunderstanding of the Socratic charge to "know thyself," for the practical sense of this aphorism for the Greeks and Romans had to do not with the establishment of knowledge but with a call to engage in specific spiritual exercises and bodily (including sexual) cultivation as part of a project of ethical living. Such a position, it might be argued, brings Foucault into conversation with the humanisms that he opposed earlier in his career. Eric Paras's *Foucault 2.0* (2006) is but one of the several recent works to argue for a Foucault "beyond power and knowledge" who had rejected many of the principles of his earlier work. However, as the work on ethics was sketchy and provisional, and unfortunately truncated by his early death, we will perhaps never know whether Foucault had undergone a major epistemological break in his final years.

Criticisms and commentaries on Foucault

As a brief visit to any database will confirm, Foucault's work inspires a prodigious amount of commentary and debate. Criticisms of Foucault tend to fall into discrete camps:

- *Empirical criticisms are usually proffered by historians or by historical sociologists.* These are often on points of detail, but may have a theoretical subtext. In the field of criminology, for example, there is a general consensus that the historical shift from torture to the prison took place over several centuries, rather than the few decades that Foucault suggests. The theoretical implication here is that we need to question Foucault's vision of penal history as one characterized by rupture and discontinuity rather than slow evolution. For example, Philip Smith (2008) argues that *Discipline and Punish* overdraws the transition from sovereign power to disciplinary power. For Foucault, only the former was deeply meaningful, with the modern age characterized by a dull bureaucratic and instrumental ethos. But Smith shows that this is not so. Technologies like the prison, the electric chair, and even panopticism itself are colorful and powerful symbols. They generate myths and emotions in society which influence their reach and power.
- *Ethical criticisms usually center on Foucault's epistemology and theory of history.* It is argued that his relentlessly skeptical perspective on history, truth, freedom, and reason is essentially relativistic. Such a position, it is claimed, does not allow for effective social critique or for the implementation of emancipatory strategies. Those making this attack are often critical modernists.
- *Humanist critiques focus on Foucault's treatment of the human subject.* The point here is that he tends to overestimate the ability of discourses to control the individual and to minimize human capacities for resistance, critical reflexivity, and agency. Such arguments might draw, for example, on Goffman's work in *Asylums*, to suggest that inmates of institutions are able to subvert regimes of power (see pp. 58–9).
- *Other critics suggest that Foucault is too middle-range in orientation.* They claim that Foucault does not have a big picture of "society." Consequently, he does not pay enough attention to inequalities between social groups (e.g., classes) and the role of social structures and discourses beyond the level of the institution or discursive field (e.g., patriarchy). It is also sometimes argued that his model of circulating, capillary power underplays the fact that some actors, groups, and institutions have more power than others. The most frequent advocates of this argument are Marxians, who have some sympathies with Foucault, but would like to incorporate his ideas within a class-based model of industrial society. They would argue, for example, that techniques of discipline and surveillance are primarily deployed by the state against the working class in order to reinforce political and ideological control.
- *Textual criticisms focus on the style of Foucault's work.* It is suggested that his writing is obscure, that his arguments are hard to grasp, and that his concepts are elusive. This kind of critique is an occupational hazard of being a French academic. It tends to be made for the most part by writers from Anglo-American social science (as opposed to philosophy and humanities traditions) who would like to be able to concretize Foucault's ideas and deploy them in a more positivistic sociology.

Foucault's advocates usually retort that such criticisms miss the point of his work. They argue enthusiastically that his ideas transcend traditional and sterile debates, go beyond rigid Marxist frameworks, and have revitalized critical cultural social science. Given such diversity of opinion, it is difficult to arrive at a balanced assessment of Foucault's work.

Jacques Derrida

The controversial Jacques Derrida is a difficult figure to classify. He is sometimes thought of as a postmodernist rather than as a poststructuralist. The latter term, however, is perhaps more accurate. Derrida's work emerges out of the structuralist tradition and then goes beyond it in a strange and paradoxical manner. Essentially he used logic and reason to launch a relentless attack on the idea that any sign system can sustain truth, logic, and coherence. Understanding Derrida's arguments can be difficult, especially for those without a background in philosophy or linguistics, and this has led some critics to claim that much of what he wrote is simply mumbo-jumbo. His proponents, by contrast, suggest he developed one of the most innovative and powerful interpretative theories of the twentieth century.

Perhaps the most influential figure behind Derrida's intellectual position is Ferdinand de Saussure, who he used as a sounding board and foil for much of his work. According to Derrida, linguistics and linguistic philosophy have traditionally been obsessed with speech rather than writing. This bias goes back to the time of the Ancient Greeks. Figures like Socrates, for example, saw truth emerging from face-to-face dialogue. Derrida complained that Saussure, too, had given to writing a "narrow and derivative function" (1976 [1967]: 30). The problem with this position, Derrida asserted, is that it conjures up the illusion of words referring to concrete objects that are directly present to speakers, being spoken by subjects who can see them. He called this the **metaphysics of presence**. Derrida suggested such a position foregrounds human consciousness and intention in the construction of meaning rather than the autonomy of the system of signs. It also contains the illusion that words and dialogue will eventually uncover a truth about the world as individual errors of perception and distortions in language are progressively corrected. He called this mistaken position **logocentrism**, insisting by way of contrast that language always contains distortions and multiple meanings, and constructs much of what it purports to describe. Derrida proposed to replace logocentrism with an understanding of language which foregrounds the role of writing. This was to be known as **grammatology** (Derrida 1976).

Drawing on Saussure and structural linguistic theory, Derrida maintained that we should approach language as a system that is independent of any given author/speaker. He also followed Saussure in asserting that signs have meanings because they are implicitly contrasted to other, absent, signs. Where he differed is in suggesting that meanings are open, plural, and without closure rather than definitive and fixed by the system of *langue*. Meaning depends upon context. Yet these are potentially infinite in number. Each reader will have their own ideas about relevant, absent contexts and will use these in multifarious and inconsistent ways. Moreover, texts will hint and suggest in inconclusive ways at the kinds of contexts and absent signs that should be used for their interpretation. The upshot of Derrida's theory is to suggest (contra Lévi-Strauss and Saussure) that meanings are endlessly proliferating. They can be thought of as expanding and contracting according to the absent perspectives and codes that are used to interpret their signs. Such thinking challenges, or decenters, the idea of a sovereign author who has produced a text with clear boundaries and a cut-and-dried message. In this sense, Derrida's work can be thought of as strongly poststructural.

We are now in a position to turn to his famous idea of **deconstruction**. This is essentially a process or method of close reading in which texts are shown to be unable to sustain definitive meanings and close down alternatives. Through a series of analyses of philosophical texts by authors like Plato, Rousseau, and Hegel, Derrida argued that alternative and contradictory readings could be made of any material. What he called **supplements** and **traces** branch off from and shadow what we assume to be the main argument. He claimed that various sections of the text are often in opposition to each other, that footnotes might contradict the main thesis, or that central categories are used in inconsistent ways and fail to withstand scrutiny. Ambiguity, uncertainty, and instability always seem to haunt efforts to generate the certain and definitive. The broader philosophical upshot of all this interpretative activity is to suggest that truth cannot be discovered through language, as language is slippery and there is an inevitable excess of meaning. Texts always mean more than writers intend them to say, and culture (contra logocentrism) eludes the efforts of human subjects to control meanings and attain closure.

Derrida did not restrict himself to treating the philosophical canon with his method. He also wrote on the work of more sociological thinkers like Marx and Marcel Mauss. In 1977–8, Derrida gave a series of lectures, later published in book form, devoted in large part to a reflection on Mauss's essay on the gift, which we discussed in chapter 5. He argued that the concept of the gift is precisely one of the categories that demonstrates fundamental ambiguity in the Western system of meaning. The study begins with a typically clever Derridean piece of analysis. The gift is introduced in the person of Madame de Maintenon, the famous mistress of Louis XIV, the Sun King. In her writings, de Maintenon claimed that the King took up all her time, while she would have preferred to give it to Saint-Cyr, the institution for the education of young women with which she was associated. The king's death in 1715 made possible her gift of her time, so, Derrida suggested playfully, might we not say that the question of the gift is therefore intimately connected to the death of the king, or the deconstruction of the traditional metaphysical "realities" of philosophy (1992 [1991]: 4)?

What is the institution of the gift, in philosophical and cultural terms? Derrida argued it is "aneconomic," or outside of the circle of exchange generated and sustained by economic relations (1992: 7). A gift is that thing which "interrupts" this system (1992: 13), precisely because it refuses the rules of the system. As we saw in our discussion of Mauss, the gift is not a commodity; that is, it is not a product within a system of rational economic exchange in which individual actors seek only their own self-interest. But neither is it wholly disinterested. In fact, some varieties of gift-giving can constitute agonistic efforts to demonstrate superior status and thereby to subordinate others. There is a paradox built into gift-giving insofar as a gift, to exist as such, must not be experienced or perceived as a gift. Indeed, even Mauss's analysis of gift-exchange is, in Derrida's view, necessarily troubled by the seeming incompatibility between gift and exchange. If a gift, something offered freely and without expectation of return, implies a necessary reciprocal counter-gift, then is it in fact a gift at all? Derrida infers that perhaps Mauss, in his desire to argue for gift-exchange as the primordial form of all exchange (and thus of the rational economic forms of exchange we all know so well in today's world), has not fully reckoned with the outsider status of the notion of gift. In arguing that the gift-exchange system preceded and laid the groundwork for the form of rational exchange in which we engage today, Mauss is reducing it to the status of original term in the business of exchange and thereby forcing the gift into a position in a significatory system to which it does not in fact belong. The gift is for Derrida one of those terms that indicates interstitial, marginal states and experiences, such as madness (1992: 35). If you found the preceding discussion of the gift hard to follow, you are not alone. Derrida is famous for losing his readers in loops of logic, allusion, and inference of this kind. Still, there does seem to be an important message here about the ambiguity and complexity of cultural systems.

JACQUES DERRIDA (1930–2004)

Derrida was born in Algeria and lived there in a Sephardic Jewish community until 1949, when he went to Paris to study for the entrance exam to the École Normale Supérieure. The Vichy government had expelled all Jews from French public schools in Algeria in 1942 and the experience profoundly affected Derrida, who had the sense his entire adult life of being neither fully French nor fully Jewish (as he person-ally rejected the Jewish faith). Like Foucault, he established a long-term friendship with Louis Althusser, who was largely responsible for Derrida's acquisition of a posi-tion as a lecturer at the ENS, which he held for 20 years. He traveled extensively and spent time at many universities outside France, beginning in the mid-1970s, but from the mid-1980s his central institutional attachment was to the École des Hautes Études en Sciences Sociales in Paris. He was very much involved in political efforts on behalf of political prisoners around the world, including Nelson Mandela in South Africa and a number of dissident Eastern bloc intellectuals. During a trip to communist Czechoslovakia in 1981, he was arrested by the state police for his political activities. The French government intervened on his behalf and he was released after a harrowing experience that he recounted often in interviews and his later biographically oriented writings. Much of his later writing is dedicated to exploring the notions of forgiveness, friendship, and cosmopolitanism. At the time of his death, he was among the most well-known intellectuals in the world.

Reference: Powell (2006)

While Derrida's work is highly specialized and centers on methods for the interpreta-tion of texts, it has exerted a huge influence on wider cultural theory. The following themes have proven especially fertile:

• Derrida's work broadly questions objectivist research models, by proposing that knowledge construction is contingent upon the resources and perspectives that are brought to bear. He also argues against the view that cultural theorists and philosophers should be engaged in logocentric, truth-finding activity, and proposes instead that playful hermeneutic and interpretative inquiry might provide a worthwhile alternative research genre. This position is foundational to philosophical justifications of poststructural and postmodern epistemologies, such as those of Bauman and Rorty, which are elaborated in chapter 14.

- Like Barthes's *S/Z* (see p. 107), Derrida's work can be thought of as illustrating the structuralist principle of infinite semiosis – the idea that sign systems in texts generate endlessly proliferating meanings. In so doing, it has also highlighted the role of the reader and their interaction with the text. Given that texts can mean just about anything, how is it that people manage to make sense of them – to fix a meaning or attain closure? Efforts to answer this question have seen his abstruse and difficult theory feed directly and indirectly into more middle-range work on processes of interpretation. Research in the media studies area looking at the reception of television, for example, has drawn upon ideas about multiple readings. We look at this issue in more detail in chapter 10.

- Derrida suggests that hybridity and ambiguity, as well as classification, are central features of cultural systems. Closure and certainty are impossible to attain, and so we can detect points of contradiction and weakness in any discourse. This idea has proven important for queer theory, postcolonial theory, and some recent thinking on race and gender (see chapters 14 and 15) in particular, as they attempt to develop theories that can encompass not only the marginal and transgressive, but also strategies through which such groups can resist or "deconstruct" dominant discourses.

Concluding Remarks

Poststructuralism offers one of the most difficult and challenging styles of contemporary cultural theory. While this can make it irritating to some readers, others find it rewarding and exciting. Those who persevere will find that poststructuralism provides a useful corrective to the more grandiose visions of structuralist theory. In so doing, it layers even more sophistication onto an already highly developed conceptual edifice. Understandings about texts, readers, discourses, power and knowledge, pleasure and deconstruction provide the cultural theorist with greatly increased powers for exploring how culture works. For this reason poststructural approaches have become widespread in disciplines like sociology and history, and are arguably dominant in fields like literary and art criticism, and media studies. Whether or not theorists fully embrace the poststructural approach, all agree that it has become a force to be reckoned with. Synergies between poststructuralism and postmodernism suggest that this will remain the case for the foreseeable future. We explore these connections further in chapter 14.

Suggested Further Reading

There are numerous introductions to Foucault's work which can be found in any good library. Yet reading about Foucault is a poor substitute for reading his own words. The problem is that Foucault's works are rather difficult; furthermore, material is still being published and translated (e.g., his lectures in the last years of his life at the Collège de France are now being made available in book form). We would suggest starting with *Discipline and Punish* (this is his most accessible book and the one which social scientists seem to like the most), followed by the first volume of *The History of Sexuality*. The two other early historical studies, *Madness and Civilisation* and *The Birth of the Clinic*, are slightly more difficult. *The Order of Things* and, in particular, *The Archaeology of Knowledge*, are very dense texts which will best be appreciated by those who enjoy heavy theory and have a strong background in philosophy. Some of the various books of interviews conducted by journalists and other intellectuals with Foucault can provide guidance to the published work and its relation to Foucault's politics. *Remarks on Marx*, for example, offers insight into the complexity of his interaction with Marxism that is not easily extracted from his published work. Derrida's works are very difficult to understand without the assistance of a guide. Jonathan Culler (1987) provides such a resource, but it will still be very tough going. *Of Grammatology* is perhaps the clearest (as well as one of the earliest) of his efforts to set forth his methodology of reading works with an eye to the absent presences they contain. *Limited Inc.* is also a good such example, and it is perhaps a livelier read in that it consists of a collection of several volleys in a very polemically charged argument between Derrida and an analytic philosopher, John Searle, on the question of interpretation. As is the case with Foucault, there are many volumes consisting of interviews of Derrida and they sometimes provide more accessible insight into his more complex published work, e.g., *For What Tomorrow . . . A Dialogue*, with the historian of psychoanalysis Elizabeth Roudinesco, shows Derrida applying his method to contemporary political topics such as the death penalty, racism, and changes in family structure.

CHAPTER EIGHT

Culture, Structure, and Agency: Three Attempts at Synthesis

The relationship between systems of meaning and human action has long been a theme in cultural theory. As we have seen in all the previous chapters, every theory must take up a position on this issue. Some, such as symbolic interactionism and ethnomethodology, allocate priority to the actor. Others, such as neo-Marxism, Parsonian functionalism, and structuralism, stress the power of systems of meaning to control human agents. During the final decades of the twentieth century, cultural theory became increasingly concerned with locating a middle ground between these opposing positions. Three of the most influential such efforts at bridge-building are those of Pierre Bourdieu, Anthony Giddens, and Norbert Elias. The first two of these scholars addressed themselves in an explicit way to ongoing debates between "micro" and "macro" perspectives during the period from the late 1960s onward. Elias's major work was completed much earlier than this, but was subsequently "rediscovered" and proposed as a potential solution to problems in social theory that were current several decades after it was developed. While these authors differ in terms of approach, we will see that in each case culture operates as a bridge between the social structure and the acting self.

Pierre Bourdieu

The French sociologist Pierre Bourdieu was arguably the most important figure in cultural theory and cultural research for the last two decades of his life and his work remains powerfully influential today. While the intellectual quality of his thought is one significant factor in accounting for this status, the ability of his work to appeal to diverse audiences is equally crucial. With Bourdieu there is something for nearly everyone:

- His work attempted to synthesize micro and macro levels of analysis. He was concerned with both subjective experience and with objective structures. This positions him as a key figure in the "micro/macro debate" and makes his work required reading for those on both sides of that fence.

- He drew upon the critical sociologies of Marx and Weber, but in a non-doctrinaire way. This allowed his theory (like that of Foucault) to appeal to the broad swathe of left-of-center thinking that rejects more orthodox Marxian visions of class society. The fact that he saw his work as part of a critical project, moreover, provides it with a competitive advantage in some academic circles over other attempts at theoretical synthesis, such as those of Giddens or neofunctionalism (see pp. 33, 136–9).
- He developed both abstract theoretical models and conducted detailed middle-range empirical studies. This provides credibility with both hard-core theorists and more methodologically driven cultural sociologists.
- His empirical work cuts over a number of fields (e.g., education, popular culture, the arts) and disciplines (e.g., anthropology, sociology), thereby maximizing his potential audience.
- He developed a number of concepts (e.g., field, *habitus*, cultural capital), which are both intellectually compelling and widely transposable to various research areas.

PIERRE BOURDIEU (1930–2002)

Bourdieu described himself during his student years in 1950s Paris as highly critical of the then-reigning school of existentialism, and attracted instead to the more empirically based philosophy and history of science epitomized by Gaston Bachelard and Georges Canguilhem. In opposition to most elite French students of the period, he turned against philosophy and took up the study of ethnography and sociology. Early on, he was inspired by Lévi-Strauss's efforts to construct a science of social life, but he distanced himself from this variety of structuralism later on. During his early anthropological fieldwork in Algeria and in studies he undertook in rural French communities like the one in which he had grown up, he found that relatively few people married in the ways predicted by the formal kinship models of Lévi-Strauss. His ideas about practice and *habitus* emerged from this experience. As his career progressed, he switched his attention from the periphery to the core, exploring the institutions and cultural codes of metropolitan France. For most of his working life, he held a chair in Paris and also enjoyed visiting status at other institutions. He intervened frequently in the arena of political debate, criticizing the mass media's role in simplifying complicated issues and serving as one of the intellectual figureheads of the massive French strike movement of the winter of 1995. By the time of his death in January 2002, he was perhaps the single most important public intellectual in France.

References: Bourdieu 1990, 2004 [2001]

Bourdieu's early writings display a number of theoretical influences, including functionalism, structuralism, and existentialism. Some passages in these works are reminiscent of Jean-Paul Sartre and others of Louis Althusser. By the late 1960s he had begun to weave these threads together in a more coherent fashion and to develop his own model of society as he worked through drafts of his most important theoretical statement, *Outline of a Theory of Practice* (1977 [1972]). Bourdieu's theory, then, emerged from a decade-long engagement with both objectivist and subjectivist social theories. Having worked from both sides of the methodological and epistemological divide he was in a unique position to develop an attempt at synthesis. Perhaps the best way to summarize this synthesis is through an explication of Bourdieu's key concepts.

Reflexive sociology

Writing in the opening pages of his *Outline of a Theory of Practice*, Bourdieu attacked structuralist understandings of society (his main target was Lévi-Strauss). He argued that these embodied a distorting objectivism that arose thanks to the position of the social scientist as an observer. From the perspective of the outsider, it was logical to try to construct abstract maps of symbol systems and to develop ideas about social rules. From here it is but a short step to claiming that social life is driven by these rules and codes in a deterministic fashion. Bourdieu argued that such understandings neglect the role of agency and practical action in social life, especially questions of strategy and subjective emotions like honor and shame. At the same time, Bourdieu wished to retain an understanding of the constraining qualities of social structure and the superiority of sociological knowledge over common sense. In other words, he did not think that folk explanations could provide an adequate account of social life. In an effort to theorize the relationship between structure and agency without reducing analysis to one level or the other, Bourdieu argued that we need a "reflexive sociology." We should think about the ways that our theoretical models are influenced by our social and social scientific locations and try to become aware of our biases. Once we have done this we can begin to move forward by constructing sociological concepts and theories which allow us to navigate a path between the perils of objectivism and subjectivism. Much of the last work Bourdieu published in his lifetime was closely focused on this effort to make his perspective as fully reflexive as possible. His last lecture course at the Collège de France directly takes on the question of whether relativizing forms of knowledge like sociology are themselves inevitably relativist and finishes with a socio-biographical "auto-analysis" that situates himself and his ideas in the social and cultural contexts in which his life and career developed (Bourdieu 2004 [2001]).

Habitus

The fruit of Bourdieu's own reflexive sociology was a shift of analytic focus away from both structure and subjective experience toward social practice. He understands practices as reflecting and reproducing both objective social relations and subjective interpretations of the world. Central to this move is the idea of **habitus**. He sees this as "systems of durable, transposable dispositions, structured structures predisposed to function as structuring structures, that is, as principles of the generation and structuring of practices" (1977: 72).

Habitus, then, is the pivotal concept in Bourdieu's effort to reconcile ideas of structure with ideas of practice. It is, however, a somewhat elusive term because Bourdieu conceptualizes it in various ways. These are as follows:

- as empirical tendencies to act in particular ways ("lifestyle");
- as motivations, preferences, tastes, and emotions;
- as embodied behavior;
- as a kind of worldview or cosmology held by actors;
- as skills and practical social competence;
- as aspirations and expectations concerning life chances and career paths.

These various aspects of *habitus* are summed up in the idea that it is a durable set of dispositions that are transposable from situation to situation. The idea of "disposition" captures the cognitive and motivational aspects of *habitus* as well as those relating to behavioral regularities. Bourdieu stresses that *habitus* is closely linked to unconscious or non-reflexive activity. He writes that *habitus* is not based on reason, but is, rather, like "the impulsive decision made by the tennis player who runs up to the net" (1990: 11). We do not stop to think how to hit the tennis ball, or whether or not we should attempt a volley, or even why we are playing tennis in the first place – we just get on with the game. *Habitus*, Bourdieu says, is something that allows us to react efficiently in all aspects of our life, not just tennis. *Habitus*, in this light, is rather like Schutz's "lifeworld" in that it allows people to get through life as competent human beings. It is a set of resources and dispositions that we carry round with us, in our minds and bodies, which we can apply in diverse social settings. It allows us to improvise, and navigate our way through encounters, episodes, and decisions. So far this all sounds very uplifting. The sting in the tail is that *habitus* is linked to systematic inequalities in society patterned by power and class. It emerges from these inequalities and produces lines of practical action which are "always tending to reproduce the objective structures of which they are the product" (1977: 72). According to Bourdieu, those in subordinate positions are not equipped with the *habitus* that will allow them to successfully enter into life-improving patterns of action. Instead, their *habitus* will equip them with the desires, motivations, knowledge, skills, routines, and strategies that will reproduce their inferior status. Bourdieu suggests that family and the school play a crucial role in the differential allocation of *habitus*. These institutions work to give people from affluent backgrounds an unfair advantage over those from the working class. In order to find out why this is so, and to see how *habitus* can reproduce inequality, we have to look at the question of cultural capital.

Cultural capital

Broadly speaking there are three kinds of capital at play in society that determine social power and social inequality. **Economic capital** describes financial resources. **Social capital** is all about who you know. It is concerned with the social ties that people can mobilize for their own advantage. A well-known example of this is the British "old-boy network," which has assisted in the reproduction of power among males who have attended elite fee-paying schools and Oxbridge colleges. These people then go on to become members of the same exclusive "gentlemen's clubs" and advantage each other's careers in areas like banking, the church, the military, and the public service. People who have been excluded from these networks will find it harder to progress, even though they may be equally talented. While economic and social capital have been investigated by others, Bourdieu's distinctive contribution was his theory of **cultural capital**. Like *habitus*, cultural capital is a concept that has several dimensions. These include:

- objective knowledge of the arts and culture;
- cultural tastes and preferences;
- formal qualifications (e.g., university degrees, music exams);
- cultural skills and know-how (e.g., the ability to play a musical instrument);
- the ability to be discriminating and to make distinctions between the "good" and the "bad."

Bourdieu sees cultural capital as a dimension of a broader *habitus*, and therefore as reflecting the social location of its possessor. In *Distinction*, a book now regarded as one of the most important social science texts of recent decades, Bourdieu (1984 [1979]) attacked the philosophical idea that aesthetic judgments could be made on the basis of universal, objective criteria about what was in good or bad taste. He showed instead that taste was socially determined. His survey research demonstrated that particular classes and occupational groups in French society (e.g., workers, academics, technicians) tended to have distinctive tastes in music, art, food, and so on. This confirmed his view that cultural capital, of which taste is but one indicator, was shaped by social location.

The idea that taste is social is hardly new, even if Bourdieu's work in *Distinction* managed to document this with previously unsurpassed levels of methodological precision. The defining twist in Bourdieu's theory is his claim that cultural capital makes a difference and helps to perpetuate social divisions and inequalities. Bourdieu argued that elite groups define what is acceptable or valued cultural capital and what is devalued. The major way this operated in the French society of his time was through placing a greater value on "high culture" than on popular culture, and by distinguishing the valuable from the trivial. By defining legitimate and illegitimate cultural capital in this way elite groups preserve the worth of their own skills and knowledge, and thereby confirm their own status. A high culture that is refined, intellectual, enduring, and serious is contrasted to a popular culture that is trivial and ephemeral.

Central to the process by which cultural capital and habitus assist in social reproduction are institutions like schools and gatekeeping mechanisms like school exams. The attraction of Bourdieu's model here is that it argues that society is formally open to mobility. There are no "rules" or elite conspiracies preventing the upward social mobility of members of subordinate groups. In theory, at least, anybody can do well in the education system. In practice, however, this is not the case. Privilege is reproduced through the subtle workings of unacknowledged cultural biases of which agents are mostly unaware.

A brief study of the French university system entitled *The Inheritors* provided perhaps the most detailed explication of this process, even though the book was written shortly before Bourdieu developed his mature theory (Bourdieu and Passeron 1979 [1964]). Here Bourdieu and his collaborator Jean-Claude Passeron set out to explain social variation in educational attainment. Having noted a correlation between social class and drop-out rates, they suggest that "Economic obstacles are not sufficient to explain how 'educational death rates' can differ so widely between one social class and another" (1979: 8). The crux of their argument is that middle-class students are advantaged in university. This is not only because of facts they learn at home (e.g., they know about Beethoven because mother plays the piano), but also because of their general attitude and demeanor in the classroom which reflects a cultural capital they have unknowingly acquired. Unlike working-class students, they tend to share the professor's unspoken expectations on things like interpersonal conduct, essay-writing style, and wider reading. They also have a romantic vision of academic training, are unconcerned about getting jobs, and despise practical knowledge, timetables, routine, and pedagogy. Thus they are able to display the flair and panache of the dilettante in their work – qualities that the (French) academic rewards. By contrast, the working-class students acquire all their knowledge in the classroom and library. They are concerned about jobs and so their work and study practices are wooden, uninspired, pragmatic, and conformist. Plagued by worries about their future prospects, they "can never completely abandon themselves to dilettantism" (1979: 62). They fail to live up to the hidden codes of the university system that are never explicated in the formal curriculum. Poor grades result, and with them an increased probability of dropping out.

An important aspect of Bourdieu's theory is the attention he gives to the question of the transposability of cultural capital. Unlike economic and social capital, cultural capital takes years to acquire and is deeply embedded in our sense of self. This makes it particularly effective as a barrier to social mobility. At the same time as making this point, Bourdieu emphasizes that groups can try to convert one form of capital into another in an effort to cement class power. Pointing to changes in France in the late 1960s, Bourdieu and Passeron suggest that the shift toward a post-industrial society was seeing the university system become more potent as a means of retaining privilege. They argued that "the reconversion of economic capital into academic capital is one of the strategies which enable the business bourgeoisie to maintain the position of some or all of its heirs" (1979: 79). The overall vision provided here is of a struggle in which social classes jockey for ownership of the various forms of capital.

Fields

Cultural capital does not work in a vacuum, but rather is a force at play in a wider social structure. The concept of the **field** is central to Bourdieu's model of complex societies. According to Bourdieu these are domains of social life such as the arts, industry, the law, medicine, politics, and so on. Within each of these fields, actors are struggling for power and status. They are helped or handicapped by their *habitus* in acquiring and deploying the particular forms of cultural capital needed for success in each area. More unusually, they can attempt to improve their lot by switching fields, cashing in their acquired prestige and transposing their cultural capital to new ventures. An example of this would be an academic who becomes a bestselling writer or journalist.

Struggles are continually taking place between fields, sub-fields, and actors within fields. In a collection of studies of the *Field of Cultural Production*, Bourdieu (1993 [1968–87]) notes that there is a long history of contest between "high" and "low" culture, between various genres (e.g., art vs. photography), and between individual artists for legitimacy and/or dominance. Disputes over the value of cultural products serve to mark out or challenge established boundaries and hierarchies. He writes: "The value of works of art in general . . . are generated in the incessant, innumerable struggles to establish the value of this or that particular work" (1993: 79). While the struggles may be about symbolic value and accompanied by a rhetoric of "art for art's sake," the rewards can be economic, with dominant artists and writers able to convert their cultural capital into economic capital. A similar picture of a tooth-and-nail fight for prestige emerges from his withering portrait of the French university system, *Homo Academicus* (Bourdieu 1988 [1984]). Here Bourdieu debunks the idea that the academic field is a domain of disinterested, collegial, intellectual activity. He points to:

- *Struggles between individuals for control of a field.* For example, we can detect empire-building activities in which leading professors attempt to make their position institutionally dominant by influencing junior appointments, training plenty of doctoral students, packing committees, trashing rivals in debate, and so on.
- *Struggles between styles of work or intellectual approaches.* Here Bourdieu (1988: 115) points as an example to a major public debate between Roland Barthes and Raymond Picard during the mid-1960s. Two camps emerged in this dispute about the correct way to interpret texts. Barthes was supported by structuralists and members of the intellectual avant-garde, while Picard had the backing of traditionalists. However, the dispute was over more than theory and method. It was really a struggle between old and new blocs in the humanities and social sciences for intellectual dominance and symbolic authority.
- *Struggles between the disciplines and faculties.* Bourdieu points, for example, to the way that the rise of social science in the twentieth century challenged the monopoly of legal disciplines to "thought and discourse on the social world." Despite this challenge, Law remains dominant. Bourdieu suggests that a factor in this relative authority may be political. In the juridical disciplines knowledge is "in the service of order and power." By contrast the social sciences confront order and power "by reducing the established order and the state, through historical comparison or speculative transposition, to the status of a special case in the gamut of realized or realizable possibilities" (1988: 69). These activities (such as this book) are perceived as "irresponsible" by those in power, and so even closer ties eventuate between government, the state, and law faculties.

Evaluations of Bourdieu

Bourdieu's supporters suggest that his work offers one of the best models of culture that we currently have available for social science research. Certainly a case can be made that his work addresses a number of key themes in contemporary theoretical debate:

- Ideas about cultural capital and habitus provide exciting insight into the form and structure of culture.
- Bourdieu points to the autonomous role of culture and cultural struggles in determining both individual and institutional outcomes.
- His work is able to powerfully theorize the relationship between culture and agency.

Nevertheless, Bourdieu has as many critics as admirers. They suggest that his work fails to deliver all that is promised – especially on the second and third of these points. A consensus has emerged among critics that Bourdieu gives too much emphasis to structure and system reproduction and not enough to agency and contingent change. William Sewell, for example, comments approvingly that Bourdieu's theory recognizes the knowledgeability of actors and their ability to be "discerning, and strategic." Yet at the same time he bemoans the "agent-proof quality" of Bourdieu's model, suggesting that "habitus, schemas and resources so powerfully reproduce one another that even the most cunning or improvisational actions undertaken by agents necessarily reproduce structure" (Sewell 1992: 15). The point Sewell is making is that Bourdieu's theory is unable to explain how change can be generated from within a system. According to Sewell, Bourdieu emphasizes homologies within *habitus* (and between *habitus* and social structure) rather than possibilities for contradiction, discontinuity, and cultural creativity. Because culture and action end up reproducing and reflecting social structure and social inequality, Bourdieu's theory of practice ends up looking rather deterministic. Some efforts have been made to make the theory of *habitus* more supple and capable of accounting for phenomenological complexity. Philip Smith (2004) has proposed that we might fruitfully look to the work of the novelist Marcel Proust as an example, albeit fictional, of a more nuanced attempt to account for the emergence of *habitus*. While much of the structural picture of Parisian class society that we find in Bourdieu can also be located in Proust's celebrated novel, *À la recherche du temps perdu*, we also find in the latter a much more nuanced effort to grapple with the contingent elements of identity construction and maintenance. The self as sexualized and motivated by desire intersects with the self formed by class relations, and "unanticipated encounters with people and objects" move selves in directions that cannot be very well tracked by purely structural models (Smith 2004: 110). The end result in Proust's account is a self that is multiple, and even chaotic and contradictory, which must be reconstructed with great analytical care and sophistication. Nick Crossley (see chapter 16) has also advocated a return to phenomenology as a way to correct problems in Bourdieu's theory of *habitus*. He suggests the perspective on habits as sometimes imitative and sometimes creative responses of the agent to the world that we find in the work of phenomenologists Maurice Merleau-Ponty and Edmund Husserl incorporates the best of Bourdieu's concept without the erasure of the very notion of the potentially innovative agent (Crossley 2001).

Another set of criticisms revolves around the broader applicability of Bourdieu's empirical findings. Tony Bennett, Michael Emmison, and John Frow (1999) conducted a replication of *Distinction* in a survey of taste and cultural consumption in Australia in the mid-1990s. A persistent finding in their work was that other variables (especially age and gender) tended to be better predictors of taste than class. They also found that boundaries between high and low cultural tastes were more permeable than Bourdieu suggests. Most notably, people of high social status were omnivorous in their tastes (see chapter 10). For example, they would listen to both classical and popular music. While these changes may reflect the egalitarian ethos of Australian society, or shifts toward postindustrialism (Bourdieu's empirical work was conducted in 1960s France), it is equally possible that Bourdieu's class-bound model made him insensitive to such possibilities.

Michèle Lamont's (1992) work also suggests that we have to be careful when generalizing from 1960s France to other contexts. Her interview study explored definitions of the "worthy person" among French and American managers and professionals, and concluded that moral criteria were used to evaluate personal worth in addition to the forms of cultural and economic capital adumbrated by Bourdieu. She also detected significant national differences. In France cultural knowledge was valued more highly, while in America economic wealth was generally seen as most important. Lamont also found that the ways that people made distinctions and drew symbolic boundaries tended to vary according to other factors, such as occupation. For example, those involved in universities or other cultural institutions tended to value cultural distinction more highly than those in for-profit contexts. Lamont uses her data to critique Bourdieu. She suggests that he "relies too heavily not just on French attitudes, but on Parisian attitudes, thereby exaggerating the importance of cultural boundaries" (1992: 181), and hints that he has projected his own life experiences into his theory as he "tends to generalize about the culture that prevails in the intellectual milieu in which he lives" (1992: 186). In her reading, Bourdieu works with an image of stable, competitive, and closed systems of distinction. What is needed in its place, she suggests, is a model which empirically investigates "open, changing and interpenetrating semiotic and social fields" (1992: 183) and the ways that people position themselves relative to these in diverse social contexts.

Anthony Giddens

Anthony Giddens's theory of structuration is widely held to present one of the most influential efforts to overcome the division of micro and macro through an appreciation of the role of culture in social life. While Giddens does not make much use of the word "culture," or even have an elaborated understanding of its composition and content, his work places an emphasis on the role of interpretation and meaning systems in human life. It should therefore be considered an important intervention in the field of cultural theory. His distinctive approach is best expressed in *The Constitution of Society* (1984). Giddens suggests that action and structure models are equally flawed. He writes: "If interpretative sociologies are founded, as it were, upon an imperialism of the subject, functionalism and structuralism propose an imperialism of the social object" (1984: 2). In attempting to overcome this dualism, he suggests we think of structure and agency as a **duality** in which both parts are mutually supporting. The theory that Giddens develops to try to capture this activity is better characterized as an assemblage of sensitizing ideas, rather than as a systematic model like those of, say, Parsons or Habermas.

At the core of Giddens's vision is a model of the active and creative human subject, and he argues vigorously against the view that humans are dummies constrained by rules and external structures (such as Durkheimian social facts). At the same time Giddens is anxious to distance himself from what he sees as the untrammeled individualism and subjectivism of ethnomethodology and phenomenology. In trying to find a path between these positions, Giddens suggests that structure needs to be thought of as something internal to the individual rather than as something external to them. He insists that in the final analysis, institutions and social systems (what we usually think of as structure) are nothing more than the aggregate product of the reflexive actions of real people on the ground. Structure for Giddens has a virtual existence in thought patterns and memory traces and is enabling rather than just constraining. He suggests that it consists of **rules and resources** (knowledge, skills, practical competence – what we might broadly think of as culture) that people acquire through socialization. Much of social life revolves around practices through which people reflexively deploy these rules and resources in going about their daily lives. While this deployment can be transformative, it more often leads to the reproduction of stable institutional settings. In an oft-quoted phrase, Giddens suggests that structure is both the "medium and outcome" of action. It is the medium insofar as human action would be impossible or chaotic without internalized skills and knowledge. It is the outcome insofar as broader cultural patterns are reproduced as they are used. The idea of **structuration** captures this image of social life as a reciprocal process tying individual actions to social forces.

ANTHONY GIDDENS (1938–)

Giddens was born in London, and after a mediocre school career attended Hull University. Here he encountered sociology for the first time and found that he had an aptitude for it. He went on to conduct postgraduate work at the London School of Economics (LSE) and then obtained an appointment at Leicester University, where Norbert Elias was also teaching. While the influence of Elias on Giddens is open to debate, it is clear that both enjoy a style of theory which asks fundamental questions about the links between individuals, culture, and society. Giddens went on to obtain more senior positions in Cambridge and back at the LSE. During the 1990s he became a key advisor to British Prime Minister Tony Blair. Many of Giddens's ideas about politics moving "beyond left and right" and finding a "third way" appealed to Blair's vision of a "New Labour" devoid of socialist influences. In 2004, Giddens obtained a life peerage and is now also known as Lord Giddens.

Reference: Bryant and Jary 1991

Aside from sharing a common knowledge or culture, Giddens suggests that there is another reason why human action tends to reproduce the social order. He claims that people need to have a sense of trust and that they fear uncertainty. He calls this the desire for **ontological security**. According to Giddens, much of social life is routinized and conventionalized so that people feel safe and can enter and negotiate encounters. He argues that Goffman's work on micro-ritual and face-to-face interactions (see pp. 56–7) captured this dynamic game of mutual assurance. Garfinkel's "breaching experiments" (see p. 64), by contrast, showed how quickly anxiety (and sanctions) would arise once conventional patterns of social interaction were violated.

Structuration theory has been criticized on various fronts. While critics seem united that it is a brave attempt at synthesis, few argue that Giddens has solved the most intractable problem of contemporary social and cultural theory. The most common complaints are:

* The theory is too voluntaristic and idealistic. It downplays the coercive and constraining qualities of both culture (e.g., as hegemony) and institutions (e.g., patterns of class or race inequality). He seems to be suggesting that society could suddenly change if only people thought and acted differently by creatively using the "structure" that is inside their heads.
* As Sewell (1992) points out, Giddens fails adequately to differentiate cultural (knowledge, skills) and material (money, guns, power) resources. There are important differences between these in terms of their ontological status and potential to impact on social life.
* His definition of "structure" is unconventional. Instead of solving the problem of structure and agency he talks around it and defines it in a novel, but idiosyncratic, way.

Modernity, self-identity, and risk

In the 1990s Giddens moved away from the advocacy of structuration theory toward an interest in contemporary social change and its impact on the self. In *Modernity and Self-Identity* (1991), he argues that we have moved into a post-traditional order in which doubt and choice surround us. Within this context we have to engage in the reflexive construction of the self instead of blindly following an identity or role that has been marked out for us. This process involves the use of knowledge and **expert systems** (psychologists, counselors, professionals, self-help books, etc.) with which individuals "negotiate lifestyle choices among a diversity of options" (1991: 5). The emphasis here is on the ways that agents select identities from the various paths that are available to them. This can involve intelligent, deliberate, and reflexive efforts to construct a rewarding biography, build intimate relationships and develop both body and mind.

The overall picture here is a rather positive one of people actively making use of cultural resources in order to cultivate the self and attain some kind of self-actualization. For this reason, Giddens's position differs from that of critical theory, which tends to understand the self-centeredness of the modern individual as a symptom of a general malaise propelled by capitalism (see pp. 197–9). Commenting on Christopher Lasch's theory of widespread narcissism, for example, Giddens suggests that "people appear as largely passive in their reactions – in this case to advertising imagery. . . . Yet powerful though commodifying influences no doubt are, they are scarcely received in an uncritical way by the populations they affect" (1991: 179). For Giddens, the proliferation of images and goods under capitalism has tended to open up rather than constrain the self: "plurality of choice is in some substantial part the very outcome of commodified processes" (1991: 200). He also sees this approach as combating poststructural theories which have claimed that the self has been decentered or dispersed (see pp. 112–13) by discourses. For Giddens, the quest for an authentic self is more central to our experience than ever.

Giddens draws particular attention to the links between this mission to construct the self and the rise of a **risk society**. This concept is most associated with the work of German sociologist Ulrich Beck (1992; also Beck, Giddens, and Lash 1994). Beck, whom we discuss in more detail in chapter 13, claims that along with the rise of ecological problems there has been a new awareness that we live in an era characterized by unpredictability and danger. He sees concerns like the greenhouse effect and nuclear and pesticide contamination as involving unknowable and unquantifiable risks. For Beck, as for Giddens, this risk society has emerged as a consequence of industrial modernity – if an unintended one. Risk society marks a development of earlier modernity, rather than a radical break, as some advocates of postmodernism maintain. It can be seen as a symptom of a wider societal shift toward increasing levels of reflexivity and auto-critique, a process which is linked to detraditionalization and the emergence of a process that Giddens and his associates call **reflexive modernization** (Beck, Giddens, and Lash 1994).

While Beck's work is concerned with the positive transformative potential of risk politics (as post-national, green, alternative, grass roots-driven, etc.) arising from environmental dangers, Giddens focuses on the ways that an awareness of biographical risk has led actors to transform and work on the self. He points out that modernity was quite successful in regulating many aspects of risk as they affected everyday life. Major dangers that had created problems for pre-modern societies, such as infectious disease, famine, and the weather, were more or less controlled. However, for the self there are many choices and uncertainties to be faced as biography is freed from tradition/ascription and expert systems offer plural, often contradictory systems of advice. This is especially the case during "fateful moments" (the term is taken from Goffman) in an individual's biography. These are often linked to the life-course, to relationships, or to questions of health and illness. In such situations individuals face uncertainty and must work out which path to take. He writes: "Living in a secular risk culture is inherently unsettling. . . . Anxieties [are] generated by risk calculations themselves, plus the problem of screening out unlikely contingencies, thus reducing life planning to manageable proportions" (1991: 181–2). The kind of politics that will emerge from this situation is a "life politics," which centers around questions of identity, lifestyle, and existential ethics. In *Beyond Left and Right*, Giddens (1994) asserts this politics is no longer about class or the distribution of economic wealth, but rather is about symbolic images, identities, and ethical visions.

Norbert Elias

Like Bourdieu and Giddens, Norbert Elias sees the self as a key tool for theorizing agency in cultural theory. His approach is historical and traces the way that the modern self has developed over the centuries. In his major work, *The Civilizing Process* (1978, 1982 [1939]), he looked at books on manners and etiquette from the past several centuries, paying particular attention to more "animal" and biological functions like eating, defecating, burping, and farting. When comparing texts from various centuries, Elias noted that the number of prohibitions increased over time. In books from the Middle Ages, for example, it was recommended not to put half-chewed food back into the communal pot, not to blow one's nose on one's clothes, and not to defecate in rooms and corridors. By the nineteenth century, elaborate rules had come into place about the ways to use cutlery, how to control bodily functions, and so on. Elias identified a trend in which more and more things came to be seen as distasteful and rude. Moreover, these things tended to be hidden from public view. Hence the rise of private bedrooms, the toilet, etc. Elias also wrote about the increasing social restraints placed on the use of violence. In medieval society people seemed to enjoy watching the torment of others in wars, public executions, and popular festivities. They also tended to be impulsive and to fight with very little provocation. In today's society, by contrast, violence and killing are strictly regulated and tend to take place behind closed doors. Executions and abattoirs are a case in point.

Elias sees a new sense of self emerging along with these changes. He suggests that in the earlier period there was less awareness of individuality and less sense of shame and embarrassment. In the later periods people became much more sensitive to the need to protect the self and police its borders; to separate out a civilized self from a spontaneous and animal self. As part of this process, they developed a capacity for higher levels of self-restraint and self-control. Elias, then, suggests that personality and culture go hand in hand, with culture equipping us with a sense of self and our emotional life.

A distinctive feature of Elias's work is that he provides a strongly sociological account of the rise of this new self, linking it to state-formation processes. As Europe came out of the relative chaos of the Middle Ages, larger, more centralized states emerged. These enforced a monopoly on the means of violence and initiated policies of internal pacification, which eliminated casual feuds and conflicts. Warriors became transformed into courtiers, with groups competing in "civilized" ways for the favor of the king and for status in courtly society. In a social context where elaborate behavioral rituals and refined manners were deemed vital indicators of rank and status, people became acutely aware of the need to develop manners. They sought to offer an impressive "presentation of self" without rude, violent, or animalistic behavior. To do this required "a constraint on the affects, a self-discipline and self-control" (1982: 7). Those who retained an older, cruder, more impulsive medieval sense of self would not have survived long in an environment where refinement and intrigue went hand in hand. Elias (1982: 4) therefore writes that: "It is by more than a coincidence that in the same centuries in which the king or prince acquires absolutist status . . . the civilizing of behavior is noticeably increased." Having been institutionalized in the court, these new ideas about manners and the self then trickled down to the lower orders. Today processes of childhood social-ization throughout society create actors with strong powers for self-monitoring and self-regulation.

NORBERT ELIAS (1897–1990)

Norbert Elias had a long and eventful life. He was born in Breslau, Poland, but came from a Jewish family of German origins. After serving in World War One, he studied both medicine and philosophy before abandoning the former. During the mid-1920s he moved to Heidelberg and switched to the study of sociology. Here he studied with Alfred Weber (Max Weber's brother) and Karl Mannheim, and began to develop an interest in culture and its links to long-term historical process. He moved to Frank-furt with Mannheim in 1929 and forged contacts with the other members of the Frankfurt School. Following the rise of the Nazis, Elias moved to Paris and then London, living in poverty and researching *The Civilizing Process*. There followed a period working in various poorly paid jobs, before finally obtaining a full-time aca-demic position at the University of Leicester in 1954 at the age of 57. However, it was only with the reprinting and translation of *The Civilizing Process* in the 1960s and 1970s that he became recognized as a major thinker.

Reference: Mennell 1992: 3–26

The work of Elias has been held up as a remarkable (and rare) example of research that spans both macro and micro sociology (see Mennell 1992: 94–5). As Elias puts it: "in order to understand and explain the civilizing processes one needs to investigate . . . the transformation of both the personality structure and the entire social structure" (1982: 287). His research covers a range of phenomena, from the emotions within the individual self, through to major historical shifts in the political order. Aside from this empirical breadth, it offers an important way for thinking about the links of agency with culture and society. What Elias's theory suggests is that human agency has slowly changed over the centuries. Whereas it used to be propelled by instincts and visceral emotions, it is now governed by reflexivity and self-awareness. We have traded in the free expression of natural drives for a different kind of freedom, one whereby we control these drives in the process of monitoring and regulating our own behavior. These changes at the level of the individual mirror and make possible changes at the levels of culture and society. For Elias, there was no point in developing a theory that privileges any one of these dimensions. Rather individual, culture, and society are tied together in complex, ever changing, and evolving networks of mutual interdependence. Elias sometimes spoke of a **figurational sociology** or a **process sociology** as a way of capturing this model. He suggested that most social theories and concepts led to an ossified, static, and reified vision of society, whilst his approach highlights permanent change, concrete reciprocal interrelationships, and the need for empirical data.

Empirical Work Influenced by Bourdieu, Giddens, and Elias

While Bourdieu's theoretical work has yet to be wholeheartedly embraced, there can be little doubt that he has been the most successful of the three theorists in sparking middle-range empirical inquiries into culture and society. Although research influenced by Bourdieu is diverse, it might be thought of as falling into the following camps:

- *Studies of cultural consumption.* For the most part, findings in this area confirm the general thrust of Bourdieu's thinking. They show that taste is driven by social location and that cultural consumption is a major dimension of contemporary stratification systems. For a review of this literature see Bennett, Emmison, and Frow (1999).
- *Studies of habitus.* This area tends to be dominated by ethnographers, especially those influenced by symbolic interactionism who are searching for newer, more high-powered theories than those developed in the 1950s and 1960s. Bourdieu's ideas about *habitus* have been adopted as a useful tool for understanding subcultures and the action patterns of their members. Much work in the sociology of the body (see chapter 16) has taken up the *habitus* as a central conceptual tool.
- *Studies of fields.* The focus here tends to be on struggles for the legitimacy of particular forms of culture or cultural capital within institutional or political settings. Following the agenda set by Bourdieu's own work, the two most significant areas at present are studies of art and art worlds, and research on academic and intellectual settings. In the former area ideas of "field" are often combined with theories about labeling and struggles for cultural recognition (e.g., of graffiti). In the second area, the concept of field is often tied to research in the sociology of knowledge tradition, with the aim of research being to identify how certain scholars and theories gain ascendancy over others.

While Elias's reputation has grown since the 1960s, the volume of work influenced by his theories remains far below that of Bourdieu. According to Stephen Mennell (1992: 279ff.), this has been the case especially in the United States, where a tradition of intellectual specialization has led to scholars who are ill-equipped to come to terms with the breadth of his vision and research agenda (see also Smith 1998). Nevertheless, his work has exerted an influence in two main areas, especially in Europe. In the field of comparative and historical research, more culturally minded scholars have drawn upon Elias's interest in long-term change. In general, historians have made the running here, with sociologists lagging some way behind in the appreciation of his work. Representative research makes use of detailed historical data to explore questions surrounding diverse topics such as punishment, sexuality, sport, death, and civility. Studies in these areas often focus on historical shifts in practices, indicating increasing concerns about privacy, reducing levels of violence and growing emotional sensitivity. We might use Elias to explain why boxers wear gloves or why the death penalty is a hidden activity involving repeated technological innovations oriented towards the painless death. Scholars interested in the sociology of emotion also now recognize Elias as a major pioneer in their field. This has been the case especially with studies of organizational culture and emotion management. These point to the way that control over emotions is central to contemporary working life.

Giddens's influence has also been mixed. Although he is regarded by many as a figurehead for the discipline (especially in Britain), his ideas seem to have generated more abstract theoretical debate than empirical applications. Efforts at systematically applying structuration theory are few and far between, although it is quite common for elements of Giddens's theory to be used by researchers. This is consistent with his own view that structuration was less a theory than a set of sensitizing concepts to guide inquiry. Applications that have been made tend to be eclectic and encompass diverse issues. Giddens's work on identity has also attracted some interest among sociologists, but for the most part has been bypassed in favor of postmodern and poststructural approaches – especially in the area of cultural studies.

It bears noting in closing this chapter that all three of the theorists we have discussed here have been recognized as important modern founders of one of the most intriguing recent developments in cultural theory, namely, the emerging field of inquiry that investigates the body as a cultural object. We return to their contributions on that topic in chapter 16.

Suggested Further Reading

Introductory texts on the scholars considered here are widely available and can be found in any good research library. Of the three, Bourdieu is the most difficult to read in the original. *The Inheritors* is a relatively accessible work. Even though it predates his mature theoretical vision, the main ideas are consistent with his later thinking. *Outline of a Theory of Practice* is obligatory reading for contemporary cultural theorists. It is a very difficult book, but at least it becomes more intelligible with each reading as the reader adapts to Bourdieu's vocabulary and style. Somewhat more approachable is *An Invitation to Reflexive Sociology*, which features Bourdieu's responses to students' questions about his work. Writings by Giddens are more reader-friendly. The first part of *The Constitution of Society* provides a time-efficient, if rather compressed, way to become familiar with the complexities of structuration theory. The later works on identity and risk are easier and, perhaps for this reason, have enjoyed quite a wide public readership. Elias is well served by Stephen Mennell's excellent introduction. The first chapters of *The Civilising Process* contain much of his more astounding data on historical shifts in manners and are entertaining as well as instructive.

CHAPTER NINE

British Cultural Studies

The field generally known as British cultural studies has become one of the dominant players in contemporary cultural theory. It is so powerful that when some people speak of "cultural studies" they often implicitly refer to this area and its progeny. British cultural studies is marked out by certain key orientations:

- It is strongly interdisciplinary in terms of research interests and theoretical influences.
- There is a primary interest in exploring culture as a site where power and resistance are played out.
- It validates the study of popular culture as well as "high culture."
- Political commitments to the concerns of the Left often influence research topics and, some critics would say, conclusions.

Theoretical Development: A Summary

The distinctive intellectual approach of British cultural studies has slowly evolved over the years. The origins of the field are traditionally dated to the work of literary critics Richard Hoggart and Raymond Williams in the late 1950s and early 1960s (Hall 1980a; Turner 1996: 12). During the late 1960s and 1970s their work was complemented by neo-Marxist **New Left** thinking. This drew upon Western Marxism (we looked at this in chapter 3) and the new social movements of the era in arguing against the reductionist, determinist, doctrinaire, and anti-humanist focus of classical Marxism. Ideas from Louis Althusser and structuralism were also incorporated and clearer understandings emerged about both the "relative autonomy of culture" and the importance of ideological frames for shaping popular consciousness. Such themes were central to early work of the Birmingham Centre for Contemporary Cultural Studies (CCCS). By the early 1980s Gramsci had replaced Althusser as the leading Marxian influence. Ideas from Foucault, Lacan, Derrida, and others were also creeping in. In the present day these have been layered with postcolonial theory, queer theory, and feminist theory. A move has gradually taken place away from Marxism toward an understanding of society as textured with multiple sources of inequality and fragmented local struggles. The result has been a dynamic and complex field that investigates issues of textuality, signification, ideology, and identity in terms of their plural relationships to systems of power. The remainder of this chapter explores some of these themes and research agendas in more depth.

Raymond Williams and Richard Hoggart

During the first part of the twentieth century, literary criticism had been dominated by aesthetes like F. R. Leavis and T. S. Eliot. They argued that the study of culture should be all about the examination of great works of high culture. These, they claimed, contained the seeds of a moral and ethical vision of the world that it was the duty of the reader to uncover. Popular culture, by contrast, was seen as trivial, debased, and deficient when measured against the standards set by the classics. Looking back, this can be seen as an elitist perspective which did little to further the serious, value-neutral study of mass culture. Coming from ordinary backgrounds and working in the adult education system, Raymond Williams and Richard Hoggart confronted a very different world. They found that existing approaches to the study of culture had little resonance with the concerns and values of middle-aged and working-class students. Consequently, they became aware of the need to understand popular culture and working-class experience in a less dismissive way.

Richard Hoggart's *The Uses of Literacy* (1957) is a seminal text which introduced this new approach at the end of the 1950s. Here Hoggart set out to investigate "changes in working-class culture . . . in particular as they are being encouraged by mass publications" (1957: 11). Hoggart begins by tracing the contours of the working-class worldview and lifestyle, exploring diverse arenas like work, the home, the family, oral tradition, and religion. He argues that "older" elements and attitudes are being challenged owing to the impact of mass publications like tabloid newspapers, paperback novels, and glossy magazines, and by new forms of entertainment like the jukebox. In Hoggart's view this influence was broadly pernicious. He writes, for example: "The mass of talented commercial writers ensures that most people are kept at a level in reading at which they can respond only to the crudely imprecise, the expected, the primary, the most highly colored" (1957: 197).

From our contemporary perspective it is easy to detect a moralistic flaw in Hoggart's book. He repeats the sins of Leavis (and, indeed, Horkheimer and Adorno) in applying normative standards to make negative judgments of contemporary mass culture. By the same token he writes with barely concealed nostalgia of a disappearing world. This was a "decent, local, personal and communal way of life", that could be found in "Working Men's Clubs, the styles of singing, the brass bands, the older types of magazine, the close group games like darts and dominoes" (1957: 265). *The Uses of Literacy* is also marred by Hoggart's tendency to enter into speculative portraits of the working-class mentality. Hoggart's major accomplishment, then, was not his research findings or application of a valid theoretical orientation. Rather, it lay in getting working-class culture onto the academic agenda and in applying the methods of literary criticism, such as close reading, to the materials of popular culture.

By contrast to Hoggart, Raymond Williams was to provide theoretically powerful models with long-term influence. In his early *Culture and Society* (1971 [1958]) he engaged in a systematic attempt to think through the idea of "culture," showing how its uses had altered over time in response to long-term economic, political, and social changes. He demonstrates that "[t]he history of the idea of culture is a record of our reactions, in thought and feeling, to the changed conditions of our common life" (1971: 285). While the data sources for this activity again tend to be Leavisite (treatments of culture in novels and philosophical essays), the book concludes with important discussions of "mass culture" and working-class culture – again putting these on the intellectual agenda.

The Long Revolution, Williams's (1961) next major work, takes up where *Culture and Society* leaves off, but is marked by a shift toward a more sociological approach to cultural analysis. Here Williams sees literature and art as only one kind of "culture" and he pushes toward an understanding of culture as an entire way of life. Williams looks at the role of institutions in not only reproducing and distributing culture, but also in changing its very form and the way we think about it. According to Williams, a "long revolution" has been taking place over the past two or three centuries involving increasing levels of industry, literacy, and democracy. These have intertwined with each other in complex ways in all spheres of social activity. The less elitist definitions and philosophies of culture that we use today reflect this process.

Today *The Long Revolution* is best remembered not so much for Williams's discussion of such long-term historical change, but rather for the concept of the **structure of feeling**. The term is elusive and rather like that of **Zeitgeist** (spirit of the age), in that it attempts to capture the particular mood or flavor of a given culture and the ways that this is experienced by people at a particular moment in history. Williams writes of the thing that he is trying to describe: "it is as firm and definite as 'structure' suggests, yet it operates in the most delicate and least tangible parts of our activity" (1961: 48). According to Williams, a structure of feeling is not an individual or personal thing, but rather is shared by a community or generation. It is acquired only through socialization and life experience and cannot be learned by formal study. Outsiders, such as cultural theorists, must do the best they can to recapture a structure of feeling using **documentary culture**. This consists of material evidence such as writings, buildings, and fashions which express "that life to us in direct terms, when the living witnesses are silent" (1961: 49). Williams argues that documentary culture, however complete, will only ever allow an approximation of a "lived culture" with its distinct structure of feeling.

During the 1970s Williams's work took another decisive theoretical turn with the publication of *Marxism and Literature* (1985 [1977]). He had always had left-wing sympathies, but had carried on his own "cultural and literary work and inquiry at a certain conscious distance" (1985: 2). Thanks to encounters with the New Left and readings of Benjamin, Lukács, Althusser, and Gramsci (all of whom are discussed in chapter 3) during the 1960s and early 1970s, Williams came to eliminate that distance and bring Marxian theory into the heart of his academic work. He speaks, for example, of the "complex relation of differentiated structures of feeling to differentiated classes"

(1985: 134), and argues vigorously that both literature and culture more broadly should be understood using concepts of hegemony and ideology. With this text the theoretical stage was set for the intellectual efflorescence at the Birmingham Centre for Contemporary Cultural Studies during the 1980s.

The Birmingham School

The Birmingham Centre for Contemporary Cultural Studies (CCCS) had been established in the 1960s with Hoggart as its first director. It became prominent from the 1970s onward under the directorship of Stuart Hall, where a period of what Durkheim would have called "collective effervescence" led to intense intellectual productivity. Some think of the research conducted in and around the Centre up until the early 1980s as constituting a sort of classical period for British cultural studies, involving the publication of key texts and the formulation of pivotal theoretical models. Many of these were the products of collaborative authorship, a practice reflecting both the communitarian norms of the Centre and a genuine sense of group belonging. By the 1990s, however, much of this energy was gone. Leading members of the group had moved on in their careers to take chairs in other locations (Hall himself moved to the Open University, from which he retired in 1997) and, as the right-wing tide of Thatcherism ebbed, it is possible that the sense of mission that had united the school also evaporated. The Centre was finally closed in 2002 in a move that some remaining department members saw as a politically motivated attack by its enemies. The research put out by the Centre was diverse, but as Graeme Turner (2002 [1996]) suggests, can be provisionally classified under three main themes:

1 Textual studies of the mass media and the ways that these operate to reproduce hegemony and ideology.
2 Ethnographic explorations of everyday life, especially those of subcultures. Broadly speaking, these sought to uncover the ways that politics, power, and inequality shaped lifestyle and fashion.
3 Studies of political ideologies such as those of Thatcherism and racist nationalism. The emphasis here was on uncovering their cultural codes and establishing why they were able to generate wide public appeal.

Textual Studies of the Mass Media

Explorations of the media were informed by a belief that they played a crucial role in ideological reproduction (e.g., Hall 1982) along the lines suggested by Gramsci's idea of hegemony (see pp. 36–8). In other words, it produces definitions of reality that prevent critical thinking. Drawing on Gramsci and Althusser, Stuart Hall claims that ideological messages in the media work predominantly by creating a false image of reality. Issues that could have been problematized were instead **naturalized** as simply a normal part of the way the world is – as an aspect of "reality." A conflict between workers and management, for example, might be reported as just an "industrial dispute," and seems to be part of the natural order of things. There is no attempt toward a deeper analysis, for example by questioning the capitalist order and the structural forces behind the struggle. Hall stresses the strategic and negotiated qualities of this cultural process, arguing that ideological struggles had a relative autonomy from class determination and that they could have major impacts of their own in reshaping social and political life. However, rather than being fully free-floating, ideologies are **anchored** in particular sets of interests, histories, and alliances. The position Hall and his colleagues tried to stake out, then, was one located between simple materialism and cultural idealism. Culture is autonomous, but at the same time is loosely tethered to social and economic bases.

Although neo-Marxism provided the basis for thinking about the social implications of the media, theories from semiotics provided the concrete tools for dissecting particular items of data. Saussure, Barthes, and Lévi-Strauss in particular were deployed in readings of messages and images. During the early 1980s British cultural studies made use of these theorists in developing powerful techniques for pulling apart media texts and uncovering the hidden ways in which they worked. Central to this agenda was a distinction between **denotation** and **connotation** taken from Barthes (see p. 105). A text might literally denote something (e.g., a strike is taking place), but also carry with it a subtle extra layer of meaning (e.g., the greedy workers threaten national stability). The power of ideology worked through this subtlety, rather than from a sledgehammer repetition of overtly political messages (e.g., a newsreader saying: "Strikers are dangerous to capitalism. They must be stopped"). Viewers would deploy their common-sense understanding of representational codes in recovering these hidden connotations, but at the same time (for the most part) not be aware of their ideological loading.

In an effort to differentiate themselves from more deterministic models of ideological process, Hall and his colleagues argued that not all people would see the same text in the same way. Central to this argument was a model of the communication process as involving both **encoding** and **decoding** (Hall 1980b), which was developed in the context of a discussion of televisual communication. Here Hall adapts the classical communication model (sender/message/receiver) to the needs of critical theory, arguing that a "complex structure of dominance" (1980b: 128) is at work in this process. Social, economic, ideological, and technical considerations shape the programs and agendas of media producers, but these have to be translated into an understandable message using ordinary language and a common stock of symbols (encoding). Viewers, meanwhile, have to make sense of the message (decoding). Hall argues that there is no guarantee of symmetry between the meanings established by encoders and decoders, allowing the possibility of misunderstanding. This is especially the case where the connotative aspects of signs are concerned. Hall writes: "The so-called denotative level of the televisual sign is fixed by certain, very complex (but limited or 'closed') codes. But its connotative level, though also bounded, is more open, subject to more active transformations, which exploit its polysemic values" (Hall 1980b: 134).

Thanks to this potential open-endedness, there are several "readings" possible of a single media item. The **dominant reading** is the one that was intended and which supports hegemonic ideologies. Here the reader derives from a media item an orthodox, politically conservative message that reflects the perspective of "political and military elites" as these are reflected in the "professional code" of broadcasters (Hall 1980b: 136). An **oppositional reading** is one that is made by someone who is aware of the dominant codes in a message and rejects them. Such a person (e.g., a British cultural studies academic!) is able to see through what is going on, formulate a more reflexive understanding of the communication process, and account for the media message in terms of an alternative code. Hall provides the example of a viewer who "listens to a debate on the need to limit wages but reads every mention of 'national interest' as 'class interest' " (1980b: 138). A **negotiated reading** is made by someone who accepts some parts of the dominant reading, but makes some adaptations which reflect their own needs and perceptions.

STUART HALL (1932–)

Stuart Hall has been the single most important figure in the history of British cultural studies. Coming from an Afro-Caribbean background, he was born in Jamaica and obtained a scholarship to Oxford. Like Hoggart and Williams before him, he went on to work as an adult education tutor. He established his reputation at a young age, working as an early editor of the *New Left Review*. Hall replaced Hoggart as Director of the Birmingham Centre for Contemporary Cultural Studies from 1968 to 1979. In this period, he shaped its intellectual and political agendas and acted as a mentor for subsequent generations of researchers. Hall is also notable as a major British public intellectual, frequently appearing on radio and television. He was an outspoken critic of "Thatcherism" – a concept that he helped to develop to explain the ideology of British Prime Minister Margaret Thatcher.

Reference: Turner 2002 [1996]: 66–7

The model provided by Hall, then, is a far cry from the rigid, mechanical, and abstract visions of ideology that have tended to dominate Marxian thinking. Attention is given to the active work of media producers and consumers in creating and reading messages, to the possibility of mistakes and opposition, and to the need for ideological messages to be translated into the multiple and autonomous semiotic codes of language and visual imagery. Arising from this perspective has been a seemingly endless stream of studies looking at the production and consumption of television (especially soap opera and current affairs) and other cultural texts (especially newspapers, magazines, and popular novels). For many of these studies the major objective has been to determine the extent to which audiences are capable of "resisting" dominant messages (see pp. 163–5). In more recent years the neo-Marxian encoding/decoding model has tended to be replaced by more poststructural frameworks. We look briefly at these later in this chapter.

Studies of Subcultures and Class Cultures

The ethnographic trend in British cultural studies looks at the ways of life of various marginal groups and sets about interpreting their social world. What makes this tradition distinctive from orthodox ethnography is that everyday action tends to be interpreted within a political framework. Social activities are often conceptualized as acts of "resistance" to a dominant social order or as creative responses to oppression and injustice. These kinds of themes are particularly central to the celebrated studies of youth subcultures by the Birmingham School, which often focused on youth music and the cultural styles attached to it. Whereas Hoggart had been dismissive of the fads and fashions of youth, seeing these as a threat to tradition and solidarity in working-class life, the ethnographies of the 1970s praised them as a vanguard of social protest. The publication of *Resistance Through Rituals* (Hall and Jefferson 1976) saw members of the Birmingham group champion the routine practices of subcultural groups (activities, dress codes, drug use, etc.) as a culture of resistance grounded in class relations. It was argued that these were symbolic and imaginative responses to objective conditions such as unemployment, consumerism, and alienation. Dick Hebdige's *Subculture: The Meaning of Style* (1979) developed this argument further. He asserts that: "Style in subculture is . . . pregnant with significance . . . interrupting the process of 'normalization'. As such, they are gestures, movements toward speech which offends the 'silent majority', which challenges the principle of unity and cohesion, which contradicts the myth of consensus" (1979: 18).

This theme is perhaps best illustrated in his discussion of punk. Hebdige points approvingly to the ways that punk made use of the garish, obscene, fetishistic, and tasteless; the ways that its dance styles like the pogo were both minimalist and absurd; the ways that the performers lacked trained musicianship, and so on. Whilst these subcultural codes might appear senseless, offensive, or infantile to outsiders, they can be interpreted as an intelligent and creative moment which confronted, mocked, and inverted mainstream norms and values. And so for Hebdige, the "sensibility which punk style embodied was essentially dislocated, ironic and self-aware" (1979: 123).

More recent work in the Birmingham tradition has refined the theoretical analysis of hegemony and resistance in youth music subculture. John Shepherd has used a socio-musicological approach to argue that specific musical structures mirror, and are the symbolic representation of, specific social structures. The pentatonicism of the feudal period in Europe, which can be heard in Gregorian chant, was organically linked to decentralized social structures, based as it was on a non-hierarchical collection of tones in which there was no principle or root tone, while the functional tonality that emerged with the industrial world established a hierarchical structure for musical composition in which the notes of a scale were subordinated to one root note (Shepherd 1991: 111, 122). In this analysis, it is quite politically significant that much African-American popular music, and especially the profoundly folk music that is the blues, is melodically deeply rooted in pentatonicism. In its very structure, Shepherd argues, this music encodes countercultural challenge to industrial American society (1991: 133–7). Andrew Goodwin (1992) has extended the Birmingham tradition on resistance and hegemony in youth music to the realm of music video and television. He has crafted a critical response to analysts of MTV and music video who see these cultural forms as wholly postmodern – i.e., disconnected from historical narratives and social relations of power and characterized purely by irony, parody, and pastiche (we discuss postmodernism in more detail in chapter 13). For Goodwin, the meaning of music video has to be understood in relation to the cultural politics of pop music itself and the political economy of the music industry. While much of music video clearly participates in hegemonic codes of meaning (e.g., the sexual objectification of women), there are nonetheless spaces for resistance within the form (e.g., Madonna's sexually explicit videos of the early 1990s in which she acts out an assertive female sexuality). Finally, Andy Bennett (with his colleague Richard Peterson) has undertaken a renovation of the very category of subculture in light of increasing recognition of the complexity of social identity. Bennett posits the **scene** as a more nuanced conceptual replacement for subculture. This concept better accounts for the fact that subcultural participants often put on and take off their identities as adherents to the values of the subculture as they enter and leave the places of one kind or another (local, global, or virtual) in which those values are shared (Bennett and Peterson 2004).

While the studies of youth subcultures are justly famed, perhaps the most widely respected work in the ethnographic genre is Paul Willis's *Learning to Labour* (1977). This book explored the issue of class reproduction through a study of working-class youths in school. He looked at a group of working-class boys using methods as varied as focus groups, observation, and in-depth interviews. He also conducted comparative studies on youths from different backgrounds. This methodological rigor probably accounts for much of the book's power and credibility with those outside of the Birmingham camp. Willis argued that "the lads" rejected the official cultural codes and ideologies of their schools. He writes: "The most basic, obvious and explicit dimension of counter-school culture is entrenched general and personalized opposition to au thority. . . . This opposition is expressed mainly as a style. It is lived out in countless small ways which are special to the school institution, instantly recognized by teachers, and an almost ritualistic part of the daily fabric of life for the kids" (Willis 1977: 11–12).

Disruptive behavior, smoking, dodging authority, avoiding the classroom and homework were all seen as valuable activities within the group. These were sources of in-group prestige and contributed to a sense of masculinity. Academic progress, on the other hand, was seen as a waste of time. For the lads the objective was to leave school as soon as possible and obtain working-class, unskilled manual labor. This would confer upon them financial rewards and membership in the adult male community. Willis also points to the ways that skills practiced in school (e.g., avoiding work and surveillance) were ones that would also be of practical use in the workplace or the construction site. In a sense, then, the culture of resistance that they had rehearsed in school turned out to be a suitable training for adult life. Yet at the same time it is dysfunctional in that it prevented the lads from becoming upwardly mobile in terms of class. In rejecting the individualistic and achievement-oriented ideologies of the school, the working-class youths had simultaneously prepared for and condemned themselves to working-class jobs.

Explorations of Political Ideologies

For the CCCS, the exploration of politics was largely confined to studies of right-wing ideologies, such as those of racism and Thatcherism. Intellectual resources from Althusser and Gramsci were used to explain how these operated to support the interests of the dominant class. During the 1980s there was a shift away from Althusser and toward Gramsci, who was seen as better able to theorize contingency and contest. Althusser, by contrast, was increasingly depicted by members of the Centre as excessively deterministic and unable to capture the cut and thrust of ideological struggle.

The influence of both Althusser and Gramsci is to be found in *Policing the Crisis* (Hall et al. 1978). Written by Hall and his colleagues, the book draws upon Stanley Cohen's idea of the moral panic (see p. 88) and situates it within a neo-Marxian framework. Hall et al. assert that a moral panic arose in Britain during the 1970s about the street crime of mugging. Although objective levels of the crime remained much as they always had been, the media highlighted incidents with sensationalist reports that the streets were out of control. Questions were asked in parliament and judges handed down tough sentences for what seemed to be minor offences. Most importantly of all, the media whipped up concern, functioning as an ideological state apparatus (see p. 48). Hall et al. suggest that the moral panic was partly linked to race politics and hostility toward migrant populations (who were often assumed to be the muggers). However, the major causal force lay in the structural crisis of the capitalist system. During the 1960s a hegemonic consensus in British society had begun to break down, to be replaced by a more authoritarian and repressive style of political control as strikes and demonstrations driven by inequality became widespread. In order for capitalism to survive it needed to be able to deal with dissent and to ideologically reconstruct a sense of national unity. A real social crisis and sense of unease were refracted and displaced by the media into a series of false moral panics that were accessible to ordinary experience. "The first phenomenal form which the experience of social crisis assumes in public consciousness, then, is the moral panic. . . . In this form, a society famous for its tenacious grasp on certain well-earned rights of personal liberty . . . screws itself up to the distasteful task of going through 'iron times'" (Hall et al. 1978: 323).

According to Hall and his colleagues, then, the moral panic over mugging operated as an excuse for tough new policing policies and laws to be introduced, and for these to gain the support of the general public. This allowed the state to clamp down on dissent that might threaten the capitalist system. Themes concerning the state, the ideology, and capitalism persisted in Hall's studies of Thatcherism during the 1980s. Here, however, a more Gramscian tone prevails than in the rather Althusserian study of mugging.

Far from realizing what Hall took to be their true class interests, during the 1980s members of the British working class had defected from socialism and voted for the anti-union, anti-welfare state, pro-capitalist Conservative Party. Why was this? Hall's answer drew upon Gramsci and his idea that forces with an interest in preserving the status quo of capitalism will actively construct new ideologies and beliefs in specific areas of struggle (see pp. 35–7). Hall (1983) gives emphasis to the way that the political ideologies of British Prime Minister Margaret Thatcher were cobbled together from a range of disparate sources and allowed her to gain hegemony. Thatcherism was seen as a clever political strategy that was appropriate to its particular time and place. This point here is to move away from the idea of dominant ideologies which persist over long periods of time, and instead to emphasize the conjunctural. This term, which is derived from Gramsci, refers to the "immediate terrain of struggle" and the "political and ideological work" (Hall 1983: 23) that goes into actively constructing ideologies, policies, and alliances. Hall suggests that Thatcherism combined a number of elements into a single philosophy. These included: traditional organic conceptions of community and family, nationalistic arguments about former greatness and national decline, authoritarian–populist themes about the need for strong leadership and control of crime, and anti-statist understandings about the need for economic deregulation and free enterprise. It was this clever synthesis of these new and old elements into a single package that allowed Thatcher to ideologically outmaneuver her critics and maintain the power of the hegemonic bloc.

The Diffusion of British Cultural Studies

The period from the early 1970s to the mid-1980s, which we have just reviewed, marks a golden age in British cultural studies. An intellectually consistent neo-Gramscian mode of analysis emerged, focused on class and culture; researchers worked in tightly knit teams with strong peer support; and theoretical agendas became rapidly more and more sophisticated. Yet at the same time as this efflorescence was taking place the seeds of a subsequent fragmentation of the field were being sown. The earliest stages of this process involved the arrival of race and gender issues on the intellectual agenda. In *Women Take Issue* (Women's Studies Group 1978), various female members of the CCCS team complained about the exclusion of women as a research topic and feminist theory from interpretative frameworks. In the early 1980s, Angela McRobbie pointed to the implicitly gendered nature of Birmingham ethnography, whose studies of working-class youths and subcultures tended to exclude or, at best, marginalize women (McRobbie 1981). By the mid-1980s there was a thriving women's studies component in the work of the School. This opened up the exploration not only of predictable areas such as the cultural construction of femininities, women's subcultures, and women's media (e.g., soap operas, women's magazines), but also took cultural studies in a new theoretical direction. Feminist theory at the time was perhaps more attuned to postmodern issues like pleasure and fantasy than the relatively modernist and rationalist Gramscian model.

While *Policing the Crisis* had considered issues of race, these were not theorized in a consistent way. Indeed, issues of race tended to be subordinated to themes of class and state. Again, it was in the early 1980s that change began to take place. In *The Empire Strikes Back* (Centre for Contemporary Cultural Studies 1982), Paul Gilroy and his colleagues argued their text was "conceived as a corrective to the narrowness of the English left, whose version of the 'national popular' continues to deny the role of blacks and black struggles in the making and remaking of the working class" (1982: 8).

In this text and Gilroy's subsequent *There Ain't No Black in the Union Jack* (1987), issues of race are placed center stage. These early studies of the topic trace out the connections of racism and race relations with the state, policing, conservative ideology, nationalism, class, the media, and cultural history. Moving into the 1990s there was a broad shift away from these traditional CCCS themes. Just like equivalent feminist work, more recent studies by Gilroy (see chapter 15 for details) and his successors have been strongly influenced by poststructuralism and by theoretical developments in the United States concerning African-American studies. The result has been that postcolonial and identity theories have become more and more central to understanding racial issues, again replacing the usual class-driven Gramscian framework of the CCCS.

Geographical expansion has also had an impact on "British" cultural studies. As it was exported worldwide, particularly to the United States, Canada, and Australia, interests arose in new national contexts. In Australia, for example, the field of "Australian Studies" is centered on the decoding of "Australian" symbols, mythologies, and histories. The result has been a plethora of texts on pioneers, bushrangers, suburbia, the beach, the barbecue, Aboriginal issues, multiculturalism, colonialism, and so on. A compact research focus on the "British" experience had provided one of the unifying themes of the Birmingham School. Once this was gone, only theoretical unity could provide a core. Yet this theoretical unity, as we have seen, was disappearing by the mid-1980s. This was not just the case in sub-fields dealing with issues of gender and race. There was a shift toward less overtly Marxian analyses of materials and, thanks to the rise of postmodernism, a trend toward more aesthetic understandings of culture and an increasing emphasis on the open-ended and indeterminate nature of signifying systems. Poststructural (and other) theories documenting the ambiguity of text have progressively become more and more prominent and have replaced the trusty encoding/decoding model. Important external influences for this shift have included de Certeau's (1988 [1974]) ideas of resistance in everyday life, Bakhtin's (1984) thinking on the carnivalesque, and Barthes's (1975b) enthusiasm for the *Pleasure of the Text*. Bakhtin and Barthes are discussed elsewhere in this book (see pp. 180–1, 107–8; also Turner 2002 [1996]: 201ff), but we need briefly to review de Certeau here.

In *The Practice of Everyday Life* the French thinker Michel de Certeau (1988 [1974]) argued that although we live in a world structured by large-scale technological, administrative, and capitalist systems, humans continually engage in small-scale subversive acts during their everyday lives. These practical actions reaffirm their identity and autonomy from dominant systems. This theme can be illustrated through his celebrated discussion of walking in the city. De Certeau suggests that the "rational organization" of the city "must repress all the physical, mental and political pollutions that would compromise it," and that it does so through "administration" and "classificatory operations" (1988: 94). However, in their movements about the city the pedestrian confronts this order. Looking closely at this activity we can see "a process of appropriation of the topographical system on the part of the pedestrian" (1988: 97). The walker can do this by means of unauthorized shortcuts or pointless detours, by walking with a particular style, or by only using streets with names that they like. Walking, in other words, is an expressive action that challenges objectifying discourses and geographies and subverts them. It could be argued that Goffman got there first (see pp. 58–9). In *Asylums* he spent some time showing how inmates respond to institutions with small acts of identity assertion. However, de Certeau's book has proven more influential for critical cultural theory and its efforts to show how seemingly innocuous everyday activities are intelligent and reflexive examples of sabotage, irony, and resistance.

With de Certeau, Barthes, and Bakhtin came a newfound interest in appropriation, pleasure, and fun in British cultural studies. Texts became seen as leaky and as containing an excess of meaning. Readers, it was alleged, were able to seize on such possibilities for alternate readings and participate in unauthorized pleasures. John Fiske's *Television Culture* (1987) exemplifies this trend. In contrast to the traditional CCCS emphasis on the oppressive and ideological qualities of television, Fiske argues (in part) that popular television is emancipatory because it allows people to locate pleasure and to generate resistant readings. Pointing to the fun that people derive from the glitzy images of Madonna music videos, television wrestling, Coca-Cola advertisements, and the action show *Miami Vice*, he suggests that "Television's playfulness is a sign of its semiotic democracy, by which I mean its delegation of production of meanings and pleasures to its viewers" (1987: 236).

Hall, among others, has criticized the extent of this move to empower users, insisting that readings of texts are still anchored in concrete social formations, locations, and production codes. Although meanings may be multiple and empowering in theory, in practice they tend to be closed off and ideological. Despite these pleas, many scholars in the area have decisively shifted their mode of analysis toward that of literary criticism. They provide virtuoso readings of mainstream texts (books, magazines, television programs, etc.) that reveal untold possibilities for emancipation, but usually without reference to concrete audiences and actual reading practices. Influences from Foucault, Lacan, postcolonial theory, poststructural feminism, and so on have all provided grist for the mill of this style of work and the movement away from class-based, Gramscian analyses. This shift is one which has decisively influenced the movement of British cultural studies from an institutional home in the social sciences toward one that is located in the Arts.

At the same time as one part of British cultural studies was cutting loose from ties to the social, another section has been moving toward engagement with cultural policy (for more discussion of this point, see Bennett 1998). Traditionally, cultural studies scholars have treated policy engagement with suspicion, seeing cultural policy as a concern for the (evil) state apparatus. More recently, there have been concerns about research funding and a growing awareness of the futility of constant critiques and decodings that get no further than the shelves of university libraries. The result has been that many cultural studies scholars have become interested in policy debates on topics like satellite broadcasting, censorship, monopolies, equity, and access. While this trend has provided increased influence with government agencies, it has perhaps blunted the political and polemical qualities of the British cultural studies tradition.

Arising from the various forces in the fragmentation and proliferation of the field has been an extensive literature of relentless self-examination. While reviews are common in all areas of cultural theory, those concerning British cultural studies are peculiarly passionate – perhaps reflecting the intense sense of political mission that once characterized the field. Works in this genre are concerned with tracing past and future directions for cultural studies and proposing diagnoses and treatments for perceived ills. The literature can be seen as both a healthy sign of reflexivity and as a token of unease at the lack of a distinctive identity and the loss of a mythical golden age.

Evaluations of British Cultural Studies

Advocates of British cultural studies (e.g., Turner 2002 [1996]) argue that it embodies several strengths. These include:

- a vigorous argument for the autonomy of culture;
- clear understandings of the links of meaning to power and social structure;
- a theoretically rich, interdisciplinary approach for decoding texts and ideologies;
- an ability to incorporate agency through an understanding of political strategy derived from Gramsci, and ideas about reading from communications and literary theory.

Critics, however, have indicated various possible flaws:

- For some critics, arguments about the autonomy of culture advanced by British cultural studies scholars are in tension with their relentless insistence that culture is centrally shaped by power. Ideas about the "relative autonomy," "articulation," and "anchoring" merely seem to postpone an inevitable economic or political determinism much as similar terms do in Althusser's work (see Sherwood et al. 1993).
- While the above criticism suggests that the field remains plagued by social structural determinism, others believe that it is not social-structural enough (e.g., Harris 1992). Here it is suggested that there is an overemphasis on the analysis of texts, semiotic systems and reading and a comparative neglect of the institutional dynamics of their production. Relatedly, Meaghan Morris (1988) attacked the "banality of cultural studies," suggesting that its political edge had been lost as study after study documented resistance and pleasure with little attention to issues of power, constraint, and control. In general, the previous criticism tends to be directed against the earlier Gramscian and Althusserian work, while this one is most often targeted at later, media-decoding exercises that are influenced by poststructuralism and postmodernism.
- Comment has also been passed on the methodologies of cultural studies. With the exception of reception studies (which are strongly influenced by American communications research norms), many interpretative projects lack the firm, value-neutral, methodological foundations which are found in more mainstream traditional academic disciplines like sociology or anthropology. As a result, readings of texts can appear as both impressionistic and as politically driven.
- The political commitments of British cultural studies can sometimes spill over into its academic analyses, with a tendency to romanticize the marginal and deviant. Dick Hebdige's early work is an example of this. Activities that might be thought of

as antisocial or illegal are described in a positive light as forms of resistance. In an effort to valorize youth subcultures, their more unpleasant aspects like sexism, violence, or racism tended to be ignored.

Notwithstanding these criticisms, British cultural studies, or just cultural studies, as it is often now known, remains an important force in contemporary cultural theory. Its future fate, however, is hard to predict. It is a vast and diverse field that lacks any obvious common ground other than a left-of-center political alignment, a generic belief that culture is linked to power and a myth of origin centered on the CCCS. Torn between policy relevance and more disinterested enquiry, between the arts and the social sciences, between modernist and postmodern theoretical frames, it may soon become diffused and fragmented to the point where it is impossible to identify any specific "school." When that day arrives, summary chapters such as this one will become a thing of the past.

Suggested Further Reading

An edited volume entitled *Culture, Media, Language* (Hall et al. 1980) contains a number of classic essays and working papers from the 1970s. It provides a useful introduction to the diverse styles of work in the classical era of the Birmingham School. Fiske's *Television Culture*, by contrast, offers an accessible introduction to the more postmodern work that was to emerge during the 1980s. The other empirical studies discussed in this chapter are also within the range of most student readers. Those on youth subculture are perhaps the most entertaining, even if many are now a little dated. Perhaps the best overview of the field is by Graeme Turner (2002 [1996]).

CHAPTER TEN

The Production and Reception of Culture

A large proportion of this book is dedicated to the exploration of rather abstract theories about culture by philosophically inclined theorists. In this chapter we look at a different, perhaps less visionary, literature that understands culture as something very concrete that is produced and consumed. It lacks the grand theoretical statements, titanic intellectual giants, and monumental landmark texts of, say, structuralism or Western Marxism. Nevertheless it is an approach that animates much contemporary inquiry. It has led to the construction of a considerable body of important middle-range theory and has been responsible for some of the most methodologically sophisticated studies of recent years. Consequently, some familiarity with this orientation is essential for understanding contemporary cultural theorizing.

Research on the production and reception of culture covers a number of fields, most notably, mass communications, film and television studies, and sociology. It has also been informed by a number of the diverse theoretical paradigms contained in this book. Despite this pluralism we can uncover some common principles which animate the perspective.

- While broader definitions of culture are not denied, it tends to be studied as it is manifested in tangible products such as a work of art, a book, or a broadcast. These can be directly experienced and measured and have a specific spatial location or temporal duration. Diana Crane (1992), for example, speaks of "recorded culture" and "cultural products" as the focus of her book entitled *The Production of Culture*. Wendy Griswold (1986) uses the term "cultural object." Such an approach differs from those that see culture as a diffuse, abstract, and intangible force pervading society. Examples of the latter would include Parsons's thinking about "values," Williams's ideas about a "structure of feeling," or Marxist ideas about a "dominant ideology," among many others (see pp. 29–30, 146, 7).
- A model derived from mass communications research sees culture as something akin to a message that is produced, transmitted, and received. Each of these stages involves cultural, technological, and social factors. The primary aim of analysis is to unpack the impact of each of these and to work out how it exerts an influence.

- A central focus is given to the concrete agency of actors and institutions. Far from being the outcome of abstract social forces, culture is grounded in proximate systems of causality. It is more likely to be explored as the output of publishing houses, broadcasting networks, or state bureaucracies, than as a response to a need for social stability or the unfolding of a long-term historical trend. These wider possibilities are not necessarily refused, but rather they are bracketed out of inquiry.
- Cultural forms should not be studied just as abstractions. Their production and consumption takes place in specific contexts and through specific technologies. We need to understand these if we are to understand the format, message, and political effects of cultural goods, e.g., whether emerging technologies such as the Internet or iPods, and new genres in existing media technologies such as reality television, allow for increased democratization and participation or simply replicate the political effects of earlier technologies.

By far the largest volume of work concerned with the production and reception of culture has emerged from the field of communications research. We begin with the foundational contribution of this field to the study of "reception" before moving on to look at questions of cultural production. We conclude by looking at some studies which have attempted to move the investigation of these issues away from a focus on the media and the arts.

The Study of Media Effects

Theoretical interest in the production and reception of culture can be traced back to communications research in the middle decades of the twentieth century. Communication is commonly seen as a process involving a sender, a receiver, and a message. A central theme in mass media research has been the exploration of the relationships between these elements. In particular there has been considerable debate about the relative power of the sender and the receiver to determine the meanings of messages. During the twentieth century there was a general shift away from models that gave primary power to senders (e.g., media institutions) and toward those which emphasize the ability of audiences to influence the interpretation of messages.

The rise of the new technologies of television, radio, and cinema during the twentieth century corresponded with the emergence of the **mass society hypothesis**. This model was adopted by those on both the Left and the Right. It suggested that industrialization and urbanization had created a "mass" of more or less undifferentiated consumers and citizens. These people were somewhat stupid, attracted to common pleasures, governed by a herd mentality, and in need of leadership. In contrast to the mass were a small, educated, intelligent, and often manipulative elite. The theory of communication associated with this vision is sometimes known as the **hypodermic model**, as it suggests that elites were able to construct meanings which were then "injected" wholesale into the mass. Another name is the **bullet model**. The theory was most often applied in the context of non-democratic regimes like Hitler's Germany, where an efficient propaganda machine was perceived to be whipping up support for the Nazis via radio and cinema. However, it also had an influence on understandings of communication in other contexts. Horkheimer and Adorno's (1972 [1947]) theory of the culture industries, for example, worked with an understanding of an undiscriminating, lowest-common-denominator American public being indoctrinated by Hollywood products (see pp. 41–3).

These kinds of models were challenged by early research findings on **media effects**. Studies on media effects aim to find out what kinds of impacts the media are actually having on their audiences. The most important early investigations were by Paul Lazarsfeld and others (e.g., Lazarsfeld et al. 1944), beginning with an exploration of the American presidential election of 1940. The findings of Lazarsfeld's various projects suggested that exposure to radio and print media had very little direct impact on voting behavior. What was important was the impact of **opinion leaders**. These were people like the head of the household, union officials in the workplace, community figures, and so on. They tended to be the highest consumers of the media. A **two-step flow** of communication took place in which the opinion leader would interpret information coming from the mass media and shape the meanings that others made from them. The opinion leader was influential thanks to factors like trust, esteem, group norms, and informal pressure to conform. The overall finding was that **personal influence** (Katz and Lazarsfeld 1956) was very important in shaping the way that messages were received. Communications coming from outside of a group or community were filtered through interpersonal and institutional (e.g., family, workplace) settings.

By the 1970s Lazarsfeld's model had become the dominant paradigm in media studies. Yet as the decade went on it became subjected to increasing critiques. In one of the most influential of these, Todd Gitlin (1978) asserted that it was flawed by a narrow measure of "effects" as short-term changes in attitudes and behavior. Wider understandings were put to one side by a methodological and definitional focus that "drained attention from the power of the media to define normal and abnormal social and political activity, to say what is politically real and legitimate and what is not . . . to establish certain political agendas for social attention and to contain, channel and exclude others" (1978: 205).

The kind of perspective advocated by Gitlin and others has come to be known as **agenda setting**. The idea here, to provide a colloquial summary, is that the media cannot tell people what to think, but it can tell them what to think *about*. It was claimed that the media was powerful because it could foreground some issues as important while marginalizing or ignoring others. This understanding was, and still is, popular with those on the Left who saw certain issues (e.g., the international arms trade, Third World poverty, illegal CIA practices, the environment) never making it into public discourse thanks to the domination of the media by capital. The media could also become important because it shaped common-sense thinking, symbolic frames, and epistemologies. Imagine, for example, a televised debate between two presidential candidates. Lazarsfeld would set out to look for a shift in voting intentions among the audience. Advocates of agenda setting, by contrast, might point to the way the broadcast naturalized a two-party system in which those who are already socially advantaged struggle for yet more power. By making such a political system seem normal, expected, routine, inevitable, or unquestioned, the media managed to reinforce a broader structural order. Gitlin (2001: 123–5) recounts a personal example of how media sources can take a complex position and turn it into something simple and amenable to the desired ideological range. He describes being interviewed by a television reporter for his thoughts on the impending Gulf War of 1991 and making a great effort to make clear both his opposition to the war and, at the same time, his support for American troops in harm's way. He was dismayed when he saw the aired interview, which had edited its content in order to present him as an uncomplicated supporter of the war.

An important variation on the agenda-setting theme was Elisabeth Noelle-Neumann's (1993 [1984]) theory of the **spiral of silence**. The idea here is that people fear being isolated. Once an issue is treated in a particular way in the media, it takes a good deal of courage to speak out against the orthodoxy and risk social isolation. The spiral of silence kicks in as one opinion becomes endlessly repeated and the perceived costs of speaking out grow. An example of this was British media discourse over the death of Princess Diana in 1997. The media ran stories about universal grief among the people and spoke endlessly of their deep love for her. The views of the many people (probably the majority) who did not share this opinion were never aired. Those who did raise them in public were sometimes subjected to harassment and hate mail. For those people who felt coolly toward Diana, it was prudent simply to keep silent (see Jack 1997; Black and Smith 1999).

New media technologies of the last few decades, which include satellite television and radio and the Internet, have substantially changed the media environment and the theoretical efforts to describe it. Contemporary versions of the pessimistic mass society framework often reject arguments about the democratic potential of these new media by pointing to two key characteristics of the current environment. The first has to do with centralized ownership and the concomitant impoverishment of content. Erik Klinenberg's study (2007) of the consolidation of ownership in the United States by a few large media conglomerates (e.g., Clear Channel Communications) demonstrates the damage done to the ability of citizens to make informed decisions about public policy and even to protect themselves in crisis situations when there is insufficient diversity in media. The second criticism points to what Gitlin (2001: 17) has referred to as **media supersaturation**. He notes that 88 percent of American children between the ages of 2 and 18 live in a home with two or more television sets, 70 percent in a home with a video game player, and nearly the same percentage in a home with a computer. This is to say nothing of the various personal communication devices (e.g., cell phones, iPods, etc.) owned by many young people. Our current media environment is characterized by **nomadicity**, which Gitlin defines as a situation in which highly mobile consumers of information are, whatever their movements, always tracked by an "underlying system [that] always knows who we are, where we are, and what services we need" (2001: 55). The resulting "torrent of information" cannot possibly be organized and, in any event, mostly focuses on the banal, effectively distracting its audience from the mundane business of the basic cultural literacy necessary for democratic citizenship.

Despite this continuing streak of pessimistic analysis, as early as the 1980s reception studies began putting power back into the hands of receivers. The most important of these were **audience ethnographies**. These were usually based on focus group, interview, or panel methodologies, and involved exploring the ways that diverse social groups "read" particular media texts – most often television programs. We turn now to that literature.

Contemporary Work on the Reception of Culture

Contemporary work exploring the consumption or reception of culture tends to be centered on three major lines of theoretical influence:

1 *The American communications research tradition which originated with Lazarsfeld.* This tends to be positivistic in orientation and organized around concepts like the transmission of information and opinion. Most often found in political science, the perspective generally operates with a pluralist model of society and quite often looks at how demographic factors and attitudes, as well as personal influence, might affect the readings of texts. A typical study here might explore whether voting behavior is changed by viewing a political broadcast.

2 *A field strongly influenced by the British cultural studies tradition (see chapter 9), which is grounded in critical theory.* This operates with an understanding of the media as part of an ideological system. Its model of culture also tends to be more semiotic and hermeneutic than the positivistic, somewhat social-psychological approach pioneered by Lazarsfeld. Rather than using a vocabulary of "attitudes" and "beliefs," it speaks of "codes" and the ways that they are read. Television programs, for example, are "texts" that have to be "decoded" by viewers who use a particular "horizon of expectations" in making sense of them. A particular emphasis is placed on the way that readings of media texts are influenced by the class locations of viewers. However, race and gender have also become recognized as structuring factors. The key point of interest here for the researcher concerns the ability of the audience to be critical of dominant ideologies and the match/mismatch between their readings and the ones that are intended. A typical study in this genre might look at the ways viewers of soap opera decode and then accept or reject the gender roles that are presented in a program.

3 *Poststructural and postmodern explorations of the role of the reader.* Although these can also focus on class, race, and gender as determinants of readings, there is a greater emphasis on the autonomy of the individual (as opposed to categories of persons) to generate their own private meanings. A major concern is with pleasure, play, and fantasy as responses to texts. In addition analysts have set about deconstructing the (modernist) categories of communication research such as "text" and "audience." A (stereo)typical study here might explore the voyeuristic sexual thrills that both male and female viewers derive from Madonna or Beyoncé music videos.

Of these three fields, the last two are probably of most interest to cultural theory. Reviewing a few recent studies provides a taste of the kind of work that goes on here.

David Morley's 1980 study *The Nationwide Audience* provides a suitable place to start. Morley sought to explore Stuart Hall's argument that class location would determine the ways that audience members decoded television programs (see pp. 147–9). Morley looked at a family television magazine program called *Nationwide*, which his expert readings told him constructed a false sense of national unity and community and masked the deep class divides that were at the heart of British society. Morley used 26 focus groups with various social backgrounds to explore readings of a single episode. He didn't find any one-to-one correlation with class. Trade union officials, for example, subscribed to the preferred (ideological/intended) reading of the text for the most part, as did bank managers. The major finding of the study was that the text of *Nationwide* could support multiple readings, but these were not entirely arbitrary. The text itself made some readings more likely than others, making counter-hegemonic readings difficult to sustain. Similar readings have been made even of the seemingly more democratic varieties of recent television that make up the reality TV genre. Mark Andrejevic (2003) argues that this genre's participatory, non-staged appearance is largely illusory, noting that reality stars are made and act out their roles in program after program (e.g., Trishelle Cannatella, who first appeared on *The Real World: Las Vegas* and then took her "drunken sexual hook-up girl" persona to *The Surreal Life* and several other reality-based programs). More, the central theme of reality television in Andrejevic's reading has to do with an active desire to watch others who are under surveillance, or to be under surveillance oneself. He invokes Foucault's notion of the panopticon (see p. 118) in describing the form of programs such as *Big Brother* (the title of which references Orwell, though it is likely that many younger viewers fail to note that fact) and still newer and more intrusive media such as the website Voyeur Dorm, where young women submit themselves to being continually in front of video cameras as a commercial porn enterprise (Andrejevic 2003: 78).

David Buckingham's 1987 investigation of the British soap opera *Eastenders*, by contrast, highlighted the role of viewer creativity and reflexivity. His study contrasted the expectations of scriptwriters and producers with the experiences of the program that were derived by viewers. Among other things, he demonstrated that, rather than passively watching the show, viewers were capable of irony and critical distance. These could enhance the enjoyment of the program, allowing the viewer to scoff at poor characterization and implausible plot lines.

Printed works, too, have proven amenable to this style of research. Janice Radway's (1991 [1984]) study of women and romantic fiction, for example, takes a feminist perspective in trying to understand how such books interact with their audience. Radway conducted discussion sessions with typical readers of such works in a Midwestern town in the United States. She concludes that it is difficult to make any simple pronouncement on the ideological effects of such texts. On the one hand, their storyline usually embodies "a simple recapitulation and recommendation of patriarchy and its constituent social practices and ideologies" (1991: 210). That is to say, they advocated marriage, family, duty, and heterosexuality as valued social goals. On the other, the women saw the very act of reading as an assertion of their own needs. They valued the time when they could put aside the demands of the family or housework and instead sit quietly enjoying their own time, space, and pleasure. In addition, their escape into the romantic books could be understood as emerging from dissatisfaction with their existing social experience. Stories about love, emotional support, and men coming to understand women's needs had an appeal precisely because many of the women's own experiences of marriage and men had been different. In this way, then, the act of reading had a critical potential within it. The fantasy world of the text could serve to highlight things that were wrong with the status quo. As Radway puts it, "women are reading not out of contentment but out of dissatisfaction, longing and protest" (1991: 214). The overall picture provided by Radway is of complexity. Ideological and oppositional forces interpenetrate in unpredictable ways as texts, readers, and acts of reading come together.

Radway's work pointed to the need to look at how texts fit in with everyday life. David Morley's later work, *Family Television* (1986), also explored this issue. Rather than investigating the content and reception of particular programs, he looked at the ways that television watching is structured as part of family routine. The point he makes is that people do not watch television programs in clinical laboratory settings. Rather, they incorporate viewing into their lives in complex ways as part of everyday practice. Studies making use of focus groups might miss this dimension of the viewing experience. Morley documents diversity in viewing activities. People might concentrate intensely on some programs and engage in another activity during others. Issues of power also featured prominently in his data, with men (predictably) taking control of viewing and video-recording choices, and imposing a regime of silence during their favorite shows. This contrasted with the subordinate orientations of women, who often had to combine viewing with other household tasks. Women also saw the home as a domain of work rather than leisure, and so would often feel guilty when taking time out for watching television. These patterns, Morley notes, are linked to socially defined roles and their intersection with the split between public and private spheres. More recent empirical studies of American (Lembo 2000) and British (Gauntlett and Hill 1999) television viewers have also documented high levels of television watching accompanied by the pursuit of some other activity (e.g., cooking, housecleaning). Lembo calls this **simultaneous viewing** and suggests the frequency of this particular variety of viewing experience would seem to make it difficult to defend arguments for simple hegemonic power effects of the medium.

Some other work in the British cultural studies tradition has been influenced by postmodernism. John Fiske's 1987 study, *Television Culture*, for example, is centrally concerned with validating popular pleasures and power of the viewer over the text. He believes that the concept of the "audience" is becoming so problematic that we should abandon it in favor of a focus on the particular moments of interpretation in which the viewer takes control and derives gratifications from their viewing (see also p. 155). The theoretical deconstruction of the audience has been taken further by John Hartley (e.g., 1987), who suggests that it is a player in a discourse, and reflects the manufactured or imagined needs of particular interest groups. Academics, broadcasting authorities, and television producers will all attempt to construct versions of the audience that allow them to get on with (and justify) their jobs. The overall approach here is rather Foucauldian, seeing "the audience" as a signifier that is actively constructed by discourses and institutions rather than as something that exists independently of particular discursive regimes. Academics, for example, might think of the audience as being made up of class or ethnic groups, while advertisers will see it as a potential market. For the television industry it is a "product" which they can use to generate advertising revenue. For all these groups, the audience is something that must be guarded, controlled, and, if possible, made predictable.

Recent studies in fan communities have demonstrated precisely how far some audiences go in negotiating the meanings of texts for themselves. Fanfic, or fan fiction, which is fiction-writing concerning characters and basic story elements taken from mass media sources by audience members, is a growing phenomenon, aided massively by the medium of the Internet. This mode of participation with media allows audiences to reshape characters (e.g., those of the cult television series *Buffy the Vampire Slayer*) significantly, and place them into plots of their own devising. In slash fiction, audience members add new erotic relationships, most often homosexual, between characters; *Star Trek*'s Captain Kirk and Mr. Spock are a common pair in this literature (Sandvoss 2005: 23). Contra Gitlin and similarly positioned writers, much recent attention to cyberfandom has demonstrated that audience readings of media products are often highly plural (Johnson 2007). The argument is often advanced that the technology in which much of fanfic takes place, i.e., the Internet, powerfully contributes to its demo-cratic potential. A significant amount of work has been done to explore this potential for counter-hegemonic participation in other computer-mediated forms, e.g., in chat rooms and Internet-based virtual worlds such as Second Life. We discuss this topic in chapter 13.

In conclusion, taken as a whole, audience ethnographies have:

- shown that viewers actively read texts and adapt them to their own uses and plea-sures – these readings are often diverse and may be influenced by various factors, such as race, gender, class, or life experiences;
- demonstrated that there is no necessary correspondence between the messages encoded into texts by their producers and those that are read by audiences;
- questioned the idea of the uniform audience as advanced by the mass society hypoth-eses; rather, they suggest there are multiple types of audience with diverse social characteristics and everyday viewing practices.

Taste Cultures and Celebrity Culture

The sociological study of taste cultures goes back at least to Pierre Bourdieu's work on distinction (discussed in chapter 8), but Herbert Gans also stakes a claim as one of the founding figures in this area with his *Popular Culture and High Culture* (1999 [1974]). Gans delineated five distinct ways of thinking about and appreciating aes-thetic/entertainment culture (**taste cultures**) in American society. Each was linked to a particular subset of the American social class system; Gans called these groups **taste publics**. Each taste culture is ultimately embedded in a certain moral way of seeing the world:

1 *High culture*: the highly educated upper and upper-middle classes, especially the professions and academia, who see cultural works from the perspective of creators and are therefore highly interested in technical questions of form and process. They appreciate works that address abstract philosophical questions and avoid easy resolution.

2 *Upper-middle culture*: the majority of the upper-middle classes, not so well-educated as the first group and not trained to read works as creators or critics, they prefer less abstract works about careers and individual achievement. As an example, Gans notes that they may appreciate the comedic films of the famed Swedish director Ingmar Bergman, but not his serious and often highly philosophical and pessimistic dramatic films, which are favored by the high culture group.

3 *Lower-middle culture*: middle and lower-middle classes in lower-status professions and white-collar jobs, they are the numerically dominant American taste public with an appreciation for work that celebrates "ordinary people" and mainstream middle-class virtues and that only rarely involves unresolved conflicts. *Life*, *Reader's Digest*, and the staple variety of television sitcoms and popular dramas are examples of works they enjoy.

4 *Low culture*: some lower-middle class members, industrial and service workers, they are frequently explicitly hostile to the taste cultures of higher-ranking classes, as they see those works as destabilizing traditional values. The moral struggles presented in the works they prefer are clear, and the "good guys" always win. Action films with heroic stars such as John Wayne or Sylvester Stallone are well liked by this group.

5 *Quasi-folk low culture*: poor and relatively uneducated and unskilled blue-collar and service workers, distinguished from the previous taste public mainly by a frequent intermingling of ethnic elements in the cultural products they enjoy. This is a reflection of the fact that this group contains many ethnic minority and recent immigrant groups.

In a revised edition of the book that appeared a quarter century after the first publication, Gans acknowledged significant change and diversification within each taste culture, but essentially reaffirmed the overall framework.

One interesting shift in taste cultures that seems to have taken place recently has to do with the phenomenon of **cultural omnivorousness**. Increasingly, elite social class members have moved from symbolic exclusion as a way to distinguish themselves (refusing to recognize lower-class genres of music as aesthetically valid or worthy of attention) to symbolic expansiveness (demonstrating interest in and knowledge of a wide variety of different music genres, including many formerly disdained by elites, e.g., rap). Bethany Bryson (1996) has augmented the terminology of Bourdieu (see pp. 131–3) to call this **multicultural capital**. In this new perspective on taste, aesthetic exclusiveness decreases with education. One of the mechanisms at work in the new-found ability of highbrows to appropriate lowbrow culture likely has to do with the fact that many genres of such lowbrow cultural production are produced by social groups of the politically marginal or oppressed (e.g., urban African-Americans and rap; rural and poor European-Americans and bluegrass); thus, embracing their cultural production can be part of a multicultural leftward political outlook, which also becomes more common as formal educational levels rise (Peterson and Kern 1996).

Much attention has been focused recently on the phenomenon of **celebrity culture**, as it has spread throughout most of the middlebrow taste cultures and even into some highbrow circles. Chris Rojek (2001: 13) points to three broad causes for the expansion of the phenomenon of the celebrity and his/her fans:

1   Democratization, which has simultaneously expanded the purview of the lowbrow and middlebrow taste cultures within which celebrity culture had its start and enlarged the pool of celebrities.
2   The decline in religion, which has drawn at least some of those with an interest in pantheons toward the celebrity firmament.
3   The commodification of everyday life, which makes information about celebrities omnipresent.

The phenomenon is now sufficiently complex, Rojek suggests, that one term is no longer sufficient. In addition to celebrities, he describes **celetoids** (celebrities of a very compressed, short-term nature – e.g., lottery winners) and **celeactors** (fictional characters who achieve celebrity-like status – e.g., Borat Sagdiyev, the fictional Kazakh reporter played by comedian Sacha Baron Cohen in *Da Ali G Show* and later in the film *Borat*) (2001: 23). He traces the connection of celebrity culture and religion in a number of fascinating forms. Celebrity death cults frequently emerge around specific deceased stars. Consider figure 10.1, which shows the tomb of the chain-smoking, hard-living, iconoclastic French singer/actor/director Serge Gainsbourg, who died in 1991 (look him up in Wikipedia). This has become a shrine. Fans leave written messages of admiration, photographs, flowers, and gifts of cigarettes and subway tickets; the latter apparently began as a reference to one of his biggest hits, *Le Poinçonneur des Lilas*, a song about a subway ticket puncher who desperately longs to escape his dismal life. This is their way of connecting in a personal way to an iconic personality and participating as both receivers and producers of a particular celebrity culture. The celebrity stalker is interpreted by Rojek as a worshipper seeking the magical power of the stars by attempting contact with them, and he reads the existence of fan narratives that doubt the deaths of particularly beloved celebrities (e.g., Elvis, Tupac Shakur) as a kind of modern parallel to primitive beliefs about shaman who undergo deep spiritual experiences that allow them to cheat death. Whole media genres such as the talk show and, more recently, the subgenre of reality television known as "celebreality TV" (e.g., *Flavor of Love*, *Celebrity Fit Club*, and *Scott Baio is 45 . . . and Single*) have emerged in response to the rise of celebrity culture.

The Production of Culture

Work on the production of culture explores the cultural and institutional factors that influence the creation of cultural products rather than the ways they are received and interpreted by an audience. As Janet Wolff (1993: 1) points out, this broadly

Figure 10.1   Serge Gainsbourg's tomb with fan messages

sociological perspective contrasts vigorously with the "romantic and mystical notion" that cultural products are "the creation of genius, transcending existence, society and time" and arrive thanks to some form of "divine inspiration." The aim here is not so much to laugh ideas about creativity and talent out of court, but rather to show how "practical activity and creativity are in a mutual relation of interdependence with social structures" (1993: 9). In a similar vein, Howard Becker (1982) speaks of **art worlds** that sustain cultural production and provide an audience for their product. He looks in particular at the subcultures and taste communities that sustain the performing arts, and writes that "all artistic work, like all human activity, involves the joint activity of a number, often a large number of people" (1982: 1). In Becker's view, the individual artist "works in the center of a network of cooperating people, all of whose work is essential to the final outcome" (1982: 25). The following précis of the production of culture literature is derived largely from a reading of Becker (1982), Crane (1992), and Wolff (1993). It provides only a brief sketch of the kinds of themes that are to be found in this vast field. Key factors influencing cultural production are provided in *italics*.

The availability of an **audience**, and expectations about it, provide perhaps the most critical variable in shaping both the decision to launch a product (e.g., a new television show) and its content. It is rarely the case that artists or culture industries create products and then wait for an audience to adapt to them. In the for-profit arena, cultural products are designed to make money by having widespread audience appeal. Even in less commercial spheres like the visual arts, performing arts, or public television, there is a hope and expectation that at least some people will take an interest in what is going on. Cultural producers will therefore shape their output to fit what they perceive to be the needs and interests of a target audience. Soap operas, for example, have traditionally included themes about intimate relationships, as these are believed to be of interest to the female audiences for whom they are intended. As Crane (1992: 47) points out, the culture that an audience receives is "designed as much as possible to reflect their tastes, interests, and attitudes . . . [and] reflects back to the consumer his or her own image." Studies in this area often look at the fit or mismatch between the perspectives of producers and audiences, the way that a particular program is appropriated by various audience segments, or the fact that existing genres change in subtle ways to meet shifts in audience needs and expectations.

A nice example of this last theme is provided by Wendy Griswold's exploration of the rising popularity of plays with trickster motifs in Jacobean theatre. Griswold (1986) shows that in the medieval period the main trickster had been an evil figure, perhaps the Devil. In the Jacobean theatre of the seventeenth century, however, the trickster role took on a new positive valence as a "gallant." The hero of the drama was often a young man who attained social advancement and wealth by means of his wits, often fooling and tricking those in authority. Griswold explains this transformation in terms of social change in seventeenth-century London and laws about inheritance. Property was usually inherited by the eldest son. This had led to a large-scale migration of younger sons to the capital in search of wealth and opportunity. The new style of drama, and new character roles, emerged in response to the needs (both real and imaginary) of this audience group. The young, downwardly mobile men could identify with a protagonist who used his wits to obtain money and status. Perceiving the popularity of this format, and keen to maximize their own income and reputation, dramatists increasingly wrote scripts aimed at this audience segment.

Technology provides an important constraint on the range of creative possibilities. A composition for a symphony orchestra would simply not be possible without the instruments on which the work is to be played. Likewise, it is unlikely that many novels would have been written were it not for the technology of printing. Closely linked to technology, its control and cost is the important area of research on the political economy of cultural production. In critical theory, the major focus here has been the power of major corporations to monopolize cultural production. The work of Horkheimer and Adorno (1972 [1947]) on the culture industries represents an early study of this kind (see pp. 41–3). The most common claim in this literature is that the search for profit leads to bland, conformist cultural output that takes few risks and seeks to maximize audience appeal. Certainly it is the case that a small number of companies control a large proportion of the market in areas like film and popular music. It is worth remembering, however, that the extent of oligopolistic control varies over time and between fields. A major factor influencing the extent of control is the cost of producing, distributing, and promoting cultural goods. A feature film, for example, requires more finance than a website. Nevertheless, the literature documents repeated efforts on the part of major corporations to control and profit from marginal fields of cultural production. Critical researchers have explored, for example, the ways that punk and other music trends have been co-opted and mainstreamed by major industries (see Hebdige 1979).

No matter how large the corporation or how big its budget, research has shown that an environment of **uncertainty** surrounds all cultural production. For example, every year produces its own multimillion-dollar Hollywood turkey: *Ishtar, Hudson Hawk, The Adventures of Pluto Nash, Gigli, Basic Instinct II*, and so on (the proof: did you, or anyone you know, pay to see any of these?). Although it is difficult to pick winners and losers, much activity by cultural producers is organized around reducing uncertainty. The most obvious strategy, as documented by Horkheimer and Adorno, has been to repli-cate formulaic products which have proven to be successful in the past (hence the ubiquitous sequel and prequel movie). Paul Hirsch (1972) suggests three other solu-tions to this question. What he calls "contact men" provide an interface between the rather anonymous corporation and concrete artists, retailers, and the media. They try to guarantee the favorable disposition of these parties. A simple example is an academic being taken out to lunch by an editor. This activity generates goodwill and may result in an improved manuscript. A second strategy is "overproduction." This involves flood-ing the market with plenty of contenders – rather like a turtle laying hundreds of eggs of which only a few will survive. The one book or CD in a thousand that becomes a bestseller will hopefully more than recoup the loss on the others. Finally, Hirsch sug-gests that corporations try to co-opt institutional gatekeepers outside of their direct control. We turn to these next.

Gatekeepers within and outside corporations select cultural products that they hope will "make it" and separate these out from those that will end up on the shelf. Crane stresses that this is a multistage process. For example, a record company must first decide to record and promote an artist. Subsequently radio stations must decide to play the disc. Both sets of gatekeepers, then, play a role in deciding the fate of the record-ing (as well as the audience, and perhaps even the performer!). Gatekeepers can be remarkably powerful in shaping the kind of work that is produced and published. For example, Wendy Griswold has documented the influence of British publishers on the rise of the Nigerian "village novel" as an entire genre in the second half of the twentieth century. This type of book was constructed around the theme of a traditional, timeless, idealized rural community. She suggests that the resulting imagined Nigerian com-munity arose thanks to "concerns of British editors who are themselves imagining what their readers want, and Nigerian authors seeking a market for their books and ideas" (1992: 719).

Cultural entrepreneurs, **patrons**, and **mediators** play a similar role to organiza-tional gatekeepers in promoting particular kinds of art. Typically, they will make use of their economic or social capital to sponsor particular forms of creative activity that they believe to be worthy or profitable. In a study of nineteenth-century Boston, for example, Paul DiMaggio (1982) looked at the way that members of social elites tried to bolster their prestige by supporting or controlling museums and symphony orches-tras. A result was that working-class culture was marginalized in the city. In a case study of French impressionism, Harrison White and Cynthia White (1965) point out that the traditionalist Academy spurned the new style. However, an emerging network of investors, critics, and dealers provided cultural credibility and financial viability for Monet and his colleagues, enabling them to continue to produce innovative works.

Gatekeepers and sponsors can both be usefully thought of as stakeholders in cultural production, as they share an interest in what is made or shown. The interactions between them are driven by complex dynamics. This is illustrated in a study of art exhibitions by Victoria Alexander (1996). She argues that the content of exhibitions is shaped by two sets of interests: those of external fund-providers and those of curators. Fund-providers such as corporations have an interest in "blockbuster" exhibitions that will maximize publicity. By contrast, affluent individuals tend to sponsor shows of art that match or dramatize their more personal tastes. Museum curators are the gatekeepers. They have to perform a juggling act in order to maintain what they (as experts) consider to be innovative or scholarly displays. For example, they might use the profits of a blockbuster to fund a smaller, specialist exhibition or try to upgrade the artistic credentials of a populist exhibition by slipping in some more challenging and confrontational artworks.

Alexander's study also points to the fact that **government policy** and **state institutions** can play a significant role in supporting cultural activity. These have increasingly replaced private patronage as the major source of finance for high-culture activities. Aside from direct grants to creators, the state supports venues for cultural display (museums, galleries, theatres, festivals) and other kinds of infrastructure. State involvement in the arts has traditionally been oriented around the promotion of high culture and the perpetuation of specific national traditions and industries. Such activities have become increasingly controversial. Many argue today that such funding decisions are arbitrary, or are influenced by the wishes of a small cultural elite, or that the works that are sponsored have no artistic merit. Consequently, the tendency over recent years has been to sponsor less elitist forms of cultural activity. Studies of state involvement often look at the processes of gatekeeping, patronage, influence, and labeling through which certain types of cultural production receive support and others are neglected. This field has increasingly come to overlap with more mainstream research on cultural policy, looking, for example, at questions of management, funding distribution, equity, and access.

Often forgotten in all this are the **social conditions of production**, that is to say, the creative milieu in which the artist works. These can have a major impact on cultural output. For example, Crane (1992: 113–15) and Becker (1982) note that the presence of networks, training academies, community organizations, established subcultures, and so on can often assist the production of cultural work, especially in peripheral and innovative spheres like jazz, alternative rock music, or experimental theatre. In the case of more mainstream cultural products, researchers usually document the importance of corporate organizational culture, profit motivations, and power relations as key factors of this kind shaping cultural output. In the study of fringe art worlds, by contrast, they tend to give emphasis to social networks, solidarities, and shared aesthetic codes.

Evaluation

Work exploring the production and reception of culture has several positive qualities. These can be summarized as follows:

- Causal links and processes can be clearly traced to specific institutions and actors.
- Rigorous methodologies are often used, especially in comparative audience research.
- Culture is treated as something concrete rather than as something that is reified and outside of human agency.
- Research projects tend to have clear research findings rather than open-ended theoretical speculations and assertions.
- There is a remarkable amount of consensus in the area, suggesting that it may be a field in which cumulative, core knowledge might be identified.

For these reasons, it is easy to see why the perspective has proven popular, especially among methodologically skilled cultural researchers. There are, however, two common criticisms of the area. The first is that cultural products often seem to be little more than the fallout of underlying social factors. The content of cultural production tends to be relentlessly accounted for with reference to the demands of audiences, the censorship of gatekeepers, technological advances, and so on. Such a position threatens the ability to theorize the autonomy of culture. Only when this sociological style of analysis is complemented by a robust model of aesthetic codes and structures, can culture become both *explicans* and *explicandum*. Griswold, for example, could achieve this by demonstrating the historical continuity of the trickster figure. Far from creating something entirely new, the playwrights of the Jacobean era adapted existing archetypes and narrative structures. Cultural forms themselves are thereby shown to be an important constraint on possibilities for cultural creativity (see also the discussion of Wuthnow, below).

A second concern is that the field tends to work with a particular, limited, definition of "culture." As we saw in the Preface to this book (pp. 1–4), and indeed throughout the text, the idea of culture refers to so much more than just "the arts" or creative products as they are conventionally defined. It can also include everyday life, ideologies, rituals, discourses, and so on. While those working in the area may justifiably prefer to stay focused on middle-range theories about concrete cultural phenomena, sympathetic outsiders suggest that the perspective needs to spread its wings. From this point of view, the next major challenge for production and reception theory is to be applied to wider contexts in cultural life. In concluding this chapter, we will look at three representative studies which contribute to this ongoing process and suggest ways in which ideas about production and reception can be extended beyond the exploration of "recorded culture" as is usually understood.

Beyond the Arts and the Media

We return first to the theory of media events advanced by Daniel Dayan and Elihu Katz (see pp. 85–6), who claim that the successful media event (televised major civic occasion) requires agreement and participation from organizers, broadcasters, and audiences. They argue: "The failure to reach consensus among the partners negotiating over the production of a media event may result either in cancellation of the broadcast or in one or another aberrant form of broadcast" (1992: 68).

Where there is a lack of enthusiasm from any of the parties, the event can fall flat. This is because the various stakeholders are required to cooperate in maintaining the correct performative genre. Organizers have to put on an event which is scripted to ceremonially enact core civic values, whether in solemn or celebratory mode. Broadcasters have to agree to treat the episode as an "event" and not just as "news." They need to suspend ordinary broadcasting schedules and provide affirming and reverential, rather than critical, commentary. Audiences need to switch into the mode of "festive viewing" and thereby demonstrate that the episode in question is indeed out of the ordinary. Their mass participation is also required in order to validate claims that the "event" has been successful – indeed, to demonstrate that anything taken to be important really took place at all.

Events are seen as failures when one or another of these groups fails to play its part. Broadcasters, for example, may refuse to cover a ceremony that the state has laid on or else treat it as another news item. Viewers may switch off in droves as yet another royal wedding takes place, or channel surf between the event and their favorite soap opera. Organizers, for their part, might fail to provide a ceremony that lives up to popular expectations. The model proposed by Dayan and Katz, then, is one that emphasizes the ways that not only media products, but also historically significant public events, can be thought of in terms of a production and reception of culture model. Just as importantly, we note in passing, they provide a basis for theorizing the autonomy of culture by insisting that such events have to follow a particular genre or script. All media events conform to one of three narrative structures: contest, conquest, or coronation. The agency of participants and broadcasters is restricted by the demands of each of these genres for a particular kind of story and mood. To broadcast a coronation as a contest would simply not make sense. Audiences, meanwhile, depend upon these genres to guide their reading and celebration of the civic occasion. Cultural production and innovation, therefore, are circumscribed by the available legitimate structures of meaning.

An analysis of the Vietnam Veterans Memorial by Robin Wagner-Pacifici and Barry Schwartz (1992) also demonstrates the wider applicability of themes relating to the production and reception of culture. In contrast to orthodox Durkheimian theory on ritual commemoration, they read the memorial as the product of a dialogue between producers and consumers, rather than as the outcome of some transcendental social need for unity and the expression of grief. According to Wagner-Pacifici and Schwartz, the memorial presented a "genre problem." Memorials usually commemorated victorious and triumphant wars. Yet the Vietnam War was widely seen as a tragedy and a failure. The process of constructing a memorial therefore involved cultural creativity, contestation, and negotiation. Getting the memorial built required activism from veterans' groups in order for the stigma of the war to be overcome. The original design contrasts with typical war memorials: it consists of black marble panels with the names of the dead written on them and is situated below ground level. Veterans' groups protested that the monument dishonored the fallen. Its design suggested there was something shameful about the war. As a result of their outcry, more traditional memorial elements were added – a statue of soldiers and a flagpole. The study by Wagner-Pacifici and Schwartz can be read as a traditional "production of culture" argument. It is, after all, about the creation of an element of recorded culture – a stone monument. Yet we would suggest that it goes further than this. As the memorial is a public symbol, they are able to use it as an index of collective memory and civic narrative. By looking at processes of production and reception, they can see how various groups in American society think about and come to terms with the past in the process of building and thinking about the memorial. The object of analysis, then, is not really the monument at all, but *ideas*, or (as Durkheim would have it) collective representations about the war, history, and American society.

Our final example takes us one step further on this path from the concrete object of recorded culture toward the production and reception of the abstract and ideal. In *Communities of Discourse*, Robert Wuthnow (1989) looks at three systems of ideas that challenged the status quo in their own day and have remained influential ever since – the Reformation, the Enlightenment, and Marxist socialism. In accounting for success and failure of these religious, philosophical, and political doctrines, he makes use of a raft of factors that would be familiar to anyone working in the production/reception of culture area. For example, he frames his analysis in terms of a "problem of articulation," arguing that "if cultural products do not articulate closely enough with their social settings," then audiences will see them as "irrelevant, unrealistic, artificial and overly abstract" (1989: 3). He also speaks about "environmental conditions" which provide "resources necessary to bring into being an innovative cultural movement" (1989: 7). Especially important are the "institutional contexts" (e.g., universities, newspapers) through which "producers of culture gain access to necessary resources, come into contact with their audiences, and confront the limitations posed by competitors and persons in authority" (1989: 7). Within this process, Wuthnow draws particular attention to the ways that ideologies are produced, selected, and finally institutionalized so that they become stable and enduring. In the case of the Reformation, these diverse background conditions included political transformations to the state as feudalism came to an end, urban growth and social unrest, the rise of print technology, patronage by powerful figures, and so on. They provided fertile conditions for cultural production and audiences attentive to the new messages.

Aware of the danger of social structural reductionism that can come from relentlessly invoking such factors, Wuthnow importantly argues that we also need to be able to understand the ways that "an ideology becomes at least partially free of contextual determination" (1989: 12). In order to do this, we need to think about the "discursive field" of the particular belief system, in particular the categories it creates and the courses of action it recommends. According to Wuthnow, constraints are imposed on these discursive possibilities by the internal structure of discourses themselves. Real-world problems and struggles have to be translated into the binary oppositions, narratives, and theoretical positions of texts. One cannot simply cook up any innovative discourse one wishes. In the case of the Reformation, secular struggles were translated into a religious idiom by Luther, with a binary rhetoric of good and evil, God and Satan structuring much of what was said.

In sum, Wuthnow's work suggests that a focus on the production and reception of culture can pay real dividends in the exploration of major systems of belief. Along with other work on the production of knowledge and ideas, such as sociological studies of science, it goes a long way toward demonstrating that these are never just free-floating abstractions. Their existence is always grounded in real actors, real institutions, and real historical settings. This is perhaps the most important lesson to be learnt from the theoretical tradition we have reviewed in this chapter.

Suggested Further Reading

Graeme Turner (2002 [1996]) provides an excellent summary of audience research as it is informed by British cultural studies. Diana Crane's book, *The Production of Culture* (1992), offers a succinct overview of the field and its major debates and is also to be recommended. Howard Becker's *Art Worlds* (1982) is surprisingly readable and is perhaps the closest thing to a classic text in the area. A characteristic of the field is that it tends to be relatively accessible to readers as it is broadly opposed to verbose "high theory." Thus the empirical studies cited here should not provide any real problems for readers once they are acquainted with the fundamental principles at play.

CHAPTER ELEVEN

Culture as Text:
Narrative and Hermeneutics

Today it is a commonplace to observe that culture or social life is like a "text" and that it has to be interpreted. For some perspectives, however, this dictum is more axiomatic than for others. Although it is central to many forms of structuralism and poststructuralism, an attention to the story-like qualities of social life is perhaps strongest in those theoretical approaches that are concerned with narrative and hermeneutics. In this chapter we focus on these. We begin by introducing some theoretical tools for interpreting stories and genre frames, before going on to look at the ways in which narrative analysis has been applied to wider social life. We then examine the challenge put forward by hermeneutics, and in particular the work of the anthropologist Clifford Geertz, before concluding with a look at one of the most recent narrative-centered theoretical frameworks, the Yale Strong Program in Cultural Sociology.

Structuralist Poetics

In chapter 6 we explored the forms of structural inquiry associated with the tradition that ran from Saussure to Lévi-Strauss. That approach, as we saw, centered on the analysis of the paradigmatic dimension of culture and took as its central tool the analysis of binary oppositions. When Lévi-Strauss looked at the Oedipus myth, for example, he had little interest in the "story" as the bearer of meaning. Rather, his primary concern was with the way that concepts could be plucked out of the narrative to uncover an underlying structure. Another significant current in structuralism, however, has been concerned with the investigation of narrative and the ways it is sustained by the sequential organization of signs. Roland Barthes asserted that we need to study syntagm as well as system (the paradigmatic), and in *S/Z* set about explaining how one particular story "worked." In *The Pleasure of the Text*, moreover, he argued that the story line was a major source of gratification for the reader, with its anticipations and denouements (see pp. 107–8).

When structuralists approach the analysis of narrative, especially conventional stories and literature, their activity is often given the name of **structuralist poetics**.

The central theme here is often not so much binary opposition, but rather plot, character, and genre. Advocates of the approach see it as a step toward a more "scientific" approach to literature, one which goes beyond traditional "evaluative" criticism and tries to set up value-free yardsticks for classifying and exploring texts. Within this tradition the work of Russian folklorist Vladimir Propp holds a canonical position, especially within the fields of literary criticism and folklore studies (Scholes 1974: 59).

Vladimir Propp

Vladimir Propp can be considered a true pioneer in the structural analysis of culture. Written in the 1920s, his (1968 [1928]) work *The Morphology of the Folktale* substantially predated that of Lévi-Strauss on myth. Propp's major interest was in the thematic organization of such popular, traditional stories. He noted certain similarities in the structure of the hundreds of tales he examined, even though the characters and precise events would vary from one to another. Propp argued that each narrative was made up of what he called "functions." These were elements of a story or plot made up from the action of a character. Propp claimed that there were never more than 31 functions in a tale and, more importantly, that they always appeared in the same order. Essentially, stories which looked very different on the surface (this one might be about a prince, that one about a woodcutter) had the same underlying structure. To give some idea of how this looks, here are the first six of Propp's "functions":

1   One of the members of a family leaves home.
2   An interdiction is addressed to the hero.
3   The interdiction is violated.
4   The villain makes an attempt at reconnaissance.
5   The villain receives information about his victim.
6   The villain attempts to deceive his victim in order to take possession of him or his belongings.

To get a feel for these functions, think about the story of "Little Red Riding Hood," who leaves her family, defies an interdiction not to enter the forest alone, is pursued and tricked by the wolf, and so on. Propp also noted that stories tended to have characters who fulfilled set roles as required by the system of functions. These were: the villain, the donor (provider), the helper, the princess (or other sought-after person) and her father, the dispatcher, the hero (seeker or victim), and the false hero. Propp suggests that it is irrelevant exactly who fills each of these roles in a given tale. What we should be looking at is the organization of stories in terms of deep, underlying commonalities rather than surface variation. Propp saw these superficial aspects of the tale as adding only charm and style to a given story rather than as being of great importance in themselves for folkloric analysis.

Like other structuralist inquiries, Propp's work demonstrates a powerful ability to uncover commonality amid apparent diversity. His particular achievement was to demonstrate that this regularity could exist in the sequential organization of stories. If there is a limitation to Propp's work it is that he was concerned mostly with the narrow study of the Russian folktale. It is not clear what wider applicability he saw arising from his findings. Several difficult questions remain to be answered. For example, does the structure of other kinds of story follow that of the folktale? How, if at all, does the structure of the folktale correspond to social forces and needs? Does the structure of the folktale indicate something beyond itself? With respect to these questions, we can detect a different emphasis in the work of Lévi-Strauss. The great French anthropologist was concerned to document the universality of the binary opposition, the need for mythologies to meditate on the dilemmas and contradictions of human existence, and links between mythology and the workings of the human mind. Propp's failure to address these bigger questions by settling for a more descriptive kind of analysis has allowed his work to be attacked as mere formalism. It has, however, provided an exemplar for structuralist poetics by substituting the aestheticism of traditional literary criticism with a more "scientific" and value-neutral mode of interpretation.

Northrop Frye

Propp was content to document the workings of the comparatively simple folktale. A major challenge for structuralist poetics has been to develop a perspective that can encompass narrative forms as they appear over a range of genres. Since the 1950s, the work of the Canadian theorist Northrop Frye has constituted the most ambitious attempt at constructing such a synthetic model. In *Anatomy of Criticism*, Frye (1971 [1957]) attempted to organize the whole of literature into a coherent framework or classification. The point of this was to move beyond the ethical and moralistic criticism of his era, which confused formal analysis with judgments about good or bad writing or the human values of the author. Frye drew in part on Aristotle's *Poetics* and suggested that structured relationships linked character, plot, and narrative genre over all forms of literature. He begins by asking what kinds of powers the characters have in various types of stories. Are they more or less powerful than ordinary people? He then goes on to ask if their powers are different in kind (supernatural) or merely in degree. These sorts of results allow Frye to construct a basic classification. In "myth," agents are superior in kind to us. These are gods and monsters with magical and miraculous powers. In "romance," the agents are superior in degree. They will be heroes capable of incredible feats of daring and courage. In "high mimesis" (note – **mimesis** means the copying or imitation of reality), such as epic stories, the characters are slightly more able than we are. They might be stronger or smarter than we can expect to be. In "low mimesis," the characters are pretty much the same as us. In the "ironic mode," the characters are inferior to us and we look down upon them. Frye argues that fiction has tended to move down the list over the past few centuries. In the religious world of the Middle Ages, myths and epic stories abounded. Now we live in a world where realism (low mimesis) and ironic despair abound in our literature. This is a perceptive observation. It replicates in the world of literary criticism the kind of point made by Weber's theory of disenchantment and secularization (see pp. 14–15).

As well as looking at character, Frye also attempted to theorize the links between genre and plot. He suggested that certain modes of literature tend to feature particular trajectories with respect to goals or aspirations. In what he calls "comic fictional modes" and Romance, for example, things usually get better. Even though the characters may experience a near-disaster at some stage, the story usually ends with a stroke of good fortune, such as a marriage, inheritance, or the death of the villain. Frye claims that the core message of such stories relates to the "integration of society" (1957: 43) and, as such, is broadly optimistic.

In tragedy, by contrast, events and circumstances move from good to bad. For example, Shakespeare's Othello starts off as the proud ruler of a prosperous city, and is married to the beautiful Desdemona. He ends up stripped of his rule and guilty of her murder. Far from being concerned with the possibility of social integration, tragedy tends to be more about "the exclusion of an individual . . . from a social group to which he is trying to belong" (1957: 39). Tragic plots, then, emphasize futility, fate, and individual isolation.

Frye's overall project is to put the study of narrative on a systematic and "scientific" footing by identifying deeper regularities that go beyond superficial distinctions in style, period, or characterization. While he has considerable sympathies with hermeneutic or interpretive approaches, his general ambition is to move the study of narrative away from subjectivism and toward a formal, comparative "archetypal criticism" of literature as a whole (1957: 342). For these reasons his project can be thought of as structural. As we will see later in this chapter, like other structuralisms, such an approach can be profitably adapted to sociological investigations as well as those pertaining to texts.

The critique of structural poetics

The approach of structuralist poetics, exemplified by Propp and Frye, has a number of strong suits. From a sociological point of view, it offers powerful evidence for understanding narratives as "social facts" which are subject to laws and empirical regularities of which authors and readers may be unaware. This allows for the possibility of constructing general theories and powerful analytic models with which to explore meanings in texts. By demonstrating the presence of structured regularities driving meaning, such an approach allows us to affirm the autonomy of culture. It also points to the dividends that can come from exploring characters and archetypes (e.g., the hero, the fool, the villain) or types of story (e.g., the morality play, the trickster story, the quest) which seem to have transcultural validity. This opens up important avenues for cross-cultural comparative research, especially in the fields of anthropology and folklore.

Structuralist poetics tends to work with the idea that fixed unambiguous meanings exist in texts and that these can be plucked out like currants from a bun. Critics assert that such an approach is too objectivist and clunky to capture the subtleties of narrative and meaning. It also neglects important questions about the role of power in the construction of texts and symbol systems. Finally, they point to the active work of readers and the need to understand the ambiguities of texts, both printed and social. The work of Derrida and Barthes has provided important ammunition for such commentaries. However, perhaps the most influential early statement of this position comes from Mikhail Bakhtin, who worked in Russia around the same time as Propp.

Mikhail Bakhtin

Bakhtin's reputation centers around two main concepts: the **dialogic** and **carnival** (we discuss this second term later in this chapter). The idea of the dialogic (see Bakhtin 1981) taps into the creative and relational aspects of the novel and was used by Bakhtin to critique Saussurian approaches to the symbolic. He dubbed such a perspective "abstract objectivism," as it failed to take into account the ways that the meanings of works can change over time or vary according to the specific cultural context within which the reader was situated. According to Bakhtin, structuralist understandings could only support a fixed or **monologic** view of meaning which framed the reader as passive. At the same time Bakhtin was careful to avoid the trap of what he called "individualistic subjectivism," which asserted that meaning was simply the product of personal mental processes (on this point the structuralists would agree with him).

The model of the dialogic proposed by Bakhtin marked out a kind of middle ground between these objectivist and subjectivist positions. He suggested that individual subjectivity and consciousness are made up of signs and meanings which are derived from our wider culture. (If this seems implausible, try thinking of what it would be like to be you without any language or cultural knowledge in your brain. Arguably, there would be nobody home!) According to Bakhtin, when we read a text there is an encounter between its objective signs and meanings and those that are subjective and interior to the individual. There is a **border zone** where the two sets of signs intermingle in a kind of dialogue, with the text producing a counter-statement from the reader in the act of interpretation. Meaning is not just something that exists in a word on a page; it is relational and depends on the interplay of text and reader.

MIKHAIL BAKHTIN (1895–1975)

Bakhtin was born into a middle-class Russian family. He studied philosophy and philology at St Petersburg University. Although he was the author of several books, few of these were published under his own name; for complex political reasons, many were attributed to other authors within the Soviet academy, and others were suppressed or amended. This has since created confusion among Bakhtin scholars, with a number of arguments taking place about the authorship of some texts and passages. It is also not clear whether Marxist elements in his writing reflect his own views or were bolted on in order to make his books politically acceptable to Soviet elites. During the 1930s, Bakhtin was exiled to Kazakhstan, where he worked as a bookkeeper. He was lucky to escape Stalin's purges and the German invasion during World War Two – many of his colleagues were not so fortunate. During the 1960s he was "rehabilitated," and before he died in 1975 was recognized worldwide as a leading cultural theorist.

References: Holquist 1981; Morris 1994

Bakhtin also stressed the role of social/historical contexts in shaping the meanings of words and signs. He suggested that these would shift over time and between social classes. As a result, words and signs would often be ambiguous and characterized by **multiaccentuality**. He saw this as a good thing. It ensured that culture was dynamic and had an inbuilt capacity for flexibility and change. Notwithstanding the empirical reality of multiaccentuality, Bakhtin suggested that there are efforts to ideologically fix the meanings of words by dominant groups. This would enforce a unitary language and interpretation known as **monoglossia**. However, social and historical forces, such as class stratification, usually worked to fragment meaning and provide alternative symbolic frames. The concept of **heteroglossia** taps into this idea of multiple sign systems and context-dependent readings surrounding a given concept. A speech act or written text could expect to encounter a tension between the centripetal meanings that allowed for mutual understanding, and the more centrifugal forces that tended toward heteroglossia. He writes: "Every concrete utterance of a speaking subject serves as a point where centrifugal as well as centripetal forces are brought to bear" (Bakhtin 1981: 272). Bakhtin looked upon heteroglossia, too, as a good thing. He thought it encouraged reflexivity about the role of language, helped generate dialogue, and desta-bilized the hegemonic meanings that went along with monoglossia. Consequently, language was rendered rich, unpredictable, and dynamic: "The word, directed toward its object, enters a dialogically agitated and tension-filled environment of alien words, value judgements and accents, weaves in and out of complex interrelationships, merges with some, recoils from others, intersects with yet a third group: and all this may cru-cially shape discourse, may leave a trace in all its semantic layers, may complicate its expression and influence its entire stylistic profile" (1981: 276).

What is particularly attractive about Bakhtin is that he is able to theorize a role for the reader and local contexts, while still acknowledging the constraining power of a collective language and symbolism on the interpretative process. The vision of words and signs moving around in complex and active patterns contrasts markedly with the rather stolid vision of Saussure's structuralism. In tone and substance it has a rather closer resemblance to poststructural theories of discursive fields, which emphasize com-plexity, multivocality, power, and ambivalence. It is hardly surprising, therefore, that Bakhtin has been enthusiastically championed in the field of poststructural literary criticism.

Umberto Eco – The Role of the Reader

The work of the Italian semiotician Umberto Eco (1984) provides another avenue for exploring these questions, offering a critique of orthodox structural poetics from within the camp. Eco is broadly sympathetic to the orthodox structuralist analysis of texts, but tries to combine this with an attention to openness, ambiguity, and the readerly. His perspective, then, is both appreciative and critical.

Eco begins by pointing out that "the author has to assume that the ensemble of codes he relies upon is the same as that shared by his possible reader. The author has thus to foresee a possible reader" (1984: 7). According to Eco, the codes and stylistic conventions used in a text will not only identify and appeal to this **model reader**, but also serve to construct them by offering actual readers clues as to how they should approach the text. Distinctive turns of phrase at the start of a book (e.g., "Once upon a time") can help the reader to understand the genre and therefore the kind of reading stance they should adopt.

Eco furthermore distinguishes between **closed texts** and **open texts**, a contrast that is broadly reminiscent of that between the readerly and writerly proposed by Barthes (see p. 107). The former tend to be populist works that "aim at arousing a precise response on the part of more or less precise empirical readers . . . at pulling the reader along a predetermined path . . . [and are] structured according to an inflexible project" (1984: 8). Although such texts can be read in diverse ways and offer possibilities for infinite semiosis, the codes within them generally work to close off alternative interpretations. By contrast, open texts are designed to generate multiple interpretations. They presume a reader who is "able to master different codes and eager to deal with the text as with a maze of many issues" (1984: 9). Ambiguity, irony, and complexity are central features of texts like these. We often find such characteristics in avant-garde literature, including Eco's own bestselling novels. In looking at the role of the reader in both open and closed texts, Eco highlights the role of anticipation, inferential leaps, fantasy, identification, and problem-solving activity, suggesting that successful narratives work to stimulate these sorts of processes by means of the skillful deployment of cultural codes. Without such active work, texts would become hopelessly dull and literal.

What Eco is suggesting then, is:

- We should not think of semiotic and narrative codes as simply the products of a transcendental cultural logic or grammar. Rather, they arise as the result of textual strategies through which real authors try to communicate with imagined readers.
- Readers have considerable freedom in the interpretative process. In exploring meaning construction, we have to look at this as well as at the structural codes of the text.
- Texts will vary in the extent to which they invite or try to foreclose the reader's interpretative freedom. We can classify them accordingly, or study the ways in which they achieve this end.

An illustration of this distinctive approach can be found in Eco's celebrated discussion of Ian Fleming's James Bond books. In a manner similar to Propp or Lévi-Strauss, Eco argues that we can identify a key semiotic structure in these closed texts. Although each is about a different scenario, all share a common core. This has two dimensions. First, a series of binary oppositions such as Bond/M, Bond/Villain, Woman/Villain, Loyalty/Disloyalty, Moderation/Excess, and so on. These structure the various scenes, encounters, and characters of the book. By the end of the book there is a resolution of these binaries, with one attaining triumph over the other. Bond will beat the villain, the villain will kill the woman, loyalty will defeat disloyalty, and so on. Secondly, the plot follows a predictable "sequence of moves" (1984: 156), much like Propp's Russian folktales. According to Eco (1984: 156), it goes more or less as follows:

1   M gives a task to Bond.
2   Villain does something.
3   Bond and Villain have first encounter.
4   Woman shows herself to Bond.
5   Bond seduces Woman.
6   Villain captures Bond.
7   Villain tortures Bond.
8   Bond beats Villain.
9   Bond, convalescing, enjoys Woman, who then dies.

Where Eco moves beyond structuralist formalism is in extending his discussion to include the impact of these codes on the reader. He suggests that the powerfully drawn binary oppositions and stereotyped villains appeal to "popular standards" (1984: 162). This is especially the case "in a time of international tensions . . . [when] . . . popular notions of wicked Communism exist beside those of the unpunished Nazi criminal" (1984: 162). By skillfully manipulating the "archetypal elements that have proved successful in fairy tales" (1984: 161), but in disguising this use and placing it in a modern context, Fleming taps into reservoirs of mythological thinking, allowing ordinary readers to enjoy the stories as they would a fable or myth. There is also a pleasure to be derived from encountering a story with a predictable plot. According to Eco, readers can relax when they know their final destination, and like to see how the author will take them there. He likens the books to a game by the Harlem Globetrotters basketball team. We know they will win – the fun is in watching the virtuosity with which they do it. This device, he suggests, "is typical of an escape machine geared for the entertainment of the masses" (1984: 161).

Eco also accounts for the appeal of Bond among a very different type – intellectuals such as himself. This group will be more detached from the immediate pleasure of the text, preferring to reflect on the skill of its construction. They enjoy the "craftsmanship" of Fleming's novels, the bravura with which he manipulates simple codes (such as those outlined above), and the stylistic flair of his writing.

Narrative and Social Process

For the most part, the analysis of narrative has been an activity of literary theorists interested in the study of texts. The field has a lot to say about cultural content and, with its robust and structural models, it provides a basis for theorizing the autonomy of cultural forms. It also has quite a bit to say about agency (in the reader and author). Yet it has almost nothing to say about how narrative intersects with broader social life. There is, however, another more sociological literature on narrative. Broadly speaking, we can detect three core themes:

1   *Studies of genres and audiences.* These aim to explain why particular narrative forms appeal to particular groups, or how these become institutionalized and widespread. Much of this literature is in the area of the production and reception of culture (see

chapter 10). The focus here tends to be on literary, media, or artistic products which have identifiable creators and consumers. Such studies often highlight processes of negotiation and interpretation that take place within defined social and historical contexts or the role of mediating institutions. They may also point to links between particular narrative forms and social or ideological function. The work of Griswold (1986) and Radway (1991 [1984]) is representative of this kind of approach (see pp. 169, 163–4). As this literature has already been discussed in chapter 10, we will not consider it further here.

2   *Explorations of narrative in qualitative methodology.* This literature has grown out of in-depth interview studies and, particularly, feminist and interactionist investigations of personal experiences that are informed by critical or poststructural theory (Reissman 1993). It is often argued that social researchers need to retrieve the forgotten voices and stories that have been excluded by positivist, mainstream social research. The emerging literature on autoethnography (see, e.g., Ellis 2004) – which is a form of ethnography wherein the author, endeavoring to fully situate herself with respect to the external object of research, explores personal narratives that shed light on her interest in and possible biases regarding the research topic – is perhaps the most recent form of this critique. While important and interesting, this approach tends to be more concerned with the research process and epistemology than with theorizing narrative forms or their social impacts. For this reason, it is not covered any further here.

3   *Studies of the narrative aspects of social and political life.* Investigations here think of social and historical events as being shaped by discourses, and point out that these often have narrative dimensions. This is because people and institutions generate stories about the world in order to make sense of it. The aim of analysis here is to map out these stories, theorize them, and trace their implications. We turn next to a brief look at some representative work of this kind.

Victor Turner and social drama

Victor Turner's (1974, 1986) work is an important point of reference for those who wish to indicate the narrative or fictive dimensions of social process in the "real world." Turner saw social life as a kind of performance characterized by imagination, play, and creativity. He suggests that although meanings are often applied post-hoc in the stories we tell about historical events (e.g., in historical stage drama), they can also be seen to influence the activities of concrete actors involved in concrete events. He argued that "meaning is not mere cognitive hindsight but something existentially emergent from the entanglement of persons" and pointed out that "narratives become scripts or arguments to be used by the instigators of new sequences" (1986: 33). In short, social life is storied in various ways and can be often thought of as a **social drama**.

In his own writings Turner focused on the ways that social dramas seemed to be processually structured. He suggests that they often exhibit plot-like characteristics and "a regular course of events which can be grouped in successive phases" (1986: 34). In his research, Turner was most concerned with crisis. He argued that it was characterized by four phases, and that the form was "universal . . . though it may be culturally elaborated in different ways in different societies" (1986: 105):

1 *Breach* involved the public violation of a particular rule or community standard.
2 *Crisis* was a period of social schism when people take sides. This can take on liminal characteristics (see pp. 74, 76–7) with established political and cultural orders subject to question.
3 *Redress* takes place as efforts at conflict resolution and arbitration come into play. Symbolic sacrifice and scapegoating may also occur.
4 *Reintegration* involves the offending social group being joined again to mainstream society, or else "the recognition and legitimation of irreparable schism" (1986: 35).

Turner emphasizes the ways that smaller narratives play a role in each of these phases. For example, judicial process during the "redress" phase will involve testimony from defendants and witnesses. From these a story will emerge as to how the schism came about. It will provide raw material for discussions on motivation, responsibility, and moral justification. Moreover, the entire episode will eventually become the subject of storytelling activity, as the "empirical social drama may continue both as an entertainment and a metasocial commentary on the lives and times of the given community" (1986: 39). This story may, in turn, influence future actors in future social crises.

The narrative analysis of politics

Perhaps the best use of Turner's ideas is by Robin Wagner-Pacifici (1986). In *The Moro Morality Play*, she applies the concept of the social drama to events surrounding the kidnapping and eventual death of Italian Prime Minister Aldo Moro during the 1970s. What was unusual about this event was that the sequence predicted by Turner did not eventuate. Events seemed to become stuck at the stage of "crisis," with neither reintegration nor legitimation of the position of the terrorists. Wagner-Pacifici argues that Moro was eventually killed by the Red Brigade thanks to a "morality-play" narrative falling into place in the Italian public sphere. This tended to see things in black-and-white terms. Goodies were goodies, baddies were baddies, and there should be no deals between them.

A possible problem with Victor Turner's work is that it tends to depict movement through the stages of the social drama as inevitable. A notable feature of Wagner-Pacifici's book is to highlight not only the possibility of an incomplete sequence, but also to foreground the need for human agency and strategy in order for a resolution to come about. She documents attempts that were made to build up and break down confrontational frameworks, to bring about negotiations, or prevent compromise. The persistence of genre frames and the propagation of narratives, then, depends on active work by real people.

While Turner's work on social drama represents the most developed approach to analyzing the impact of narrative on public life, Northrop Frye's structuralist poetics (which we discussed above) is now being realized to offer untapped potential. Philip

Smith (2005) applied a model derived from Frye's *Anatomy of Criticism* to Western media and civil discourses on Arab leaders. The analysis focused on the way that the United States was prepared to support a war against Saddam Hussein and Iraq in the early 1990s and then again in 2003, but opposed military intervention against Colonel Nasser's regime at the time of the Suez Crisis in 1956. In objective terms, the three situations seemed remarkably similar, involving oil, Arabs, and military/geopolitical threats, yet foreign policy and public opinion outcomes had differed radically. The answer, at least in part, lay in the genres used to understand or frame each event by the media and public sphere. During the 1950s, Nasser was depicted in a heroic and romantic narrative by influential sources like *Time* magazine. Themes of ascent saw him bringing development and independence to his country. Biographical stories framed a rise to wisdom and made use of romantic plot devices, like the "trial" or "ordeal," to account for a character transformation from impetuous youth to wise and charismatic leader. A military conflict emerged between Britain, France, and Egypt in 1956, when Nasser nationalized and took control of the Suez Canal. However, events were seen in terms of "low mimesis" in the United States. The nationalization was understood in terms of a "business as usual" motif. Alongside the pre-existing romantic frame, this provided cultural legitimacy for negotiations and prudence rather than intervention, war, and loss of life. In the better-known cases of the 1990–1 Gulf War and the 2003 Iraq War, a different genre was established early on in the United States. In the run-up to the Gulf War, an apocalyptic framework depicted Saddam Hussein as an evil, Hitler-like figure, his army as powerful, and his invasion of Kuwait as a danger to world peace and security. In 2003, the apocalyptic genre returned, only this time narrative details of the threat had changed to Saddam Hussein's alleged links to Al-Qaeda terrorists (who were responsible for the attacks on the United States on September 11, 2001) and the possession of weapons of mass destruction. These more elevated (high-mimetic) representations of events could justify human sacrifice, thus providing the cultural groundwork for war that had been absent during the Suez crisis. Smith constructs a general framework for understanding national responses to conflict according to narrative genres and the scale of mimetic intensity where low mimetic, realist genres (protagonist and antagonist remain relatively close, actor motivations are mundane, and the object of struggle is understood as local) are at one end and high mimetic, apocalyptic genres (greater moral distancing of protagonist and antagonist, the idealization of actor motivations, and the globalization of the object of struggle) are at the other (Smith 2005: 24).

Ronald Jacobs (1996) has also used Frye's approach to narrative alongside Habermas's ideas about the public sphere (see pp. 43–4) to explore the Rodney King crisis. In 1991 the African-American motorist Rodney King was stopped by the police and beaten. An amateur cameraman captured the event and the tape was aired on television, creating an outcry about police brutality and racism. The police officers were tried in 1992, but were found not guilty of any crime. Riots resulted in protest at the decision, with a widespread loss of faith in the police, city hall, and justice system. Eventually, reforms were made, and the Police Chief resigned, thus resolving the crisis. Jacobs notes that diverse narrative frames helped people to make sense of events and evaluate the situation, and that "both meanings and outcomes depend on the interaction between events and their narrative understandings" (1996: 1267). While all agreed that it was a "crisis," he writes that "the Rodney King crisis was socially constructed as several different problems in several different public spheres" (1996: 1266).

Drawing on Frye's ideas about character and plot, Jacobs indicates the ways that various players, such as the public, the mayor, and the Police Chief Daryl Gates, were framed as heroes and villains in both mainstream and African-American media. He argued that the contending narratives could be classified in terms of two main genres: tragedy and romance. Tragic narratives tended to focus on entrenched racism in the police, white indifference, or insincerity and the existence of an irreconcilable split in the community. These suggested that the problem indicated by the Rodney King beating and the acquittal was permanent. Romantic narratives pointed to the future with optimism. They saw the crisis as an opportunity for the cleansing of racism and a wider community renewal.

Like Wagner-Pacifici and Smith, Jacobs urges that narratives are far more than just commentaries on events. Rather, they have an impact as genre "influences social outcomes because of the way it informs competing expectations" (1996: 1267). In the case of the Rodney King crisis, the romantic narrative that carried the day in the mainstream press was a driving force in allowing politicians to legitimate and implement reform strategies. It suggested that their activity would be successful, worthwhile, and meet with public approval.

Bakhtin on the Carnivalesque

Aside from tracing the implications of particular narrative frames for particular events, like the studies above, it is also possible to begin with a genre or narrative form and explicate its less specific, transhistorical, social, or political consequences. Perhaps the greatest work in this field is Mikhail Bakhtin's *Rabelais and his World* (1984). Here, Bakhtin situates the work of medieval writer Rabelais (and later authors like Shakespeare and Cervantes) within a broader social context. According to Bakhtin, writers like Rabelais were able to develop their genre by drawing upon a preexisting folk tradition of storytelling and everyday behavior. Using a mixture of literary and historical data, Bakhtin highlights the ways that the aesthetics of the popular carnival infuse the work of Rabelais. This focused on the sensual, the grotesque, the embodied, and the excessive, and so great attention in the genre is paid to prodigious feats of eating, excreting, strength, laughter, and sexuality. Bakhtin looks upon the genre favorably, suggesting that it is politically subversive because it celebrates ambiguity over hierarchy, the debased over the exalted, the open and public over the secretive and official. He writes: "The genres we have examined . . . have . . . great power of travesty . . . bringing an atmosphere of freedom, frankness and familiarity . . . they helped to create an absolutely gay, frank, and fearless speech that was necessary for the attack undertaken by Rabelais against Gothic darkness" (1984: 195). For Bakhtin, carnival affirms the importance of solidarity among ordinary people and the vitality of their popular culture. He claims, for example: "We have tried to understand Rabelais precisely as part of the stream of folk culture, which at all stages of its development has opposed the official culture of the ruling classes and evolved its own conception of the world, its own forms and imagery (1984: 473).

As the quotations just provided might suggest, it can be argued that Bakhtin's analysis of the carnival genre is rather value-laden. And although he celebrates the carnivalesque as a form of popular resistance to authority in all ages, he fails to consider in a serious way the limited political possibilities of such undirected popular activity. In its favor, the analysis stands out as a pioneering attempt to capture, via a "thick description" (see the discussion of Geertz below), a particular mode of social and cultural life. Along with the work of de Certeau (see pp. 154–5), it has exerted a considerable influence on the efforts of British cultural studies to valorize popular culture and popular pleasure as a form of coded resistance to authority. Students of ritual process have also made profitable use of Bakhtin's work, pointing to links between the carnivalesque and Victor Turner's ideas about liminality (see pp. 76–7).

Hermeneutics

There are strong affinities between the hermeneutic tradition in social science and those advocating the centrality of narrative. **Hermeneutics** as an area is concerned with issues of meaning and mutual understanding. Traditionally, it has tended to be subjective, humanistic, individualistic, aesthetic, philosophical, and phenomenological in orientation. In the context of literary criticism, for example, it has been centrally concerned with theorizing whether the reader can recover the meanings and thoughts held by the author. Narrative theory, by contrast, has tended to be more objectivist in orientation. As we have seen in the first part of this chapter, there is a focus on the text, its form, structures, and social implications, with no interest whatsoever in the subjective intentions or mental state of the author. More recently, hermeneutics has taken on board lessons from structuralism, poststructuralism, and narrative theory, and so the boundaries between hermeneutics and other forms of cultural inquiry have begun to be broken down.

It is often forgotten that important early arguments to this same effect were made by Wilhelm Dilthey, a German philosopher whose work bridged the fields of historical/textual criticism and social philosophy in the late nineteenth century. He was to exert an influence on Max Weber's writings on *Verstehen* (see pp. 12–13), which can also be seen as an important milestone in the translation of hermeneutic philosophy into social science. Dilthey argued that interpretation was not just about getting inside someone's head, but could also involve establishing the intellectual situation and social milieu within which they were working. In other words, hermeneutics was compatible with a broader cultural enquiry. More recent intellectual heirs of this perspective include Hans-Georg Gadamer and Paul Ricoeur, who draw on existentialism and phenomenology in developing theories and methodologies of interpretation. They place a central emphasis on reconstructing the systems of meaning that informed the act of writing. While some of these would be personal and psychological, others can be located in a broader, publicly available culture which the author would have drawn upon in creating a text. Reconstructing these frameworks can play a vital role in establishing a framework or **horizon of interpretation** through which the text can approached and understood with some accuracy by the reader. Our readings of Shakespeare, for example, are likely to be better served by knowledge of Elizabethan manners, customs, stagecraft, class structures, and linguistic conventions than by a speculative effort to get inside of the immortal bard's head. The arguments proposed by Gadamer and Ricoeur provide important philosophical groundwork for legitimating hermeneutic inquiry in the social sciences. Yet the largest single influence has been the work of the anthropologist Clifford Geertz and his efforts to read society as a text.

Clifford Geertz

In his younger days Geertz was a student of Talcott Parsons. As his career progressed, he moved away from Parsonian theory. This in itself was not uncommon. What was unusual was the way that Geertz did this. As we saw in chapter 2, most critics of Parsons argued that he was too cultural and that his model of society overemphasized the role of culture. In *The Interpretation of Cultures* Geertz (1975 [1973]) took another path. He claims there that Parsons was not cultural enough and went on to outline an alternative vision.

In "Ideology as a Cultural System" (1975: 193ff.), Geertz suggested that Parsons's model tended to understand culture as a response to social strains and as a mechanism for dealing with them (see chapter 2). For Geertz, this provided a rather limited understanding of the role and power of culture and had little more than "the most rudimentary conception of the processes of symbolic formation" (1975: 207). In contrast, he argued that culture is an active and constitutive dimension of social life rather than just a dull mechanism for ensuring social integration. He sees it as a providing "symbolic templates" or "blueprints" through which people can make their world meaningful on both cognitive and emotional levels (1975: 216–17).

In thinking through the implication of this shift, Geertz began to move away from the Parsonian vocabulary of "norms" and "values" for describing cultural life, and worked instead on a richer understanding of the stuff of culture. And so it was that during the 1960s Geertz came to an understanding of culture as an incredibly complex texture of signs, symbols, myths, routines, and habits that cried out for a hermeneutic approach. He writes, for example, that "man is an animal suspended in webs of significance he himself has spun. I take culture to be those webs, and the analysis of it to be therefore not an experimental science in search of law but an interpretive one in search of meaning" (1975: 5).

The view Geertz proposes here is clearly a majestic and enthralling one. Culture is all around us and invades every aspect of life. It is at once concrete and diffuse, deep and superficial. If this is the case, though, then what kind of method will allow us to tap into and capture this complexity and texture? Geertz (1975: 3ff.) famously proposes that the answer lies in the hermeneutics of **thick description**. The method attempts to "draw large conclusions from small, but very densely textured facts" (1975: 28). In other words, there is to be a concerted interpretative and ethnographic focus on small, real-time events, rather than a grandiose effort at "discovering the Continent of Meaning and mapping out its bodiless landscape" (1975: 20). Clearly, Geertz is attacking the kind of structuralist work advocated by Lévi-Strauss here. He asserts that analysis should be grounded in the mucky data of lived experience, with the cultural theorists making the effort to capture and textually reproduce the threads of meaning that inform the social action in specific contexts.

Doing thick description requires the analyst to write in such a way as to capture the workings and rhythms of the cultural system on the page. The reader is to be drawn in by the wealth of detail and provided with a sense of "being there" that is both intellectual and emotional. In describing the Balinese cockfight, for example, Geertz (1975: 412ff.) provides vivid and compelling descriptions of the birds, their owners, the gamblers, the spectators, and the fighting activity. He also talks us through the system of symbols and emotions that informs the ritual gathering and the actions of the participants. The overall effect is more like a novel than a conventional, dry, and dispassionate anthropological account. It is as if he is trying to win the reader over, and bring us round to seeing the world in Balinese terms, by offering a set of Balinese spectacles with which to see. As he puts it, "societies, like lives, contain their own interpretations. One has only to learn how to gain access to them" (1975: 453).

Geertz's great achievement is to alert us to the textual qualities of cultural life and to call upon cultural theorists to provide rich and persuasive detail in their accounts. By contrast to Geertz's eloquent writing, many other approaches toward culture can look crude, formalistic, and robotic. Some questions have been asked, however, about his general approach. The technique of thick description requires considerable writing ability – and social scientists are not often praised for this skill! Geertz's approach may also seem "unscientific" to some readers. It can look impressionistic or unsystematic (see Crapanzano 1986: 72). Just as good novels refuse any simple interpretation, so Geertz's anthropological accounts afford tantalizing glimpses of alien symbolic orders, but never offer a concise punchline. After reading the same cockfight essay, two people will likely disagree about the key features of Balinese culture, even if both feel that Geertz has taught them a great deal about it. Related to this literary delivery is Geertz's reluctance on occasion to make use of general theory or attempt to construct general models. This tendency can lead to events being explained in purely local, and therefore somewhat relativistic and tautological, terms (see Alexander 1987). The cockfight, Geertz shows us, can be understood as an exemplary product of Balinese culture once we really understand the textures and themes of that way of life. Is this really surprising? If we are primarily interested in the unique qualities of each setting, then Geertz's approach has much to offer. But if we think cultural theory is about creating models and templates that can be used to explain diverse phenomena in varying cultural environments, then a thick description needs to be combined with other, less culture-bound interpretive frames.

A final comment on Geertz relates to his impact on the discipline of anthropology. Geertz is a modernist in that he believes anthropology to be a discipline that can generate improved understandings and interpretations. This, after all, is the task at the center of the hermeneutic agenda. In his vision, the theorist is an interpreter, translating the meaningful worlds of the culture they study into the idiom of their readers. Yet his writings have proven to be a crucial steppingstone between conventional ethnography and the rise of a postmodern, deconstructivist movement in anthropology. Geertz's work, after all, highlighted the fact that anthropology was a textual practice rather than a "scientific" one. There are other convergences with the postmodern agenda, too. Geertz's embrace of explanation at the level of the "local" is consistent with postmodern calls for the end of grand narratives and grand theory. Moreover, his methodology of thick description unwittingly subverts received wisdom about the omniscience of the anthropologist's eye. While continuing to privilege his own interpretation, Geertz also suggests that thick description can embrace multiple perspectives held by actors in a given setting. When combined with his emphasis on the centrality of writing to anthropology, this idea was to prove more dangerous than he realized. A little over a decade after the publication of *The Interpretation of Cultures*, scholars influenced by postmodernism, poststructuralism, and standpoint epistemology were pushing the envelope and claiming that there was no single "truth" that could be uncovered by anthropological research or writing.

The landmark collection of essays entitled *Writing Culture* (Clifford and Marcus 1986) saw various authors argue that their disciplinary knowledge was inextricably bound up with techniques of representation. Anthropological texts could be relativized as a form of creative, even fictional, writing. The focus of attention shifted inwards from the "tribe" to the "text" with particular attention given to the tropes and narrative devices through which these constructed expert authority. Consistent with critical poststructural and postmodern theories (see chapter 14), power relations were held to be central to knowledge construction, with the expert vision of the anthropologists and the "truth" of their texts exposed as a partial reflection of colonialism, sexism, and so on. James Clifford, perhaps the most important advocate of this perspective, writes that "the poetic and the political are inseparable, that science is in, not above, historical and linguistic processes" (1986: 2). In this vision, ethnographic texts are "inherently partial." They present only a particular vision of what is really going on and can never transcend their own cultural bias. No matter how good the writing, the ethnographer will only be able to present a particular interpretation of reality that is marked by exclusions, absences, and rhetorical choices. The upshot of this vision was a more dialogical understanding of the research and writing process with an accompanying epistemological shift. Culture was no longer "out there" waiting to be recorded. Rather, it was seen as something that was actively constructed through the activities of the ethnographer. Clifford, for example, writes that "culture is not an object to be described, neither is it a unified corpus of symbols and meanings that can be definitively interpreted. Culture is contested, temporal, emergent. Representation and explanation – both by insiders and outsiders – is implicated in this emergence" (1986: 19). What is required, then, is a study of representations and the ways that these fabricate the reality that they purport to describe. Culture can now be seen as a field of contesting representations and discourses that struggle for recognition, authority, and voice.

The shift from Geertz's "thick description" toward the style of work embodied in *Writing Culture* is typical of the fate of hermeneutics in general. While it remains an important intellectual field, it has frequently found itself outpaced and colonized by the newer interpretative possibilities offered by poststructuralism and postmodernism. In chapters 13 and 14, we explore in more detail their impact on cultural theory. Before we move along, though, we need to discuss an emerging approach which takes a different path out of Geertz from that adopted by poststructuralist and postcolonial anthropology. The Yale Strong Program taps into Geertz's emphasis on narrative and description, but endeavors to blend those tools with elements taken from Durkheimian theory and structuralism. The result is an effort at systematic cultural theory that resists the poststructuralist idea that culture and representation are simply reducible to power.

Yale Strong Program in Cultural Sociology

The phrase "strong program" originates with the approach to the study of scientific knowledge championed by scholars such as David Bloor and Barry Barnes, who argue that science should be understood not simply as the business of discovering the truth of the natural world, but as an eminently cultural practice informed by eminently cultural conventions and structures. For Bloor and his colleagues, it is not just bad science that is marked by the cultural; correct science is equally immersed in it, and we need to understand precisely how in order to understand more fully science's place in human activity. What the Yale Strong Program does is take this perspective and apply it to the discipline of sociology more broadly. As Bloor and his colleagues reject the simple determination of scientific knowledge by the natural world alone, so Jeffrey Alexander and his colleagues reject the determination of the content of culture by social structure alone. The central theoretical principles of the Yale Strong Program can be summed up as follows:

- a commitment to cultural autonomy from power and social structure;
- an effort to move away from the systems-level explanation of a Parsonian variety with a focus on cultural pragmatics, public performance, and contingency;
- the use of theoretical influences combining Geertz with strands such as Durkheim, structuralism, and Victor Turner so as to generate more generalizable theory;
- a belief that societal rationalization as described by authors like Weber and Foucault has been incomplete – social life is never fully rational but remains deeply meaningful and often mysterious, with eruptions of the sacred and ritual;
- the belief in the role of civil society and civil discourse as a pivotal domain for both cultural struggles and solidarity formation.

With this theoretical arsenal, Alexander has taken on, among other topics, 9/11, the Holocaust, and the Watergate crisis, demonstrating how the narrative structures of these events emerge and how control of the means of symbolic production affects precisely what kinds of narratives emerge as dominant. The raw event that was the mass extermination of Jews in Nazi Germany, for example, requires a narrative structure to become "the Holocaust." The initial narrative informing this event is broadly progressive and driven by the American state's near complete control of the definition of events. It locates the importance of the Jewish killings as one of a number of evils beneath the aegis of a broader Nazi evil that has been defeated, thus framing the killings within a context of "liberation" from a conquered enemy (Alexander 2004: 38, 40). The new and radically evil category of "the Holocaust" emerges as new groups (critics of the conduct of the Allies in World War Two, the nation of Israel, Jewish political and cultural groups in the United States and elsewhere) gain access to the **means of symbolic production** and enlarge the circle of perpetrators of the deeds (2004: 60–6). No longer is it a matter of a delimited act, performed by a small sub-set of people in only one country, against a specific group, ethnically and socially differentiable from "normal" Americans and Europeans. It now becomes a "sacred-evil," something of such enormous dimensions that it becomes inexplicable in the familiar language of guilt and innocence (2004: 50). Similarly, the events associated with the cultural symbolic structure known simply now as "Watergate" do not by mere definition constitute a political and cultural crisis of the first order for the American polity. They have to be made into such a thing through performance and specific symbolic processes. Alexander analyzes the televised Senate Select Committee hearings in May 1973 to demonstrate the construction of the Watergate narrative, which relied heavily on invocation of specific sacred categories in the discourse of American civil society that were opposed to profane categories: rational/irrational, open/secret, trusting/suspicious, rule-regulated/arbitrary, law/power.

Philip Smith's work on war (discussed above) uses this same set of binary categories as a key to understanding narratives about conflict in democratic societies. War would seem to be the most rational of actions, driven wholly by realpolitik. Smith argues, however, that war is a ritual activity oriented by cultural codes and narratives defining the civilized and the barbaric, the trustworthy and the risky. He has also challenged Foucault's influential account of growing instrumental rationality and control (see chapter 7), showing in a study of the history of punishment that power and its technologies are meaningful. He shows, for example, that prisons are seen as spooky, the guillotine and electric chair are totemic items that still inspire dread and awe, and that ideas about individual dignity have often placed a limit on disciplinary technique (Smith 2007). Other contributors to the Yale School have explored the cultural universe of the Salem Witch Trials (Reed 2007), the South African Truth and Reconciliation Commission (Goodman 2006), and the Lewinsky scandal of the Bill Clinton presidency (Mast 2006) with elements of this narrative theoretical toolkit underpinned by Durkheimian ritual categories.

Criticisms of the Yale School have argued that it is based in a cultural idealism that makes it difficult to adequately account for the materiality of culture (McLennan 2004) and that it might be unable to account for dynamics in cultural structures and narratives due to its significant reliance on Saussurean and Durkheimian binary categories (Emirbayer 2004). While it is still too early to know how effectively the Yale School will satisfy such critics that it has spoken to the relevant issues, it certainly seems clear at this point that it represents one of the more intellectually ambitious of recent theoretical frameworks for cultural analysis.

Suggested Further Reading

Readers familiar with James Bond movies will find Eco's discussion a great introduction to structuralist approaches in narrative analysis. Start here if you are unconvinced by the first part of this chapter. Geertz is a terrific writer, and his essays on thick description and the cockfight are stylistic classics as well as important theoretical statements. Read them! Bakhtin's conceptual writings are very difficult, but several anthologies are available with helpful commentary. His empirical study of Rabelais is somewhat easier and more fun. If you are short of time, look at just the first 30 or so pages of the works by Frye and Propp mentioned here. These get to the point quite quickly. We can also recommend an old book by Robert Scholes entitled *Structuralism in Literature* (1974). This provides a user-friendly guide to structuralist poetics, and will offer a next port of call for many readers. For the Yale Strong Program, the "Strong Program" essay by Alexander and Smith is the perfect starting point. It can be found in the same volume, Alexander's *The Meanings of Social Life*, that contains the pieces on Watergate and the Holocaust and also at the Yale Center for Cultural Sociology website. You can then move on to any of the substantive essays and books discussed above.

CHAPTER TWELVE

Psychoanalytic Approaches to Culture and the Self

The relationship between cultural and psychoanalytic theory is a complex one. There are clear affinities in as far as both see social life as essentially about meanings and emphasize the need for interpretation. The relationship becomes strained over two themes. First, psychoanalysis (in its traditional form at least) has tended to focus on the pathologies of the individual rather than on collective phenomena. Secondly, there is a tendency toward psychological and biological reductionism in much psychoanalytic thought. Moves that have been made by some psychoanalytic thinkers aimed at breaking down these barriers mark out one of the major achievements of twentieth-century cultural theory. This work has now reached a stage where it sometimes seems impossible to delineate certain psychoanalytic theories from cultural theory more broadly conceived. Before we can discuss these more recent theorists, we need first to review the work of the founder of psychoanalysis – Sigmund Freud.

Sigmund Freud

Freud challenged the assumption that the self was merely what can be seen on the surface. He argued that identity, personality, and mental function were far more complex than anyone had previously imagined. First, he claimed that there was a basic split between the conscious mind and a hidden, unconscious mind. These were in constant interaction. Existing alongside these two levels was a split in the psyche between the id, the ego, and the superego. These terms refer to aspects of the self rather than to concrete parts of the brain's anatomy. The **id** is the realm of diverse, primitive instincts that wish for immediate gratification. The **ego** maintains a stable sense of self and is adaptive to reality. It is the seat of reason and common sense. Feelings of conscience and morality can be found in the **superego**. This is derived from society, and in particular from parental socialization and authority.

In Freud's understanding the self was very much about sexuality, instinct, and pleasure. According to his theory of the **pleasure principle**, the self is continually seeking to satisfy biological and instinctive needs grounded in the id. These are associated with sensual pleasure. Infants are able to satisfy these through the stimulation of orifices (breastfeeding, defecation, genital manipulation), but as we grow up and attain a sense of selfhood we have to put these drives under some kind of control. They then become buried or **repressed** in the unconscious, where they will sometimes generate neuroses, perversions, obsessions, and other psychic pathologies. Freud suggested that much of modern life, both individual and collective, was miserable and unhappy thanks to our need to continually frustrate our innate sexual drives. For men at least, one of the most important repressed desires involved the **Oedipus complex**. This takes its name from the Greek myth (see also p. 98) in which Oedipus kills his father and marries his mother. According to Freud, the male infant is attracted to its mother, in part thanks to the mother's ability to fulfill its infantile sensual needs. The possibility of union with the mother is denied by the more powerful and authoritarian father. Castration anxiety, hatred of the father, and the repression of desire for the mother follow.

SIGMUND FREUD (1856–1939)

Freud was born in Freiburg near the Czech/German border, but moved to Vienna as a child. He was a brilliant schoolboy and consistently finished top of his class. In 1873, he entered the University of Vienna and began a study of medicine. During a visit to Paris in 1885, he developed an interest in hysteria and nervous conditions. During the 1890s, he worked toward theories which could understand these as the product of mental processes, rather than physiological ones, as was commonly believed at the time. He went on to write about phenomena as diverse as dreams, slips of the tongue, sexual dysfunction, phobias, and religion. All these were seen as the products of the fertile and complex unconscious mind, with its hidden dreams, fantasies, and drives. In 1938 he left Vienna for London in order to escape Nazi rule. He died from a deliberate overdose of morphine in 1939.

Reference: Gay 1989

As a practicing clinician, much of Freud's writing is concerned with the discussion of individual cases and neurological conditions. Nevertheless, in his later work especially, he applied his psychoanalytic theories to exploring the wider culture of modernity. Here he began to shift away from a model which privileged sexuality and suggested that **life and death drives** (Eros and Thanatos) were central to the organization of modern society. While Eros was concerned with love, friendship, creativity, and solidarity, Thanatos was implicated in aggression and destruction. *Civilisation and its Discontents* (1961 [1930]) is perhaps his most important effort to explore culture in a more collectivistic way. Here, Freud draws an analogy between the development of civilization (by which he means modern, bureaucratic society) and the development of the individual. In both cases, instincts and the self come to be controlled as a precondition for orderly life (Norbert Elias knew of Freud's work and made an analogous, if more sociological, argument; see pp. 140–1). Freud claimed that there was a deep contradiction between the need of civilization for order, control, and cooperation, and the instinctual demands of the libido for sensual gratification and the expression of aggressive drives. He writes: "it is impossible to overlook the extent to which civilization is built upon a renunciation of instinct, how much it presupposes precisely the non-satisfaction (by suppression, repression or some other means) of powerful instincts. This cultural frustration dominates the large field of social relationships between human beings" (1961: 51–2).

Freud emphasized the ways that instinctual drives were either repressed or underwent sublimation – a process involving their displacement to spheres beneficial for civilization, such as work or love for the family. Yet such a process was rarely fully successful and frustration, aggression, guilt, and unhappiness could all too often arise for the modern individual.

Post-Freudian Theories of Self and Society

Psychoanalytic theory has not stood still since Freud's death. In many ways, *Civilisation and its Discontents* sets the scene for this shift with its interest in macro-sociological issues and the links between pathology and modernity. General characteristics of more recent psychoanalytic theory include (see Elliott 1994: 19):

- a decreased emphasis of individual psychological pathologies as the cause of neuroses and a compensating interest in relations between people or between people and objects;
- a focus on the way that society and its cultural organization are implicated in the problems experienced by selves;
- an understanding of modern people as emotionally damaged, isolated, and suffering from impoverished identity. This has replaced the Freudian image of sexual and neurotic malfunction.

Even though much psychoanalytic theory is still of interest primarily to the specialist, or is not really very cultural (e.g., object relations theory), a good deal has filtered through into mainstream cultural theory. We consider below those thinkers whose works are most relevant to the concerns of this book.

The Frankfurt School

We last encountered the Frankfurt School in chapter 3, where we drew attention to their analysis of the culture industries and consumerism and the critique of instrumental reason and modernity. A further distinguishing feature of their work was a fusion of post-Freudian psychoanalytic theory with Marxian political economy. This theme was most developed in the writings of Fromm and Marcuse.

Like Freud, Erich Fromm argues that modern society restricts human freedom, but is more specific in placing the blame squarely at the foot of capitalism. In *The Sane Society* (Fromm 1968 [1956]), he argued that the economic ordering of society led to the creation of particular kinds of subjects. In an ideal world, we would be able to relate to each other in healthy ways by thinking reflexively and rationally about our selves and our society. This will allow us to engage in an authentic existence. This potential is cut off by consumerism, which offers shallow fantasies, and illusions to substitute for genuine efforts at self-understanding. Attempts to generate a true self-conception are further impeded by structures of power in institutional life, which deform and stunt the development of the self. Fromm writes that, in the modern world, "Happiness becomes identical with consumption of newer and better commodities, the drinking in of music, screen plays, fun, sex, liquor and cigarettes" (1968: 356), and goes on to argue that "alienation and automatization leads to an ever-increasing insanity. Life has no meaning, there is no joy, no faith, no reality" (1968: 360). The solution to this "robot-ism" advocated by Fromm was a "humanistic socialistic communitarianism" (1968: 363), which would involve economic change and foster "bonds of brotherliness and solidarity" (1968: 362).

As a fellow-member of the Frankfurt School, it is hardly surprising that Herbert Marcuse sees the world in much the same way as Fromm. Yet while Fromm's solution to social and personal pathologies spoke of the need for greater social reflexivity, Marcuse emphasized the need to resexualize and eroticize life so as to uncover what he called "libidinal rationality." The resulting transformations of libidinal energy would lead to the emergence of genuine interpersonal relationships.

Like most other cultural Marxists, Herbert Marcuse was puzzled by the failure of capitalism to produce revolution. Drawing, no doubt, on his encounters with wealth and the leisure society in 1960s southern California, Marcuse (1972 [1964]) provided an answer in his text *One Dimensional Man*. The book suggested that consumerism was an insidious force which was heading off revolutionary potential and social critique. Writing in the tradition that extended from Marx's thoughts on fetishism and alienation through to Horkheimer and Adorno's *Dialectic of Enlightenment* (see pp. 41–3), Marcuse alleged that people had been seduced by commodities and comfort. They were content in their material affluence and happy to wallow in the false freedoms provided by leisure, domesticity, and sexual opportunity. Subjectivities, he asserted, had been shaped by the needs of the capitalist system. Rather than attaining the "true" perspective afforded by critical reason, the **one-dimensional man** was a shallow person living an illusory life, voluntarily seeking to fulfill **false needs**. Marcuse writes that "Most of the prevailing needs to relax, have fun, to behave and consume in accor-dance with the advertisements, to love and hate what others love and hate, belong to this category of false needs" (1972: 19).

Fusing his understanding of Freud with this neo-Marxist thinking, Marcuse made the innovative argument that as part of a process of ideological control, libidinal ener-gies are controlled and channeled through a process of **repressive desublimation**. This involves their being directed toward superficial sexual activity, or else used in ways that reproduce rather than challenge the established system. As he puts it: "Technical progress and more comfortable living permit the systematic inclusion of libidinal com-ponents into the realm of commodity production and exchange" (1972: 71). For this reason, Marcuse proposed the rediscovery of an authentic, non-repressive sexuality as an important antidote to alienation under capitalism.

Marcuse's book is rightly considered an important intervention in the study of consumerism and the self. Much of its influence came from its timing. Denunciations of mainstream suburban life and calls for sexual freedom were popular with 1960s counter-cultural radicals in the United States. Although *One Dimensional Man* was probably more widely read than properly understood, the aging Marcuse found himself a doyen of the campus activists and student intellectuals of that era.

Jacques Lacan

For those influenced by structuralism, poststructuralism, and discourse analysis, Jacques Lacan's (1977) writings from the 1950s and 1960s are the key to theorizing the association of culture and psychoanalysis. One of the reasons for this is that his broadly poststructural approach shifts responsibility for the construction of the self away from biological drives (as advocated by Freud) toward language and culture. According to Lacan the unconscious was structured like language. It was a domain of signs, signifiers, and concepts that had to be decoded using techniques similar to those pioneered by Saussure.

In his *Ecrits*, Lacan sets out to challenge or destabilize the concept of the coherent, unitary self, and replace it with an idea of the self as a fiction or fantasy. Central to this argument was the concept of the **mirror stage**. Lacan suggests that during the "mirror stage, the infant comes to look at itself in the mirror and thereby creates the illusion of self-unity" (Elliott 1994: 29). This fictitious, narcissistic identity is subsequently elaborated upon by language and culture, which Lacan calls **Symbolic Law**. This works to prohibit Oedipal desires and locate the child within an imaginary world of symbolic and linguistic meanings. Far from being neutral, the world of language is one which is patriarchal in nature – and for this reason Lacan thinks of it as the **Law of the Father**.

Jacques Lacan (1901–1981)

Lacan was born in Paris and trained in psychiatry in the 1920s. During the 1930s he allied himself with Freudian theory and began to develop his ideas about the mirror phase. In the 1950s he began to give his famous weekly seminars. Over the years these were to be attended by leading French intellectuals like Sartre, Lévi-Strauss, Barthes, Althusser, Julia Kristeva, and Luce Irigaray. Here he would demonstrate his brilliance and charisma through wide-ranging attacks on alternative intellectual positions. During this period he also became increasingly interested in the role of language in structuring the unconscious. France had previously been resistant to Freud, but by redefining psychoanalysis in this new, more cultural way, Lacan was able to find an audience for his ideas. He rose to become one of the most influential intellects in France. According to the authorities, his "subversive" teachings played a major role in instigating the student riots of 1968.

Reference: Grosz 1998: 14–17

A key signifier within the Law of the Father is the **phallus**. This represents male author-ity and sexuality, and replaces Freud's somewhat biological focus on the penis. For Lacan, male dominance and identity are invested in the symbolic power of the phallus, while women are defined in terms of its absence. All things considered, Lacan's work gives a central role to language and culture, as they work upon both the conscious and unconscious mind in order to construct desire and provide people with what are known as **subject positions**. These are the imaginary senses of self that people adopt as they go about their lives.

Lacan's work can be seen as paralleling that of Foucault and Lévi-Strauss (see pp. 93, 113) in that it insists on decentering the subject. The idea here is that we are not sovereign over our own sense of identity. Nor do we have much choice about our desires or destinies. Rather we are constructed by discourses and other cultural forces. These provide for our sense of selfhood and the roles we occupy. There is no timeless essence of true selfhood to any of us, but rather the self is a fabrication and fiction.

Lacan's work has been highly influential in the area of cultural studies, providing a sophisticated theory with which to explore how contemporary subjectivities and desires are related to cultural, social, and ideological forces as well as those of biology. It has, however, been criticized by postmodernists for its emphasis on the repressive and nega-tive dimensions of culture and symbolism as they impact upon the self. In perhaps the most influential text of this ilk, *Anti-Oedipus*, Gilles Deleuze and Félix Guattari (1984 [1972]) suggest that Lacan's theory neglects the positive dimensions of fantasy and desire. In their reading, Lacan's theory overemphasises the power of the Law of the Father and Symbolic Law to regulate and control the creative excesses of the human mind. We return to their theory later in the chapter.

Post-Lacanian Psychoanalytic Cultural Theory

By deftly combining psychoanalytic theories of the self with structuralist understand-ings of culture, Lacan's work has exerted a distinctive impact on cultural theory, espe-cially in the areas of psychoanalytic feminism and literary and film criticism. Work in this poststructural tradition has several key features (see Elliott 1994: 102–3):

- There is a focus on the ways that identities (or subject positions) are created by lan-guage, texts, and the ways these relate to power.
- Ideas of essential, fixed, or true selves are problematized. There is a focus on the shifting, multiple, and constructed qualities of the conscious and unconscious self.
- Desire, fantasy, and illusion are understood to reproduce inequalities because they are constructed by symbolic structures that are, in turn, shaped by relations of power.

One of the earlier and most influential attempts to apply Lacan's theory in a sociologi-cal way was Louis Althusser's exploration of subjectivity and the Ideological State Apparatuses, or ISAs (we also looked at this theory in chapter 3). Althusser (1971) suggests that ideology works through state institutions to **interpellate** (locate, construct) people in subject positions. Along with these come the illusion of freedom and misrecognition of the true, objective nature of self and society. People are unaware of their membership in a class, the structuring power of capitalism, and so on. This process enables capitalism to be reproduced by preventing class awareness and critical thinking.

Althusser's model clearly borrows from Lacan in its understanding of the role of culture and language to construct human subjects. It is, however, rather crude by the standards of psychoanalytic discourse. Within that tradition people had long been seen as multiple and split, and the self as full of unresolved tensions and unrealized fantasies. Freud, for example, had seen individuals as **polymorphously perverse**, that is to say as inherently bisexual, incestuous, and pleasure-seeking. The self was such a complex entity precisely because these various forces had been repressed and locked away in the unconscious. With Althusser, issues of sexuality, fantasy, contradiction, and desire are ignored. The subject positions he talks about seem to be rather dry and robotic roles within state bureaucracies or industrial combines. Later theorists, however, have tried to combine his emphasis on social reproduction, power, and the self with a more sophisticated use of the psychoanalytic tradition.

Lacanian psychoanalytic feminism is very much situated on this terrain and represents perhaps the most dynamic contemporary field of psychoanalytic cultural theory. Lacan, to recap, argued that language and culture worked to reinforce patriarchy and was structured around the Law of the Father and the authority of the phallus. Women were, in a sense, excluded from language and defined by the lack of phallic authority (see Elliott 1994: 132). This line in his thinking has appealed to some feminist analyses, with Lacan being used as a tool for diagnosing the pathologies of patriarchal culture. For example, in *Psychoanalysis and Feminism*, Juliet Mitchell (1974) drew on Lacan to explore the ways that modern culture empowers men as active and creative while marginalizing women as lack and the Other.

Julia Kristeva's work (e.g., 1982 [1980]) has also taken from Lacan in a broadly appreciative way (see Grosz 1998: 147 ff.), and she has been perhaps the most influential theorist in this area. Drawing on Freud, she suggests that the pre-Oedipal (male) infant identifies strongly with its mother. That is to say, before it develops a coherent sense of self it thinks of itself as being at one with its mother. In the course of development it comes to realize its separation from the mother, and has to suppress its feminine side as the symbolic and the Law of the Father takes control. However, a female aspect of the self remains repressed beneath this layer of power. The broad canvas that Kristeva paints is of a contest between what she calls the "semiotic" and the "symbolic." The former is about pleasure, the subversive, the feminine, and the unruly. It is a space structured by the maternal body, while the "symbolic" is about order, coherence, authority, stability, system, and patriarchy.

Much of Kristeva's work is taken up with identifying and classifying these moments when the "semiotic" is able to break through the "symbolic" and be expressed. Her particular concern is with avant-garde literature, usually by male authors. She scours this for subversions of the phallocentric symbolic order. The interest here is in the transgressive, the insane, the sensual, the disgusting, and the mystical. And so the point of research is to find those moments when structures of (patriarchal) meaning become unstable or are undercut by the visceral, irrational, emotional, and embodied. She dubs the methodology behind this quest **semanalysis**. This idea has since been influential in psychoanalytic feminist film and literary criticism, where a good deal of effort is made to identify and decode such hidden female moments in texts.

Despite such uses, feminist responses to Lacan have been ambivalent. While they have generally applauded his demonstration that culture is patriarchal and that gender and sexuality are constructed by language and society (rather than biology), it has also been argued that his theory is ideological in as far as it reproduces the distortions of wider culture. In Lacan's theory, as in language generally, men are positioned in terms of power and discourse; women as the absent Other. Women are framed only as the "not male" or as having an "absent phallus." There is no specifically female conceptual space. Even Kristeva has been subject to such a critique. She sees the semiotic as a characteristic of male writing, and in so doing, "disembodies femininity from women, and claims that the avant-garde explores femininity without noticing that femininity as expressed in men cannot adequately represent women's femininity" (Grosz 1998: 166). In contradistinction to such a position, many poststructural psychoanalytic feminists have attempted to create a theory that is more gender-neutral or woman-centered. The aim here is to avoid depicting women as an absence or as deficient males, and instead to locate a realm of specifically female value which is inaccessible to, or irreducible to, masculine experience and knowledge.

Luce Irigaray (1985 [1977]) has been an important contributor to this literature. Her major quest is not only to identify female experiences and moments, but also to use these to critique and undermine dominant representational systems. According to Irigaray, systems of representation that privilege the masculine and evaluate women according to male discourses are **phallocentric**. She seeks to "cast phallocentrism, phallocratism, loose from its moorings in order to return the masculine to its own language. Which means that the masculine would no longer be 'everything.' That it could no longer, all by itself, define, circumvent, circumscribe, the properties of anything and everything" (1991: 128).

In this effort to escape from the phallocentrism of Lacan's model, Irigaray looks to hysteria, laughter, and especially the female body as the locus of a specifically female experience. She points in particular to the female orgasm (*jouissance* – see also p. 108), and the way it cannot be encapsulated in a phallocentric conceptual structure as an absence or lack. For Irigaray female sexuality, especially that derived from (phallus-free) masturbation, provides the foundation for a female conceptual space and pleasure that stands outside of dominant discourses and representations. The result of this process is a valorization of productive excess, and a celebration of the language of paradox, ambivalence, and ecstasy in contradistinction to the hierarchy, logic, and power characterizing phallocentric systems of representation. In such a novel language "there would no longer be either subject or object . . . that syntax would involve nearness, proximity, but in such an extreme form that it would preclude any distinction of identities, any establishment of ownership, thus any form of appropriation" (1991: 136).

Postmodern Psychoanalytic Cultural Theory

As we move from poststructural toward postmodern psychoanalytic theory, more and more attention is given to such issues of desire and pleasure alongside attacks on the concept of the unitary subject as the repository of desire. *Anti-Oedipus*, by Gilles Deleuze and Félix Guattari, is perhaps the most important text in this tradition. The book, which, as the title implies, is critical of the Freudian emphasis on the Oedipal complex in understanding identity, celebrates schizophrenia, fragmentation, and desire as radical tendencies in contemporary culture. The schizophrenic is elevated to a kind of heroic status as the carrier of an unregulated, non-Oedipal self. In schizophrenia, Deleuze and Guattari detect fluidity, unpredictability, and multiplicity, which threaten the order and authority necessary for capitalist reproduction. This desire no longer resides in individual subjectivities, but rather circulates in random and incoherent ways through human bodies and psyches that operate as "desiring machines." They write, for example, that "schizophrenia is the universe of productive and reproductive desiring machines, universal primary production as the essential reality of man and nature . . . desire constantly couples continuous flows and partial objects that are by nature fragmentary and fragmented. Desire causes the current to flow, itself flows in turn, and breaks the flows" (1984: 5).

The rise of capitalism depended on the regimentation and control of desire. This channeled it into fixed territories of time and space, alienating and impersonal commodity forms, or routines and bureaucracies. Deleuze and Guattari (the former a philosopher, the latter a renegade psychoanalyst) see institutional psychoanalysis not as a potential therapy for the maladies created by capitalism, but rather as itself implicated in producing those maladies. Indeed, in their view, the central category of Freudian psychoanalysis, the unconscious, is an invention designed to facilitate the regulation of individual desire. Traditional psychoanalysis is a reactionary political mechanism "constituted to prevent people from speaking . . . when one is analyzed, one has the impression of speaking . . . but whatever one says, it is seized in a kind of tourniquet, an interpretive machine, the patient will never have access to what he really has to say . . . this code is constituted by Oedipus, castration, the family novel" (Deleuze 2002 [1973]: 381–2). Desire does not arise from the lack created by Freudian (and Lacanian) separation from primal plenitude and entrance into the phallic Law. Rather, desire, which is not personal but always relational and collective, is already there, bursting out all the time in all directions, ultimately uncontrollable. For Deleuze and Guattari, endlessly proliferating schizophrenic desire holds out a transgressive and anarchic potential which will enable it to break down the psychological and cultural boundaries established by capitalism and maintained by ideological machinery like that of traditional psychoanalysis. They allege that the events of May 1968, when French students brought the country to a standstill, were an indicator of a new, progressive schizo-politics.

Sherry Turkle (1979) perceptively reads *Anti-Oedipus* as a celebration of "naturalism." This was the idea that society was linked to oppression and only a return to a pre-social, spontaneous, and pre-symbolic order could bring authenticity and freedom.

A similar current runs through Kristeva's contrast between the "semiotic" and the "symbolic." Lacan's ideas about the Law of the Father provided an important resource for such thinking, with their emphasis on the repressive qualities of culture. However, a critique of Lacan and psychoanalysis is also present in Anti-Oedipus (Turkel 1979: 151). Deleuze and Guattari see the professional obsession with the Oedipus complex as a dangerous thing. Its analytic focus on repression and order has interfered with our ability to understand productive desire. Moreover Lacan, like Freud, tends to see identity formation and power originating in the family system. This downplays institutional relationships structured by politics and capitalism.

Jean-François Lyotard, considered by many to be the foremost commentator on postmodernism, has also explored the connections between desire, culture, and the capitalist economy. For Lyotard (1974), the ideological works through the multiplication of desire and libidinal energies rather than their repression and distortion. In this respect his work has clearer parallels with Foucault's History of Sexuality (1990) or Bataille's ideas about heterology (see pp. 118–119, 75) than with psychoanalytic work such as that of the Frankfurt School. The image he conjures up is of society regulated by, and regulating, modes of desire that energize the system of production and consumption. For Lyotard, capitalism thrives on this channeling of desire and libidinal energies through the proliferation of signs and commodities. Rather than calling for resistance to capitalism, Lyotard suggests we should seize moments of pleasure from this flux of desire, enjoying the multiplicities and intensities of desire as they circulate and expand in late capitalism. This position, it has been commented, is insufficiently critical. Unlike other forms of psychoanalytic cultural theory, it fails to distinguish between potentially "good" and potentially "bad" forms of desire or provide criteria for their evaluation.

Psychoanalytic Theory and Imagination

In the past few years, Anthony Elliott has emerged as an important voice in psychoanalytic cultural theory. He has been critical of the Lacanian reading of Freud on a number of counts, not least of which has to do with Lacan's emphasis on repression and the stultifying vision of the self that arises from it. Elliott borrows from Cornelius Castoriadis's reading of Freud the radical potentiality of the concept of **imagination**. This is "[t]he core of all psychical productions for Freud," something that precedes the subject's entry into language (Elliott 2004: 76). It is the source of creative and endless fantasies about the individual, her relationship to self, to other people, and to history (Elliott 2001: 74). For Castoriadis and Elliott, then, the contemporary self has to be understood not as the repressed construct of Lacan, but as a hopeful and fundamentally creative entity. Much of this resonates with Deleuze and Guattari's critique of Lacan, but Elliott disagrees with them about the disappearance of the unitary subject. Instead, he sees the self moving back and forth between fragmentation and integration in a kind of dialectical process, constantly moving on from each moment of seeming stasis to a new beginning.

Elliott has also used psychoanalytic cultural theory to explore themes in celebrity and fandom (see chapter 10 for more on these topics). His book on John Lennon (1999) explores the ways in which the former Beatle's career and evolving perspective on his own celebrity were driven by the effort to deal with the loss of his parents. Early in the period of his fame, Lennon basked in the narcissistic glow of his celebrity image, but as his perspective on celebrity grew more critical along with other elements of his politics, he sought to use his fame as a tool for promoting a cultural politics of selfhood that privileged the radical imagination. Ironically enough, Lennon's murder may have been a consequence of the fact that his own political intervention into the culture of celebrity entailed his refusal to cultivate the public's adulation. As he sought instead to withdraw to a certain degree into the ordinary life of a father and husband, some of his fans (including his murderer Mark David Chapman) saw him as a traitor to the outspokenly radical celebrity tradition he had helped establish (Elliott 2004: 167).

Some Concluding Comments

For contemporary cultural theorists, psychoanalytic theory has clearly offered the most elaborate and attractive discourse on the self. It is an area marked by continuing theoretical innovation that has attracted a number of formidable thinkers to its ranks. It should be noted, however, that reservations are often expressed about this approach. These include the following points:

- *Many of the central claims of psychoanalysis remain untested.* Positivists suggest that it is akin to a religion rather than a science. Its central concepts (e.g., the unconscious) do not always seem amenable to empirical observation.
- *It is a field marked by internal division with innumerable factions and cliques.* In addition, some scholars believe themselves to be scientists, others clinicians, and still others interpreters or social commentators. In other words, there is no core consensus or agenda or identity. This tends to undercut the claims made within the area to have uncovered some basic truths about humanity and culture.
- *Like other major fields (e.g., Marxism), psychoanalytic theory has constructed its own language.* Learning this takes years of study and so texts can be extremely difficult for outsiders to understand.
- *It operates with an a priori belief that people are repressed, neurotic, sick, and so on.* This relentlessly grim and pessimistic view makes the theory difficult to apply in an appreciative account of human creativity. The work of Giddens or Bourdieu (see chapter 8), for example, suggests that it makes sense to think of people today in a very different way.
- *There are enduring problems with the application of a model designed to cure troubled individuals to the sociological analysis of collective phenomena.* Slippages and ambiguities often occur in this movement from micro to macro levels of analysis. These can sometimes involve woolly ideas that invoke a nebulous collective mind, gross generalizations about how modern people think and feel, or an unsatisfactory picture of culture as simply an aggregate of individual minds and their pathologies.

Suggested Further Reading

Much original work in the psychoanalytic tradition can be very, very difficult to read without years of training. In some cases it is incomprehensible to all but the initiated. Anthony Elliott has written several very good books summarizing psychoanalytic theory and its contribution to thinking about society (1994, 2004). Elizabeth Grosz's (1998) book on Lacan and feminism is more difficult, but is probably the best introduction to that literature. Among original works, Freud's *Civilization and its Discontents* is important, lucid, intelligible, and brief. It is a landmark work in twentieth-century thought, so please try to read it.

CHAPTER THIRTEEN

The Cultural Analysis of Postmodernism and Postmodernity

In the area of cultural theory, few concepts have generated as much anxiety and controversy as that of postmodernism. Debate revolves around a series of related terms: postmodernism, postmodernity, postmodernization, and globalization. By the end of this chapter and the next, you should have a good grounding in these complex themes. It is helpful to begin here with some basic definitions:

- **Postmodernism** has several dimensions. It refers, first, to an aesthetic and artistic style that rejects the aesthetic and artistic codes of modernism. It also encompasses a philosophical and theoretical position that emerges from poststructuralism and rejects the tenets of modernist thought.
- **Postmodernity** refers to a stage of social development which is thought to be beyond that of modernity. A synonym here is the postmodern era. The key idea is that there has been a decisive and radical shift to a postindustrial economy organized around culture and cultural consumption, the media, and information technology.
- **Postmodernization** refers to the process of social change which drives the transition from modernity to postmodernity.
- **Globalization** is the process by which the world is becoming more and more interconnected, with existing political, cultural, and economic boundaries being superseded. Many discussions of postmodernity involve some discussion of globalization.

A further useful analytical distinction can be made between literatures that *advocate* or make use of the principles of postmodernism, and those that seek to *explain* postmodernism and postmodernization. We can distinguish, for example, between "postmodern sociology" and a "sociology of postmodernism." The former embraces, proselytizes, and applies the perspectives advocated by postmodern theory. The latter takes the postmodern and postmodernization as the objects of analysis. It sets out to trace their characteristics and explain their emergence – often using conventional "modernist" social and cultural theories. In this chapter, we are concerned with this second literature. In line with the theme of this book, our primary aim is to identify the codes of postmodern *cultural* production and to introduce theories and critiques of cultural shifts toward a postmodern society. In chapter 14 we look in more detail at postmodernism as a theoretical or philosophical stance.

Before going any further, we need to put some content into the empty box of "the postmodern." Perhaps the quickest way to do this is to list some of the qualities of postmodern culture and postmodern society on which everyone seems to agree, regardless of their particular explanations and discussions (see, for example, Bauman 1992; Frow 1998; Hebdige 1986; Lash 1990a):

- Culture and the mass media have become more powerful and important in society than previously.
- Economic and social life revolve around the consumption of symbols and lifestyles, rather than the production of goods through industrial labor.
- Ideas about reality and its representation are made problematic.
- Image and space have replaced narrative and history as organizing principles of cultural production.
- Stylistic features like parody, pastiche, irony, and pop eclecticism become more prevalent.
- A consumption-based cityscape dominates urban form. Rather than being organized around economic production, this has as its central dynamic the provision of entertainment, leisure, and lifestyle services. Shopping malls, pleasure parks, and themed residential complexes are examples of this.
- Hybridity comes to replace rigid boundaries and classifications.

In the course of this chapter, we will encounter various theories and discussions of these diverse and sometimes puzzling phenomena.

Postmodernism in Architecture

The field in which the concept of the postmodern first came to be firmly established was that of architecture. As debates about architecture have long held a central place in discussions on postmodernism among cultural theorists as well as architects and planners, some familiarity with such issues is required. It is also a useful place to begin thinking about the differences between aesthetic modernism and postmodernism.

Somewhat tongue in cheek, the architectural critic Charles Jencks (1977: 10) dates the end of modern architecture to July 15, 1972 at 3:32 p.m. At that moment, several blocks of the Pruitt–Igoe housing scheme in St Louis, Missouri were blown up. The development consisted of uniform concrete housing blocks, had been repeatedly vandalized, and was notoriously crime-prone. Repeated efforts to fix up the development had failed. Jencks suggests that the demise of the scheme is emblematic of wider problems with modernism in architecture. The Pruitt–Igoe scheme had been designed according to principles of "rationalism, behaviorism and pragmatism" (1977: 10), but had not provided a safe or enjoyable place to live. Jencks suggests that modern architecture has several key characteristics:

- *Form tends to be univalent.* There is an emphasis on the monumental and repetitive use of a few materials and shapes. This is exemplified in the "international style": the glass and steel skyscrapers of Mies van der Rohe and Le Corbusier, with their towering, anonymous, curtain-wall façades.
- *Buildings are constructed according to the metaphor of the industrial machine.* They are serious buildings that signify things like power and rationalism. Form and design are subservient to function.
- *Designers had utopian ideas.* Influenced by artistic, political, and philosophical doctrines, they believed that architecture could play a heroic role as part of a wider project of social and moral engineering.

According to Jencks, the eventual failure of modernist architecture, symbolized by the demise of the Pruitt–Igoe development, has much to do with these characteristics. The design never responded to human needs for environmental diversity and community formation. It also failed to connect with symbolic needs. He asserts that most people found the metaphors of modern architecture (e.g., building as "machine" or "factory") rather alienating.

A broadly similar point is made by the star architect Robert Venturi and his collaborators in the influential text *Learning from Las Vegas* (1977 [1972]). Their claim is that architects need to be "more understanding and less authoritarian" in orientation. Venturi turned to the casinos, hotels, and strip malls of Las Vegas for lessons. Although these had traditionally been condemned as populist and ugly, he argues that such evaluative distinctions should be inverted. To the contrary, he asserts that the architecture of Las Vegas is vibrant, anti-elitist, and communicates effectively to ordinary people. One reason for this was that ornament (e.g., billboards) was a key feature of design. In contrast to this is a modern architecture which is obsessed with "space, structure and program . . . a dry expressionism, empty and boring" (1977: 103). Here, ornament is neglected and the building symbolizes through a code that only experts can read.

What, then, is postmodern architecture? The core elements of this style can be derived from the writings of Jencks (1977), Venturi et al. (1977), and the critic Fredric Jameson (1984), the last of whom we discuss below:

- There is an emphasis on playful rather than serious design. The casinos of Las Vegas, for example, are buildings which are fun to look at rather than grandiose social statements.
- "Radical eclecticism," the "hybrid," and "adhocism" (Jencks 1977: 87, 92) are to replace monumental uniformity. This might involve the use of multiple styles simultaneously, perhaps mixing and matching themes from different eras. For example, we might find a fake Tudor mansion with a Greek temple-style front porch.
- Buildings copy other styles and engage in an ironic pastiche rather than attempting to have a personal stylistic signature. Again, the Las Vegas casinos, which amusingly mimic New York, Ancient Egypt, and so on, provide a nice example of this.
- Design is fragmented, with parts of the building operating in aesthetic and functional isolation from each other, each with their own style and micro-environment.

- There is an effort to create buildings which appeal to ordinary people, with semiotic codes that they can understand and enjoy. Jencks writes that buildings should be "sensual, humorous, surprising and coded as a readable text" (1977: 101).
- Curves and blind alleys are used, rather than rectangles and straight lines. As a result, such buildings can be confusing to navigate.

These characteristics, it should be noted, are broadly consistent with themes in postmodern social theory that we discuss in the next chapter. These include the critique of rationality and expert authority, the decline of grand narratives and the triumph of play and the local.

Postmodernism in Art and Literature

Similar developments have taken place in the fields of art and literature, where postmodernists have pitched themselves against what they see as the ills of modernism. The aesthetic codes of modernism, for the most part, favored work that was deeply serious, internally consistent, innovative, abstruse, abstract, and authored by an individual "genius." To a lesser extent, it has also celebrated reason, order, and knowledge and carried with it some kind of message or commentary that it thought to be important about the world. Figures who have been associated with modernism and whose work embodies these traits include:

- composers like Schoenberg, Berg, Stravinsky, and Webern;
- artists like Picasso, Matisse, Klee, Mondrian, and Pollack;
- writers like Joyce, Beckett, Pound, and Eliot.

Postmodern work in these fields is, for the most part, driven by a different aesthetic. It tends to be playful and fragmented, to make use of pastiche and borrowings, to celebrate the irrational and (sometimes) to be readily accessible for interpretation without expert knowledge. There is often no clear moral or message in the work. Such creative products are often ironic in tone, mocking and challenging established aesthetic practices and concepts (e.g., authorship, the value of the arts). Postmodern work can also frequently challenge the boundaries between high and low culture, suggesting not so much that that the latter is valid as form of expression, but rather that the distinction itself is no longer useful or viable. In fields like literature and cinema, we will often find a refusal of the traditional sequential plot and the clear moral message. We might find a jumbled story line in place of a grand narrative and high levels of **intertextuality** (when one film or book refers to or borrows from another) which challenge the idea of a bounded artistic creation with an omnipotent author.

Postmodernity in Social Theory

Discussion of postmodernity in social theory began with the work of the French philosophers Lyotard and Baudrillard. Both are difficult to read and, like many theorists, make extreme claims but present limited supporting evidence. Later ideas about post-modernity were taken over by middle-range theorists who attempted to make them relevant to their particular disciplinary concerns.

Jean-François Lyotard

Intellectual debates about postmodernism often find a point of departure in the writings of the French social philosopher Jean-François Lyotard (1984 [1979]). According to Lyotard, societies are organized not just around technologies but also around dis-courses. He drew particular attention to the role of narratives in social life. In non-industrial societies, myths and stories had a religious quality and assisted in the reproduction of the social order. With the coming of the Enlightenment, a new set of narratives came into place alongside the rise of science. These emphasized the impor-tance of progress, reason, knowledge, and technology in bringing freedom from igno-rance, want, and oppression. Such narratives gave social life a sense of purpose. They legitimated the social order and provided a framework within which to evaluate human activity.

Lyotard suggests that we have now entered a new, postmodern era. Science, technol-ogy, complex administrative systems, and computers have become developed to a stage where "knowledge has become the principle force of production over the last few decades" (1984: 5). This shift has had a qualitative as well as a quantitative dimension. The utopian, visionary, humanistic and consensus-based discourses that once ani-mated social life have lost their authority. These discourses were ultimately based on the idea that one mode of legitimation, that of science, was superior to all others, and that all realms of human communication could finally be reduced to that scientific mode of legitimation. But we now know that this is not the case. Lyotard calls this the **decline of grand narratives**. He believes that "the grand narrative has lost its credi-bility, regardless of what mode of unification it uses, regardless of whether it is a specu-lative narrative or a narrative of emancipation" (1984: 37). Most people no longer believe that science, reason, or "truth" will provide answers to social problems or allow us to build a better world. Nor do they think that we can locate a single theory or worldview that can successfully unify all knowledge and experience (e.g., Marxism). Moreover, Lyotard argues that nobody imagines the possibility of a "God's-eye" place from which to construct knowledge that is true or universally valid. As a result knowl-edge (and society) fragments into local and multiple fields, with grand humanistic visions falling by the wayside.

Lyotard invokes the philosopher Ludwig Wittgenstein's notion of the **language-game** to sketch out his vision of the failure of the grand narratives. Wittgenstein had demonstrated that the meaning of words in a given language cannot be adequately accounted for by reference to a fixed, context-free definition. No dictionary can ever include along with the formal definition of a word the virtually limitless social contexts in which it can be used in different ways. He gives the example of the context in which two workers on a building site use words such as "block" and "slab" to communicate much more than could be found in the formal definition of those terms. When one worker calls out a term to the other, the other knows because of the context that this is a call to action ("Bring me one of those") rather than simply an observation ("That object is a slab"). The example is simple but powerful. Language use depends on knowledge not just of abstract meanings of words, but of the specific form of action, or game, in which they are being used at any particular time. Lyotard appropriates this relativistic perspective on language to contend that no narrative is ever fully reducible to another, as each one in effect constitutes its own language-game. The rules governing different narratives are incommensurable. What the purported triumph of the scientific and emancipatory grand narrative has brought about is the realization that no single narrative can trump all others and that the end of that scientific grand narrative, consensus, is in fact unattainable. Drawing also on Nietzsche, Lyotard argues that conflict, dissent, and heterogeneity are unavoidable in discourse, but his conclusion from this is not simply pessimistic. Instead, he maintains that the desire for justice remains powerful in human societies and that we will now simply have to find a way toward it without the consoling illusion of consensus (1984: 66). Lyotard's major innovation, perhaps, is in theorizing the role of narrative and the linguistic in the process of rationalization. It is also important to note that he places a major emphasis on the shift to a "postmodern," post-industrial society rather than the move from tradition to industrial modernity that had interested earlier scholars.

Jean Baudrillard

Like Lyotard, Jean Baudrillard was a major early influence on the development of theory about the postmodern. As long ago as the late 1960s, Baudrillard (1998 [1970]) argued that we lived in an era where society is no longer based on the exchange of material goods with use values (à la Marxism). Rather, he suggested, it involves commodities as signs and symbols which have entirely arbitrary and conventional significance within what he calls "the code." The idea of "the code" draws on Barthesian notions of culture as a collective grammar of signifiers (see pp. 103–8). For Baudrillard, our consumer society is one in which people seek to affirm their identity and difference, and experience pleasure through the purchase and consumption of a shared system of signs. He writes: "consumption is an order of significations, like language or like the kinship system in primitive society. . . . The circulation, purchase, sale, appropriation of differentiated goods and signs/objects today constitute our language, our code, the code by which the entire society communicates and converses" (1998: 79–80).

Baudrillard went on to suggest that "the code" has become dominant to such an extent that we have to question some of the most basic distinctions that have informed social and cultural thinking. According to him, distinctions between "culture" and "reality" and between the "sign" and that which is symbolized no longer make sense. In the past, signs and symbols masked some underlying reality or provided a gloss or commentary upon it. Now, however, "a neo-reality has everywhere been substituted for reality, a neo-reality entirely produced by combining elements of the code" (1998: 126). Events in the "real" world are increasingly material expressions of models and mythologies that have originated in an autonomous cultural sphere. The terms he used to capture this strange dynamic are those of **simulation** and the **simulacrum**. Examples of these that have been provided by various researchers include:

Figure 13.1   Sleeping Beauty Castle, Disneyland, Paris

- Theme parks like those owned by the Walt Disney Company. Disneyland is often cited by postmodern theorists as an example of a simulation writ large, or a "real fake," as Umberto Eco (see chapter 6) calls it. Here we have a multibillion-dollar infrastructure designed around themes from Disney movies and cartoons. There are real jobs, real buildings, and real hotels. Yet, at the same time, the engine behind all this is a set of iconic characters and images from celluloid invented by artists. As Baudrillard would point out, the "real" is built upon a myth or fantasy, as in the case of the Sleeping Beauty Castle at the Disneyland Resort in Paris (figure 13.1), which is an idealized fairytale castle reflecting generations of thought about how such places should look.
- Themed housing developments which originate on the architect's drawing board and replicate mythologized versions of the past. They might try to copy Olde English villages, Mediterranean fishing ports, and so on.
- Television programs and media events which end up intervening in real life. The 1991 Gulf War, for example, was a conflict in which both sides derived information from television coverage and adjusted their war policies to make them television-friendly. Documentary programs which track the lives of ordinary people, but end up changing those lives, are another example of this process. In both these cases, the situation being reported is a situation that is generated by the media itself.
- "Primitive" tribes in Third World tourist destinations whose living conditions, dress, and activities are carefully styled so that they remain "primitive" and so live up to tourist expectations.

Aside from pointing to consumerism and the media, Baudrillard placed special emphasis on the work of planners and computer simulations in helping to generate the world in which we live. This perspective possibly reflected his experiences in the technocratic France of the 1960s. Baudrillard tended to be rather fatalistic and nihilistic about the impact of the changes he observed. He saw them as challenging to human agency and spoke of the "death of the social" and "implosions." According to Baudrillard, we have witnessed the end of "the social," as social life becomes caught up in a giant black hole of **hypersimulation**. Henceforward, we are doomed to experience each other only as players in a field of signs, and to passively experience spectacles and simulacra that reflect upon each other.

In several of his most important works of the late 1970s, Baudrillard's debt to the Durkheimian/Maussian lineage in cultural theory is evident. During this period he developed the notion of **symbolic exchange** to refer to a mode of interaction characteristic of pre-modern, pre-industrial societies such as those described in classic Durkheimian works like *The Elementary Forms of Religious Life* and *The Gift* (see chapter 5). It is according to Baudrillard a form of social interaction in which all giving of any kind (whether of objects or meaningful bits of communication) calls for and receives commensurate return, and a kind of symbolic balance is thereby maintained. Even death is seen in the primitive world as a participant in this system of total exchange, wherein life and death are equal partners each of which gives and receives. In perhaps its most vivid form, Baudrillard claims, we see this in rituals of communal cannibalism of the dead in some primitive societies: "By offering her a piece of flesh, the brother gives his wife to a dead member of the family, in order to bring him back to life. By nourishing her, this dead man is included in the life of the group. But the exchange is reciprocal. The dead man gives his wife, the clan's land, to a living member of the family in order to come back to life by assimilating himself to her and to bring her back to life by assimilating her to himself" (Baudrillard 1993 [1976]: 131).

The industrial era is fundamentally based in Baudrillard's view on the repudiation of this need for total exchange. Capital relies precisely on imbalances in exchange; some accumulate great deficits in trade, others great surpluses. The modern world even shakes up the primitive equilibrium of life and death by overbalancing the scales in favor of life and doing all it can to remove death completely from our cycle of exchange. The world of simulation in which we now live, while different from the productivist world in the ways just summarized, nonetheless fails to return us to the world of symbolic exchange. Although there are some transgressive contemporary practices and experiences which momentarily escape the totalitarian system of simulation, such as suicide and terrorist acts, Baudrillard seemed clear that we were doomed to live in a world devoid of the form of exchange he saw as most fully human.

Up until around the late 1980s or early 1990s, Baudrillard made connections to existing cultural theory and wrote mostly in an academic genre. In much of his later work, such as *The Perfect Crime* and *Impossible Exchange*, Baudrillard (1996 [1995]; 2001 [1999]) adopted an aphoristic, ironic, paradoxical, and fragmentary style. He seemed to give up on classic scholarly analysis and instead presents us with elusive, evocative texts that read as much like a strange poetry as conventional social or cultural theory. He sometimes noted in interviews that this was something of a deliberate attempt to emulate Nietzsche's embrace of fragmentary and aphoristic writing late in his life. As Bryan Turner (1993: 85) points out, this style "simulates the condition it wishes to convey rather than producing a critical style in opposition to postmodern culture." In contrast to his earlier works, these later writings have been read by some (e.g., Callinicos 1989: see below) as an uncritical celebration of the postmodern which is in need of a reality check.

Two important empirical branches of contemporary research that have engaged Baudrillard's conceptual language, and which Baudrillard himself discussed, are that focused on the Internet and computer-mediated communication (CMC), and that treating the topic of tourism.

Computer-mediated communication and virtual reality
Sherry Turkle's study, *Life on the Screen* (1995), was one of the first concentrated looks at how interaction in environments of simulation and virtuality, such as online MUDs (Multi-User Domains), affects conceptions of identity. In these environments, users can essentially create their own identities, freely playing with gender, race, sexuality, and other ascribed identity markers. They can also quickly discard one identity and take up another. Ultimately, in Turkle's view, we have to shift the frame of our investigation in this new scenario to recognize that the relations between subjects in this kind of environment are complicated by another relation: that of the user to the computer technology she is using. The postmodern descent into simulation as basically indistinguishable from the real world is fueled by a relationship to computer technology that Turkle calls "opaque." This is a way of thinking about the computer that she argues is epitomized by "the Macintosh mystique," the desire to interact with the technology at a surface, hands-on level without the need for any real knowledge of the functioning of the technology itself. Just as we might interact with another person in a way motivated by the desire to accomplish certain goals without necessarily knowing much about what is going on inside the other person's head, so we have learned to approach computer technology in the same way (Turkle 1995: 34–5). An almost inevitable result is the increasing murkiness of the boundary between a simulated world and the real world. Turkle documents this at length, describing MUD users who spend as much time online as in the real world and see their online relationships and lives as just as substantial as any real world relationships. In one passage, she describes a user who spent more time organizing and orchestrating his MUD marriage to another character than many actual engaged couples might (1995: 194–6).

Since the publication of Turkle's book more than a decade ago, there has been a great deal of study of CMC with varying affiliations with postmodernist theory. CMC technology has also become quite a lot more sophisticated, which tends in itself to make the case for a Baudrillardean reading of CMC stronger. In today's virtual worlds such as *Second Life*, textual communication is increasingly being replaced by real-time voice interaction, removing one more distinction between virtual world and reality. The increasing fusing of fantasy and real economies is evident in the fact that skilled players in developing countries can bring in earnings approaching a living wage in their countries by acquiring coveted powers that First World players purchase on e-Bay. Dennis Waskul's reading of online sexual interaction follows postmodernist theory in recognizing how, in both text-based and video-format online sex, the sexual body is always virtual, but he also notes that almost all cybersex participants recognize the difference between sexual contact online and in real life and rate the latter as superior (2003: 117). It has also been pointed out that the particular variety of simulation present in the dominant style of video game perhaps does tell us something about the origins of the technology itself. The emergence of the popular "first person shooter" games, of which *Doom* is perhaps the best-known example, has been seen as obviously connected to the non-virtual reality of the military research motivations of much early video game technology (Kline et al. 2003: 107, 144). Recent research on massively multiplayer online games (MMOs), such as *World of Warcraft*, which has more than nine million global players, seems to demonstrate a profound attachment of users to the mythological forms and structure they encounter in these "synthetic worlds" (Krzywinska 2006; Castronova 2005). Inasmuch as narratives about the Internet and CMC generally have also been heavily encoded in mythical symbolism of "the techno-logical sublime," a "history-ending" rhetoric that accompanies virtually every new form of communicative technology (Mosco 2004: 117), this should perhaps not be too surprising.

Tourism

Tourism has been the object of interest by cultural scholars at least since Dean Mac-Cannell's book on the topic (1999 [1976]), but the field has massively grown in the past few decades and the phenomenon itself has significantly changed. Here, as with the literature on CMC, we find some affirmations of Baudrillardean concepts and some contestation. MacCannell insisted that tourists sought (what they considered to be) the authentic and tried to get beyond the routine and stage-managed holiday experience to encounter the real people and places they visited. This is why some leading guide-books insist they are for "travelers" and not "tourists." Much seems to confirm this observation that tourists, rather than giving themselves up to a relativist play of signs, continue to seek authenticity in their tourist experiences, even if they know that it is, of necessity, constructed. More, many forms of tourism seem to be fundamentally predicated on embodiment and physical experience (e.g., sport, adventure and extreme tourism, sex tourism, ecological tourism) and would likely present difficulties to Bau-drillard's theory of simulation. On the other hand, though, one can locate elements of virtuality and simulation in many of those same varieties of tourism. Much Caribbean sex tourism, including that of the Bahamas and even communist Cuba, has relied on the construction of a virtual colonial Caribbean of the past, complete with eroticized and commodified images of dark-skinned colonial subject Others and the mobilization of a colonial fantasy for the tourist (Sheller 2004: 20). The Palm Islands in Dubai, three artificially constructed tourist islands off the coast of the country, are certainly an example of simulation even in their actual physical shape (all are designed to look like palm trees), and the architectural intent of building on the islands in 22 different civilizational themes portends a simulation of the global, the sense of "going around the world without leaving Dubai" (Junemo 2004: 187). Casual tourists at beach sites who photograph the busy activity of fisherman to commemorate their edifying encoun-ter with Nature likely are unaware of how often the fishermen's activities are pure performance for their benefit (Baerenholdt et al. 2004: 60). Perhaps the clearest kind of tourism to lend itself to the use of Baudrillard's theory is virtual tourism, or tourism undertaken via television, video, or the Internet. The Travel Channel and websites such as virtualtourist.com can provide one with a significant amount of visual and aural tourist experience. Although it does not seem to be the case that virtual tourism supplants tourism involving actual physical displacement so much as it accompanies it, we are arguably still in a realm that Baudrillard tried to speak to when we see a tourist in a café in Italy, checking out possible sites to visit that evening on his laptop (Molz 2004: 170).

Daniel Bell

Postmodern ideas about the growing power of knowledge and culture in contemporary society were decisively prefigured in the works of Daniel Bell, written in the 1960s and early 1970s (Turner 1993: 78ff.). Today, Bell is increasingly being seen as a theorist of postmodernity *avant la lettre*. While he is clearly modernist in sensibility and theoretical style, his works such as *The Coming of Post-Industrial Society* (1973) and *The Cultural Contradictions of Capitalism* (1976) document the decisive shift from an industrial modernity to one based on information. In these works, Bell suggests that in the second half of the twentieth century the continued growth of capitalism depended on information technology and knowledge created in major research centers like universities and hi-tech corporations. At the same time, citizens were being converted into consumers with ever-expanding demands for goods and entertainment. Bell suggests that a contradiction exists between culturally driven, hedonistic demands for consumer goods, and the sober needs of the state and the economy. While the latter were still driven by an ascetic rationality that derived from the Protestant ethic (see p. 13), the consumer demanded pleasure and instant gratification. The net picture was of culture becoming unchained. It had become more autonomous and more powerful in driving both demand (consumerism) and production (knowledge, technology).

The neo-Marxist critique of postmodernism

In theorizing the postmodern, the early running was made by French theorists. During the 1980s the Anglophone nations began to catch up. Perhaps the most significant development of that era was a wave of neo-Marxist cultural commentary, which was:

- broadly hostile to the aesthetic codes of postmodernism;
- keen to demonstrate how the forces of capitalism were at the heart of contemporary cultural shifts;
- concerned to document the relationship between these shifts and the possibilities for human emancipation.

Fredric Jameson: postmodernism as the cultural logic of late capitalism

One of the earliest and most influential accounts of postmodernism was an article published in 1984 in the *New Left Review* by the leading literary critic Fredric Jameson. The essay provides an important starting point for all those interested in the aesthetics of the postmodern and their links to capitalist development. Jameson sees postmodernism and capitalism to be so intimately linked that: "every position on postmodernism in culture . . . is at one and the same time, and necessarily, an implicitly or explicitly political stance on the nature of multinational capitalism today" (1984: 55).

Jameson's essay features a seminal discussion of the Bonaventure Hotel in downtown Los Angeles. The outside of the building is broadly modernist, consisting of reflecting glass towers. The interior, by contrast, is strongly postmodern in terms of its spatial configuration. The entrances and exits are hard to find, there are staircases and corridors leading nowhere, and there is no central space, such as a foyer or lobby. The space, in short, is fragmented and "decentered." Jameson claims that such transformations of space are a mutation that has arisen along with postmodernism. Such new spatial arrangements have also replaced "history" as an organizing principle of society. Jameson sees this as a negative move because he considers that having a sense of history is central to developing a genuine understanding of who we are. These new spaces are also dangerous in that they defy our abilities to navigate them and thereby overwhelm our cognitive faculties. They deny us the ability to become active, autonomous, critical agents in charge of our own destinies, as "we do not yet possess the perceptual equipment to match this hyperspace" (1984: 80). Such dystopian aspects of the building are also reflected in a design which turns inward upon itself. Unlike modernist architecture, it refuses contact with the city (remember those hard-to-find entrances and exits), and makes no claim to fulfill any wider civic responsibilities. Rather, it sets itself up as a fully self-contained hyperspace – a new, confusing form of space which is cut off from society. Jameson sees these negative characteristics as inherent not only to postmodern architecture, but also to other postmodern cultural products.

This thematic is further illustrated in his discussion of art. Jameson compares a picture of peasant clogs by Van Gogh with an Andy Warhol screen print. The former (modernist) picture shows a pair of dirty wooden clogs. According to Jameson, we can connect these with a coherent interpretation and a depth hermeneutic. They can be read as symbols of the hardships of an authentic of peasant life. Warhol's picture, by contrast, is a screen print showing a jumble of various high-heeled shoes. Such a postmodern work refuses any stable interpretation. It might be read as a celebration of consumerism, or as its critique. Perhaps it reveals the artist's own fetishistic tendencies. Or maybe it is an ironic parody upon them. The work of art seems to exist only as a playful series of surfaces and to lack any clear moral vision, narrative, or framework through which we can interpret it. Instead, it exhibits "a new kind of flatness or depthlessness" (1984: 60). For all their entertainment value, postmodern works like Warhol's *Diamond Dust Shoes* fail to generate powerful and authentic emotions. Jameson speaks of this as the waning of affect – an understanding which draws on Benjamin's thinking about post-auratic cultural production (see pp. 39–41).

In explaining the rise of artistic postmodernism Jameson makes use of a neo-Marxist framework. He suggests that we have entered a phase of late capitalism characterized by the relentless circulation of signs and symbols and global information flows. The hedonistic consumption of images is central to this stage of capitalism. Postmodernism reflects the new image-based economy in that it is the "cultural logic of late capitalism." It also operates in ideological ways to prevent people from connecting with their history and collective identity. It generates confusion and celebrates the superficial. In order to combat postmodernism, he suggests we need to come to terms with its new spatial logic and develop critical tools for reading postmodern cultural artifacts.

David Harvey and flexible accumulation

The geographer David Harvey (1989) provides another neo-Marxian take on post-modernism. Like Jameson, Harvey hangs his analysis on a periodization of phases in capitalist development. For much of the twentieth century, we were in an era of **Fordism**. Named after automobile manufacturer Henry Ford, the concept refers to the industrial mass production of standardized goods. In Ford's case, his automated assembly-line production system churned out millions of identical cars, most notably the famous Model "T" Ford. Harvey suggests that we have now entered an era with a different logic of production. This was a response to a crisis in capitalism that emerged during the early 1970s. Markets were saturated with goods, tax revenues were down, and inflation was out of control. Capitalists responded with a system Harvey calls **flexible accumulation**. This term is broadly analogous to the concept of **post-Fordism** used by other scholars. The key to flexible accumulation is an ability to rapidly change product lines and to manufacture small batches for niche markets. In order to do this, manufacturers make use of smaller numbers of adaptable multi-skilled workers, information technology, and computerized production systems. They also deploy advertising and other strategies in order to continually generate shifts in demand for new and trendy products. By incessantly changing product lines, and by encouraging fads and fashions, the wheels of consumerism and capitalism are kept turning. This helps to postpone what Harvey predicts will be an eventual meltdown of the capitalist system.

Consistent with a Marxist logic, Harvey sees these capital-driven trends spilling over into wider cultural life and determining its broad contours. We live in a world where the media, fads, fashions, and images are increasingly important. The result is a culture characterized by superficiality in which products relentlessly replace each other and where the pursuit of empty style has replaced the search for authenticity, history, and narrative.

Scott Lash: postmodernism as de-differentiation

Scott Lash is broadly sympathetic to Marxian understandings of postmodernism, interpreting it as a product of the capitalist phase he had earlier designated as "disorganized capitalism." However, his work is rather eclectic and also draws upon Weber and Durkheim as well as Marx. Making use of their contributions to classical sociological theory, Lash points out that the rise of modernity was associated with a process of differentiation. This was all about the separation of spheres of social life from one another. As he puts it: "Modernization is a process of cultural differentiation, in which (1) the cultural differentiates from the social, and (2) cultural forms which were previously rather indistinct differentiate from one another" (1990b: 153). Examples of this process include the separation of religious and secular art, and the distinction between the arts and the sciences. Lash claims that postmodernism is a critique of modernity which is all about **de-differentiation**. For example:

- boundaries between culture, economy, and politics are collapsing;
- within the cultural sphere itself, Kantian distinctions between the aesthetic and the moral are also being problematized;
- distinctions between high and low culture are becoming harder to make;
- academic disciplines are no longer distinct from one another.

The concept of de-differentiation is Lash's most novel idea. Other parts of his work provide extended discussions of themes we have already encountered elsewhere. Key claims include:

- We are living in a world where signs and spaces are increasingly shaping our lives (Lash and Urry 1993), or in a "semiotic society" (Lash 1990b).
- Postmodern artworks are post-auratic in Benjamin's sense (see pp. 39–41), and issues of authorship are made problematic.
- The idea of "reality" is under attack.
- Images and spectacles are replacing narratives and history as core features of cultural life. It is a "visual rather than a literary sensibility" (Lash 1988: 314).

Where Lash differs from Harvey, Jameson, and most other neo-Marxist critics is in suggesting that postmodernism has a critical and emancipatory potential. Rather than denouncing postmodernism, he suggests that as future struggles are going to be fought out on this "cultural terrain" the critical project has to come to terms with it.

In order to do this, Lash identifies two distinct kinds of postmodernism – "spectral" and "organic" (Lash 1990b). The former corresponds to conventional understandings of the postmodern. It is about play, the simulacrum, individualist consumerism, and superficiality. The latter is linked to the rise of new social movements (women, greens, gays, etc.) and is based on reflexivity, the search for meaning, and collectivism in the face of advanced capitalist society. Lash argues that only organic postmodernism is capable of engendering an oppositional politics. He sees hope in the fact that class shifts in contemporary capitalism have provided a large potential audience for this form of postmodernism – including intellectuals, academics, and those who work in the information economy. Furthermore, Lash (e.g., 1988) embraces the idea that postmodernism can support tolerance and difference. Drawing on postmodern "gender-bending" advertisements, he suggests that postmodernism has worked to destabilize identities and generate ambivalence. Space has thus been opened up for exciting new subject positions that challenge the normative orders imposed by modernist cultural values.

Further Critiques and Debates

The neo-Marxist critique of postmodernism and postmodernization represents perhaps the most important line of attack. There is also an endlessly proliferating, non-partisan literature which has relentlessly subjected these concepts to scrutiny. This tends to circle around three main themes: the timing, the definition, and the scope of the transition to postmodernity.

Problems of timing

Implicit in the concept of "postmodernism" is the idea that it somehow comes after modernism. Yet when we look closely at various domains, we see that artistic modernism reached a high-water mark at divergent points (see Calhoun 1995: 106; Frow 1998: 40).

- In literature, we think of the work of writers like T. S. Eliot, James Joyce, and Virginia Woolf, and work that reached a peak of innovation in the 1920s and 1930s.
- In architecture, as we have seen, the focus is on the International Style, which arose in the 1920s and continued strongly until the 1970s.
- In music, the paradigm of modernity is associated with the Vienna School. This arose around Schoenberg in the early 1900s but was already being challenged by the "postmodern" work of John Cage and others in the 1940s.

Our understanding of the arrival of the postmodern will vary according to which of these fields we privilege. Looking to social rather than artistic transformations does not help, either. Harvey (1989), for example, dates the shift to the postmodern to the oil crisis of the early 1970s. Yet his fellow Marxist Jameson draws on Ernest Mandel's model of stages of capitalist development and points to the early 1960s.

Compounding this uncertainty yet further is the fact that, for many authors, the postmodern is simply an extension or logical progression of the modern. This means it is possible to trace intimations of postmodernity back several centuries. We can point, for example, to the rise of commodity fetishism and the narcissistic isolated individual in the nineteenth century (see Callinicos 1989: 149), or to the predominance of supposedly postmodern features (irony, play, etc.) in the aesthetic systems of the seventeenth-century baroque (Turner 1990). Such forerunners of the present threaten the idea of a radical break, or even the validity at any attempt at periodization. Craig Calhoun (1995) likewise dubs postmodernism a kind of "pseudohistory" and suggests that "the positing of an epochal change is problematic" (1995: 103). In his reading, theorists of postmodernity often work with simplistic caricatures of artistic modernism, ignoring its complexity and the existence of anti-modern trends in earlier thought.

Problems of definition

Problems of definition are closely related to those of periodization. Even supporters of postmodernism agree that there are multiple understandings. Bauman (1992: vii), for example, points out that "postmodernity means many different things to many different people." He goes on to suggest that for some it means an architectural style, for others the blurring of reality and television, for yet others consumerism and a proliferation of choice, while for philosophers it refers to a radical, skeptical state of mind. Bauman makes a virtue of a necessity by claiming that "incoherence is the most distinctive among the attributes of postmodernity" (1992: xxiv). He argues that this helps to prevent the emergence of a false, totalizing vision and encourages the proliferation of partial observations and narratives. We discuss these sorts of themes further in chapter 14.

While advocates like Bauman see multiplicity and contradiction as a sign of vitality, critics suggest it merely indicates confusion. A representative attack in this vein has been by John Frow (1998), who claims that "postmodernism" has no clear meaning. Most efforts at definition, he argues, seem to be in academic essays like his own. These set out to find a post hoc meaning for concepts that they have found themselves using. He suggests that the term "postmodernism" has proven to be productive simply because of the binarisms implicit within it. These mark it out as being different from, and after, modernism. Therefore endless academic books and papers come into being which work within and fill out these preexisting parameters. This discourse works in the following way: "First you assume the existence of a historical shift in sensibility, which you call the postmodern, then you define it by opposition to whatever you take the modern to have been, finally, you seek to give a content to the postmodern in terms of this opposition" (1998: 15). Frow claims that a lack of clear thinking is manifested in the disconnected lists of things postmodern (the movie *Bladerunner*, the O. J. Simpson trial, Disneyland, irony, MTV, the simulacrum, and so on) that authors inevitably provide in place of a clear and concise definition. Thanks to the lack of conceptual precision, authors debating in the field often talk past one another in a pointless form of "shadowboxing" (1998: 27).

Problems of extent

The issue at hand here concerns the scale and scope of social change. Critics suggest that arguments that we are living in an entirely new social and cultural order are exaggerated and tend toward hyperbole. Craig Calhoun argues that much of the literature presents little or no evidence for extravagant claims that the industrial economy has become less important or that we have entered a post-materialist information age. At best, he suggests, authors like Harvey have documented a "shift – not the first – in the internal organization of capitalism" (1995: 113). Likewise, Alex Callinicos acknowledges that there has been a decline in industrial labor, but goes on to argue that: "The fact that fewer people are employed in material production does not in any case alter the fact that no one can survive without the industrial goods manufactured by these people . . . rising living standards and the associated expansion of mass consumption entail a proliferation of material goods" (1989: 127).

He further points out that arguments about the rise of post-Fordist production (which we have seen are often linked to sociological accounts of postmodernization) neglect continuing demand for standardized products (e.g., white goods) which do not have to be tailored to a specific lifestyle niche in order to be marketable.

The culture written about by postmodernists is one that celebrates cosmopolitanism, diversity, and consumption. Jean-François Lyotard epitomizes this view when he writes: "Eclecticism is the degree zero of contemporary general culture: one listens to reggae, watches a western, eats McDonald's food for lunch and local cuisine for dinner, wears Paris perfume in Tokyo and 'retro' clothes in Hong Kong" (1984: 76). Alex Callinicos (1989: 162) suggests such arguments gloss over questions of access, pointing out: "it is a bit rich that Lyotard should ignore the majority of the population even in the advanced economies to whom such delights as French scent and Far Eastern travel are denied." However Lash (1990b), as we have seen, suggests that postmodernism has indeed reached the working classes as a form of superficial consumerism of precisely this type.

In response to this kind of criticisms and debates, those who suggest change has taken place tend to be rather more cautious now than in the past. Steven Seidman (1994: 1), for example, concedes that "the chief signs of modernity have not disappeared" and that things like the industrial economy, professions, trade unions, political parties, state regulation and utopian visions of the public good remain important. He goes on to suggest that we think of the "modern" and "postmodern" as analytical abstractions that can be used to highlight current social trends and sensibilities. For Seidman, while the postmodern is gaining in importance, we need to be sensitive to the fact that it is by no means dominant in all spheres.

Globalization and Culture

In order to round off this chapter, we need to finish with a detour into the literature on globalization. This is because discussions about postmodernity often overlap closely with those about this process. A major reason for this is that the social forces associated with the postmodernization of culture (e.g., the Internet and other media, consumerism, tourism, the transnational corporation) have also played a core role in generating a world that is more and more interconnected. By bringing cultures into contact, globalization has also encouraged recognition of relativism, reflexivity, difference, and the critique of Western modernity. As we will see in chapter 14, these are all key aspects of postmodern theory.

Globalization can be thought of as a process involving three key dimensions (Waters 1995). These are as follows:

1   Economic globalization is associated with the rise of world finance markets and free-trade zones, the global exchange of goods and services, and the rapid growth of transnational corporations.
2   Political globalization is about the way that the nation-state is being superseded by international organizations (e.g., the United Nations, the European Union) and the rise of global politics.
3   Cultural globalization is about the flow of information, signs, and symbols around the world and reactions to that flow.

While discussion of globalization took off in social science during the 1980s, it is important to remember that the process has been going on for millennia. The movement from small-scale hunting and gathering societies toward the modernist nation-state, for example, can be seen as a step toward a global society. For this reason, much orthodox social and cultural theory can be understood as relating to the issue. The theories of Durkheim, Marx, and Weber provide diverse accounts of the ways that forms of social organization extending over ever larger regions of time and space followed one another during the broader span of history. Notwithstanding the fact that we can reconstruct past theoretical traditions in this way (see Waters 1995), most attention in research on globalization is focused on contemporary settings. In the field of cultural globalization, in particular, themes relating to capitalism, commodities, time/space distanciation, and information flows lead to an inevitable convergence between the globalization, postmodernization, and postmodernism literatures.

Mike Featherstone argues that much writing on the cultural impact of globalization centers around two contending hypotheses or models (Featherstone 1995: 6). The first model suggests that we are living in a world characterized by increasing **Americanization, McDonaldization**, and **homogenization**. Early arguments in this genre were often proposed by academics on the Left and featured denunciations of Americanization. They stressed **cultural imperialism** and the way that the culture of the United States was being exported to the rest of the world along with its free-market ideologies (e.g., Schiller 1976). Particular attention was given to the export of United States-sourced media and entertainment products, such as Disney cartoons. More recent adaptations of this position have pointed to the way that local difference is eroded by the rise of global cultural preferences and administrative systems. These are tied to a generic, rootless, and ever-expanding capitalist rationality, and its associated commodities and technologies, rather than to a distinctively "American" value system.

Perhaps the best-known theory in this tradition is George Ritzer's (1996) concept of McDonaldization, which draws on the work of Marx and Weber. The idea here is that the principles of fast-food organizations are "engulfing more and more sectors of society and areas of the world" (1996: 16). These principles can be summed up as efficiency, calculability, predictability, and control. Ritzer points to sites like universities, funerals, tract housing development, and motels as current areas of McDonaldizing activity. While he sees some benefits in terms of service delivery and affordability, there is also a downside. The practical consequences of change include a narrow means–end rationality without any vision of larger social goals, the deskilling of work and other activities into easy tasks, the provision of prepackaged, standardized modular options, the ruthless application of market principles, and the erosion of authenticity and meaning in social life. According to Ritzer all this has negative implications. He writes: "If the world were less McDonaldized, people would be better able to live up to their human potential" (1996: 15).

According to Featherstone, during the 1980s and 1990s, this sort of thinking, with its pessimistic emphasis on uniformity and the loss of authenticity as the outcome of globalization, came to be increasingly challenged. A second model emerged which stressed the incredibly complex interplay of the **global** and the **local**. While these terms are often used, their exact meaning is elusive and most discussions set about problematizing the binary distinction rather than its explication. Broadly speaking, "the global" refers to the spatially extensive social and cultural forces associated with globalization (e.g., consumerism, satellite communications, culture industries, migration), while "the local" refers to small-scale, geographically confined traditions and ways of life (e.g., ethnic traditions, language, religion). Scholars in this area generally point to the way that processes of globalization have seen global and local cultures brought into contact with each other. These collisions have brought about complex and unpredictable results, with major outcomes in any sphere including possibilities for hybridization and difference, as well as homogenization.

- In some cases homogenization takes place. For example, there are many common tastes, preferences, and lifestyles among the affluent middle classes of all developed nations. This has tended to eliminate or minimize the impact of local cultures and lifestyles. In many cases findings in this area are consistent with mainstream socio-logical theory on processes of modernization, which suggest that the "rest" catches up with the "West."
- Hybridization can arise from the mixing of cultures and lifestyles. This is the theme exemplified by Lyotard's notion of the urban cosmopolitan (see above, pp. 222–3), and Homi Bhabha's images of postcolonial migrants, who share qualities of both core and periphery (see pp. 236–7). A major theme here can be the way that global forces and products are adapted or modified by local conditions.
- Difference and the local can also be reaffirmed through globalization. Ethnic reviv-als, struggles for indigenous rights, religious fundamentalism, and racist backlashes can all be seen as defensive reactions to globalization. They have arisen from a desire to defend and preserve valued ways of life against what are taken to be the perni-cious effects of foreign and global influences.

Over recent years, scholars have tended to focus increasingly on the last issue of differ-ence and suggest that it has perhaps been the major outcome of cultural globalization (see Featherstone 1995: 12ff.). Postcolonial scholars in particular have suggested that the process has opened up space for the periphery to have a voice, with the monolithic power and authority of the center subject to question from multiple competing centers. The image here is of an endlessly proliferating babble of voices, with established hier-archies and points of reference destabilized and with affirmations of difference providing the only common ground. In this context, Western cultural values are relativized as just another form of the local that has been brought into contact with others through globalization.

Two scholars have contributed notable and influential conceptual innovations to the globalization discussion in the past decade or so, and we cannot conclude this section without discussing them. Both Manuel Castells and Ulrich Beck should probably be placed in the second of Featherstone's two groups, but the sheer scope of their explora-tions defies easy categorization.

Castells's massive three-volume work on the information age and the network society has already become something of a modern classic barely a decade after its first publica-tion. His argument is broadly that what is called globalization in the media and else-where is in fact a set of revolutionary changes in both information technology and organizational structure and culture, each of which contributes to and pushes further change in the other. The **network society** is connected via both the new communicative medium of the Internet and a new spirit of business enterprise that he calls the Cisco model, by which he means a commercial model in which firms employ the same networking interdependency characteristic of the Internet itself to the organization of their businesses. But the network society is not in fact global, at least not in the sense that we mean that it is to be found everywhere. There is a global elite which inhabits the **space of flows** (a very fluid sense of place created by electronic networking and easily accessible travel), but the global dispossessed live in a much more traditional world of exploitation and quotidian misery (Castells 2000 [1996]). Castells describes the contemporary world as islands of networked elites surrounded by seas of the disconnected poor. The responses of many of the latter to the rise of network society will entail rejection of the abstract universalism it posits and a protective retreat into the construction of ethnic and cultural local community that can take a wide array of forms, from Islamic fundamentalism to Catalonian cultural nationalism. The very core of democracy is, in Castell's view, threatened by the effects of **informational politics**. Mass media and the drive for audiences and profits comes to define democratic politics, and a perverse cycle is created wherein scandal becomes the central trope of media coverage of politics and politicians are driven to scandal precisely by the need to channel more and more money into those media sources that will ultimately decide if they will be elected or not (Castells 2004 [1997]).

Cosmopolitanism is Ulrich Beck's main contribution to the theoretical vocabulary on globalization. Tracing the history in European thought of this notion, he points out how we find the fundamental duality he wishes to explore in the concept already there in its first articulation, in Greek Stoicism. For the Stoics and for Beck, cosmopolitanism means that each individual is a member both of some delimited political community and of the global community of all humans. These two bases for identity and relations with others are not presented by Stoicism in an "either/or" but rather in a "both/and" relationship (Beck 2006: 45). But while the Stoics spoke from a time near the beginning of the rise to dominance of what Beck calls "the national outlook," Beck elaborates his version of the concept at what he sees as the period of its decline and fall. Not only are more and more people forced to acknowledge the latent cosmopolitanism of their lives and the lives of others, but social scientists and other analysts of society and culture necessarily come to realize that the conceptual tools of the national era are no longer up to the task for which they were intended. A social science that does not endeavor to theoretically free itself from the limitations of the national outlook finds itself in the same situation as the German citizen who is unable to adequately make sense of his German co-citizen with a "non-German" last name. Both continue fruitlessly to ask "but where do you *really* come from?" because they are working with an outmoded notion of origins (Beck 2006: 25).

For Beck, even most of the social science purportedly directed to a multicultural politics fails to free itself sufficiently from this framework and ends up merely recapitulating nationalist discourses within one nation. Instead of real cosmopolitan identity, we get a hodge-podge of ethnically based identities that are taken as essential objects and opposed to one another. The "both/and" operation that cosmopolitanism must perform today, according to Beck, is to affirm the Other as at one and the same time different and the same (2006: 58). Both crude universalism and crude cultural relativism are rejected in favor of a richer grasp of cultural reality. He provides the Hmong people living in the West as an example. How should they be identified? Are they Chinese? Vietnamese? Laotian? American? Canadian? French? Cosmopolitanism accepts that they can be several of these all at once (2006: 64).

Beck's work has some affinities with recent work on racial and ethnic identity that have taken up notions of racial hybridity and *métissage*; we discuss these in chapter 15. He has also attracted some critics. These tend to agree with the utility of cosmopolitanism as a utopian political ideal, but doubt that it has been sufficiently defined as a theoretical category. One group of critics points to four central problems:

- The indeterminacy of the concept (Beck himself admits the difficulty of providing a robust definition).
- The difficulty in precisely identifying who is and who is not cosmopolitan and in establishing an ideal type of the category.
- The disagreement over the attributes of cosmopolitanism. It is not clear if the cosmopolitan is to be defined chiefly through her practices (like the eclectic cultural consumption of world music and food styles); her progressive beliefs and attitudes (e.g., tolerance of strangers, anti-racism, environmentalism); her spatial movements (around the world for work or leisure); or her national and racial background (e.g., a hyphenated identity). Beck seems to introduce all such themes without imposing any real analytic order or sense of priority on these.
- The demonstrable weakness of the political aspect of cosmopolitanism, vividly seen in the lack of real agency and power afforded to individuals as "global citizens in so far as they do not vote, have no representatives or constitution, etc." (Skrbis et al. 2004: 118).

Suggested Further Reading

We are not aware of any textbooks or readers that provide a focused and balanced discussion of all the themes we have considered here. Thankfully, several of the studies referred to in this chapter are difficult but not impenetrable. Fredric Jameson's (1984) essay is a classic which should be read. Lash's (1990a) anthology covers many of the core themes in the literature and will provide a sense of the issues at stake. A study of Jencks (1977) will also help the reader develop a feel for what is going on. Although they are not pitched at textbook level, we can also recommend two insightful books by Krishnan Kumar (1995) and Bryan Turner (1994) to readers looking for a sociological take on postmodernity. Lyotard's *The Postmodern Condition* and Baudrillard's *Symbolic Exchange and Death* are less daunting than most of the rest of their writing, but still demanding. Mike Gane (1991a, 1991b) has written a number of reliable and readable secondary sources on Baudrillard as well as compiling a book of interviews with him that do much to make sense of some of his denser work (1993).

CHAPTER FOURTEEN

Postmodern and Poststructural Critical Theory

In the previous chapter we looked at work that explored aesthetic postmodernism and the alleged transition to a postmodern era. Here we are concerned with a literature that embraces key elements of a postmodern and poststructural philosophical and analytic position, while also retaining a commitment to core elements of critical theories ranging from Western Marxism (see chapter 3) to feminism and queer theory. This has recently become a major force in contemporary cultural theory and has taken over from Marxism as one of the dominant voices of the intellectual Left. We are concerned here, of course, with a massive field full of complex and overlapping intellectual positions. However, the chapter paints with a broad brush, and so exegesis will center not so much on itemizing differences and internal debates as on detecting the essential family resemblances which run through this style of work. This includes the following characteristics:

- the critique of the cultural foundations of science and Western modernity;
- a commitment to the centrality of texts and discourses in the construction of social order;
- a belief that cultural theory is part of a moral and political enterprise;
- a recognition of the perspectives, voices, and cultures of subordinate groups.

The following discussion will explore these themes.

The Critique of Modernity

In the previous chapter we saw how writing on postmodernization was concerned with documenting a historical shift from a modern to a postmodern era. Theorists who adopt a postmodern position go somewhat further and criticize the value systems and beliefs of modernity. While Lyotard was content, for the most part, to record the decline of the grand narratives of modernity (see pp. 211–12), postmodern theorists endorse their consignment to the dustbin of history either with enthusiasm, or else with a pragmatic regret. Charles Lemert, for example, suggests that this move is a rational response to a changing world. He writes: "Postmodernism, if it is about anything, is about the prospect that the promises of the modern age are no longer believable because there is evidence that for the vast majority of people worldwide there is no realistic reason to vest hope in any version of the idea that the world is good and getting better" (1997: xii).

For many, the articulation of a postmodern philosophy is inevitably caught up in this sort of critique of modernity and its optimistic beliefs about human progress, reason, universalism, and science. This position has been articulated most forcefully by Zygmunt Bauman in *Modernity and Ambivalence* (1991). He suggests that modernity was all about the control of contingency (chance, diversity). It had a "dream of order" and was obsessed with controlling, regulating, and classifying. The result was a society that attempted to create order through regulations, institutions, laws, and moral codes. These tried to identify universally applicable standards for truth, justice, and reason and to stamp out relativism, uncertainty, and ambiguity. While this all sounds very noble, there was an unfortunate downside to these ambitions. In the act of creating order through classifications, modernity also produced binary oppositions. These led to the identification of the **other** – that which did not fit into the positive side of the binary and which had to be subjected to power and control. Bauman writes: "[A]bnormality is the other of the norm, deviation the other of law-abiding, illness the other of health, barbarity the other of civilization, animal the other of the human, woman the other of man, stranger the other of the native, enemy the other of friend, 'them' the other of 'us', insanity the other of reason, foreigner the other of the state subject, lay public the other of the expert" (1991: 14).

According to Bauman, then, modernity inevitably set up and legitimated hierarchies of oppression. It also led to the persecution of ambivalence. Social groups that could be assigned to more than one category, or which fell between the cracks of modernity's ordering principles, were subject to assimilationist policies or (as in the case of Europe's Jews) to persecution and extermination. The point that Bauman makes is representative of the critique of **totality** or **totalism** which is common in the postmodern literature. This refers to intellectual and administrative systems that try to capture social life as a whole; that attempt to understand and control it within a single coherent intellectual or legislative framework. Postmodernists generally assert that efforts to understand and be sensitive to fragmentation, difference, and the local are less dangerous and more fruitful.

The Suspicion of Science

Associated with the assault on modernity's ordering principles has been a critique of science. During the Enlightenment, attacks were launched in the name of science on religion, folk knowledge, and superstition. The philosophies of modernism, such as Marxism ("scientific socialism") and positivism, argued that scientific knowledge and experts could uncover universal truths and work selflessly for the common good. Postmodernists see these claims as highly problematic. Drawing in large part on Foucault's critiques of power/knowledge, they suggest that science has by and large operated as an ideology through which disciplinary discourses are supported (Bauman 1991: 242). It is linked to domination, objectification, and control rather than emancipation and truth. An important background influence here has been Thomas Kuhn's book *The Structure of Scientific Revolution* (1970). Although a conventional historian of science rather than a postmodernist or critical theorist, Kuhn undermined the idea that scientific knowledge was produced in an intellectual vacuum and that observations alone led to theories. On the contrary, he argued that our theories and intellectual frameworks, what he called **paradigms**, shape the way we see the world. More recent sociological work on science has also challenged its claims to objectivity and infallibility. Ethnographic studies, for example, have demonstrated that many scientific findings are artifacts of laboratory practice, social networks, struggles for prestige and funding, and so on.

Building on this work, postmodernists have challenged the underpinning ontological and epistemological foundations of science. For postmodernists, the fundamental divisions between, say, reason and emotion, or objective knowledge versus personal experience, are questionable. It is increasingly being argued that knowledge is produced as a consequence of identity and social location. Science is a discourse of dominant white males, and a task of postmodern and poststructural theory is to recover subaltern voices – such as those shaped by race, gender, or sexuality.

An illustrative and important book in this broad tradition is Sandra Harding's *The Science Question in Feminism* (1986). Writing from a feminist perspective, Harding's main point is that, far from being neutral or transcending social relations, scientific activity and scientific knowledge have been "epistemologically and politically regressive" (1986: 243). Cloaked in a universalistic myth, they have, in fact, served to represent male interests and ways of thinking. Harding paints a picture in which "emotions, feelings and political values" (1986: 245) are marginalized by the scientific worldview. In her opinion, it is not just the case that we need to weed out "bad science" (e.g., sexist research projects), but rather that the entire conceptual framework of science is faulty.

Harding draws on standpoint epistemology in making her argument. This is the theory that knowledge production is profoundly influenced by social location. The questions that are selected for investigation, the theories that are constructed to understand the world, and even research findings, reflect experiences and political locations. She also draws from postmodernism and its attack on totalizing theories, with their argument that reason and method will allow us to fully comprehend the world. Consequently, Harding suggests that what we need is a scientific enterprise that is more reflexive about its own limitations. She asserts that moral and political discourses should no longer be separated from scientific activity. We should also be more attentive to questions of difference, and attempt to make space for diverse voices within science rather than continuing to operate with a universalistic mythology. We examine theoretical work in standpoint epistemology that specifically describes how race and gender positions influence knowledge in chapter 15.

While Harding does not altogether give up the idea of comparatively evaluating different forms of knowledge and even arguing that some perspectives produce better scientific knowledge than others (2004: 131), the critique of science in postmodernism is closely linked to relativism. This is a philosophical position which argues that there is no absolute and objective viewpoint from which we can detect the truth. Rather, all knowledge is derived from a particular perspective and is supported by particular doctrines and institutions. While accusations of relativism are often used against post-modernism (see below), many postmodern theorists are quite comfortable with the label. They see it as consistent with the postmodern proposition that we cannot privi-lege any particular vision, but rather should document, juxtapose, and challenge all visions, demonstrating how they are incomplete, biased, or socially constructed in various ways. This intellectual move has been facilitated by a declining faith in the grand narrative of science – a process documented by Lyotard (see pp. 211–12) – and the work of Foucault, who insisted that there were multiple, contending "truths" that the intellectual should work to uncover (Lemert 1997: 139).

According to Bauman (1992: 105–6), the rise of relativism has seen the role of intel-lectuals shift. Under modernity, they were **legislators** who had responsibility for devel-oping universal classifications and objective knowledge. Under postmodernity, such a task is seen as both impossible and undesirable. As a consequence, their role has changed to that of **interpreters**. Bauman sees Geertz as emblematic of this position (see pp. 189–92). In a world without absolute standards, the cultural theorist becomes a sort of translator and mediator whose role is to generate dialogue and reflexivity between and within diverse social spheres. Postmodern cultural theorists generally prefer to think of themselves as interpreters, too. They understand themselves not as scientists of but rather as carriers of discourses that encourage the open exchange of ideas and healthy, reflexive critique.

The Attack on General Theory

As we saw in the discussion of Sandra Harding and Zygmunt Bauman, a critique of totalizing knowledge is closely linked to the attack on science and modernity. Accord-ing to Steven Seidman (1991: 68), for example, the "epistemic suspicion" which is "at the core of postmodernism . . . challenges the basic aim of disciplinary discourses to create general – indeed universally valid conceptions of society, history and moder-nity." He suggests that we should replace efforts at general theory (a theory of every-thing) with theoretical constructions that are more local and contextual. These should be responsive to the needs and struggles of marginalized groups in particular settings.

Central to this position is the belief, derived in part from Foucault, that we should relentlessly interrogate our conceptual categories for evidence of power/knowledge. We should attempt to uncover the hidden biases behind the concepts that we use and the ways that they work to reproduce relationships of domination. Efforts at the con-struction of a general or universal theory are to be feared because they are part of modernity's failed project. This project was inevitably about control as much as under-standing, in as far as attempts to construct knowledge were also (sometimes inadver-tently) attempts to repress or convert difference. Where it claimed to detect truth, general theory ended up reproducing power. As Bauman puts it: "Truth is, in other words, a social relation (like power, ownership or freedom): an aspect of a hierarchy built of superiority-inferiority units . . . an aspect of the hegemonic form of domination. The part of the world that adopted modern civilization as its structural principle and constitutional value was bent on dominating the rest of the world by dissolving its alterity and assimilating the product of dissolution" (1991: 232).

In this postmodern perspective we need to rethink our understanding of knowledge as something that is outside of power. Rather than celebrating efforts at understanding that arise from general models and grand theories, we need to exercise caution and be aware that our ideas are potentially dangerous. Abandoning ideas about "truth" and "reason" might provide an important initial step on this journey. Constant reflexivity about the intellectual tools that we use is another major aspect of this process.

Textuality

Attacks on science suggested the impossibility of an objective understanding of the world. This has in turn led to an interest in the texts and representations through which knowledge claims are constructed. Knowledge is seen as the product of textual strategies and ways of writing. Thus rhetoric and discourse shift to the fore as objects of analysis (see Brown 1990). Consequently, postmodernists are interested in exploring the ways that language is involved in processes of definition, classification, and control. Unlike earlier studies of ideology, there is no particular emphasis here on documenting the "false" nature of particular worldviews. Rather the aim is to explore discourses and their consequences. Divisions between society and text have been made as problematic as those separating truth and rhetoric (see Lemert 1997: 101ff.). Thanks to the work of scholars like Foucault, it is argued that the social world is marbled with discourses. "Real" institutions and practices (e.g., the prison, punishment) can be seen, in a sense, as expressions of underlying discursive patterns. Consequently, we have to "read" the social and uncover the linguistic and textual practices with which it is inscribed. Research now can be seen less as a scientific exercise and more as a kind of literary criticism or decoding exercise.

Ever attentive to the power of language, postmodern and poststructural theorists are keen to avoid the mistakes of modernists and positivists. A reflexive awareness of the ways the language intervenes in the construction of knowledge has led to the adoption of complex textual forms by some postmodern writers. The aim of these is to head off logocentrism (see pp. 123–4) by foregrounding the distorting and constructive role of language in academic activity. These writing strategies can include:

- juxtaposing various descriptions of the same episode;
- adopting diverse narrative personas;
- building dialogue and debate into an argument;
- writing in modes that are unconventional in academic fields, such as using real (or fake) diary excerpts, or scripting dramas;
- breaking up, mutating, or hybridizing words to demonstrate their ability to carry multiple meanings simultaneously (e.g., Homi Bhabha's "DissemiNation" [1990b]).

These various trends are well illustrated in Michael Mulkay's (1985) work in the field of the sociology of science. The challenge he sets himself is to write about science and scientific communication without replicating the "empiricist monologue" that is common to both scientific and social scientific writing. In order to do this, he uses drama, dialogue, and parody – even pretending at one point to be the book speaking to the reader. Another prominent work in this vein is Malcolm Ashmore's (1989) book on reflexivity and scientific knowledge. This kind of writing can appear absurd, irritating, or self-indulgent to outsiders, but the intent is serious. Authors such as Mulkay and Ashmore suggest that, by highlighting the use of language and by violating conventional expectations about its use, we can become more reflexive about textual practices and their implications. From a postmodern perspective, such unorthodox writing styles are more honest than mainstream social-scientific writing that adopts a pseudo-objectivist pose.

The Rise of Pragmatism and Attacks on Foundationalism

As we have seen, postmodern theorists are highly suspicious of attempts to organize or understand society on the basis of universal values, methods, or perspectives. The modernist effort to locate a set of originating values or definitive principles or "the truth" is denounced as **foundationalism**. Marxism, liberalism, functionalism, structuralism, and so on can all be read as foundationalist projects, although each was foundationalist in its own special way. Drawing on Derrida, in particular, postmodernism asserts that the central binary oppositions of modernist thought (true/false, mind/body, reason/emotion, etc.) are less stable than we might suppose. It is also argued that there is no guarantee that foundational concepts like freedom or democracy actually bring about a better society. Nor can ideological blueprints for policies, institutions, and interventions. Given the fact that universal principles have been rejected, some kind of criteria need to be deployed for guiding and evaluating our society. But just what?

The theorist Richard Rorty (e.g., 1989) has perhaps been the most significant thinker in providing a solution to this issue. Rorty suggests that we should use pragmatic criteria for making sense of and directing social change and social policy rather than extolling ambivalent and empty values. Drawing on the American pragmatist tradition of philosopher John Dewey as much as on Derrida's anti-foundationalist philosophy, Rorty claims that we should try to see "what works" rather than endlessly debating about the best abstract principles for running our societies. According to this sort of position, most social criticism is vague, obscure, doctrinaire, and full of jargon. What is needed in its place is a dose of common sense and healthy suspicion of authority. Rather than engaging in philosophical disputes about, say, capitalism versus communism, it is better to look at the world around us for evidence about what to do next.

While Rorty speaks with a kind of breezy American optimism, Bauman's response to the loss of foundationalist certainty exudes a more bleak sensibility. He suggests that we are living in an era of contingency, which he has named "liquid life" (2005), where uncertainty, the ephemeral face of celebrity, and the need to quickly dispose of the "outdated" in order to keep up with the pace of change reign. Those who cannot keep up are cast aside and we seemingly have no choice but to play the game of the post-modern condition. Where there is no faith, no ready-made solution to uncertainty and ambivalence, and only an all-pervading radical doubt, we need to have "nerves of steel" (1991: 245). Bauman's faint hope for our "dark times," echoing the position of Adorno (see chapter 3), is that his own and other critical voices, which are largely ignored in the midst of the anarchic consumerist frenzy of postmodern liquidity, will be preserved as a kind of "message in a bottle" for future generations. These future recipients of today's postmodern critical observations might be better positioned than the present generation to create new forms of solidarity and community (2005: 141).

Social Theory as a Moral and Political Enterprise

Postmodernists generally attack the idea of cultural theory as a morally neutral enter-prise aiming at disinterested social inquiry, but rather take it to be an emancipatory activity. To be sure, they query the idea that there can (or should) be universal moral standards that can guide human activity. Yet the point of this is not simply nihilistic. Rather, they see critical postmodern theory as forcing people to make their own moral and ethical choices without the crutches of habitual belief or deference to moral author-ity. Bauman refers to a resulting "ethical paradox of the postmodern condition," which "restores to agents the fullness of moral choice and responsibility while simultaneously depriving them of the comfort of the universal guidance that modern self-confidence one promised" (1992: xxii). He notes that we may not know what form the new eman-cipatory political frameworks toward which postmodern critical theory points will take, but we are nonetheless morally obliged not to give up the "critical" in "critical theory" (2005: 143, 153).

Moral issues also invade the research enterprise and its methodologies. As we have seen, postmodernists argue that no research – not even that of bench scientists – can be truly value-free or denuded of power relationships. Therefore intellectuals and researchers have a duty to be explicit about their values and identities and understand their work as inherently political. Rather than being written out of the research process, these are foregrounded. For this reason, claims are frequently made that intellectuals have a duty to enter into the public domain and engage in debates with others. They should also seek to work with (rather than upon) the people they study. These sorts of claims echo those that have been made by critical theorists and feminists for some time. However, with postmodern research the arguments that are proposed tend to favor more specific and local struggles rather than attempts at global emancipation. Among the more important of these are attempts to explore, retrieve, and give voice to identities which have become subordinated, and efforts to explore and deconstruct the discourses that create their subordination. We discuss this in the next section.

The Analysis of Identity and Difference

Writing about the arts, Cornel West (1994) argues that intellectuals should be engaged in a "new cultural politics of difference." This involves the alignment of cultural creators and theorists with disempowered minorities and the construction of works of art which focus on themes of race, gender, difference, and empowerment. According to West, the core features of the new cultural politics of difference are "to trash the monolithic and homogenous in the name of diversity, multiplicity and heterogeneity; to reject the abstract, general and universal in the light of the concrete, specific and particular; and to historicize, contextualize and pluralize by highlighting the contingent, provisional, variable, tentative, shifting and changing" (1994: 65).

Something similar has been going on in postmodern and poststructural social and cultural theory too, with numerous efforts being made to document diversity and particularity. Social changes during the last decades of the twentieth century paved the way for a renewed focus on identity and difference as key components of postmodern social theory (Lemert 1997: 35). These included the rise of new social movements, the reemergence of ethnicity and the continuing vitality of traditional cultures. Such events challenged "modernity's long-standing claim to be THE universal culture of human progress" (1997: 35). A related claim is that an alleged decline of Western hegemony and the rise of globalization has undermined the authority of Western/Enlightenment intellectual constructs and opened up space for alternatives. Lemert again writes: "the destabilizing of the modern world is associated with a curious, but undeniable, energizing of identity as the topic of widespread political interest" (1997: 128).

Over recent years the study of **identity** and **difference** has become a crucial hallmark of thinkers influenced by postmodern and poststructural theory. "Identity" refers to who people think they are, either individually or collectively, and the ways that this is culturally constructed. Ideas about "difference" try to capture the diversity of forms of human identity and experience. It is almost invariably opposed to the "universal."

Craig Calhoun identifies two ways in which poststructural theory urges us to take difference seriously:

1   *Differences of value.* The emphasis here is on recognizing that humans and cultures may have diverse values and modes of moral reasoning that cannot be subsumed within a single, Enlightenment-derived model. Often these differences of value may be incommensurable and not amenable to any easy synthesis.
2   *The value of difference.* The point here is to understand that "there is an intrinsic advantage to the production of cultural variation. It can lead to "reflective self-awareness" and "creativity" (1995: 75). In other words, difference can create a better world.

Calhoun argues that an attention to these aspects of difference has implications for the way that we do theory. We need to try to generate "polyphonic discourse, not a monological statement . . . a discourse in which many voices shed light on a problem from different vantage points" (1995: 88). A theory which recognizes difference should replace efforts at closure and general explanation. We need also to be more attentive to the social and historical contexts within which difference is constructed, and explore its implications. Thinking along these lines about the theoretical implications of difference has been especially important in the new empirical areas that have come into prominence over recent years: queer theory, postcolonial theory, and African-American studies.

Within queer theory, a major agenda has been not only to trace the ways in which dominant representations of gender and sexuality serve to marginalize gays and lesbians, but also to deconstruct these dominant representations. A key aim has been to avoid essentialist understandings of homosexuality and to destabilize the kinds of binary opposition that define the homosexual in contrast to the heterosexual (Seidman 1997: 149ff.). For the most part, this calls for the study of the collective representations and discourses through which such binaries are encoded, rather than a study of individual identities and struggles for liberation. Thanks to the influence of thinkers like Lacan (see pp. 199–200) and Foucault (see pp. 115–21), identity is seen as a signifier at play in cultural fields rather than as a biological or psychological quality of individuals. Derrida's deconstructivist techniques (see p. 124) are also often drawn upon, frequently to problematize the boundaries of the homo- and heterosexual. Judith Butler's work (e.g., 2006 [1990]) is perhaps the best-known example of this position. Butler argues that the cultural regime in which we live inscribes heterosexual orientations as "normal" and links sexed subjects (men and women) to sexed bodies (male and female). This linkage is inherently political insofar as it is part of a power/knowledge regime. According to Butler's model, performativity (what people do) is important for maintaining this gender order. She looks to drag (men dressing as women) as a deconstructive performative practice which problematizes taken-for-granted subjectivities and gender binarisms. She sees it as an activity through which individuals can create alternative gendered identities and spaces. Thanks to its play on difference, it simultaneously makes use of and subverts the core binary opposition that maintains heterosexual power. We explore Butler's work in more detail in chapter 15.

In postcolonial studies, the most noted exponent of the deconstructive method is Homi Bhabha (e.g., 1990a, 1990b). For Bhabha, colonialism and postcolonialism are very much about identities and the ways that these are constructed and deconstructed by discourses. As Edward Said (1978) documented in his earlier (broadly modernist) work *Orientalism*, colonial hegemony was cemented by a series of binary oppositions which contrasted the rational West to an irrational, sexual, and childlike East. Bhabha suggests that postcolonial social relations and theoretical discourses are breaking down these binarisms. He argues that ambivalence is at the heart of the nation. Following Derrida's theories of writing, he suggests that the nation sets out to define or "narrate" itself and its boundaries, but can never be fully comprehensive and ends up producing ambivalence, contradiction, and uncertainty. Bhabha writes: "The address to nation as narration stresses the insistence of political power and cultural authority in what Derrida describes as the 'irreducible excess of the syntactic over the semantic'. What emerges as an effect of such 'incomplete signification' is a turning of boundaries and limits into the in-between spaces through which the meanings of cultural and political authority are negotiated" (1990a: 4).

What Bhabha is saying here is not just that cultural difference and the "Other" are produced by dominant discourses, but also that ambivalence and in-between groups arise as an unintended product of their cultural logic. These inhabit and emerge into the spaces and contradictions in a national discourse. Like other postcolonial theorists,

Bhabha (e.g., 1990b: 315ff.) sees difference, ambivalence, and **hybridity** as powerful tools for combating dominant discourses and structures of power. It is the last of these that he hints is the most potent. Rather than simply setting up an alternative discourse which affirms difference, hybridity works to transgress existing discourses and reveal the incomplete and contingent nature of nationalist ideologies. Hybridity, he says, exists at the borderlines and intersections of national narratives and self-definitions (note the similarity to Butler's analysis of drag, above). An example of this that Bhabha uses is the postcolonial migrant. Such people can destabilize traditional identities and violate supposedly mutually exclusive categories because they are simultaneously of both the East and West. A number of influential cultural theorists of racial identity, e. g., Paul Gilroy, Orlando Patterson, and Orville Lee, have further elaborated on hybridity and related conceptual tools. We examine this work in chapter 15.

Within African-American studies there is also a powerful impetus to valorize perspectives which have been marginal or neglected, and to confront and challenge the worldviews of dominant discourses. Often this quest involves the effort to evaluate African-American experiences using African-American standards. A study of the Harlem Renaissance by Houston Baker (1987) exemplifies this style of work. The Harlem Renaissance was an artistic movement in the 1920s involving black Americans. Baker notes that it has often been judged a failure, and attributes this to the imposition of alien evaluative categories. He writes that "the very histories that are assumed in the chronologies of British, Anglo-American and Irish modernisms are radically opposed to any adequate and accurate account of the history of African-American modernism, especially the discursive history of such modernism" (1987: xvi).

Abandoning dominant frameworks, Baker seeks instead to approach the Harlem Renaissance using a different set of categories more closely related to African-American history. He speaks, for example, of the "minstrel mask" and the ways that this impacted upon African-American modernism. The effort to move beyond the sorts of stereotypes displayed in minstrel shows had long been a key theme in black cultural expression and academic discourse. Similarly, there was an enduring effort to develop African-American nationalism and collective identity and to validate the vernacular. For Baker, the Harlem Renaissance has to be understood as a product of this wider social, cultural, and political project. It can be considered a success when viewed in this more appropriate lens as part of a decades-long struggle whose roots lie in the history of oppression and slavery. Indeed, it is best thought of as a "sounding strategy" through which a minority group generated solidarity and made "audible signs of the human will's resistance to tyranny" (1987: 105, 107).

Postmodern and Poststructural Critical Cultural Theory: Evaluation and Critique

For many critics, especially those influenced by Marxism, postmodern theory encourages a distant and aesthetic gaze which does not support critique and which glosses over real inequality and suffering. We have already seen this kind of argument raised against postmodern art in Jameson's attack on *Diamond Dust Shoes* (see p. 218). A broadly similar point was made by Jürgen Habermas in an early commentary on post-modernism in the arts. According to Habermas, postmodernism can be broadly described as "neoconservatism" (1981: 13), which arose from a disillusion with the project of aesthetic and artistic modernism. This disillusion emerged from the failure of modernism to mediate the effects of societal modernization and provide cultural and moral constraints on the rationalization of everyday life. According to Habermas, the neoconservative orientation of the postmodernists magnifies this failure. It gives up altogether on attempts to connect art with politics or emancipation, and insists on the purely private nature of aesthetic experience. He suggests that this move has been premature and argues that "instead of giving up on modernity and its project as a lost cause, we should learn from [its] mistakes" (1981: 11).

Allegations of conservatism raised against postmodern art have also been voiced against postmodern cultural theory. Alex Callinicos, for example, claims that postmodern intellectuals like Baudrillard have abandoned "the traditional task of theo-retical enquiry, of uncovering the underlying structure responsible for the way things seem" and have substituted a kind of "intellectual dandyism" (1989: 147). At the root of this problem is the postmodern insistence that the "real" does not exist outside of discourse, and that the world must therefore be understood in aesthetic terms. Accord-ing to Callinicos, Baudrillard's idea of the simulacrum suggests that we live in a world which is pure simulation – there is nothing beyond the image, no reality hidden beneath immediate sensory experience. Such postmodern understandings reject as absurd a "depth model of interpretation" which would hunt for an "underlying essence" and proposes instead that we engage in attractive, but intellectually shallow, descriptions of simulacra which straddle the boundary of literature and philosophy.

While these sorts of denunciations are often made, it is worth noting that they tend to be directed against soft targets, such as Baudrillard's travel writing or Warhol's pop art. As we have seen in this chapter, most of the leading figures in postmodern and poststructural critical theory have made the analysis and denunciation of power a key aspect of their work. Far from denying oppression and "reality," they have tried to develop tools so that we can better understand them. They have tried to speak on behalf of minority voices and question those that are invested with authority and power in the contemporary world.

A more telling criticism, perhaps, is that postmodern social philosophy amounts to a relentlessly critical and deconstructive enterprise. It has been said that it continually denies the possibility of truth and reason, and uncovers power and contradiction wher-ever it looks. For modernists, this ironic and relativistic gaze threatens to undercut the epistemological and moral foundations that are required for an emancipatory politics. Such a critique is nicely captured up by Zygmunt Bauman (1992: ix), who says: "It [postmodern theory] is often blamed for not being positive enough, for not being posi-tive at all, for not wishing to be positive and for pooh-poohing positivity as such, for sniffing a knife of unfreedom under any cloak of saintly righteousness or just placid self-confidence." Of course, Bauman goes on to defend postmodernism, suggesting that its suspicion is a healthy "siteclearing operation" which is dismantling the distortions and pretensions of modernist thinking.

Craig Calhoun (1995) remains skeptical. He questions the emancipatory potential of postmodernism. In his view there is no clear practical strategy advanced for engaging inequality, capitalism, and so on, even if the diagnosis is insightful. Moreover, the relentless emphasis on difference makes it difficult to see how collective identity, and hence collective action, can emerge that transcends ethnic, racial, or other identity boundaries. Finally, the decentering of the subject (see pp. 93, 113) "poses a challenge for a theory desiring to address agency and moral responsibility" (1995: 124). While offering a useful counter to an individualistic liberal humanism, postmodernism does not have an adequate account of human freedom and choice.

Finally, we have to confront the issue of relativism. Postmodern and poststructural perspectives undermine our conventional notions of truth. They suggest that knowledge and values reflect interests, experiences, standpoints, and identities. Thus a complete, accurate knowledge of the world is impossible. Indeed, there is no universally valid knowledge or system of morality, only perspective. Modernist critics suggest that such a position is dangerous. It leaves us with no way of evaluating which interpretation or research finding is more accurate. By exposing them as discursive conventions of modernity, it also threatens to undercut basic ideals like human rights, democracy, or freedom that have facilitated human emancipation. Far from encouraging rational debate and inclusion, it undermines the possibility of appeal to objective facts and universal values. This leaves the door open for demagogues, racists, and bigots to propagate their views and dismiss those of others out of hand.

Despite these various attacks, the perspective we have reviewed in this chapter continues to grow in authority and clearly has much to offer contemporary cultural theory. These benefits are summarized below:

- Questions of morality, value, and politics are given a central role in theoretical inquiry.
- Genuine efforts are made to incorporate minority views and perspectives.
- The perspective recognizes the central and autonomous role of culture (as discourse, text, difference, and identity) in shaping social life.
- Intellectual models shaped by modernism, universalism, and scientism are subject to healthy suspicion and critique.
- Attention is given to the local. This encourages the study of specific research sites and issues rather than sweeping general theories.

These are important achievements. By interrogating familiar intellectual categories and approaches, postmodern and poststructural critical theories have challenged complacency and opened up new directions for cultural research. This reflexivity and sensitivity will provide an important resource as we move into the global, multicultural, postmodern world that lies ahead.

Suggested Further Reading

There are several excellent readers available that contain essays of postmodern and poststructural social theory. One such starting place is Steven Seidman's edited collection *The Postmodern Turn*. Charles Lemert's *Postmodernism is Not What You Think* offers an honest, friendly, accessible, and enthusiastic review of the area by one of its leading partisans. *Intimations of Postmodernity* and the more recent *Liquid Life* are perhaps the best examples of Bauman's work. The critiques by Callinicos (1989) and Calhoun (1995) cover the spectrum of outsider opinion, ranging from hostility (Callinicos) to cautious appreciation (Calhoun).

CHAPTER FIFTEEN

Cultural Theories of Race and Gender

In the previous chapter, we discussed some of the ways in which postmodern and poststructural critical theory frame identity and difference as important conceptual categories in the description of culture. This chapter will look at other work in the cultural theorizing of identity and difference along two of its major axes, those of race and gender.

So central are these two topics to the study of culture that most theoretical traditions have had something to say about them even when they do not make them their sole focus. Nonetheless, we feel this chapter is merited as a way of recognizing the significant amount of cultural theory produced in the past several decades that has taken race and/or gender as the *central* categories of its vision and understood culture as fundamentally intertwined with notions of racial and gender classification.

Race

Much of the theoretical attention to the topics of race and gender has been focused on them as more or less invariant structural variables marking social stratification. With respect to race, this tradition is venerable, especially in the American context. Even today, many scholars, including some of the most visible, exploring the topic concentrate on social structural aspects and have comparatively little to say about racial identity and the cultural processes by which definitions of race are constructed and maintained. William Julius Wilson's important work on the black underclass and the way in which major economic restructuring post-1960s reinforced patterns in racial stratification is exemplary here (1978). Similarly, there has been much written on the topic of racism as a political and social problem that nonetheless has relatively little to offer to a theoretical discussion about the make-up of the category of race. The work of Joe Feagin(2000) and Eduardo Bonilla-Silva (2003) is broadly of this persuasion.

Cultural theory on race differs from this work not necessarily in that it is uninterested in how race contributes to stratification and inequality, but certainly in that it is focused on race as an eminently cultural object, something constructed by means of particular narratives, symbols, and cultural structures to contribute to meaning and identity. This kind of work is relatively recent, emerging since the 1970s and often in close relationship to the social and political struggles of racial minority groups that intensified in many parts of the world in and following the 1960s. We look in what follows at cultural work on race under three broad substantive themes: racial knowledge and identity, racial formations, and racial hybridity.

Racial knowledge and racial identity in interaction

Patricia Hill Collins is one of the most prominent of a number of thinkers who make a case not unlike that made by Sandra Harding (see p. 230), on perspective and epistemology, but with an added twist. As Harding argues that knowledge is shaped by the gendered position from which one sees, so Collins and other racial standpoint theorists believe that it is also informed by racial identity and perspective. Georg Simmel's essay on the stranger provides a foundation in classical social theory for Collins here. The **stranger**, for Simmel, was a person residing in a given community who nevertheless was not really fully a member of that community. The model type for Simmel's argument was the European Jew in the late 1800s. Although there were large numbers of Jews in many European cities, they often lived in ghettos isolated from the rest of the society, and were targeted for discrimination and social exclusion. In addition to facing these considerable disadvantages, though, Simmel argued that the stranger's experience brought a knowledge perspective that was freer of local prejudices and structural limitations, and this enabled the stranger to understand the workings of the culture in which she lived better than "insiders." Collins's argument is that African-American women are, for all intents and purposes, contemporary strangers. Because of their unique position outside mainstream white American culture, they are able to see the workings of social exclusion more clearly than insiders to that culture. They also are almost naturally suspicious and aware of the constructed nature of either/or binary methods of classification, since their position at the negative pole of two such binary systems (male/female and white/black) provides them with much experience of the costs of such thinking. They share with non-African-American women a certain attachment to the value of lived experience rather than abstraction (see discussion of Dorothy Smith below), but they additionally bring the cultural legacy of African societies and slavery to their epistemological stance. This leads to a strong valuing of dialogue in knowledge claims and an ethics of caring and personal accountability that Collins claims is unique to African-American women (Collins 2000 [1990]: 260–6). This singular knowledge perspective, ironically, can greatly enrich the broader culture which systematically excludes it on the occasions on which it manages to elude subordinate status and get inside the mainstream institutions of society. In this vein, Collins talks about the value of the perspective of the **"outsider within**," e.g., African-American female university professors like herself (Collins 1986).

Others have explored the nuances of racial knowledge by looking at the actual lived ways in which a racialized self emerges in specific interactional contexts. Elijah Anderson does not follow Collins into standpoint theorizing, but, in his deep ethnographic work in poor African-American neighborhoods of Philadelphia, he has substantially investigated how particular perspectival bodies of racialized knowledge are constructed and used. His primary theoretical contribution from this work is the description of a face-to-face interactional culture that he calls the **code of the streets**.

This code is, in Anderson's argument (1998, 1999a), a piece of culture that emerged largely because of the recognition among its adherents that the mainstream institutions of order and justice (the police and the courts) will not adequately protect them. This realization, intermingled with inner-city poverty and the sense it produces that one has little of which one can boast beyond the respect of others, creates a code of interpersonal communication in which one is constantly in a heightened state of awareness for evidence of challenge or disrespect. Even maintaining eye contact for too long as one passes someone on the street can be the prelude to violence in this culture. Like DuBois (see chapter 1) before him, Anderson notes that poor African-American families and individuals are not monolithic in cultural terms; there are many who adhere to the middle-class culture of restraint and avoidance of conflict in public living in the same neighborhoods with the firm adherents to the code of the streets. However, even the "decent" are required to learn and use the code in interaction with adherents to the code if they want to avoid being dominated by them, as they too know that the police will be reluctant to do their job in these neighborhoods. They therefore must learn how to "get ignorant" when necessary (Anderson 1998: 272). Adults in the "decent" community also have to tolerate a certain amount of superficial playing with other elements of the code (e.g., the ostentatious demonstration of expensive jewelry and clothing) on the part of their children, as they recognize how status works in the streets. For these reasons, it is often hard when seen from the outside for onlookers to tell the difference between the "decent" and the "street" individual.

Anderson has also studied African-American business executives and discovered similar code-switching abilities among this group. Just as "decent" poor African-Americans can shift into the code of the streets when necessary and then back out when danger is past, so many African-American executives move between two discourses on race depending on whether they are interacting with other African-Americans or with European-Americans. With the latter, they may remain silent on racially charged issues, e.g., when affirmative action policies are criticized, while in interaction with the former they express a different position. This ambivalence, which leads Anderson to recall DuBois's concept of double consciousness (see p. 24), helps them to survive in what is often felt to be a relatively insecure work environment, but Anderson notes that it is often accompanied by a fair amount of alienation (1999b).

Other recent efforts have been made to frame racial identity in broader, less situation-specific ways according to the logic of cultural theories discussed elsewhere in this book. Michèle Lamont (see p. 136) has looked at how the production of **cultural repertoires** that construct symbolic moral boundaries between groups works differently for working-class African- and European-Americans. Both engage in this work of morally distinguishing themselves from other groups, but European-Americans privilege an identity centered on the value of discipline and ascetic work, while African-American identity foregrounds care, warmth, and solidarity. Not only their own racial group but members of outgroups are defined according to the differing logics of these cultural repertoires (Lamont 2000). Ron Eyerman (2004) uses the narrative theory of the Yale Strong Program (see pp. 192–3) and in particular the idea of **cultural trauma** to situate slavery in the formation of African-American identity. A cultural trauma is a collective memory of some overwhelmingly negative situation experienced by members of a particular social group that is understood as ineradicable and threatening to the very existence of society. In his argument, at least two distinct narratives of this traumatic experience and its meaning emerge in African-American culture – one progressive, modern, and pointing to the integration of African-Americans into American society; the other tragic, redemptive, and pointing toward black nationalism.

Racial formation

The term "racial formation" is fundamentally associated with the work of Michael Omi and Howard Winant (1994). They present a theory of race that criticizes three dominant approaches in the sociological study of race that have attempted to reduce it to, respectively, ethnicity, class, or nation. Instead, Omi and Winant see race as a much more tenacious and autonomous category in the understanding of societies, like those of the modern West, that were built on conquests of indigenous peoples and the institution of slavery. The socio-historical processes that began with those efforts by one group to dominate another include as a central element what they call **racial formations**. These literally bring racial groups and ideas into existence as part of a cultural effort to legitimize and bolster the existing social structural inequalities. Racial formation in the United States, for example, involved a process of turning all the Africans brought here from many different countries and cultural groups into the monolithic category "blacks." That racial designation literally did not exist prior to this historical period, and it emerged in direct response to the ideological needs of one group seeking to effectively dominate another. **Racial projects** are specific narratives and representations concerning racial categories that are designed to "reorganize and redistribute resources along particular racial lines" (Omi and Winant 1994: 56). These projects can be politically conservative, reactionary, liberal, or radical, but in each case they are embedded in a socio-historical context that Omi and Winant call, after Gramsci, "hegemonic" (see p. 36). The situation in the Western capitalist world was one of racial domination from the epoch of slavery right up until roughly the mid-twentieth century, when some political reforms in favor of oppressed racial minorities materialized. But just as Gramsci read the situation of the European working class of the 1930s as defined by a mere shift in the nature of the class struggle rather than the experience of its end, so Omi and Winant, and more recently Winant alone (2004), see the result of civil rights reforms in the capitalist world as the establishment of a new stage in the struggle of racial groups rather than the abolition of racism.

   Their suggestion that race should be conceived as a marker of social and political interests and struggles for domination, and their rejection of highly cultural theories that see race as always and only ethnicity, make it possible to see Omi and Winant in part as critics rather than defenders of a cultural approach to the subject. Yet though their debt to Marxian categories is clear, they move beyond crude Marxism and stay in the realm of cultural theory in their recognition of the fact that conflict can emerge along lines that are not neatly reducible to static notions of social class. Indeed, they argue that the racial conflicts in much of the Western world have been fundamentally transformed, though not resolved, by explicitly political interventions at the level of law and social policy that Marx would likely have seen as mere ideological effects of class relations.

Although Omi and Winant focus on the formation of the racial categories of **subaltern** (this term too comes from Gramsci) or dominated groups, this broad theoretical perspective can be used to understand the category of the dominant group as well. This is the task of the emerging body of scholarship known as **whiteness studies**. The idea here is that the category of whiteness has, by virtue of the inherent logic of its function in racist symbolic systems, managed to pass, illegitimately, as non-constructed and non-racial. In fact, whiteness should be understood as "a site of elabo-ration of a range of cultural practices and identities, often unmarked and unnamed, or named as national or 'normative' rather than specifically racial" (Frankenberg 2001: 76). It is the members of this category who have the greatest stake in racially organized societies, as that organization places them at the top of a social hierarchy, and it is only because of the consolidation of their power that the category becomes invisible in the first place. The task of studying whiteness, then, is a part of the analysis of racial forma-tion of any society in the West today, but a part made still more urgent and difficult because of the particular role this category plays in the establishment of the entire racial system.

The central thrust of whiteness studies is intimately connected to the analysis of postcolonialism discussed in the previous chapter (see pp. 236–7). Ultimately, it was colonialism that historically made it possible for whiteness to emerge as an unmarked and purportedly autonomous category, opposed by the marked and dependent racial-ized Other. A good deal of the work in this area can seem purely historical and without explicitly formulated theoretical principles because of its concern with the historical processes by which whiteness and the racial systems it has engendered emerged. None-theless, the best of this work is quite informed by a concern for conceptual language.

David Roediger's account (2005) of how some Southern (e.g., Italian) and Eastern (e.g., Hungarian) European immigrants to the United States of the end of the nineteenth century were initially perceived as racially separate from already present Americans of European descent demonstrates how careful analysis of racial categories must be to avoid importing categories from the present into the past as theoretical tools. In adher-ing to the tenet of whiteness as a historical accomplishment, not something given by any fact of complexion of skin, Roediger describes how these groups that scholars now refer to as "white ethnics" could not have been perceived as such, simply because that term did not appear until the 1960s. He argues that too much of the desire to read the reception of those groups in those terms is perhaps motivated by the requirements of a certain simplistically optimistic narrative about the quick assimilation and acceptance of all in America. In reality, these groups were made sense of by a notion of **racial inbetweenness**. They were visibly not African-Americans, although some of the derogatory terms used to refer to them indicated some collapsing of the difference between them and African-Americans, e.g., the term "guinea," which was used to refer to Italians but has its origins in the designation of Africans from that coast (Roediger

2005: 37). But they were also distinguished from, and seen as inferior to, existing European-American groups in the US by those same groups. Moreover, much information exists that the new immigrant European-Americans identified themselves as something other than white or black, and in more than a few situations politically identified themselves more with African-Americans with reference to their own social exclusion. Roediger recounts episodes of, for example, the lynchings of Italian-Americans in the south at the turn of the century for fraternizing too closely with African-Americans to further demonstrate why the idea of a clear and static racial line between white and black is suspect. Even official national policy on immigration during this period was marked by the sense that these new immigrants were not racially white. The 1924 Johnson-Reed Act that limited the number of new immigrants from any country to 2 percent of the number of people already in the US from that country (and which therefore much more greatly reduced immigration of the more recent immigrant groups) explicitly cited the desire to preserve the "racial status quo" of the country (Roediger 2005: 139). In short, Roediger's work shows how the boundary between white and non-white is permeable and often problematic. Whiteness is not simply or even centrally about skin color, but also about the label that is applied to groups and individuals as they negotiate available cultural categories.

Diasporic racial identity, hybridity, and the end of "race"

In the previous chapter, we discussed Homi Bhabha's use of the notion of **hybridity** (see p. 237). A significant amount of recent cultural work on race has also made use of this and related terms, including a few of the more prominent thinkers in the field. In the remainder of this section on race, we discuss the work of Paul Gilroy, Orville Lee, and Orlando Patterson.

Paul Gilroy

The notion of **diaspora** has long been associated with a particular ethnic group, Jews, and their scattering from their homeland as depicted in the Old Testament. Paul Gilroy (2000) suggests that it might well serve us as something more. He uses it as a theoretical concept for understanding the complexity of identity in the case of what he calls the black Atlantic. This is the widely dispersed population of people of African descent whose ancestors were removed from the African continent by the European and American slave trade.

Gilroy criticizes what he sees as the obsession with identity in much contemporary analysis of race and history. What many of those analyses overlook is the implication of the concept of identity in dangerously politicized notions of exact sameness. The premier political mobilization of identity in the twentieth century, he argues, was in fascism and Nazism, where a radically simplistic and ahistorical effort was made to bind significantly differing populations in Germany, Italy, France, Spain, and other European countries under a single racialized and nationalized banner, to massively destructive ends. Later in the century, projects of ethnic cleansing in Rwanda and the former Yugoslavia similarly utilized identity in this manner, tying a mythical racial identity to a particular place as the fuel to ignite cataclysmic conflict with those seen as interlopers.

The dangers of such notions of identity can elude even the good intentions of those who mobilize them. Gilroy points to Nelson Mandela's efforts in the immediate wake of the fall of apartheid in South Africa to tie black and white South Africans together in a mythologized relation to South African soil and argues that this effort too inevitably runs up against the more complex facts of the contents of the consciousness of individual South Africans. While Mandela certainly cannot be ideologically aligned with his racist white opponents, Gilroy shows that the discourse on identity that he invokes relies on the same uncomplicated tie to place that grounds the racist narrative of South African identity. It celebrates "the nation" and downplays the migration histories and complex cultural flows that have long characterized the peoples living there. Similarly, he criticizes the "ideology of antiracism" for its careless move into extreme reductivism (Gilroy 2002 [1992]). In the struggle against the racist right, Gilroy argues, the anti-racists have too frequently accepted nearly the same vision of racial identity and experience held by their opponents. In this view, racial and ethnic categories become rigid, almost naturalized, and essentially insurmountable. Black nationalist and other racially conceived separatist social programs follow from this theoretical position.

Against the rootedness and simplicity of the forms of racialized and nationalized identity, the notion of diaspora "points toward a more refined and more wieldy sense of culture" (Gilroy 2000: 122). Drawing on an analogy to agricultural variation, Gilroy notes that two identical seeds cultivated in two different places will ultimately develop into different kinds of plant because of differences in weather and soil. The situation with racial identity is made still more volatile and indeterminate by the fact that single "seeds" may pass through several different combinations of "climate and soil" in a lifetime. He describes, among others, the complex example of the mid-eighteenth-century freed slave and abolitionist Olaudah Equiano, who was born in what is now Nigeria, sold into slavery and taken to the Americas, then to England to be educated, then to the Caribbean, then to the American colonies, and finally back to England. How can we make sense of his identity in any simple manner drawing from only his "place of origin"? Another of Gilroy's examples will be more quickly recognized by younger readers: Bob Marley. How should the great reggae musician be understood culturally? Is he Jamaican? Caribbean? African? Pan-African? All or none of the above? Gilroy's suggestion is that we are bound to be misled if we rely on faulty notions of origins in trying to make sense of his highly complex identity.

Most recently (2005), Gilroy has sustained his argument for a radical sense of multiculturalism by criticizing what he calls the **postcolonial melancholia** of much of British society. He derives the term not directly from Freud, but from its adaptation by two post-World War II German psychoanalysts who were seeking to make sense of the broad social sense of "loss of [the] fantasy of omnipotence" following the death of Hitler (2005: 99). Like Germans who refused to move on to build a new and constructive sense of identity after the collapse of the narcissistic nationalist myth of the Nazis, contemporary Britons are unable to move beyond a cultural depression over the loss of the mythical power of their former Empire and its racial simplifications to a positive affirmation of the real multiculturalism already present in much of British society. He argues that both this real multiculturalism and the melancholia of lost British identity, as well as the limits of the embrace of "pure" forms of ethnic identity that is evident in some parts of Britain, can be seen at play in the pop culture phenomenon of Ali G. This comedic parody of a middle-class and visually white – or just maybe Pakistani – British youth who seems to believe himself something of a cross between a Jamaican-descended urban black Briton and an African-American hip hop artist manages to make uncomfortable everyone with an investment in clearly defined boundaries in racial identity. Meanwhile, those who recognize what Ali G reveals ("British culture['s] . . . perverse attachment to numerous forms of destructive hierarchy") and the actual multiculturalism at work in his depiction (a middle-class British Jewish comedian/actor named Sacha Cohen playing a white Briton who identifies completely with a black-dominated youth culture) are overcome with laughter (Gilroy 2005: 135). The basic idea here is that "traditional" British society is already multicultural to its roots, as Stuart Hall (1997) makes clear in tracing something so traditionally British as the cup of tea to its colonial history: the tea itself comes from India and Sri Lanka, the sugar that sweetens it from plantations in the Caribbean.

Orville Lee

Like Gilroy, Orville Lee deliberately includes intellectual institutions and practices in the cultural machinery that produces and reproduces race and racial identities. But Lee has been perhaps still more rigorous in this regard. He discusses the discipline of sociology (from within which he himself writes) as profoundly implicated in the production and reproduction of static and rigid racial categories (Lee 2004). In an implicit nod to Pierre Bourdieu (see pp. 128–34), he takes much of the existing sociology of race, especially in its racial standpoint variations (e.g., Patricia Hill Collins), to task for essentially encouraging the adoption by subordinated groups of exactly the categories of identity that help subordinate them. Bourdieu (1991a [1982]) gave the label "symbolic domination" to this acceptance on the part of the dominated of the reality of the worldview that makes them such. Even well-meaning political policies such as race-based affirmative action programs run the risk of reifying racialist categories in using them toward the laudable goal of providing resources to relatively deprived populations.

In place of this way of theorizing race, Lee proposes an approach with strong affinities to that of Gilroy. One of the more promising bodies of work on race in recent years, he notes, is that concerned with **race practices**. Here, racial identity is seen as the result of Geertzian performance (see pp. 189–92). Lee stresses the similarity of racial belief and religious belief in that both require active performance and agency on the part of individuals and are not simply given by non-cultural factors. The complex empirical facts call for a movement in the study of race away from the crude binary of an objectively raced body and the cultural ideas that produce racial stratification to a cultural theory that recognizes that even the former is already a cultural production. There are no black or white bodies. There are only bodies that are already hybrids, and some in fact already choose to inhabit those bodies in explicitly hybrid ways, e.g., the golfer Tiger Woods's preference for defining himself as "cablinasian," which is a combination of Caucasian, black, (American) Indian, and Asian (Lee 2004: 248).

Most recently, Lee and colleague Sarah Daynes have further honed this theory with the notion of the **racial ensemble** (Daynes and Lee 2008). Four elements make up the racial ensemble that emerges in any manifestation of racial classification:

- a phenotype, or the empirically observable characteristics of an organism;
- the perception of that phenotype by observers;
- racial ideas;
- racial practices.

Only the first of these terms is in any way reducible to the pre-cultural world. Perceptions of phenotype are inevitably selective and informed by cultural frameworks of what is and what is not racially meaningful (e.g., why does skin color appear to us a more meaningful component of the phenotype than, say, foot size or amount of hair on the arms and hands?). Already existing racial ideas influence the perception of phenotype, which also tend to act back in a confirming fashion on the racial ideas. Racial ideas inform racial practices, which in turn tend to support and confirm the racial ideas that give rise to them.

Provocatively, Daynes and Lee argue that the sociology of race should proceed no differently from the sociology of religion, as both are concerned with the study of an idea and the ways in which that idea is constructed despite the inability of empirical reality to fully justify belief in it. They mine the cultural thought of Maurice Halbwachs and Sigmund Freud, two thinkers we discussed in earlier chapters, to sketch out this perspective. Collective memory, which as Halbwachs (see pp. 72–3) showed is rooted in membership in particular social groups, is frequently invoked in discourse on race, and Daynes and Lee note, in agreement with Halbwachs, that those memories are always at least as much about the socially constructed present realities as they are about what actually happened in the past. When people invoke racial pasts, whether positively or negatively presented, we should inquire more thoroughly into the ways in which those pasts depend on present conditions. Finally, they note that psychoanalysis (see chapter 12) might contribute something useful to our reading of race insofar as the conceptualization of race may well be tied to deeply unconscious desires and wish-fantasy. It is no coincidence that much thinking about race has been linked to thinking about sexuality, and specifically the sexuality of differently raced individuals. This unconscious root in pre-scientific fears of the problematic category of sexual desire helps drive race as an idea well beyond the point at which it runs out of purely intellectual gas.

Orlando Patterson
The sociologist Orlando Patterson has produced a theoretically and methodologically wide-ranging and eclectic body of work on race, focusing on the African-American situation and the legacy and meaning of slavery. Rather than trying to summarize the breadth of his thought, we would perhaps do better to look closely at a few of his efforts on specific topics that highlight particularly innovative theoretical approaches to race.

The consequences of slavery for African-Americans have been massive, though Patterson notes that we need to be culturally sophisticated in our analysis to see precisely what contributed to these consequences and in some cases even to see properly the consequences at all. He connects the contemporary crisis in African-American gender relations – i.e., the fact that declining marriage rates, rising divorce rates, and massive increase in female-headed families are particularly high among African-Americans – to

slavery's destruction of the paternal role (see also DuBois's discussion of this relationship, pp. 23–4). That African-American male slaves were so thoroughly dispossessed
of any authoritative position vis-à-vis their wives and children by the institution of
slavery has resulted in the relative disappearance of narratives of effective fatherhood
in African-American culture. Evidence for this is present, Patterson argues, in survey
data that suggest that European-American men and women, and also African-
American women, agree that socially irresponsible and negative behavior (e.g., marital
infidelity) is most offensive when engaged in by men, while African-American men tend
to see things differently. They are more inclined to see such behavior as forgivable on
the part of men, in Patterson's argument due to their acceptance of a cultural narrative
constructed as a response to African-American male disempowerment under slavery
(Patterson 1998: 132). Instead of seeking female companionship and familial responsibility, many young African-American men are instead led by their collective cultural
and historical experience to prefer the **"cool pose" culture** of the urban street, which
has much in common with Elijah Anderson's code of the streets. Patterson says we find
this most stereotypically represented in the male figure that emerges in much hip hop
culture and rap music: contemptuous of ascetic work ethics and narratives of adult
male responsibility, concerned mainly with material success to be achieved in ways
that demonstrate cunning and ruthlessness, quick to engage in risky and violent behavior while under the influence of drugs and alcohol, and eager to use women sexually
but extremely suspicious of commitments to them.

Understanding the attractiveness of the "cool pose" stance for young African-
American men necessitates a careful reading of their representation in American
culture. Borrowing conceptual terminology from Nietzsche (see pp. 19–21), Patterson
argues that all societies need to maintain a balance between two opposed principles,
the Apollonian and the Dionysian, the former the emblem of order and reason, the
latter representing emotion and passion. Dionysus, he argues, is dangerous but necessary, as too much social order and a too narrow rationality can lead toward totalitari-
anism. In the contemporary United States, a specific cultural balance between Apollo
and Dionysus has been reached that bears heavily on racial difference. Young African-
American males disproportionately have been called on to perform the Dionysian role
of frenzy and violence that counterbalances the Apollonian discipline and order of
middle-class work and family culture. In this "cultural division of labor" (Patterson
1998: 272), it is the function of young African-American men to play the dual parts
accruing to the Dionysian: that of the heroic and attractive demigod (e.g., boxing
legend Muhammad Ali, basketball great Michael Jordan, and now perhaps his heir-
apparent as basketball superstar LeBron James), and that of the violent, sexually
depraved demon (e.g., Willie Horton, a convicted murderer who was infamously used
by the campaign of George H. W. Bush during the 1988 US presidential campaign to
make his opponent appear to be a coddler of criminals). Ellis Cashmore's sociobiogra-
phy of boxer Mike Tyson provides a detailed exposition of the latter figure, an African-
American young man celebrated precisely for his ability to destroy opponents like "a
Serengeti lion rip[ping] into a warthog" and whose frequent encounters with the criminal justice system only further fascinate a public that does not so much admire him as
stand in fearful awe of his ferocity (Cashmore 2005: 43). In some cases, Patterson

notes, the two roles are played by one individual. O. J. Simpson, he of one-time football and movie superstardom and now of unpunished murderer infamy, is the central example discussed by Patterson, but we might also add the charismatic former star of the music and movie worlds, Tupac Shakur, who at various times in his short life was accused of murder, rape, and assorted other violent crimes. Patterson argues that the spectacle of young men of color leading violent and often criminal lives in the worlds of rap music and sport provides white America with the vicarious whiff of transgression that it needs in order to continue to submit to Apollonian discipline. In that sense, then, it is culturally functional. The associated cost, however, is the destruction of the lives of many of those young athletes and artists and the recruitment by attraction of other young African-American males into those same role positions.

Patterson has also looked at historically more virulent evidence of racial inequality with novel theoretical materials. He has studied the mass lynchings of African-Americans that took place across the post-Civil War South of the United States as ritualistic human sacrifices by adopting the Durkheimian work on sacrifice of Marcel Mauss and Henri Hubert (see pp. 69–72, 74). They had demonstrated that sacrifice makes up one of the most basic rituals that societies have for dramatically acting out and reinforcing communal membership and boundaries. Successful rituals are communally sanctioned events with broad participation, and Patterson argues that lynchings in this period frequently met this definition. Six central elements of sacrifices are indicated by Mauss and Hubert:

- They involve ritualistic "drama, celebration, and play."
- They are performed in sacred places, or the places in which they are performed are made sacred by the sacrifice itself.
- They frequently use fire as a means of destruction and consumption of the victim.
- The stake to which the victim is tied (and the source from which it is obtained) takes on a special sacred status.
- They are accompanied by moral narratives that frame the victim as a mediator between worlds of sacred and profane, with victim as representative of good, evil, or both.
- The remains of the victim are frequently cannibalized or otherwise preserved. (Patterson 1998: 182–3)

Patterson then reads mass lynchings as satisfying each definitional point. He recounts the festive atmosphere recorded at many mass lynchings and the fact that many were carried out near churches or at bridges (ancient symbols of magical power). Trees from which victims were hanged or stakes at which they had burned were likewise sacralized by members of the lynching group, who often took pieces of the object home with them. More gruesomely, they often took pieces of the victim's body as souvenirs. Patterson even suggests that the burning of the victims permitted a kind of cannibalism by inhalation of the smoke given off by the body. It is ultimately though the particular cultural frameworks concerning collective violence and the reading of Christian sacrificial theology according to the narrative of "Christ triumphant," which were already in place in the South prior to the period of heavy racially specific lynching, that play the key role in providing the specific meaning these lynchings had for European-American Southerners, according to Patterson. Prior to Civil War defeat, such religious lynchings (and this is indeed what they are for Patterson) did take place, but the victims were more often white than black. The context of total political defeat in the war spurred the emergence of the narrative of the "Lost Cause" and provided a clear and accessible scapegoat for European-American Southerners. Patterson's reading here provides an example of how deeply rooted cultural frameworks can affect seemingly unrelated practices, given a conducive social context.

Like Gilroy and Lee, Patterson has evinced suspicion at the continuing utility and legitimacy of the very use of the term "race" to describe different social groups. All three frequently place the term in quotation marks to indicate its suspect status. Patterson has in fact explicitly called for its abandonment, and expressed incredulity that scholars still find useful terms such as "black" and "white," which reveal nothing useful socio-logically but denotatively and connotatively advantage one term over the other (recall that angels and good guys in Western movies wear white, while devils and villains are clad in black). He recommends using "Afro-American" and "Euro-American" in the American context and similar more accurate terms in other contexts (1997: 173).

Let us briefly sum up the cultural sociological research on race that we have examined in this first half of the chapter before turning to a look at gender. The various works and theorists discussed above offer the following general insights into the analysis of race:

- An outsider status frequently gives racial minorities special forms of culture and knowledge that are unavailable to members of dominant racial groups.
- Particular interactional competencies, identities, and performances are often central to racial culture and identity.
- The very concept of race might well be radically questioned, with many suggest-ing that it is a cultural construction that should be avoided altogether or substan-tially modified because it is problematic, overly binary, and closely linked to the reproduction of power.

Gender

Interest in gender as an element of culture extends at least as far back as the time of the classical social theory discussed in this book's opening chapter. Max Weber's spouse Marianne was a significant contributor to the public discussion and analysis of the social situation of women in Western society, whose books were read and reviewed by some of Weber's intellectual peers. It is, however, really in the years following the emergence of second wave feminism in the 1960s and 1970s, which broadened femi-nism's political critique of gender stratification beyond the narrowly legal question of suffrage, that we see the first signs of the massive growth in the volume and intensity of thinking about gender and culture which continues to the present.

As in the section on race, we discuss this new cultural theory of gender under a number of substantive headings: gendered knowledge perspectives, the relationship between the concepts gender and sex, and the cultural examination of the deeply gendered topics of motherhood and reproduction.

Gender and knowledge

Contemporary cultural theory concerned with gender has, like that dealing with race, focused much attention on the implications this variable has on the production of knowledge. Gender standpoint theorists such as Sandra Harding (see p. 230), Dorothy Smith, and Donna Haraway have attempted not only to trace the ways that gendered identity shapes how one perceives and organizes the world, but also to argue that one can comparatively evaluate these gendered knowledge perspectives and find some more inclusive, complete, and just than others.

Smith's perspective is that of a materialist feminist informed by ethnomethodology and discourse analysis (see pp. 63–6). Together, those two theoretical orientations have led her to significant inquiry into the knowledge and experience of women and the specific institutional means in the contemporary world by which that knowledge and experience are marginalized. Her grounding in micro-interactional theory leads her to understand social reality as something fundamentally found in the concrete experience of the everyday, yet she believes that the material purity of that real social life is distorted in the contemporary world by a relatively new, abstract, and non-experiential form of knowledge about the world. Increasingly, official, formalized, and abstract **texts** are what mediates social interaction, whether these be the contracts into which we enter, the doctor's reports that inform us of our health status, the checking and credit card statements that we compile through our economic activity, or the books that we read to inform ourselves about things like cultural theory. Texts in Smith's sense are diverse in many ways, but united by one central characteristic: they all produce facts, which are purportedly objective and authoritative accounts of something. **Facticity**, or the production of facts, is problematic for Smith because she understands this way of knowing, which claims objectivity, as in fact gendered and male. The texts produced by the male-dominated institutions that broadly dictate the patterns of our lives should not simply be accepted as true, but rather examined for their contribution to male hegemony and female subordination. Smith sees the actual function of texts in their contribution to the **relations of ruling**. In a close examination of the textual process by which a decision is made that a woman, K, is mentally ill, Smith (1990) reads the institutional transcript of an interview with a friend of K who testified to some of her allegedly insane behaviors and notes that the behaviors are all presented free of a broader context that might allow the reader a different interpretation of their meaning. The text also allows no process by which K or other present individuals might fill in that contextual and experiential data. So, for example, when Angela describes K as weeping frequently over "little things," her account cannot be challenged by K's own explanation of the causes of her weeping (1990: 26–7). The transcript of Angela's interview nonetheless presents itself not as merely one account among others, but as an authoritative document which, with other such documents, produces the effect of defining K as mad.

Although Smith's approach to texts might seem to have some affinities with the postmodernist criticism of the role of textuality in producing knowledge that we discussed in chapter 14, it can be distinguished from the latter in its rejection of relativism. She presents female knowledge as not simply different, but inherently more experiential, materially rooted, and ultimately more accurate than male knowledge. But as women are excluded from the abstract, institutional realm dominated by men, they are simultaneously secluded in the realm of everyday "dirty work" that allows the institutional realm to exist even while the latter refuses to acknowledge its dependence on women's work. Smith calls her brand of intellectual inquiry into the functioning of that textual, institutional world **institutional ethnography** (Smith 2005). The goal here is precisely to demonstrate the invisible material factors that allow texts of institutional authority to be produced. Even feminist analysis must guard against falling into this mode of representation by sticking as closely as possible to the material reality of women's existence.

Donna Haraway's work, like that of Harding, has been especially influential in, and relevant to, the burgeoning field of science studies. Like other feminist thinkers on scientific knowledge, she sees science as necessarily enmeshed in the social fact of the gendered bodies of scientists. The idea of science as "the view from nowhere" is rejected as an illusory belief in a kind of knowledge that ignores the inevitable perspectival limits of all knowers. But she also rejects theoretical projects like that of the strong program in the sociology of scientific knowledge (see p. 192) as dangerously relativist and cynical about truth claims. Instead, she proposes **situated knowledges**. These are partial perspectives that have to account for their location and that, by their very local nature, can be webbed together into a more holistic account of the world than that approached by traditional science. Objectivity is thus not completely a fiction, but neither is it something that can be attained via the **god trick** of the view from nowhere. Some situated perspectives are in fact better than others at accounting for their positions and endeavoring to understand the perspectives of other knowers. These are subjugated knowledges, in principle "least likely to allow denial of the critical and interpretative core of all knowledge" (Haraway 2004a [1991]: 88). They also best understand the inherent moral nature of knowledge claims and build an emancipatory political project into their vision of the world. Here, Haraway merges her interest in the philosophy of science with a feminist and socialist political platform. In *Primate Visions* (1989), she provides a precise example of how scientific knowledge in the study of primates is produced differently by men and by women and why this has important consequences in how we define basic notions such as nature, culture, human, animal, male, and female. The male-dominated field of primatology has, in Haraway's reading, significantly contributed to and profited from colonialism and the cultural systems of racial and gender hierarchy on which it was based, while female primatologists have challenged that way of interpreting the primate world. Male researchers tended to read their own preconceptions concerning human sexuality into the world of apes, for example, characterizing female primate sexuality as fundamentally passive and classifying females as juvenile or adult solely according to their capacity to breed, while categorizing males with a much more complex set of social factors. Female scientists informed by feminism responded to this not simply by positing "mirror-image reverse account[s] or method[s]" (Haraway 1989: 310), for example, arguing for a more active female primate sexuality, but rather by attacking the gendered nature of the very scientific terms determined by male scientists to be most relevant to the study of primates. Why do so many of the terms and concepts center on sexuality, given the fact that primates, like humans, have rich and varied social lives that include, but are certainly not completely defined by, sexual behavior? Haraway suggests a feminist science must be focused on destabilizing categories and bodies of knowledge that have been constructed from a very specific and gendered identity position.

One of the central concepts used by Haraway to demonstrate her understanding of the complexity of identity that traditional conceptions of gender radically simplify is that of the **cyborg**. Literally a being part human and part machine taken from the language of science fiction, the cyborg becomes for Haraway something of a metaphor for discussing the socially constructed nature of category distinctions such as culture/nature, male/female, human/machine, and human/animal. All such oppositions, she argues, have as part of their functioning the Othering of one of the paired terms and the assertion of relations of domination between the two. The idea of the cyborg, for Haraway, offers the possibility of escaping this (Haraway 2004b).

Gender and sex

A classic distinction in the literature on gender is that between the latter term and sex. In the formulation that social scientists have broadly relied on since roughly the early 1970s, sex is seen as having to do with anatomical and "natural" distinctions in genitalia (one has either a penis or a vagina), while gender is considered to have to do with behavioral traits that are intended to line up with sex categories and that are socially learned (one wears dresses or jackets and ties). A good deal of feminist cultural work over the past 30 or so years has documented the way that both sex and gender reproduce inequality. There have been numerous studies on the split between the public and private spheres, with the former occupied largely by men. Others have examined the ways that women are expected to subordinate themselves in everyday interaction. Explorations of domestic violence, rape and sexual harassment, and housework and workplace inequalities further document how cultural understandings about gender roles can have serious negative consequences. Still others have shown how the sexed female body is subject to domination, surveillance and control by men, medicine, and the law (see below). That said, a good deal of cutting-edge theoretical work today is concerned with the difficult task of deconstructing sex and gender rather than exploring the routine outcomes of these taken for granted cultural categories.

Judith Butler, whose interest in drag as a transgressive identity practice we briefly discussed in the previous chapter (see p. 236), flatly argues that sex too is a social category that has little, if anything, to do with the natural, and much to do with discourse about nature. She borrows heavily from Foucault (see pp. 115–21) in arguing that distinguishing the actual physical body from the body as a perceived object seen by subjects immersed in cultural ideas about bodies is far more difficult than we might like to think. Bodies in fact only come into existence for us as a result of our process of signifying their meanings and marking them with gender (Butler 2006 [1990]). From the very moment we imagine the unborn child, our notions of his/her body, and thus his/her sex, are already saturated in gendered culture. Butler shows how even the reasoning of the purportedly objective cell biologists studying sex at the chromosomal level fails to elude this culture. One such group of scientists at MIT in the late 1980s believed they had discovered the particular sequence of DNA on the Y chromosome that determined the sex of an individual, which they called the TDF, or testis-determining factor. In examining two groups of abnormal individuals (the first with XX chromosomes yet medically determined as male because of their genitalia, the second with XY chromosomes yet classified as females for the same reason), the MIT biologists were able to make sense of the seeming anomalies by arguing that the TDF of the XX males had transposed itself somewhere else and that the Y chromosomes of the XY females in fact had no TDF. Butler noted, though, that they had to admit that the exact same DNA sequence could be found on the X chromosomes of the XY females. How then could TDF determine sex? Because, they claimed, the TDF was *active* in the males and *passive* in the females. Butler's response is to invoke Aristotle's ancient argument, which we now see as clearly absurd, to the effect that a great amount of excitement in the male during intercourse produces male (active) children, while less excitement produces (passive) females. In other words, like Aristotle, the MIT scientists fell back on cultural notions of gender in order to describe their seemingly natural data (2006 [1990]: 137).

Butler observes that even some of the other poststructuralist cultural theorists from whom she borrows fail to take seriously enough the all-encompassing quality of our immersion in discourses about sex. She analyzes a relatively little-read text from Foucault which presents the journal of Herculine Barbin, a French hermaphrodite of the mid-1800s who was initially classified female, then abruptly reclassified as a male before committing suicide at the age of 30. Butler argues that even someone as aware of the purview of discourse as the author of *Discipline and Punish* allows himself to fall into a celebration of Barbin's sexual experience that seems to presume the possibility of an emancipatory escape from the binary discursive categories that make us sexed and gendered. But in Butler's view this is akin to the desire of the biologists to find a sexed body prior to gendered culture. Impossible tasks, as we are always already implicated in culture. There simply is no space to which we can retreat and theorize sexual difference without the "contamination" of our pre-existing cultural categories of sexual difference, and so all efforts to claim to be doing that should be viewed with considerable suspicion.

The theoretical position we find in Butler's work is further bolstered by the often harrowing experience of people who are born intersexed, i.e., with sexual anatomy that does not conform to stereotyped male or female genitalia or that seems at odds with other physical characteristics (e.g., a female with vagina, breasts, and undescended testes; or a male with a penis, breast development, and an ovary). Anne Fausto-Sterling famously suggested in the early 1990s that such individuals were the clearest evidence that a merely binary system for sex was too simple and more categories were needed to encompass the true empirical variety we find in the world. She suggests that the traditional medical manner of dealing with the intersexed, which is to surgically alter them in such a way as to make them better conform to one or the other of the two existing sex categories, has mostly to do with cultural prejudice and in most cases actually harms the individuals, psychologically if not physically. The "heretical bodies" of the intersexed must be made normative, at risk of endangering the sexual system of categorization (Fausto-Sterling 2000: 8). Like Butler, Fausto-Sterling describes some of the domains in which contemporary biological science seeks to ground traditional theories of sexual development in the human organism and demonstrates how inextricably entangled they are in cultural predispositions about gender. A region in the posterior part of the brain, the corpus callosum, is believed by some scientists to be directly linked to the sex of an individual, yet Fausto-Sterling argues that efforts to fix and measure it are affected by the predisposition scientists have to the two-sex model, and that they might well come up with different measurements if they went to that task with something other than the male/female sex binary as background knowledge and presumption. We even have historical precedents for seeing that binary as something malleable. Thomas Laqueur (1990) has argued that previously in the West, sex was one rather than two. Women were seen as having the same genitals as men, only on the inside instead of the outside, and this understanding lasted through the eighteenth century.

Butler has discussed transsexuality as another phenomenon mired in misunderstandings about identity based in the discourse of gender binarism. A diagnosis of gender identity disorder (GID) may lead to a program of intervention to alter an individual's gender from one binary category to the other, and in this sense it is seen as radically deconstructive of the naturalness of gender by many. Butler, however, carefully describes the ways in which the very existence of a condition such as GID relies on the binary system of gender. What is in fact always an empirically complex life experience for an individual has to be fitted within a narrative of "born biologically male but identifies as female" or the inverse. Scenarios in which no gender category is naturally given and an individual identifies with neither of the two binary gender categories of our system are simply disallowed (Butler 2004a).

Motherhood, pregnancy, abortion

Historical and anthropological work has long made the case that gendered activity and identity can differ significantly from one culture to another and even within the same culture historically. Yet new cultural theory has in the past several decades contributed to innovative ways of understanding precisely how fundamental aspects of gender are produced and how they change, especially in relation to emerging technologies.

The practice of mothering and the association of these nurturing practices with women, and specifically with the biological mothers of children, is one of the central topics to explore here. Nancy Chodorow, a sociologist with psychoanalytic training, made an enduring contribution to the cultural study of motherhood with her 1978 book *The Reproduction of Mothering*. She argued for the durable existence of female mothering in a combination of family structure and process, on the one hand, and macro-social structures linked to capitalism, on the other. The features of the family, and specifically its gendered division of labor, incorporate the larger social structure and directly communicate it to children in the development of their psychic structure. The fact that it is overwhelmingly women who provide primary childcare has differential effects on the psychic development of male and female children. Mothers treat female children as more "continuous" with themselves, while they recognize male children as different from themselves. The female children reciprocate by bonding more closely and for a prolonged period of time in pre-Oedipal fusion with the mother, while male children move early to individuate and construct an autonomous ego (Chodorow 1978: 166–7). There is, Chodorow notes, no real evidence that such parenting is optimal for the children, but it certainly is useful for a broader social world in which a fairly rigid distinction between highly achievement-motivated, work-focused men and familial-focused women is evident. Just a few years after Chodorow's book, social psychologist Carol Gilligan wrote another classic in this field that pointed to the ways in which these psychosocial developmental factors created a gendered binary in moral reasoning. Her argument is that girls learn, consistently with their development as parental caregivers, to make moral judgments from a fundamentally relational perspective that recognizes the moral as rooted in responsibility for others, while boys see morality as founded in universal and abstract individual rights and non-interference with others (Gilligan 1982).

More recently, Sharon Hays has argued that the notion that biological mothers naturally care best for children should best be understood as an **ideology of intensive mothering**. For Hays, this belief has no foundation in biology. She cites Margaret Mead and other anthropologists who catalogued numerous examples of non-Western and/or pre-modern societies in which nurturing mothering, up to and including breast-feeding of children, was and is carried out by individuals who are not the biological mothers of the children. Studies of pre-industrial Europe also reveal an attitude toward children and mothering very different from ours. We find, for example, children categorically seen as "demonic" and "animalistic" and biological mothers eager to protect themselves from the depredations of voraciously feeding infants (Hays 1996: 20, 22). Even within the contemporary Western world, there is cultural diversity regarding definitions of motherhood, as Patricia Hill Collins has shown in her description of "blood-mothers" (biological mothers) and "othermothers" (female relatives or close friends of the biological mother who assist with childcare in families with no father) in the African-American community (Collins 2001: 178).

So how does the ideology of intensive mothering come to be? Echoing Chodorow, Hays argues it has largely to do with the utility of a specifically gendered division of labor for the development of modern capitalism and the state. Modern capitalism requires a workforce wholly dedicated to the business of the public sphere and this in turn requires other subjects with a full-time dedication to the realm of the private sphere of home and family. Hays also describes how this ideology of intensive mothering gives rise to contradictions. Mothers feel compelled to try to live up to the exacting demands of the ideology by emotionally giving themselves fully to children and exhausting themselves keeping up with all the expert knowledge on child-rearing, but they are also caught in a world where they are frequently also in the workforce (some willingly, some by necessity), where individualistic, economic tough-mindedness is rewarded. Many women therefore develop intricate ideological rationalizations for their necessary immersion in the work world, defining that work activity as a boon for their childcare abilities, e.g., work serves as a way to refresh them for time with their children, or day care opens up new developmental opportunities for the children (Hays 1996: 122).

As ideas about motherhood are rooted in broader cultural narratives and values, so too are ideas about the function most frequently associated with motherhood, that of reproduction. Kristen Luker's study (1984) on the abortion debate in the United States delineated how political positions on abortion were deeply rooted in broader cultural perspectives on the meaning of sexuality and women's reproductive ability. Pro-choice women tend to see sexuality and fertility as separable, while pro-life women link the two inextricably. Differing cultural contexts can significantly change the perception of a woman's reproductive capacity. For example, Alexandra Halkias (2004) has shown that Greek women inhabit a cultural sphere that frames contraceptive methods other than withdrawal as unnatural because they intrude on largely male-produced discourses of emotional, spontaneous Greek sexual freedom. As a practical response, women there come to see abortion as a more natural mode of controlling their reproductivity, and many women have multiple abortions even as the Greek state deplores declining birth rates.

Still more recent reproductive technologies further demonstrate the cultural factors at play in defining motherhood, fatherhood, femininity, and masculinity. The Baby M case of the 1980s (in which a couple contracted another woman to bear a child conceived with the sperm of the male partner because of the female partner's risky health status, and the birthing woman subsequently refused to give up the child) showed how motherhood consists not only of biological but also legal narratives, and gave us the new category of "surrogate motherhood." Assisted reproductive technology (ART) clinics have still more radically transformed the categories. Charis Thompson's investigation into the literal making of parents and children at these sites reveals the complicated cultural work necessary to construct familial relations and identities in this new technological environment. In one fascinating example she provides, we find an infertile woman who has a close friend donate an egg that will be fertilized with the sperm of the first woman's husband and implanted in her womb to grow to term. Explicit and careful cultural work is done by the involved people and the clinic staff to be sure to construct relational connections (those implicating legal kinship) between the first woman and the child and merely custodial ones (not implicating kinship) between the second woman and the child. The relative time of the egg's presence in the two women's bodies and the fact that both women are Italian-American (and therefore of the same ethnic stock, which means a genetic link, however weak, can be forged between the infertile woman and the child) are deployed as modes of appropriately constructing parenthood (Thompson 2005: 167). In the near future, we may well see the emergence of artificial wombs that could carry children to term, bringing us perhaps to cyborg motherhood à la Haraway (Aristarkhova 2005). The produced nature of these once taken-for-granted notions is certain to become more apparent with each new technological advance.

Evaluations of Cultural Theories of Race and Gender

As the topics of this chapter are highly visible in political debates in many societies, it is no surprise that much of the evaluation of cultural work on race and gender points to its political importance and engagement. Proponents of this kind of work see the relativizing of categories that are frequently linked to biological explanation as conducive to the dismantling of structures of inequality built up around notions of racial and gender identity. Critics however argue that too much work in this area allows its politics to dominate its intellectual rigor and objectivity. As is the case with the racial civil rights and feminist social movements that accompanied the rise of cultural theorizing on race and gender, there is much internal conflict in both areas. A fair amount of this conflict can be made sense of by comparing the strengths and weaknesses of standpoint cultural theories of race and gender to those of theories based on poststructuralist ideas such as hybridity. Standpoint theories, such as those of Patricia Hill Collins or Dorothy Smith, are intimately concerned with the dimension of power in race and gender and they frequently give detailed accounts of the elements that make up those raced and gendered perspectives and identities. These strengths are however countered by a number of weaknesses:

- They can be read as attempting to generalize ideal types such as "the black woman's perspective" that ultimately come undone when closely examined.
- They sometimes get bogged down in fruitless attempts to find "the most disadvantaged perspective" from which to theorize, and they can even wind up appearing self-refuting as a result. Smith's critique of texts, for example, can be read as leading in the final analysis to the necessary rejection of all academic scholarship in so far as even that of thinkers like Smith herself emerges from established educational institutional sites and is published in sources that privilege just the expert knowledge that she wants to criticize.
- They have a tendency to rely on political rather than purely intellectual criteria for criticizing other theories. When this is carried far enough, the results can be frustrating. Whiteness studies frequently attacks other ways of theorizing racial identity as politically reactionary, and in response some other scholars of race have accused whiteness studies as a de facto means by which black and other minority scholars studying minority racial groups are displaced as the focus of racial inquiry in favor of whites studying whites. (Omi 2001: 266)

The more poststructuralist and postmodernist theories, such as those of Paul Gilroy or Judith Butler, offer responses to some of the weaknesses of standpoint theories as their strengths. They reject essentializing and seek complexity in identity. They are also suspicious of the game of positing one identity position as more truthful than others. However, they too can sometimes elide the distinction between theoretical argument and political claim. Butler, for example, very clearly situates her work primarily as an intervention into the politics of feminist activism. Theories of hybridity and diaspora in race theory are sometimes criticized as offering ammunition for conservative ideological visions of a "race-free society" in which existing racial inequalities are simply ignored and/or accepted. We all know that the reality of race and gender on the streets is very different from the more relaxed, tolerant, and cosmopolitan feel of the campus. Out in the "real world" of wrenching inequality, it may well be the case that clinging to problematic categories rather than deconstructing them is the best way to undertake a critical cultural analysis. Hence the same critical points regarding the implications of relativism that we noted at the end of the previous chapter can apply to much of the poststructuralist-influenced theory described in this chapter.

Suggested Further Reading

Many of the particular studies referenced in this chapter are eminently readable. On race, *Theories of Race and Racism* is a well-rounded volume put together by Les Back and John Solomos with selections from several of the key theorists discussed here. Sandra Harding's edited volume *The Feminist Standpoint Theory Reader* contains essays by a number of the thinkers summarized in the section on gender and knowledge. *The Haraway Reader*, which was prepared by the author herself, contains well-chosen selections from each of her books. Butler is probably the single source in this chapter who is the most difficult to read. There is a *Judith Butler Reader* with an introduction by Sarah Salih that adequately summarizes her intellectual trajectory, but this is not much lighter sledding than Butler herself.

CHAPTER SIXTEEN

The Body in Cultural Theory

Since at least the mid-1990s, much attention has been focused on the human body as a cultural object and on embodiment as a crucial component or even the very ground of cultural experience. So significant has this theme become in the study of culture that a good deal of the work we have discussed in other chapters under other thematic headings has been reread as having something to contribute to the theory of the body. For example, if we revisit classical cultural theory from a century ago, we can excavate some exciting ideas about the relationship of culture to the body. Durkheim noted that intensive and coordinated bodily actions like dance were central to the ritual activity that generated religious beliefs and social solidarity. Marx theorized the appropriation of bodily labor by capitalism. Weber observed that religious figures like prophets often underwent ascetic ordeals like fasting. More recently, Goffman spoke of bodily displays of deference and demeanor as pivotal to the interaction order. But it is only in recent years that this body component of their theory has been explicitly brought to the front stage of cultural theory. Of all the biggest names in cultural theory, only Foucault (see pp. 115–21) put the body so explicitly at the center of his work that this could not be overlooked. In this chapter, we will focus more explicitly on cultural theory of embodiment and work regarding the body. We trace out more fully the contributions on this topic of a few of the thinkers we have already introduced in earlier chapters as well as discussing the work of other scholars not yet encountered in this book.

The historical fact that the discipline of anthropology took up the close study of the body and its social construction and modification from virtually its moment of origin, while sociology took the better part of a century to do so, tells us something important about the dualistic mind/body way of thinking that has long informed the Western intellectual manner of considering bodies. The traditional object of study for the anthropologist was the pre-modern social group, which was seen as less mentally advanced and more centered in the physical than the "intellectual" modern societies generally studied by the sociologist. Traditional sociological definitions of culture have frequently tended to ignore the incorporated and the physical and to envision modern societies as somehow having gotten beyond the ways in which primitive societies relied on bodies as carriers and symbols of culture.

But this has been changing. Chris Shilling (2003 [1993]: 35) has attributed the increase in theoretical interest in the modern body as a cultural and social object in the past few decades to four broad social changes:

1   The focus on the body of second-wave feminism beginning in the 1960s.
2   The general aging of the populations of Western societies and the accompanying rise in public concern for providing for the health of all those aging bodies.
3   The shift (noted especially by postmodernists) from productivist to consumerist societies.
4   An increasing lack of certainty as to the definition of the body, attached to techno-logical advancements that have made it possible to alter bodies in more and more ways.

One might also expand on Shilling's third causal factor by noting that the emergence of consumer societies has itself coincided with the rise of modern youth culture and the general cultural privileging of youth in its many embodied characteristics. So it is not a coincidence that concern for the body has very often meant concern for *youthful* bodies, and much of the theoretical work in this field has been quite concerned to note this connection.

The Somatic Society: The Body and Social Order

Bryan Turner's *The Body and Society* (1996 [1984]) marks the beginning of the explicit contemporary theoretical preoccupation with the body. But Turner did not come to this topic from nowhere. His effort to provide an embodied cultural theory starts with the work of Foucault on discipline and governmentality (see pp. 116–20) and Max Weber on rationalization (p. 13). Parsonian functionalism (see chapter 2) also plays a key role in Turner's framework. Although he would not coin the term until later, Turner was already in the mid-1980s presenting his vision of the **somatic society**, a social order in which major public and personal problems are manifested in and through bodies (1996: 1). The basic theoretical framework of *The Body and Society* focuses on the problem of order in society. All social systems, Turner argues (1996: 38, 108), must effectively regulate and discipline the bodies of its members in four ways:

1   Bodies must be reproduced to populate the society over time.
2   Bodies must be regulated in public space to prevent disorders such as crime.
3   Bodies must be trained to exercise internal restraint against unhealthy desires.
4   Bodies must be represented externally in such a way as to facilitate orderly interaction.

In each of these four domains, a breakdown in effective order produces illness. By this term, Turner means not simply a disorder in individual bodies, but a disorder in society itself in as much as the relationship between the body and the broader cultural and social order is such as to deny easy separation between the two. A sick body is not simply a body with something awry at the biological level; it is a body that has been marked culturally as insufficiently dedicated to reproduction, disorderly, unrestrained, or as an unhealthy representation (Turner 1996: 124). Here we see Turner's reading of Foucault and Weber, both of whom described the development in the West of elaborate cultural frameworks for the ascetic regulation and disciplining of bodies. While the dominant vision of the body in modern science has been the biomedical view, which reduces the body to biology and seeks the causes of malfunctions in biological processes, a new "biopsychosocial" approach to medicine has emerged that recognizes health and illness as concepts that touch also on the social and cultural (Hancock et al. 2000: 16). Cultural causes are now recognized as implicated in some illnesses, and this makes clearer the overlap of medical and moral categories of reasoning. If one develops heart disease after years of eating fast food hamburgers, or contracts a venereal disease from careless and unprotected sex with strangers, or lung cancer from years of cigarette smoking, what cultural calculus should be used to discuss these facts? Turner suggests that a broad movement toward rationalization of bodily maintenance should be understood as the central causal factor for many of these illnesses. Changes in the scientific discourse on nutrition, for example, and the subsequent rationalizing of food production and consumption have produced many of the diseases of abundance from which Westerners now suffer (Turner 1992: 186).

In his more recent work, Turner has continued to elaborate on this vision of somatic society. The reality of globalization is somatically apparent in the rapid spread of the "new plagues" (e.g., AIDS, bird flu), which is made possible by the great facility with which many individuals move about the globe and thereby greatly increase the contact networks in which these and other diseases exist. Older diseases that seemed confined to certain parts of the world population have recently reappeared elsewhere as a consequence of the permeability of borders, globalized labor markets, and tourism. Broad social and cultural patterns concerning gender and class distinction can be traced in bodies, as the First World poor are more inclined to obesity as a result of the cheap fatty foods on which they survive, while women diet more frequently than men because of the gendered politics of courtship. The state of political and human rights is visible in the way in which the bodies of the disabled are understood, in as much as we now are better aware of how much of the business of defining bodies as "disabled" has to do with social exclusion and the normalization of social competence linked to specific embodied capacities, e.g., the ability to speak to others in the socially appropriate register, rhythm, etc. (Turner 2004: 113, 185, 202; Paterson 2001).

Body Techniques, the Corporeal Schema, and Sensual Sociology

As we saw in chapter 8, Pierre Bourdieu was quite concerned with embodiment in his elaboration of the concept of the *habitus*. For Bourdieu, the body literally comes through experience and social structure to bear the imprint of a class *habitus*, and he described this process vividly in his discussion of the differing sporting and exercise cultures to which inhabitants of different social classes are drawn and into which they are trained. Working-class sports tend to the heavily physical, even brutal and violent – e.g., football, boxing, and weightlifting – while middle-class and elite sports are often less physically rigorous and focused on the social networking in which they are involved – e.g., golf and skiing. At bottom, Bourdieu argues, we see in these different class *habitus* different relationships to our own bodies. The working classes tend toward an instrumental relation to the body, where the body is a tool to be used to attain some external end, and the middle classes view their bodies as ends in themselves to be cultivated for aesthetic and social reasons (Bourdieu 1991b [1978]).

It has generally not been made clear enough how much Bourdieu's theoretical treatment of the body owes to the work of Marcel Mauss (see pp. 69–72). The very term *habitus* was invoked by Mauss in his seminal essay on **body techniques**. In that work, he argued for a need to catalogue the ways in which, from society to society, humans learn to deploy and use their bodies just as they would other tools, the body being in fact "man's first and most natural instrument" (Mauss 1979 [1950]: 104). *Habitus*, Mauss contended, is the best term to get at the social and cultural nature of the habitual and customary ways in which people use and inhabit their bodies, as he saw the central distinctions in how people do so as rooted not in merely individual difference, but in differences of "societies, educations, proprieties and fashions, prestiges" (1979: 101). It is a social and cultural fact, not a merely individual one, that some people learn how to spit or to squat and others do not. This is precisely the central point in Bourdieu's understanding of *habitus*, i.e., these embodied ways of being vary by social class, gender, and other such categories of social identity. In his essay on body techniques, and elsewhere, Mauss presented a framework for understanding what he termed the "total person" (in French, *l'homme total*). The study of the total person had to be a triple endeavor, geared to the social, psychological, and biological elements of the human being, ideally all considered holistically and not separately.

Two contemporary efforts at theorizing the body with direct reference to the concept of the *habitus* can be found in the work of Nick Crossley and one of Bourdieu's students, Loïc Wacquant. Like Bourdieu, Crossley is dissatisfied with dualistic approaches to embodiment that radically separate mind and body. He also shares Bourdieu's concern to avoid rigid oppositions between determining structures and creative action. A satisfactory theoretical understanding of embodiment must account for the body's relationship to culture and society in a more fluid way. Bourdieu endeavored to achieve this with the *habitus* by defining it at once as a structur*ed* and a structur*ing* structure, i.e., as a long-lived element of human identity that is both the product of an already-existing set of objective social and cultural facts and the ground of possibility for new experience and practices. Ultimately, though, Crossley finds that Bourdieu's formulation does not fully capture the complex relationship between embodiment and culture, and it is even in danger of falling back into the structure/agency binary from which it seeks to escape because its account of the construction of the *habitus* is dangerously close to a purely structuralist account that implicitly rejects real creative capacity (Crossley 2001: 95).

Crossley borrows several conceptual elements from the phenomenologist Maurice Merleau-Ponty (briefly mentioned in chapter 4) in his attempt to overcome these problems. For Merleau-Ponty, the body has to be understood as fundamentally outside of stock dualisms precisely because of its unique status for us as, at one and the same time,

Figure 16.1   Pretty woman? or aged crone?

both an external object and the subjective condition through which it is possible to have relations with objects, including the body itself (e.g., you experience your leg as an object by touching it with your hand or looking at it with your eyes). The idea of a mind/body distinction in which the body is a kind of machine animated by the mind is fundamentally mistaken for Merleau-Ponty. Perception, the interaction of our lived body with the ambiguous environment around it in such a way as to make it meaningful, is revealed here to be prior to the subject/object distinction, as it is acts of perception themselves that give birth to perceived objects and perceiving subjects. Crossley illustrates this with the famous ambiguous image of a woman who can be seen as young and attractive or old and unattractive depending upon how one orients one gaze on the image (figure 16.1). We see it one way or the other not because of any a priori act of judgment by an independent subject, nor because the object itself imposes itself on us in a necessary way (as stimulus-response determinists argue), but rather only after an embodied act of looking at it and then relationally making sense of it in one way or the other, e.g., seeing the dark horizontal line approximately at the center of the image as either her mouth or her necklace (Crossley 2001: 71). Instead of the isolated subject/body and an external world of objects to which it responds, Merleau-Ponty presents the notion of the **corporeal schema** to better understand how embodied experience works. We experience our bodies and other elements of our environment that we can include in that schema in a pre-reflective manner that does not require explicit thought or knowledge. You are able to scratch your head as you read this without reflection on where your head is or how to move your arm up there to do the scratching. Similarly, once you learn how to drive, you are able to brake, put on the turn signal, and parallel park in a way that subsumes the car itself into your corporeal schema (Crossley 2001: 123).

We develop our corporeal schema by acquiring bodily **habits**. This is a key term in Merleau-Ponty and in Crossley's adaptation of his theory. Habits are embodied, learned skills that are acquired not intellectually but by doing something. Some habits are learned by imitation of others (e.g., brushing one's teeth as a child), others arise through "innovative and creative praxes" or combine imitation and innovation (e.g., the specific way one has to push and turn a key to make the sticky lock on the front door open). Ultimately, though, all action becomes part of an embodied individual's being by becoming habituated. We constantly learn new habits and our corporeal schema is constantly changing, albeit slightly and slowly. Crossley calls this situation a "moving equilibrium" (2001: 137). Agency is not opposed to, but in fact only realizable through, habit. And ultimately, though many if not most of the habits individuals have will be shared among other members of the groups to which they belong, an individual's corporeal schema or bodily *habitus* is never completely identical to that of any other individual because their experiences are not exactly the same.

From these roots in phenomenology, Crossley has proposed a systematic way of studying the body socially as embodied culture. He suggests that all societies have a particular range of what he calls **reflexive body techniques (RBTs)**, which differ from Mauss's body techniques in that the latter frequently have some practical or symbolic purpose beyond the body itself (e.g., a particular way of sitting or greeting others), while the former are only those techniques directed toward the body itself and its maintenance and modification. RBTs therefore tell us important things about how particular societies conceptualize and mark bodies (Crossley 2005: 9). Crossley breaks the field of RBTs down into three components (core, intermediate, and peripheral zones) and presents some preliminary findings from British society that show, among other things, that virtually all varieties of RBTs, except some of the more peripheral (e.g., large numbers of tattoos), find women more frequently involved in them than men. We will return to the topic of gender distinction in body techniques later in this chapter.

Loïc Wacquant's study of the sport of boxing (2004) is the central forum for his thinking about the body. As one of Bourdieu's closest associates, he is heavily indebted to Bourdieu's categories regarding embodiment, but he pushes and elaborates on them considerably in his own work. The first thing one learns from Wacquant's account is that, whatever sportscasters might say about "natural talents," there is nothing at all natural about attaining a pugilistic *habitus*. In fact, the individual well-suited to brawling in the streets is generally a poor candidate to be a successful boxer, as the spontaneous and disordered embodied temperament of the former is not often given to the ascetic practice and routine needed for production of the latter. Wacquant exhaustively describes the various kinds of labor (ring work, floor work, table work, road work) required to condition a given body to behave as a boxer's body. Even the most basic elements, the punches, require a "thorough physical rehabilitation" (2004: 69). Emotion work is also involved, as a boxer has to be able to control the effect that anger and fear have on his actions in the ring. Time and rhythm are essential technologies for the shaping of the *habitus*. Wacquant details how training enables the body literally to incorporate the three-minute interval that is a fight round into its manner of operation, pacing and reserving strength for use throughout that unit of time. The effective production of this *habitus* (and Wacquant follows Bourdieu in arguing that this is the case for all *habitus*, not just for the pugilistic one) requires an elimination of the body/mind dualism. The boxer constructs what John Dewey called a "body mind complex" in which the two are so thoroughly integrated into a machinery for action that the well-trained fighter can go on fighting even when he has been beaten into a semi-conscious state (Wacquant 2004: 96–7).

Wacquant fills out the Bourdieusian notion of **physical/bodily capital** by demonstrating how individuals cultivate and manage this capital through careful practices and strategies. As we summarized in chapter 8, Bourdieu's notion of cultural capital includes embodied elements, e.g., the cultural elite not only know about highbrow music forms, they frequently play the piano, the violin, the cello, or some other musical instrument associated with such highbrow music. This embodied cultural capital comes from specific training and an environment supportive of that training. Wacquant demonstrates not only the specific methods for producing the capital of the pugilist, but also how different realms of *habitus* formation overlap in specific ways for specific individuals. The pugilistic *habitus* of two boxers in his gym, one from the working class, the other from the underclass, develop differently as a result of their different initial class *habitus* (2004: 131).

In Wacquant's account, the acquisition of a bodily *habitus* and the accurate description of that process are necessarily phenomena that exceed discourse. Most of what boxers must learn to attain the pugilistic *habitus* has to be learnt by doing, not by verbal instruction, which recalls Merleau-Ponty's notion of habits. Fully understanding this process on the part of the cultural analyst requires a similar commitment to embodiment and a rejection of body/mind dualism. Wacquant's call for a **sensual sociology** is a methodologically radical move, pointing toward the ultimate inadequacy of written texts standing alone as intellectual statements on embodied culture. Ideally, we need all the elements that go on in the process of acquisition in the account of that process. The actual sights and sounds of the gym, which are so crucial to the actual crafting of the pugilistic *habitus*, suggest the need for video and audio sources in researching that process.

Body Projects/Options/Regimes, Body Pedagogics, and Corporeal Realism

Chris Shilling has been one of the most prolific cultural theorists of the body in recent years. In reflecting on the ways in which our attitudes toward our bodies seem to have changed as we have entered high modernity, he suggests we have come to understand our bodies as ongoing processes that can be intervened in and changed in specific ways as part of our construction of self-identity. Individualization is almost certainly a powerful cause of this reorientation in our thinking about bodies, as traditional cultural frameworks of meaning give way to individual responsibility and the creeping sense of loss of control over many areas of modern life drives many to an investment in the one thing over which they seemingly do have some control: their own bodies (Shilling 2003: 4, 6). He provides three categories with which to understand these efforts:

1 **Body projects.** Derived from Giddens (see pp. 136–9), these are efforts to use modern highly rationalized and technological knowledge and apparatuses to mold and cultivate one's own body. They range from the relatively simple (dietary restrictions) to the more complex (heavy exercise routines).
2 **Body options.** While projects "help us explore the possibilities of living in one body," body options greatly expand the realm of possibilities for redirection to a "direct and radical assault on the limitations connected to being a body" (Shilling 2003: 189; Mellor and Shilling 1997). For example, the expansion and development of virtual reality and surgical technologies make it possible, perhaps even likely, that individuals who so desire might be able fundamentally to alter their bodies and do so with some frequency.
3 **Body regimes.** Shilling locates these primarily in a medieval context of religiously induced radically ascetic disciplines, but he notes too that some contemporary extreme forms of self-denial and discipline (e.g., individuals who undergo rigorous training campaigns to get in shape for grueling sporting competitions) should perhaps be grouped together with them (Shilling 2003: 191; Mellor and Shilling 1997).

Others have followed Shilling in such efforts to classify body projects according to some such scale of differentiation. For example, Michael Atkinson (2003: 25–7) has elaborated his own set of four kinds of project explicitly derived from a starting point in Shilling's conceptual language:

1 **Camouflaging projects.** These are everyday, impermanent and relatively minimal efforts to alter bodies, e.g., using make-up or cologne, in ways that help it better adhere to collective standards of bodily presentation.
2 **Extending projects.** Still basically mundane but slightly more involved, these have as their intent the surpassing of limits presented by the physical body, e.g., the use of eyeglasses or prostheses.
3 **Adapting projects.** These involve more invasive and permanent physical alteration of the body in the interests of adhering to collective standards of bodily maintenance and health, e.g., dieting and weight loss.
4 **Redesigning projects.** Still more invasive and permanent, these include the most radical transformations of the physical body – e.g., tattoos, cosmetic surgeries, sex reassignment – and entail the greatest level of commitment.

More recently, Shilling has argued for a notion of **body pedagogics** that would seek to analyze the specific means and processes by which members of a culture learn its central embodied techniques as a way of making the study of cultural change sensitive to the new interest in the body (Shilling 2007: 13).

Shilling has been more systematic than any of the other major thinkers on the body in explicitly setting out and elaborating the existing field of body theories as a prelude to presenting his own theoretical framework. He summarizes what he sees as the three dominant traditions in the cultural theory of the body as the social constructionist theories of the body under control (e.g., Foucault and Bryan Turner), the phenomeno-logically oriented theories of the lived body (e.g., Nick Crossley), and structuration theories of the body (e.g., Giddens and Bourdieu). Each has strengths, and this is especially so of the third, which Shilling sees as an attempt at a kind of middle way between the extreme determinism and the extreme agency of the other two. However, none of the three manages to encompass all the various aspects of the relation of the body to society. Shilling argues that we need a theory that understands "the body as a multi-dimensional medium for the constitution of society," by which he means an acknowledgement that the body is at once something that produces society, something that is produced by society, and something that serves as a mechanism for placing individuals in specific relations of attraction and repulsion with one another in society. He suggests this comprehensive theory of the body can be assembled by drawing on certain elements in a rather disparate group made up of several classic theorists and one more recent thinker. In Marx, he argues, we find the body as the site of economic relations and the object that bears the brunt of capitalism's destructive force; in Durkheim, the body as the bearer of marks of collective symbolism and moral commu-nity; in Simmel, the body as the source of sociability, which is the primordial desire to playfully interact free of any greater purpose than the interaction itself; and in Elias (see pp. 140–1), the body as the site for the broad cultural shifts that make up what Shilling called the civilizing process (2003: 208).

This theory is grounded in what Shilling calls **corporeal realism**, a term he relates to the critical realism of Roy Bhaskar (see p. 51). Corporeal realism entails a recognition that both society and the body exist as real things, not simply as ideas or discourses as some would have it, but also that they are emergent phenomena. This means they are not to be understood as unchanging structures, but as generative and changing phenomena that have to be examined in relation to one another and in history. Like Bhaskar, Shilling situates his theory within a critical perspective, which is to say that he sees it as connected to a project of "human flourishing" (2005: 13, 15). Thus, theo-rizing about the body should be closely associated with the broad political project of human liberation.

Much of the contemporary cultural study of the body meets Shilling's challenge here. He has, however, made the further suggestion that a good deal of this work is in fact under-theorized and too reliant on pure empirical description (2005: 200). While it is true that relatively few thinkers have to this point presented full-blown cultural theo-ries of the body, some would suggest that a focus on description is part and parcel of the move to the body itself, i.e., that the very desire to materialize cultural theory in rooting it in the body is a de facto move away from the cultural in the form of norms, beliefs, discourses, and narratives. It is also the case that a good deal of the work on the body does not wears its theory on its sleeve, though it is nonetheless clearly situated in the critical theory and its variants we have discussed in earlier chapters of this book (e.g., chapters 3, 9, 14, and 15).

In the remainder of this chapter, we take a brief tour through some of the central topical areas in new cultural work on embodiment. While some of this work might seem at first glance amenable to Shilling's criticism, we will try to indicate as we proceed the ways in which the studies tie into broader cultural theoretical arguments. Very often, these arguments concern whether particular bodily practices contribute to human liberation in the form of self-expression and self-realization or are merely more sites for ideological and practical oppression and induced conformity.

Body Modification and Technologies of the Body

As we have already seen, all human cultures allow for or even prescribe the modification of the bodies of their members in accordance with procedures that carry meaning in those cultures. These practices range from the mundane (the removal of undesired hair) to the much more extraordinary and technically involved (the changing of one's sex via surgical procedure). In cases both mundane and extraordinary, they can involve **technologies** that make it possible to extend the function or ability of the body. Prosthetic limbs are perhaps the most obvious example, but as Tia DeNora has shown, even something as seemingly non-material as music can act as a technology to change bodies, e.g., in the form of Muzak at labor sites that sonically program work rhythms right into the bodies of workers (DeNora 2000: 104). Body modifications are also frequently associated with specific status positions in the social order, i.e., who you are sociologically will have much to do with what kinds of body modification you are likely to be engaged in. And it is likewise the case that the particular modifications you undertake will have much to do with placing you firmly into one or another social category, e.g., much body work is also gender work in the sense that it helps the body more stereotypically fit into either male or female categories.

Even as recent developments have created more cultural space for deliberation about male bodies (e.g., in fitness magazines), men remain in a markedly different position vis-à-vis body techniques and modification than that typically held by women, as indicated in Crossley's work on RBTs. Even when talking about body care, men tend to use a language of instrumentalization instead of aesthetics (e.g., they use skin moisturizer for health reasons, not simply for appearance), as many men perceive a kind of broad cultural taboo regarding consideration of bodily appearance (Gill et al. 2005: 49–50). Gendered differences are a more or less constant theme in consideration of most aspects of contemporary body culture.

Many of the forms of decorative body modification (tattoos, piercings, scarrings) that have become increasingly popular in many parts of the First World in recent years have their origins in primitive societies, as it was European sea travel to the South Pacific and other such previously unexplored parts of the globe that provided the first extended contact between Westerners and groups who ritually modified their bodies in these ways (Atkinson 2003: 30). The distinction between the meanings of such modifications in the two different kinds of society is one of great interest to cultural theory on the body. One way of characterizing the difference is in terms of **thick/hot** societies and **thin/cool** ones (Turner 2000). In the former (traditional) societies, social relations are marked by density and intensity. In the latter, relations are less concentrated and more distant. The meanings of tattoos and other similar body marks become less stable as we move from thick/hot to thin/cool societies, and members have greater freedom to mark bodies, in very idiosyncratic ways if they like, or to refrain from doing so. Body marks that were once a central and obligatory element in the construction of collective memory (i.e., as indicators of who belongs to which group and has undergone which rites of passage) have become optional tools for the narcissistic expression of individualism. Atkinson (2003) echoes this in his reading of the historical progression of tattooing in the West and its gradual incorporation into broader segments of the population, starting in the circus world and then moving in order from the working class to the "rebel" youth culture of the 1950s and '60s to the new age and finally to the supermarket. Of course, however individual, narcissistic, and consumerist such marks may be, they always take place in social contexts. Crossley (2005) borrows terminologically from Howard Becker (see pp. 62, 168, 171) to talk of the tattoo world, which consists not only of individuals seeking to pursue particular body projects via tattooing, but also of tattoo shops/parlors, tattoo artists, other tattoo aficionados and publications about tattoos, and a larger commercial culture.

We should also perhaps be careful to avoid collapsing tattooing into the same category with other elements of expressive individual identity in contemporary society. The fact that they are bodily, and therefore have a more permanent status than, e.g., clothing, indicates that it might be too easy to consider tattoos and piercings as part of a fashion culture, since fashion requires constant change as an essential element of its definition. Moreover, unlike putting on a new pair of jeans, one endures pain, sometimes for weeks or months afterward, with a tattoo or piercing, and some argue these facts move them outside the realm of purely consumer culture (Sweetman 2001). They may, in at least some of their contemporary forms, represent oppositional political or subcultural identity, as they did in many cases in the Western world before massive adoption by its middle-class youth in the last 15–20 years. Some women tattoo parts of their bodies that are in their view overly sexualized by men (frequently breasts) as a way to reclaim those parts of their bodies from the unwanted gaze of the lascivious. Piercings and brandings in the genital area are frequently markers of homosexual or other sexually non-normative identities. Some subcultural members even go so far as to mark the parts of their body generally not covered by clothing in ways (e.g., extreme stretching of ear lobes) that they feel proclaim their status as "visibly queer" and therefore incompatible with and antagonistic to mainstream cultural life. This has been referred to as a process of "**self-stigmatization**" that is intended as a radical attack on sexual normalization (Pitts 2003: 107).

Like the visibly queer, body modification devotees who align themselves with **Modern Primitivism** present an intriguing cultural phenomenon. This movement was first widely exposed in a 1989 publication that carried photos and descriptions of a number of iconic subcultural figures such as Fakir Musafar, an American from South Dakota who took up what he calls "shamanistic body play" as a way to connect himself to pre-modern spiritual practice (Vale 1989). Many members see themselves as descendants of the body art traditions of indigenous populations such as those of Borneo, Melanesia, and North America, and explicitly attempt to copy those aesthetics, while others more self-consciously invent their own "neo-tribal" body modification practices.

Individuals in both camps frequently see their body projects as a symbolic and political rejection of modernity and an embrace of the "natural" and "primal." While some thinkers with affinities to postmodernist theory see these practices as a willful and welcome embrace of a kind of hybridity in the form of bodily marks, others have criticized them as participating, whatever their intentions, in the reification of precisely the kinds of binarism (primitive/civilized) that they purport to want to escape. Some even see this "romanticized . . . possibility of escape from the West" as a de facto ally of the racist Othering of non-Western peoples that was born with colonialism (Klesse 1999: 35). The subcultural and radical thrust of primitivism has also perhaps been blunted significantly by the fact that it has become something of a consumer object, as "primitivist fashion" has made its way into mass media women's magazines and other mainstream sources (Pitts 2003: 144).

Cosmetic surgery is another body modification practice that is taking up an increasingly important role in many contemporary societies. While reconstructive surgery designed to repair serious deformities can be traced back to the Renaissance, the cultural shift that made it acceptable to apply risky surgical techniques to modify the body in situations that were not catastrophic is what made modern cosmetic surgery possible. Beginning in the early twentieth century, the fact that people with attractive appearances frequently enjoy higher status was made a much more explicit element of many Western societies. Women entering the workforce in increasing numbers meant more of them were exposed to gender-specific criticisms regarding attractiveness and aging, while the fact that service sector and office work greatly expanded meant that an attractive appearance became a more explicit advantage occupationally (Sullivan 2004: 29). The fact that cosmetic surgery was linked at its birth to the specific cultural imperatives that women face regarding beauty and attractiveness tells us much about its contemporary context as well. Many feminist scholars see cosmetic surgery as profoundly implicated in a broader cultural system that constantly informs women of their need to be thinner, younger, and more sexually enticing from a male heterosexual perspective (e.g., Blum 2003; Bordo 2004 [1993]). Stories like that of Kelly, a British woman who had accrued £30,000 in debt by age 22 from a series of breast augmentation and subsequent corrective surgeries, are more frequent now than ever (Elliott and Lemert 2006: 1). Others, however, have noted an increasing male interest in cosmetic surgery. Some men, in the face of a perceived crisis in traditional masculinity and male power, use an interpretive strategy for making positive sense of surgical "bodywork" that is rooted in those traditional norms of masculinity seen as under siege. The earlier response of the traditional masculine male was rejection of plastic surgery as a "feminine" thing, but more now embrace it as a way to better "produce appearances of a traditionally 'in control' male" (Atkinson 2006: 252). So it is perhaps not that new modes of masculinity are being invented as men embrace the cosmetic surgery culture, but rather that the practice is adapted to existing understandings of masculinity.

The explosion of workout culture and the ascetic dietary regimes that often accompany it demonstrate another important contemporary mode of body modification. It has become more or less accepted in many Western middle-class cultures that individuals spend at least part of their time free from their working responsibilities actively working to maintain their bodies in gyms, sports facilities, etc. Much like tanning in some segments of the middle and upper classes (although this is changing with increased health warnings of skin cancer), working out seems in at least some ways to provide men and women who work predominantly in office and white-collar occupational settings to approximate the perceived and perhaps romanticized beneficial effects of the physical labor of the working classes. While the working-class man hones his biceps by loading trucks, the middle-class professional man does so by interacting with Nautilus machinery. But working out is not only about health considerations; it is also, and perhaps even more so, about moral and aesthetic ones. As obesity is frequently morally equated by some with laziness or even a quasi-criminal propensity for risky behavior, some may well be interested in working out at least in part as a contribution to the work necessary to keep others from making negative moral judgments of them (Saguy and Riley 2005). Many others are pursuing aesthetic projects of various types. These projects are generally gendered in fairly clear ways. As stereotypical male body images involve muscularity and size, while the stereotypically ideal female body type is generally much smaller, typical male workouts emphasize weight training to a significantly higher degree than women, whereas women tend to concentrate more on cardio exercises designed to burn excess weight. This can produce the spectacle of gendered self-segregation in gyms as treadmill and stationary bike areas fill up with female bodies and the male bodies are all to be found in the weight room (see figure 16.2(a)(b)). Predictably, this leads those sympathetic to critical cultural theories to view the rise of workout culture as old wine in new bottles. What looks like an increased interest in personal health is understood as one more way to enforce gender hierarchies.

Dedicated bodybuilders push workout culture further than casual exercisers. They can rightly be considered a body subculture whose particular body projects reveal much of a broader nature about the body as an aestheticized, technologically produced piece of culture. Lee Monoghan's (2000) study of bodybuilding subcultures demonstrates how much of the aesthetic vocabulary is only gradually learned as part of initiation into the subculture. Bodybuilders are, in other words, not born, but rather frequently transition from the world of more casual gym exercisers into the dedicated subculture. Much as in Howard Becker's (1973 [1963]) classic study of marijuana users learning how to define what is initially perhaps a not very pleasant experience as something uniquely desirable, so Monoghan shows how dedicated bodybuilders learn over time to see larger and larger physiques not as strange or freakish but as admirable and even worth pursuing at the risk of significant personal injury, i.e., with the aid of steroids. Bodybuilding culture has to be studied at the micro level and with micro theories of interaction (see chapter 4) in order to fully understand how individuals are brought into the culture's way of seeing things. Whereas non-bodybuilders might see champion bodybuilders as obese, especially when they are in street clothes, other members of the subculture recognize the ascetic effort (long hours in the gym, considerable investment in food and supplemental vitamins, care to sleep sufficiently and avoid excessive partying) and potential risk that the individual has endured to achieve the aesthetic. Bodybuilding requires a very high and specialized degree of knowledge about diet and metabolism; one must know how to maximize the amount of protein in the body throughout the day and supplement at just the right intervals with respect to

Figure 16.2(a)   Women working out in the gym

Figure 16.2(b)   Men in the weight room

exercise to achieve maximum physical gains. Bodybuilding subculture also creates its own highly specific and nuanced body of knowledge surrounding the use and abuse of steroids. These are seen as a risk that one might legitimately run in order to bypass otherwise insurmountable barriers (e.g., the limits to muscle size and growth in a small-framed man). In this sense, bodybuilders acknowledge the risk society indicated by Giddens and Beck (see pp. 138–9), but they claim the ability to minimize the risks through their knowledge of the "proper" use of drugs and their capacity to maintain control of the increased aggression with which they admit the drugs provide them.

Female bodybuilders raise other intriguing questions about the culture of body modification involving the technology of weight training. Women who seek to grow significantly muscularly larger directly challenge standard expectations of gendered bodies, and the significance of the challenge is evident in the constant attempt to frame female bodybuilding, both in the media sources dedicated to them and in the culture of professional female bodybuilding itself, as typically feminine. In bodybuilding magazines, women are constantly told that weight training will make them more heterosexually desirable and competent and many professional female bodybuilders go to great lengths to enhance typically feminine aspects of their appearance (e.g., hair, make-up) and frequently hold gender ideologies with distinctly conservative elements (Schulze 1997; Fisher 1997). The cultural imperative to maintain connection with distinctly feminine gender identity elements carries over also into the realm of sexual "schmoozing" that some female bodybuilders engage in to generate income for their bodybuilding careers. This practice also exists in the male bodybuilding community, where it is called "hustling" and consists mostly of being paid for dates or nude photograph/film sessions, generally with a homosexual orientation. For female bodybuilders, however, the stigma of homosexuality is greatly feared and so the vast bulk of this "schmoozing" work is heterosexually oriented (Fisher 1997).

Commodification, Old Age, and Death of the Body

We introduced **commodification** as a broad cultural process as it is presented in Western Marxism in chapter 3, and it has popped its head up here and again in some subsequent chapters (see pp. 167, 216). It is a central theoretical concept for much of the recent work on the body. Turner indicated its importance in *The Body and Society* in emphasizing the complex ways in which representation of bodily images is affected by consumer capitalism. Bourdieu's interest in sporting *habitus* has led to a consideration of commodification in the way in which professional athletics provides a cut-throat market for the buying and selling of the bodies of the socially disadvantaged. But media representations and sport are hardly the only realms in which we find bodies commodified. One of the core such forms in modernity is found in the sex trade. Though by no means a new cultural practice, the exchange of sexual access to bodies for money is facilitated by cultural shifts in the direction of globalization. Sex tourism, in which the bodies of poor Third Worlders become commodities for relatively wealthy First World seekers of physical pleasure, is on the increase, despite some international political efforts to clamp down on it. Within the First World, sex workers engage in very specific bodily practices to hide their everyday miseries and make their bodies more marketable. Strippers often put their earnings back into the enterprise of obtaining top market value for their bodies by getting breast- and/or buttocks-enhancement surgery and both strippers and prostitutes who are drug-addicted do significant body work to hide parts of their bodies that betray that fact from potential clients (Epele 2002). Some of those who use their bodies in this sexual economy claim to come out of the transaction personally empowered, e.g., exotic dancers who feel they enhance the sexual experience of clients without themselves having to have sexual contact with them (Rambo et al. 2006: 224–5), but the dominant perspective seems to resonate with Marx's arguments about the inevitable alienation that comes from commodification (see pp. 7–8).

Recent developments in medical technology have facilitated other and still more radical varieties of body commodification. The national and international markets in organs, especially kidneys, have been studied in their cultural ramifications by numerous scholars. Nancy Scheper-Hughes has shown how we might use the concept of **commodity fetishism** (see p. 35) to understand better how the international black market in organs functions. As patients who were previously denied organ transplants (e.g., the very elderly or those with other serious health conditions that make the transplant unlikely to have long-term positive effects) come to understand such medical procedures as consumer products, those who are willing and able to pay are being catered for by an illegal network of providers who often obtain organs from the poor through unethical methods (Scheper-Hughes 2000, 2002). The phenomenon of biotech companies harvesting body parts from the Third World and using them to isolate useful genes which they then patent and use to make products that are frequently sold back to the Third World countries further roots the Marxian idea of alienation in the body. Cultural frameworks of exclusion and fear of a greater spread of hybridity via the use of such transplants and other such biotech products can drive decision-making frameworks. Even some physicians seem to indicate a reticence about certain organs or materials, as in the example of a doctor who responds to a program of organ donation for prisoners condemned to death by remarking: "I wouldn't like to have a murderer's heart in my body" (Lock 2002: 72).

The phenomenon of commodification perhaps also contributes to an understanding of how aging and death are integrated into the contemporary cultural landscape of the body. As in the case of the disabled, much thinking about aged bodies has taken them as somehow debilitated and inferior to other "normal" bodies. The bodies of the old are frequently seen as having entered a "second childhood" and their bodies are compared to those of children, which are defined in the adult-centered ideology of the West by their deficiencies vis-à-vis adult bodies: lacking in self-control, prone to confusion and credulity, sexually immature. The aged body's sexuality is particularly powerfully affected by this symbolic framework, as the aged are frequently seen by others as essentially asexual beings (Hockey and James 1995). The social devaluation of the aged body is seen in still more radical form in the increased likelihood in at least some societies that elderly hospital patients will be labeled with "Do Not Resuscitate" orders that define them as sufficiently burdensome to the system as not to merit intervention in the event of cardiac or respiratory failure (Biggs 2002). But just as one can argue that adult bodies can easily be understood as deficient in comparison to children's bodies in some ways (e.g., decreased flexibility and ability to fall without injury), so too it is being increasingly suggested that symbolically making sense of aged bodies as deficient has to do with a particular cultural worldview that can and might change. The idea of **the posthuman body** (see Donna Haraway's discussion of the cyborg, p. 255), which is defined by "its connectedness, not only to reproductive technologies, intelligent machines, and prosthetic extensions, but also to changing informational patterns" in such a way as to radically challenge fundamental paradigms for the traditional under-standing of bodies (e.g., the inescapability of sexual binarism), effectively makes it pos-sible to think of aged bodies in the same terms that define youthful bodies (Katz and Marshall 2003). Seniors are and will be increasingly understood in this perspective as hyper-sexualized and consumerist, and new technologies (especially the exploding market in treatments for sexual dysfunction) will help them fit this mold. Of course, if instead of no representations of the aged in media we find a proliferation of older bodies that are extraordinarily youthful and in fact show very few signs of aging at all, we might well ask how much has actually changed.

Still, despite efforts to culturally reframe old age and defer the aging process, the simple fact that the body does age makes it something that cannot be wholly subjected to rational control. Eventually, no matter how much we exercise, how well we eat, and how much we avail ourselves of technological anti-aging "fixes," our bodies inevitably deteriorate and eventually die. The death of the body was famously described by Peter Berger (1967) as the ultimate "marginal situation" that poses a severe crisis in meaning for both individuals and cultures. In modernity, the religious cultural systems that Berger argued have traditionally been so successful at integrating the death experience into a larger framework of meaning begin to give way, and, as Anthony Giddens (1991) has argued, this brings death as a bodily fact home all the more radically for the narcis-sistic subjects who inhabit the contemporary world. Death in this context is understood culturally as the falling away of personhood, literally the transformation of the body from subject to object. This is a process of some duration for many, for example, the terminally ill, in which the individual slowly loses both her sense of a discrete, bounded body (as, e.g., bowel function becomes less controllable) and the physical capacity to use her body in the pursuit of her intentions (Lawton 2000: 7). Dying alone, and the increasing removal or sequestration of the dying process from public view and discus-sion, have become dominant themes of the culture of death in the West, according to some (Elias 1985 [1982]; Seale 1998), but others argue that we have actually seen an encouragement that the dying be represented and heard since at least the early 1960s, most evident in the omnipresence of death in the media, even if it is often fictional death (Williams 2003). Of course, this also means that death and dead bodies too can become commodities, as Eric Klinenberg (2002) demonstrates in his analysis of how the nar-rative concerning the deadly 1995 Chicago heatwave focused on images of the dead at the Medical Examiner's Office (which were used to sell the story in the form of news-paper and television coverage) instead of on the reasons that the tragedy happened and why it affected poor and elderly populations most acutely.

It has also been suggested that we might do well to understand death and the body in relation to another cultural fact of bodies that is frequently connected to death in popular discourse, namely sleep. Simon Williams maintains, in borrowing from Elias, that both sleep and death have undergone privatization and sequestration in the modern world and that both are now culturally understood as experiences to defer, or even to eliminate completely with technological fixes if possible. Thus, the massive growth of varieties of "sleep sickness," e.g., sleep apnea and restless leg syndrome, is connected to our cultural desire to avoid sleep in the same way and with the same motivations that we try to avoid death. The closer study of what Williams calls **the dormant body** and its meaning in culture would make still more nuanced and comprehensive our new cultural theory of the body (Williams and Bendelow 1998; Williams 2003).

Evaluation

The promise of embodied cultural theory is significant. Concepts such as the somatic society, body techniques, body projects and pedagogics, and the corporeal schema, and frameworks such as that of sensual sociology offer cultural theory new ways to integrate formerly rigidly separated fields of inquiry and to make more complex the relations between binary pairs that frequently stifle nuanced analysis, e.g., nature/culture, body/mind, and structure/agency. Much of this work also provides a ready response to materialist accusations of the purported hyper-idealism of some cultural theory, as bringing the material back into analysis of modern culture in a big way is one of its obvious features.

This is not to say cultural theory of the body faces no obstacles. It certainly is the case that even much of the work on the body that avoids Shilling's charge of under-theorization is highly pluralistic and non-unified, and it may be that thorough integration of the research that exists on the body awaits the emergence of theoretical consensus, if not in the form of one specific theoretical model, at least in the emergence of some small set of well-defined and complementary theories like, e.g., the Marxist, Weberian, and Durkheimian paradigms that dominated mainstream sociological theory for much of the twentieth century. Shilling may be correct in claiming that we can already locate three dominant theoretical traditions in body theory (social constructionist, phenomenological, and structuration), but it is not clear that these three traditions have achieved enough coherence internally or in their relationships to one another to effectively organize thinking and research in the way they are so organized in more established fields of inquiry.

Despite these challenges, it seems safe to say that this is one of the growth areas in cultural theory and we are well advised to keep our eyes on it in the years to come.

Suggested Further Reading

Unlike the case in some other areas, there are a number of very good general reference books on cultural theory of the body that provide solid introductions to most or all of the topics introduced in this chapter. Shilling's *The Body and Social Theory* and *The Body in Culture, Technology & Society* are both wide-ranging and well written, and we found them to be invaluable sources in researching this chapter. *The Body*, a volume compiled by Mariam Fraser and Monica Greco, has selections from many of the theorists and on many of the themes noted here. Turner's *The Body and Society* is foundational and eminently accessible, so anyone seeking a basic layout of the field would do well to read it.

References

Afary, Janet and Anderson, Kevin. 2005. *Foucault and the Iranian Revolution: Gender and the Seductions of Islamism*. Chicago. University of Chicago Press.

Alexander, Jeffrey. 1987. *Twenty Lectures*. New York. Columbia University Press.

Alexander, Jeffrey. 1988. (ed.) *Durkheimian Sociology*. Cambridge. Cambridge University Press.

Alexander, Jeffrey. 2004. *The Meanings of Social Life: A Cultural Sociology*. New York. Oxford University Press.

Alexander, Jeffrey and Colomy, Paul. 1990. "Neofunctionalism Today," pp. 33–67 in G. Ritzer (ed.), *Frontiers of Social Theory*. New York. Columbia University Press.

Alexander, Jeffrey and Smith, Philip. 1993. "The Discourse of American Civil Society," *Theory and Society* 22, 2: 151–207.

Alexander, Jeffrey and Smith, Philip. 2005. (eds.) *The Cambridge Companion to Durkheim*. Cambridge. Cambridge University Press.

Alexander, Victoria. 1996. "Pictures at an Exhibition," *American Journal of Sociology* 101, 4: 797–839.

Althusser, Louis. 1971. *Lenin and Philosophy and Other Essays*. New York. Monthly Review Press.

Anderson, Elijah. 1998. "Drugs and Violence in the Inner City," pp. 259–78 in Michael Katz and Thomas Sugrue (eds.), *W.E.B. DuBois, Race, and the City: The Philadelphia Negro and Its Legacy*. Philadelphia. University of Pennsylvania Press.

Anderson, Elijah. 1999a. *Code of the Street: Decency, Violence, and the Moral Life of the Inner City*. New York. W. W. Norton & Co.

Anderson, Elijah. 1999b. "The Social Situation of the Black Executive: Black and White Identities in the Corporate World," pp. 3–29 in M. Lamont (ed.), *The Cultural Territories of Race: Black and White Boundaries*. Chicago. University of Chicago Press.

Anderson, Perry. 1979. *Considerations on Western Marxism*. London. Verso.

Andrejevic, Mark. 2003. *Reality TV: The Work of Being Watched*. Lanham. Rowman and Littlefield.

Aristarkhova, Irina. 2005. "Ectogenesis and Mother as Machine," *Body & Society* 11, 3: 43–59.

Ashmore, Malcolm. 1989. *The Reflexive Thesis: Wrighting Sociology of Scientific Knowledge*. Chicago. University of Chicago Press.

Atkinson, Michael. 2003. *Tattooed: The Sociogenesis of a Body Art*. Toronto. University of Toronto Press.

Atkinson, Michael. 2006. "Masks of Masculinity: (Sur)passing Narratives and Cosmetic Surgery," pp. 247–62 in Dennis Waskul and Phillip Vannini (eds.), *Body/Embodiment: Symbolic Interaction and the Sociology of the Body*. London. Ashgate.

Back, Les and Solomos, John 2000. (eds.) *Theories of Race and Racism*. London. Routledge.

Baerenholdt, Jorgen Ole, Haldrup, Michael, Larsen, Jonas, and Urry, John. 2004. *Performing Tourist Places*. London. Ashgate.

Baker, Houston. 1987. *Modernism and the Harlem Renaissance*. Chicago. University of Chicago Press.

Bakhtin, Mikhail. 1981. *The Dialogic Imagination*. Austin. University of Texas Press.

Bakhtin, Mikhail. 1984. *Rabelais and his World*. Trans. H. Iswolsky. Bloomington. Indiana University Press.

Barthes, Roland. 1973 [1957]. *Mythologies*. St Albans. Paladin.

Barthes, Roland. 1973. *Le Plaisir du texte*. Paris. Éditions du Seuil.

Barthes, Roland. 1975a [1970]. *S/Z*. London. Cape.

Barthes, Roland. 1975b [1973]. *The Pleasure of the Text*. New York. Hill and Wang.

Barthes, Roland. 1984 [1964]. *Elements of Semiology*, pp. 77–165 in *Writing Degree Zero and Elements of Semiology*. London. Jonathan Cape.

Barthes, Roland. 1991 [1981]. *The Grain of the Voice: Interviews 1962–1980*. Berkeley. University of California Press.

Bataille, Georges. 1997a [1941]. "Madama Edwarda," pp. 223–36 in F. Botting and S. Wilson (eds.), *The Bataille Reader*. Oxford. Blackwell.

Bataille, Georges. 1997b [1949]. "The Meaning of General Economy," pp. 182–7 in F. Botting and S. Wilson (eds.), *The Bataille Reader*. Oxford. Blackwell.

Baudrillard, Jean. 1993 [1976]. *Symbolic Exchange and Death*. London. Sage.

Baudrillard, Jean. 1996 [1995]. *The Perfect Crime*. London. Verso.

Baudrillard, Jean. 1998 [1970]. *The Consumer Society*. London. Sage.

Baudrillard, Jean. 2001 [1999]. *Impossible Exchange*. London. Verso.

Bauman, Zygmunt. 1991. *Modernity and Ambivalence*. Cornell. Cornell University Press.

Bauman, Zygmunt. 1992. *Intimations of Postmodernity*. London. Routledge.

Bauman, Zygmunt. 2005. *Liquid Life*. Cambridge. Polity Press.

Beck, Ulrich. 1992. *Risk Society*. London. Sage.

Beck, Ulrich. 2006. *The Cosmopolitan Vision*. Cambridge. Polity Press.

Beck, Ulrich, Giddens, Anthony, and Lash, Scott. 1994. *Reflexive Modernization*. Cambridge. Polity Press.

Becker, Howard. 1973 [1963]. *Outsiders*. Glencoe. Free Press.

Becker, Howard. 1982. *Art Worlds*. Berkeley. University of California Press.

Bell, Daniel. 1973. *The Coming of Post-Industrial Society*. New York. Basic Books.

Bell, Daniel. 1976. *The Cultural Contradictions of Capitalism*. New York. Basic Books.

Bellah, Robert. 1970. *Beyond Belief*. New York. Harper and Row.

Benjamin, Walter. 1973 [1936]. *The Work of Art in the Age of Mechanical Reproduction*, pp. 211–44 in H. Arendt (ed.), *Illuminations*. London. Fontana.

Benjamin, Walter. 1997 [1935–8]. *Charles Baudelaire*. London. Verso.

Bennett, Andy and Peterson, Richard. 2004. (eds.) *Music Scenes: Local, Translocal, and Virtual*. Nashville. Vanderbilt University Press.

Bennett, Tony. 1998. *Culture: A Reformer's Science*. Sydney. Allen and Unwin.

Bennett, Tony, Emmison, Michael, and Frow, John. 1999. *Accounting for Taste*. Melbourne. Cambridge University Press.

Benton, T. 1984. (ed.) *The Rise and Fall of Structural Marxism*. London. Macmillan.

Berger, Peter. 1967. *The Sacred Canopy*. New York. Doubleday.

Bhabha, Homi. 1990a. "Introduction: Narrating the Nation," pp. 1–7 in H. Bhabha (ed.), *Nation and Narration*. London. Routledge.

Bhabha, Homi. 1990b. "DissemiNation: Time, Narrative, and the Margins of the Modern Nation," pp. 291–322 in H. Bhabha (ed.), *Nation and Narration*. London. Routledge.

Bhaskar, Roy. 1991. *Philosophy and the Idea of Freedom*. Oxford. Blackwell.

Bhaskar, Roy. 1998 [1979]. *The Possibility of Naturalism: A Philosophical Critique of the Contemporary Human Sciences*. London. Routledge.

Bhaskar, Roy. 2000. *From East to West: Odyssey of a Soul*. London. Routledge.

Bhaskar, Roy and Callinicos, Alex. 2003. "Marxism and Critical Realism: A Debate," *Journal of Critical Realism* 1, 2: 89–114.

Biggs, Hazel. 2002. "The Ageing Body," pp. 167–84 in M. Evans and E. Lee (eds.), *Real Bodies: A Sociological Introduction*. New York. Palgrave.

Black, Elizabeth and Smith, Philip. 1999. "Princess Diana's Meaning for Women," *Journal of Sociology* 35, 3: 263–78.

Blum, Virginia L. 2003. *Flesh Wounds: The Culture of Cosmetic Surgery*. Berkeley. University of California Press.

Blumer, Herbert. 1969. *Symbolic Interactionism*. Englewood Cliffs, NJ. Prentice Hall.

Bonilla-Silva, Eduardo. 2003. *Racism without Racists: Color-Blind Racism and the Persistence of Racial Inequality in the United States*. Lanham. Rowman & Littlefield.

Bordo, Susan. 2004 [1993]. *Unbearable Weight: Feminism, Western Culture and the Body*. Berkeley. University of California Press.

Bouglé, Célestin. 1971 [1899]. *Essays on the Caste System*. Cambridge. Cambridge University Press.

Bourdieu, Pierre. 1977 [1972]. *Outline of a Theory of Practice*. Cambridge. Cambridge University Press.

Bourdieu, Pierre. 1978. "Sport and Social Class," *Social Science Information* 17(6): 819–40.

Bourdieu, Pierre. 1984 [1979]. *Distinction*. Cambridge, MA. Harvard University Press.

Bourdieu, Pierre. 1988 [1984]. *Homo Academicus*. Cambridge. Polity Press.

Bourdieu, Pierre. 1990. *In Other Words*. Stanford. Stanford University Press.

Bourdieu, Pierre. 1991a [1982]. *Language and Symbolic Power*. Cambridge. Polity Press.

Bourdieu, Pierre. 1991b [1978]. "Sport and Social Class," pp. 357–73 in Michael Schudson and Chandra Mukerji (eds.), *Rethinking Popular Culture*. Berkeley. University of California Press.

Bourdieu, Pierre. 1992. *An Invitation to Reflexive Sociology*. Chicago. University of Chicago Press.

Bourdieu, Pierre. 1993 [1968–87]. *The Field of Cultural Production*. Cambridge. Polity Press.

Bourdieu, Pierre. 2004 [2001]. *Science of Science and Reflexivity*. Chicago. University of Chicago Press.

Bourdieu, Pierre and Passeron, Jean-Claude. 1979 [1964]. *The Inheritors*. Chicago. University of Chicago Press.

Brown, Andrew, Fleetwood, Steve, and Roberts, John Michael. 2002. (eds.) *Critical Realism and Marxism*. London. Routledge.

Brown, Richard Harvey. 1990. "Rhetoric, Textuality, and the Postmodern Turn," *Sociological Theory* 8: 188–98.

Bryant, Christopher and Jary, David. 1991. *Giddens's Theory of Structuration*. London. Routledge.

Bryson, Bethany. 1996. " 'Anything but Heavy Metal': Symbolic Exclusion and Musical Dislikes," *American Sociological Review* 61: 884–99.

Buckingham, David. 1987. *Public Secrets: Eastenders and its Audience*. London. British Film Institute.

Burns, Tom. 1992. *Erving Goffman*. London. Routledge.

Butler, Judith. 2004a. *Undoing Gender*. New York. Routledge.

Butler, Judith. 2004b. *The Judith Butler Reader*. London. Blackwell.

Butler, Judith. 2006 [1990]. *Gender Trouble*. New York. Routledge.

Caillois, Roger. 2001 [1958]. *Man, Play and Games*. Urbana. University of Illinois Press.

Caillois, Roger. 2003. *The Edge of Surrealism: A Roger Caillois Reader*, ed. C. Frank. Durham. Duke University Press.

Calhoun, Craig. 1992. (ed.) *Habermas and the Public Sphere*. Cambridge, MA. MIT Press.

Calhoun, Craig. 1995. *Critical Social Theory*. Cambridge, MA. Blackwell.

Callinicos, Alex. 1989. *Against Postmodernism: A Marxist Critique*. Cambridge. Polity Press.

Cashmore, Ellis. 2005. *Tyson: Nurture of the Beast*. Cambridge. Polity Press.

Castells, Manuel. 2000 [1996]. *The Rise of the Network Society*. London. Blackwell.

Castells, Manuel. 2004 [1997]. *The Power of Identity*. London. Blackwell.

Castronova, Edward. 2005. *Synthetic Worlds: The Business and Culture of Online Games*. Chicago. University of Chicago Press.

Centre for Contemporary Cultural Studies. 1982. *The Empire Strikes Back*. London. Hutchinson.

Chodorow, Nancy. 1978. *The Reproduction of Mothering: Psychoanalysis and the Sociology of Gender*. Berkeley. University of California Press.

Clifford, James. 1986. "Introduction," pp. 1–26 in James Clifford and George Marcus (eds.), *Writing Culture*. Berkeley. University of California Press.

Clifford, James. 1988. *The Predicament of Culture*. Cambridge, MA. Harvard University Press.

Clifford, James and Marcus, George. 1986. (eds.) *Writing Culture*. Berkeley. University of California Press.

Cohen, Stanley. 1973. *Folk Devils and Moral Panics*. London. Paladin.

Collins, Patricia Hill. 1986. "Learning from the Outsider Within: The Sociological Significance of Black Feminist Thought," *Social Problems* 33, 6: S14–S32. Repr. in Sandra Harding (ed.), *The Feminist Standpoint Theory Reader*. New York. Routledge, 2004.

Collins, Patricia Hill. 2000 [1990]. *Black Feminist Thought: Knowledge, Consciousness, and the Politics of Empowerment*. New York. Routledge.

Collins, Randall. 1975. *Conflict Sociology*. New York. Academic Press.

Collins, Randall. 2004. *Interaction Ritual Chains*. Princeton. Princeton University Press.

Concise Oxford English Dictionary. 1980. Oxford. Oxford University Press.

Coser, Lewis. 1971. *Masters of Sociological Thought*. New York. Harcourt Brace Jovanovich.

Coser, Lewis. 1992. "Introduction," pp. 1–34 in Maurice Halbwachs, *On Collective Memory*. Chicago. University of Chicago Press.

Crane, Diana. 1992. *The Production of Culture*. Newbury Park. Sage.

Crapanzano, Vincent. 1986. "Hermes' Dilemma," pp. 51–76 in James Clifford and George Marcus (eds.), *Writing Culture*. Berkeley. University of California Press.

Crossley, Nick. 2001. *The Social Body: Habit, Identity and Desire*, London. Sage.

Crossley, Nick. 2005. "Mapping Reflexive Body Techniques," *Body & Society* 11, 1: 1–35.

Culler, Jonathan. 1983. *Roland Barthes*. London. Fontana.

Culler, Jonathan. 1987. *On Deconstruction*. London. Routledge and Kegan Paul.

Dayan, Daniel and Katz, Elihu. 1992. *Media Events*. Cambridge, MA. Harvard University Press.

Daynes, Sarah and Lee, Orville. 2008. *Desire for Race*. Cambridge. Cambridge University Press.

De Certeau, Michel. 1988 [1974]. *The Practice of Everyday Life*. Berkeley. University of California Press.

Deleuze, Gilles. 2002 [1973]. "Cinq propositions sur la psychanalyse," pp. 381–90 in Gilles Deleuze, *L'Île déserte et autres textes*. Paris. Éditions de Minuit.

Deleuze, Gilles and Guattari, Félix. 1984 [1972]. *Anti-Oedipus: Capitalism and Schizophrenia*. London. Athlone Press.

DeMarco, Joseph. 1983. *The Social Thought of W.E.B. DuBois*. Lanham. University Press of America.

DeNora, Tia. 2000. *Music in Everyday Life*. Cambridge. Cambridge University Press.

Derrida, Jacques. 1976 [1967]. *Of Grammatology*. Baltimore. Johns Hopkins University Press.

Derrida, Jacques. 1988 [1977]. *Limited, Inc*. Evanston. Northwestern University Press.

Derrida, Jacques. 1992 [1991]. *Given Time: 1. Counterfeit Money*. Chicago. University of Chicago Press.

Derrida, Jacques and Roudinesco, Elisabeth. 2004 [2001]. *For What Tomorrow . . . : A Dialogue*. Palo Alto. Stanford University Press.

DiMaggio, Paul. 1982. "Cultural Entrepreneurship in 19th Century Boston," *Media, Culture and Society* 4: 33–50.

Douglas, Mary. 1966. *Purity and Danger*. London. Routledge and Kegan Paul.

Douglas, Mary. 1970. *Natural Symbols: Explorations in Cosmology*. London. Barrie and Rockcliff.

Douglas, Mary. 1978. *Cultural Bias*. London. Routledge and Kegan Paul.

Douglas, Mary and Wildavsky, Aaron. 1982. *Risk and Culture*. Berkeley. University of California Press.

DuBois, W. E. B. 1961 [1903]. *The Souls of Black Folk*. New York. Fawcett Publications.

DuBois, W. E. B. 1996 [1899]. *The Philadelphia Negro: A Social Study*. Philadelphia. University of Pennsylvania Press.

Durkheim, Émile. 1966 [1897]. *Suicide*. New York. Free Press.

Durkheim, Émile. 1968 [1915]. *The Elementary Forms of Religious Life*. London. Allen and Unwin.

Durkheim, Émile. 1984 [1893]. *The Division of Labor in Society*. New York. Free Press.

Durkheim, Émile and Mauss, Marcel. 1963 [1903]. *Primitive Classification*. Chicago. University of Chicago Press.

Eagleton, Terry. 2000. *The Idea of Culture*. London. Blackwell.

Eagleton, Terry. 2003. *Sweet Violence: The Idea of the Tragic*. Oxford. Blackwell.

Eagleton, Terry. 2006 [1976]. *Criticism and Ideology: A Study in Marxist Literary Theory*. London. Verso.

Eco, Umberto. 1984. *The Role of the Reader*. Bloomington. Indiana University Press.

Elias, Norbert. 1978 [1939]. *The Civilizing Process. Vol. 1: The History of Manners*. Oxford. Basil Blackwell.

Elias, Norbert. 1982 [1939]. *The Civilizing Process. Vol. 2: State Formation and Civilization*. Oxford. Basil Blackwell.

Elias, Norbert. 1985 [1982]. *The Loneliness of the Dying*. London. Blackwell.

Elliott, Anthony. 1994. *Psychoanalytic Theory*. Oxford. Blackwell.

Elliott, Anthony. 1999. *The Mourning of John Lennon*. Berkeley. University of California Press.

Elliott, Anthony. 2001. *Concepts of the Self*. Cambridge. Polity Press.

Elliott, Anthony. 2004. *Social Theory Since Freud: Traversing Social Imaginaries*. London. Routledge.

Elliott, Anthony and Lemert, Charles. 2006. *The New Individualism: The Emotional Costs of Globalization*. London. Routledge.

Ellis, Carolyn. 2004. *The Ethnographic I: A Methodological Novel about Autoethnography*. Lanham. AltaMira.

Emirbayer, Mustafa. 2004. "The Alexander School of Cultural Sociology," *Thesis Eleven* 79, 1: 5–15.

Epele, Maria. 2002. "Excess, Scarcity and Desire among Drug-Using Sex Workers," pp. 161–80 in Nancy Sheper-Hughes and Loïc Wacquant (eds.), *Commodifying Bodies*. London. Sage.

Eribon, Didier. 1991. *Michel Foucault*. Cambridge, MA. Harvard University Press.

Erikson, Kai. 1966. *Wayward Puritans*. New York. Wiley.

Essed, Philomena and Goldberg, David Theo. 2002. (eds.) *Race Critical Theories: Text and Context*. Oxford. Blackwell.

Evans-Pritchard, E. E. 1974. "Introduction," pp. v–x in M. Mauss, *The Gift*. London. Routledge and Kegan Paul.

Evans-Pritchard, E. E. 1956. *Nuer Religion*. Oxford. Clarendon Press.

Eyerman, Ron. 2004. "Cultural Trauma: Slavery and the Formation of African American Identity," pp. 60–111 in J. C. Alexander, R. Eyerman, B. Giesen, N. J. Smelseret, and P. Sztompka, *Cultural Trauma and Collective Identity*. Berkeley. University of California Press.

Fausto-Sterling, Anne. 2000. *Sexing the Body: Gender Politics and the Construction of Sexuality*. New York. Basic Books.

Feagin, Joe. 2000. *Racist America: Roots, Current Realities, and Future Reparations*. London. Routledge.

Featherstone, Mike. 1995. *Undoing Culture*. London. Sage.

Fisher, Leslee. 1997. "'Building One's Self Up': Bodybuilding and the Construction of Identity among Professional Female Bodybuilders," pp. 135–64 in Pamela Moore (ed.), *Building Bodies*. New Brunswick. Rutgers University Press.

Fiske, John. 1987. *Television Culture*. London. Methuen.

Foucault, Michel. 1967 [1961]. *Madness and Civilization*. London. Tavistock.

Foucault, Michel. 1970 [1966]. *The Order of Things*. London. Tavistock.

Foucault, Michel. 1972 [1969]. *The Archaeology of Knowledge*. London. Tavistock.

Foucault, Michel. 1973 [1963]. *The Birth of the Clinic*. London. Tavistock.

Foucault, Michel. 1988. *Politics, Philosophy, Culture: Interviews and Other Writings, 1977–1984*. London. Routledge.

Foucault, Michel. 1990 [1976]. *The History of Sexuality*. New York. Vintage Books.

Foucault, Michel. 1991a [1975]. *Discipline and Punish*. London. Penguin.

Foucault, Michel. 1991b [1981]. *Remarks on Marx*. Los Angeles. Semiotext(e).

Foucault, Michel. 2005 [2001]. *The Hermeneutics of the Subject: Lectures at the Collège de France, 1981–82*. New York. Palgrave.

Frankenberg, Ruth. 2001. "The Mirage of an Unmarked Whiteness," pp. 72–96 in B. Rasmussen, E. Klinenberg, I. Nexica, and M. Wray (eds.), *The Making and Unmaking of Whiteness*. Durham. Duke University Press.

Fraser, Mariam and Greco, Monica. 2005. *The Body: A Reader*. London. Routledge.

Freud, Sigmund. 1961 [1930]. *Civilization and its Discontents*. New York. W. W. Norton and Company.

Frisby, David. 1984. *Georg Simmel*. London. Tavistock.

Frith, Simon, Goodwin, Andrew, and Grossberg, Lawrence. 1993. (eds.) *Sound and Vision: The Music Video Reader*. Routledge.

Fromm, Erich. 1968 [1956]. *The Sane Society*. London. Routledge and Kegan Paul.

Frow, John. 1998. *Time and Commodity Culture*. Oxford. Oxford University Press.

Frye, Northrop. 1971 [1957]. *Anatomy of Criticism*. Princeton. Princeton University Press.

Gane, Mike. 1991a. *Baudrillard's Bestiary: Baudrillard and Culture*. London. Routledge.

Gane, Mike. 1991b. *Baudrillard: Critical and Fatal Theory*. London. Routledge.

Gane, Mike. 1993. *Baudrillard Live: Selected Interviews*. London. Routledge.

Gans, Herbert. 1999 [1974]. *Popular Culture and High Culture: Analysis and Evaluation of Taste*. New York. Basic Books.

Garfinkel, Harold. 1967. *Studies in Ethnomethodology*. Englewood Cliffs, NJ. Prentice Hall.

Gauntlett, David and Hill, Annette. 1999. *TV Living: Television, Culture and Everyday Life.* London. Routledge.

Gay, Peter. 1961. "Sigmund Freud: A Brief Life," pp. ix–xxii in S. Freud, *Civilization and its Discontents.* New York. W. W. Norton and Company.

Geertz, Clifford. 1975 [1973]. *The Interpretation of Cultures.* London. Hutchinson.

Giddens, Anthony. 1984. *The Constitution of Society.* Cambridge. Cambridge University Press.

Giddens, Anthony. 1991. *Modernity and Self-Identity.* Stanford. Stanford University Press.

Giddens, Anthony. 1994. *Beyond Left and Right.* Cambridge. Polity Press.

Gill, Rosalind, Henwood, Karen, and McLean, Carl. 2005. "Body Projects and the Regulation of Normative Masculinity," *Body & Society* 11, 1: 37–62.

Gilligan, Carol. 1982. *In a Different Voice: Psychological Theory and Women's Development.* Cambridge, MA. Harvard University Press.

Gilroy, Paul. 1987. *There Ain't No Black in the Union Jack.* London. Hutchinson.

Gilroy, Paul. 2000. *Against Race: Imagining Political Culture Beyond the Color Line.* Cambridge. Belknap Press of Harvard University Press.

Gilroy, Paul. 2002 [1992]. "The End of Antiracism," pp. 249–64 in Philomena Essed and David Theo Goldberg (eds.), *Race Critical Theories: Text and Context.* Oxford. Blackwell.

Gilroy, Paul. 2005. *Postcolonial Melancholia.* New York. Columbia University Press.

Gitlin, Todd. 1978. "Media Sociology," *Theory and Society* 6, 2: 205–54.

Gitlin, Todd. 2001. *Media Unlimited.* New York. Metropolitan.

Goffman, Erving. 1959 [1956]. *The Presentation of Self in Everyday Life.* New York. Doubleday.

Goffman, Erving. 1967. *Interaction Ritual.* Chicago. Aldine.

Goffman, Erving. 1968 [1961]. *Asylums.* London. Penguin.

Goffman, Erving. 1974. *Frame Analysis.* New York. Harper and Row.

Goffman, Erving. 1979. *Gender Advertisements.* London. Macmillan.

Goodman, Tanya. 2006. "Performing a 'New' Nation: The Role of the TRC in South Africa," pp. 169–92 in Jeffrey Alexander, Bernhard Giesen, and Jason Mast (eds.), *Social Performance: Symbolic Action, Cultural Pragmatics, and Ritual.* Cambridge. Cambridge University Press.

Goodwin, Andrew. 1992. *Dancing in the Distraction Factory: Music Television and Popular Culture.* Minneapolis. University of Minnesota Press.

Gouldner, Alvin. 1970. *The Coming Crisis of Western Sociology.* London. Heinemann.

Gramsci, Antonio. 1992 [written 1929–33]. *Prison Notebooks Volume 1.* New York. Columbia University Press.

Greenfeld, Liah. 1996. "Praxis Pietatis: A Tribute to Edward Shils," *The American Sociologist* (Winter): 67–82.

Griswold, Wendy. 1986. *Renaissance Revivals.* Chicago. University of Chicago Press.

Griswold, Wendy. 1992. "The writing on the mud wall," *American Sociological Review* 57: 709–24.

Griswold, Wendy. 2003. *Cultures and Societies in a Changing World.* Thousand Oaks. Pine Forge.

Grosz, Elizabeth. 1998. *Jacques Lacan: A Feminist Introduction.* London. Routledge.

Grusky, David B. and Galescu, Gabriela. 2005. "Is Durkheim a class analyst?" pp. 322–59 in Jeffrey Alexander and Phil Smith (eds.), *The Cambridge Companion to Durkheim.* Cambridge. Cambridge University Press.

Habermas, Jürgen. 1978 [1968]. *Knowledge and Human Interests.* London. Heineman.

Habermas, Jürgen. 1981. "Modernity versus Postmodernity," *New German Critique* 22 (Winter): 3–14.

Habermas, Jürgen. 1984 [1981]. *The Theory of Communicative Action.* Boston. Beacon Press.

Habermas, Jürgen. 1989 [1962]. *The Structural Transformation of the Public Sphere*. Cambridge, MA. MIT Press.

Halbwachs, Maurice. 1992 [1925]. *On Collective Memory*. Chicago. University of Chicago Press.

Halkias, Alexandra. 2004. *The Empty Cradle of Democracy: Sex, Abortion, and Nationalism in Modern Greece*. Durham. Duke University Press.

Hall, Stuart. 1980a. "Cultural Studies and the Centre: Some Problematics and Problems," pp. 15–47 in Stuart Hall, Dorothy Hobson, Andrew Lowe, and Paul Willis (eds.), *Culture, Media, Language*. London. Unwin Hyman.

Hall, Stuart. 1980b. "Encoding/Decoding," pp. 128–38 in Stuart Hall, Dorothy Hobson, Andrew Lowe, and Paul Willis (eds.), *Culture, Media, Language*. London. Unwin Hyman.

Hall, Stuart. 1982. "The Rediscovery of Ideology: The Return of the Repressed in Media Studies," pp. 56–90 in Michael Gurevitch, Tony Bennett, James Curran, and Janet Woollacott (eds.), *Culture, Society and the Media*. London. Methuen.

Hall, Stuart. 1983. "The Great Moving Right Show," pp. 19–39 in Stuart Hall and Martin Jacques (eds.), *The Politics of Thatcherism*. London: Lawrence and Wishart.

Hall, Stuart and Jefferson, Tony (eds.). 1976. *Resistance Through Rituals*. London. Hutchinson.

Hall, Stuart, Critcher, Chas, Jefferson, Tony, Clarke, John, and Roberts, Bryan. 1978. *Policing the Crisis*. London. Macmillan.

Hall, Stuart, Hobson, Dorothy, Lowe, Andrew, and Willis, Paul. 1980. *Culture, Media, Language*. London. Unwin Hyman.

Hamilton, Peter. 1983. *Talcott Parsons*. London. Tavistock.

Hancock, Philip et al. (eds.). 2000. *The Body, Culture, and Society: An Introduction*. Buckingham. Open University Press.

Haraway, Donna. 1989. *Primate Visions: Gender, Race, and Nature in the World of Modern Science*. London. Routledge.

Haraway, Donna. 2004a [1991]. "Situated Knowledges: The Science Question in Feminism and the Priviledge of Partial Perspective," pp. 81–102 in Sandra Harding (ed.), *The Feminist Standpoint Theory Reader*. New York. Routledge.

Haraway, Donna. 2004b. *The Haraway Reader*. New York. Routledge.

Harding, Sandra. 1986. *The Science Question in Feminism*. Ithaca. Cornell University Press.

Harding, Sandra. 2004. "Rethinking Standpoint Epistemology: What is 'Strong Objectivity'?," pp. 127–40 in Sandra Harding (ed.), *The Feminist Standpoint Theory Reader*. London. Routledge.

Harris, David. 1992. *From Class Struggle to the Politics of Pleasure*. London. Routledge.

Hartley, John. 1987. "Invisible Fictions: Television Audiences, Paedocracy and Pleasure," *Textual Practice* 1: 121–38.

Hartouni, Valerie. 1997. *Cultural Conceptions: On Reproductive Technologies and the Remaking of Life*. Minneapolis. University of Minnesota Press.

Harvey, David. 1989. *The Condition of Postmodernity*. Oxford. Blackwell.

Hays, Sharon. 1996. *The Cultural Contradictions of Motherhood*. New Haven. Yale University Press.

Hebdige, Dick. 1979. *Subculture: The Meaning of Style*. London. Methuen.

Hebdige, Dick. 1986. "Postmodernism and the Other Side," *Journal of Communication* 10, 2: 78–89.

Heritage, John. 1984. *Garfinkel and Ethnomethodology*. Cambridge. Polity Press.

Hertz, Robert. 1960. *Death and the Right Hand*. London. Cohen and West.

Hirsch, Paul. 1972. "Processing Fads and Fashions," *American Journal of Sociology* 77: 639–59.

Hockey, Jenny and James, Allison. 1995. "Back To Our Futures: Imaging Second Childhood," pp. 135–48 in M. Featherstone and A. Wernick (eds.), *Images of Aging: Cultural Representations of Later Life*. London. Routledge.

Hoggart, Richard. 1957. *The Uses of Literacy*. London. Chatto and Windus.

Holquist, Michael. 1981. "Introduction," pp. xv–xxxiv in M. Bakhtin, *The Dialogic Imagination*. Austin. University of Texas Press.

Horkheimer, Max and Adorno, Theodor. 1972 [1947]. *Dialectic of the Enlightenment*. London. Allen Lane.

Hubert, Henri. 2005 [1905]. *Essay on Time: A Brief Study of the Representation of Time in Religion and Magic*. Oxford. Berghahn.

Irigaray, Luce. 1985 [1977]. *This Sex Which Is Not One*. Ithaca. Cornell University Press.

Irigaray, Luce. 1991. *The Irigaray Reader*, ed. Margaret Whitford. Cambridge, MA. Basil Blackwell.

Jack, Ian. 1997. "Those Who Felt Differently," *Granta* 60: 10–35.

Jacobs, Ronald. 1996. "Civil Society and Crisis," *American Journal of Sociology* 101, 5: 1238–72.

Jameson, Fredric. 1984. "Postmodernism, or the Cultural Logic of Late Capitalism," *New Left Review* 46: 53–92.

Jay, Martin. 1984. *Adorno*. Cambridge, MA. Harvard University Press.

Jencks, Charles. 1977. *The Language of Postmodern Architecture*. London. Academy Editions.

Joas, Hans. 1996 [1992]. *The Creativity of Action*. Chicago. University of Chicago Press.

Johnson, Derek. 2007. "Fan-tagonism: Factions, Institutions, and Constitutive Hegemonies of Fandom," pp. 285–300 in J. Gray, C. Sandvoss, and C. L. Harrington (eds.), *Fandom: Identities and Communities in a Mediated World*. New York. New York University Press.

Junemo, Mattias. 2004. " 'Let's build a Palm Island!': Playfulness in Complex Times," pp. 181–91 in Mimi Sheller and John Urry (eds.), *Tourism Mobilities: Places to Play, Places in Play*. London. Routledge.

Katz, Elihu and Lazarsfeld, Paul. 1956. *Personal Influence*. Glencoe, IL. Free Press.

Katz, Stephen and Marshall, Barbara. 2003. "New Sex for Old: Lifestyle, Consumerism, and the Ethics of Aging Well," *Journal of Aging Studies* 17: 3–16.

Kaufmann, Walter. 1959 [1950]. *Nietzsche: Philosopher, Psychologist, Antichrist*. New York. Meridian Books.

Kertzer, David. 1989. *Ritual, Politics and Power*. New Haven. Yale University Press.

Klesse, Christian. 1999. " 'Modern Primitivism': Non-Mainstream Body Modification and Racialized Representation," *Body & Society* 5, 2–3: 15–38.

Kline, Stephen, Dyer-Witherford, Nick, and De Peuter, Greig. 2003. *Digital Play: The Interaction of Technology, Culture, and Marketing*. Montreal. McGill-Queen's University Press.

Klinenberg, Eric. 2002. "Bodies That Don't Matter: Death and Dereliction in Chicago," pp. 121–36 in Nancy Scheper-Hughes and Loïc Wacquant (eds.), *Commodifying Bodies*. London. Sage.

Klinenberg, Eric. 2007. *Fighting for Air: The Battle to Control America's Media*. New York. Metropolitan.

Kristeva, Julia. 1982 [1980]. *Powers of Horror*. New York. Columbia University Press.

Kroeber, A. L. and Kluckhohn, Clyde. 1952. *Culture: A Critical Review of Concepts and Definitions*. Cambridge, MA. Peabody Museum.

Krzywinska, Tanya. 2006. "Blood Scythes, Festivals, Quests and Backstories: World Creation and Rhetorics of Myth in *World of Warcraft*," *Games and Culture* 1, 4: 383–96.

Kuhn, Thomas. 1970. *The Structure of Scientific Revolution*. Chicago. University of Chicago Press.

Kumar, Krishnan. 1995. *From Post-Industrial to Post-Modern Society*. Oxford. Blackwell.

Lacan, Jacques. 1977. *Ecrits: A Selection*. London. Tavistock.

Lamont, Michèle. 1992. *Money, Morals and Manners*. Chicago. University of Chicago Press.

Lamont, Michèle. 2000. *The Dignity of Working Men: Morality and the Boundaries of Race, Class, and Immigration*. Cambridge, MA. Harvard University Press.

Laqueur, Thomas. 1990. *Making Sex: Body and Gender from the Greeks to Freud*. Cambridge, MA. Harvard University Press.

Lash, Scott. 1988. "Discourse or Figure? Postmodernism as a Regime of Signification," *Theory, Culture and Society* 5: 311–36.

Lash, Scott. 1990a. *Sociology of Postmodernism*. London. Routledge.

Lash, Scott. 1990b. "Learning from Leipzig – or Politics in the Semiotic Society," *Theory, Culture and Society* 7: 145–58.

Lash, Scott and Urry, John. 1993. *Economies of Signs and Spaces*. London. Sage.

Latour, Bruno and Woolgar, Steve. 1979. *Laboratory Life*. Princeton, NJ. Princeton University Press.

Lawton, Julia. 2000. *The Dying Process: Patients' Experience of Palliative Care*. New York. Routledge.

Layder, Derek. 1994. *Understanding Social Theory*. London. Sage.

Lazarsfeld, Paul, Berelson, Bernard, and Gaudet, Hazel. 1944. *The People's Choice*. New York. Columbia University Press.

Leach, Edmund. 1974. *Lévi-Strauss*. London. Fontana.

Lee, Orville. 2004. "Race After the Cultural Turn," pp. 234–250 in M. Jacobs and N. Hanrahan (eds.), *The Blackwell Companion to the Sociology of Culture*. Cambridge, MA. Blackwell.

Lembo, Ron. 2000. *Thinking Through Television*. Cambridge. Cambridge University Press.

Lemert, Charles. 1997. *Postmodernism is Not What You Think*. Oxford. Blackwell.

Lévi-Strauss, Claude. 1963 [1958]. *Structural Anthropology*. Boston. Basic Books.

Lévi-Strauss, Claude. 1964. *Mythologiques*. Paris. Plon.

Lévi-Strauss, Claude. 1966 [1962]. *The Savage Mind*. London. Weidenfeld and Nicolson.

Lévi-Strauss, Claude. 1969 [1949]. *The Elementary Structures of Kinship*. Boston. Beacon Press.

Lévi-Strauss, Claude. 1973 [1955]. *Tristes Tropiques*. London. Jonathan Cape.

Lewis, David L. 1993. *W. E. B. DuBois: Biography of a Race, 1868–1919*. New York: H. Holt.

Lock, Margaret. 2002. "The Alienation of Body Tissue and the Biopolitics of Immortalized Cell Lines," pp. 63–92 in Nancy Scheper-Hughes and Loïc Wacquant (eds.), *Commodifying Bodies*. London. Sage.

Lockwood, David. 1996. *Solidarity and Schism*. Oxford. Clarendon Press.

Lukács, Georg. 1971. *History and Class Consciousness*. London. Merlin Press.

Luker, Kristin. 1984. *Abortion and the Politics of Motherhood*. Berkeley. University of California Press.

Lukes, Steven. 1975. "Political Ritual and Social Integration," *Sociology* 9, 2: 289–308.

Lynch, Michael and Bogen, David. 1994. "Harvey Sacks' Primitive Natural Science," *Theory, Culture and Society* 11, 4: 65–104.

Lyotard, Jean-François. 1974. *Économie Libidinal*. Paris. Minuit.

Lyotard, Jean-François. 1984 [1979]. *The Postmodern Condition*. Manchester. Manchester University Press.

MacCannell, Dean. 1999 [1976]. *The Tourist: A New Theory of the Leisure Class*. Berkeley. University of California Press.

Maffesoli, Michel. 1993 [1982]. *The Shadow of Dionysus*. Albany. State University of New York Press.

Maffesoli, Michel. 1996 [1988]. *The Time of the Tribes*. London. Sage.

Marcuse, Herbert. 1972 [1964]. *One Dimensional Man*. London. Abacus.

Marx, Karl. 1956. *Capital*. Moscow. Progress Publishers.

Marx, Karl. 1978a [written 1844]. *The Economic and Philosophical Manuscripts of 1844*, pp. 66–125 in R. Tucker (ed.), *The Marx–Engels Reader*. New York. Norton.

Marx, Karl. 1978b [1852]. "The Eighteenth Brumaire of Louis Bonaparte," pp. 594–617 in R. Tucker (ed.), *The Marx–Engels Reader*. New York. Norton.

Marx, Karl and Engels, Friedrich. 1978 [1848]. *The Communist Manifesto*, pp. 473–500 in R. Tucker (ed.), *The Marx–Engels Reader*. New York. Norton.

Mast, Jason. 2006. "The Cultural Pragmatics of Event-ness: the Clinton/Lewinsky Affair," pp. 115–45 in Jeffrey Alexander, Bernhard Giesen, and Jason Mast (eds.), *Social Performance: Symbolic Action, Cultural Pragmatics, and Ritual*. Cambridge. Cambridge University Press.

Mauss, Marcel. 1974 [1925]. *The Gift*. Trans I. Cunnison. London. Routledge and Kegan Paul.

Mauss, Marcel. 1979 [1950]. *Sociology and Psychology: Essays*. London. Routledge.

McCarthy, Thomas. 1984. "Translator's Introduction," pp. vii–xxxix in Jürgen Habermas, *The Theory of Communicative Action*, vol. I. Boston. Beacon Press.

McLennan, Gregor. 2004. "Rationalizing Musicality: A Critique of Alexander's 'Strong Program' in Cultural Sociology," *Thesis Eleven* 79, 1: 75–86.

McRobbie, Angela. 1981. "Settling Accounts with Subcultures: A Feminist Critique," pp. 112–24 in Tony Bennett, Graham Martin, Colin Mercer, and Janet Woollacott, *Culture, Ideology and Social Process*. London. Open University Press.

Mellor, Philip and Shilling, Chris. 1997. *Re-forming the Body: Religion, Community, and Modernity*. London. Sage.

Mennell, Stephen. 1992. *Norbert Elias*. Oxford. Blackwell.

Mitchell, Juliet. 1974. *Psychoanalysis and Feminism*. London. Allen Lane.

Molz, Jennie Germann. 2004. "Playing Online and Between the Lines: Round-the-World Websites as Virtual Places to Play," pp. 169–80 in Mimi Sheller and John Urry. *Tourism Mobilities: Places to Play, Places in Play*. London. Routledge.

Monoghan, Lee. 2000. *Bodybuilding, Drugs, and Risk*. London. Routledge.

Morley, David. 1980. *The Nationwide Audience*. London. British Film Institute.

Morley, David. 1986. *Family Television*. London. Comdeia.

Morris, Meaghan. 1988. "The Banality of Cultural Studies," pp. 14–26 in Patricia Mellenkamp (ed.), *Logics of Television*. London. British Film Institute.

Morris, Pam. 1994. "Introduction," pp. 1–24 in *The Bakhtin Reader*. London. Edward Arnold.

Mosco, Vincent. 2004. *The Digital Sublime: Myth, Power and Cyberspace*. Cambridge, MA. MIT Press.

Mulkay, Michael. 1985. *The World and the Word*. London. George Allen and Unwin.

Needham, Rodney. 1963. "Introduction," pp. vii–xlviii in Émile Durkheim and Marcel Mauss (1963 [1903]), *Primitive Classification*. Chicago. University of Chicago Press.

Nietzsche, Friedrich. 1954 [1873]. "On Truth and Lie in an Extra-Moral Sense," pp. 42–7 in W. Kaufmann (ed. and trans.), *The Portable Nietzsche*. London. Penguin Books.

Nietzsche, Friedrich. 1967 [1872]. *The Birth of Tragedy*. New York. Vintage Books.

Nietzsche, Friedrich. 1967 [1887]. *On the Genealogy of Morals*. New York. Vintage Books.

Nietzsche, Friedrich. 1967 [1888]. *Ecce Homo*. New York. Vintage Books.

Nietzsche, Friedrich. 1974 [1887]. *The Gay Science*. New York. Vintage Books.

Noelle-Neumann, Elisabeth. 1993 [1984]. *The Spiral of Silence*. Chicago. University of Chicago Press.

Nora, Pierre. 1996 [1984]. (ed.) *Realms of Memory*. New York. Columbia University Press.

Omi, Michael. 2001. "(E)racism: Emerging Practices of Antiracist Organizations," pp. 266–93 in B. Rasmussen, E. Klinenberg, I. Nexica, and M. Wray (eds.), *The Making and Unmaking of Whiteness*. Durham. Duke University Press.

Omi, Michael and Winant, Howard. 1994. *Racial Formation in the United States from the 1960s to the 1990s*, New York. Routledge.

Paras, Eric. 2006. *Foucault 2.0: Beyond Power and Knowledge*. New York. Other Press.

Parsons, Talcott. 1966. *Societies: Evolutionary and Comparative Perspectives*. Englewood Cliffs, NJ. Prentice Hall.

Parsons, Talcott. 1968 [1937]. *The Structure of Social Action*. New York. Free Press.

Parsons, Talcott. 1970 [1951]. *The Social System*. London. Routledge and Kegan Paul.

Parsons, Talcott. 1971 [1966]. *The System of Modern Societies*. Englewood Cliffs, NJ. Prentice Hall.

Parsons, Talcott and Shils, Edward. 1962 [1951]. (eds.) *Toward a General Theory of Action*. New York. Harper and Row.

Parsons, Talcott and Smelser, Neil. 1966 [1956]. *Economy and Society*. London. Routledge.

Paterson, Kevin. 2001. "Disability Studies and Phenomenology: Finding a Space for both the Carnal and the Political," pp. 81–97 in Sarah Cunningham-Burley and Kathryn Backett-Milburn (eds.), *Exploring the Body*. New York. Palgrave Macmillan.

Patterson, Orlando. 1997. *The Ordeal of Integration: Progress and Resentment in America's "Racial" Crisis*. Washington, DC. Civitas/Counterpoint.

Patterson, Orlando. 1998. *Rituals of Blood: Consequences of Slavery in Two American Centuries*. New York. Basic Books.

Peterson, Richard and Kern, Roger. 1996. "Changing Highbrow Taste: From Snob to Omnivore," *American Sociological Review* 61: 900–7.

Pitts, Victoria. 2003. *In the Flesh: The Cultural Politics of Body Modification*. New York. Palgrave Macmillan.

Pollner, Melvin. 1991. "Left of Ethnomethodology," *American Sociological Review* 56, 3: 370–80.

Powell, Jason. 2006. *Jacques Derrida: A Biography*. London. Continuum.

Propp, Vladimir. 1968 [1928]. *The Morphology of the Folktale*. Austin. University of Texas Press.

Radway, Janice. 1991 [1984]. *Reading the Romance*. Chapel Hill. University of North Carolina Press.

Rambo, Carol, Sara Renee Presley, and Don Mynatt. 2006. "Claiming the Bodies of Exotic Dancers: The Problematic Discourse of Commodification," pp. 213–28 in Dennis Waskul and Phillip Vannini (eds.), *Body/Embodiment: Symbolic Interaction and the Sociology of the Body*. London. Ashgate.

Ratzinger, Joseph and Habermas, Jürgen. 2007. *The Dialectics of Secularization: On Reason and Religion*. Fort Collins. Ignatius Press.

Reed, Isaac. 2007. "Why Salem Made Sense: Culture, Gender, and the Puritan Persecution of Witchcraft," *Cultural Sociology* 1, 2: 209–34.

Reissman, Catherine Kohler. 1993. *Narrative Analysis*. Newbury Park, CA. Sage.

Riley, Alexander. 2005. "The Rebirth of Tragedy out of the Spirit of Hip Hop: A Cultural Sociology of Gangsta Rap Music," *Journal of Youth Studies* 8, 3: 297–311.

Riley, Alexander. 2008. "On the Role of Images in the Construction of Narratives about the Crash of United Airlines Flight 93," *Visual Studies* 23, 1: 4–19.

Ritzer, George. 1996. *The McDonaldization of Society*. Thousand Oaks, CA. Pine Forge Press.

Roberts, Julian. 1982. *Walter Benjamin*. London. Macmillan.

Roediger, David. 2005. *Working Toward Whiteness: How America's Immigrants Became White: The Strange Journey from Ellis Island to the Suburbes.* New York. Basic Books.

Rojek, Chris. 2001. *Celebrity.* London. Reaktion.

Rorty, Richard. 1989. *Contingency, Irony, Solidarity.* Cambridge. Cambridge University Press.

Rose, Nikolas. 1998. *Inventing our Selves: Psychology, Power, and Personhood.* Cambridge. Cambridge University Press.

Rose, Nikolas. 1999 [1990]. *Governing the Soul: The Shaping of the Private Self.* London. Free Association Books.

Rose, Nikolas. 2006. *The Politics of Life Itself: Biomedicine, Power, and Subjectivity in the Twenty-First Century.* Princeton. Princeton University Press.

Sacks, Harvey. 1992 [1964–8]. *Lectures on Conversation: Volume 1.* Oxford. Blackwell.

Saguy, Abigail and Riley, Kevin. 2005. "Weighing Both Sides: Morality, Mortality and Framing Contests over Obesity," *Journal of Health Politics, Policy, and Law* 30, 5: 869–921.

Sahlins, Marshall. 1976. *Culture and Practical Reason.* Chicago. University of Chicago Press.

Said, Edward. 1978. *Orientalism.* London. Routledge and Kegan Paul.

Sandvoss, Cornell. 2005. *Fans: The Mirror of Consumption.* Cambridge. Polity Press.

Saussure, Ferdinand de. 1986 [1916]. *Course in General Linguistics.* La Salle, IL. Open Court Publishing Company.

Scheper-Hughes, Nancy. 2000. "The Global Traffic in Human Organs," *Current Anthropology* 41, 2: 191–224.

Scheper-Hughes, Nancy. 2002. "Commodity Fetishism in Organs Trafficking," pp. 31–62 in Nancy Scheper-Hughes and Loïc Wacquant (eds.), *Commodifying Bodies.* London. Sage.

Schiller, H. I. 1976. *Communications and Cultural Domination.* New York. Sharpe.

Schleifer, Ronald. 1987. *A. J. Greimas and the Nature of Meaning.* London. Routledge.

Scholes, Robert. 1974. *Structuralism in Literature.* New Haven. Yale University Press.

Schulze, Laurie. 1997. "On the Muscle," pp. 9–30 in Pamela Moore (ed.), *Building Bodies.* New Brunswick. Rutgers University Press.

Schutz, Alfred. 1973. *Collected Papers.* The Hague. Martinus Nijhoff.

Schwartz, Barry. 1998. "Postmodenity and Historical Reputation," *Social Forces* 77, 1: 63–103.

Scruton, Roger. 1985. *Thinkers of the New Left.* Longman. Harlow.

Seale, Clive. 1998. *Constructing Death: The Sociology of Dying and Bereavement.* Cambridge. Cambridge University Press.

Segal, Robert. 1996. (ed.) *Structuralism in Myth: Levi-Strauss, Barthes, Dumezil, and Propp.* London. Routledge.

Seidman, Steven. 1991. "Theory as Narrative with a Moral Intent," pp. 47–81 in S. Seidman and D. Wagner (eds.), *Postmodernism and Social Theory.* New York. Blackwell.

Seidman, Steven. 1994. *The Postmodern Turn.* Cambridge. Cambridge University Press.

Seidman, Steven. 1997. *Difference Troubles.* Cambridge. Cambridge University Press.

Sewell, William. 1992. "A Theory of Structure," *American Journal of Sociology* 98, 1: 1–30.

Sheller, Mimi. 2004. "Demobilizing and Remobilizing Caribbean Paradise," pp. 13–21 in M. Sheller and J. Urry (eds.), *Tourism Mobilities: Places to Play, Places in Play.* London. Routledge.

Shepherd, John. 1991. *Music as Social Text.* Cambridge. Polity Press.

Sherwood, Steven, Smith, Philip, and Alexander, Jeffrey. 1993. "The British are Coming . . . ," *Contemporary Sociology* 22, 2: 370–5.

Shilling, Chris. 2003 [1993]. *The Body and Social Theory.* London. Sage.

Shilling, Chris. 2005. *The Body in Culture, Technology and Society.* London. Sage.

Shilling, Chris. 2007. (ed.) *Embodying Sociology: Retrospect, Progress and Prospects.* Oxford. Blackwell.

Shils, Edward. 1975a. "Introduction," pp. vii–xliii in *Centre and Periphery: Essays in Macrosociology*. Chicago. University of Chicago Press.

Shils, Edward. 1975b. "Centre and Periphery," pp. 3–16 in *Centre and Periphery: Essays in Macrosociology*. Chicago. University of Chicago Press.

Shils, Edward. 1975c. "Charisma," pp. 127–34 in *Centre and Periphery: Essays in Macrosociology*. Chicago. University of Chicago Press.

Shils, Edward and Young, Michael. 1975 [1956]. "The Meaning of the Coronation," pp. 135–52 in E. Shils, *Centre and Periphery: Essays in Macrosociology*. Chicago. University of Chicago Press.

Simmel, Georg. 1978 [1900]. *The Philosophy of Money*. London. Routledge and Kegan Paul.

Simmel, Georg. 1986 [1907]. *Schopenhauer and Nietzsche*.

Simmel, Georg. 1997. *Simmel on Culture*, ed. D. Frisby and M. Featherstone. London. Sage.

Skrbis, Zlatko, Kendall, Gavin, and Woodward, Ian. 2004. "Locating Cosmopolitanism: Between Humanist Ideal and Grounded Social Category," *Theory, Culture and Society* 21(6): 115–36.

Smelser, Neil. 1959. *Social Change in the Industrial Revolution*. London. Routledge and Kegan Paul.

Smith, Dorothy. 1990. *Texts, Facts, and Femininity: Exploring the Relations of Ruling*. London. Routledge.

Smith, Dorothy. 2004 [1974]. "Women's Perspective as a Radical Critique of Sociology," pp. 1–13 in Sandra Harding (ed.), *The Feminist Standpoint Theory Reader*. New York. Routledge.

Smith, Dorothy. 2005. *Institutional Ethnography: A Sociology for People*. Lanham. AltaMira.

Smith, Philip. 1991. "Codes and Conflict," *Theory and Society* 20: 103–38.

Smith, Philip. 1994. "The Semiotic Foundations of Media Narratives," *Journal of Narrative and Life History* 4, 1–2: 89–118.

Smith, Philip. 1998. "The New American Cultural Sociology," pp. 1–14 in P. Smith (ed.), *The New American Cultural Sociology*. Cambridge. Cambridge University Press.

Smith, Philip. 1999. "The Elementary Forms of Place and their Transformations," *Qualitative Sociology* 22, 1: 13–36.

Smith, Philip. 2000. "Culture and Charisma," *Acta Sociologica* 43, 2: 101–11.

Smith, Philip. 2004. "Marcel Proust as Successor and Precursor to Pierre Bourdieu: A Fragment," *Thesis Eleven* 79, 1: 105–111.

Smith, Philip. 2005. *Why War? The Cultural Logic of Iraq, the Gulf War, and Suez*. Chicago. University of Chicago Press.

Smith, Philip. 2008. *Punishment and Culture*. Chicago. University of Chicago Press.

Smith, Philip and Alexander, Jeffrey. 1996. "Durkheim's Religious Revival," *American Journal of Sociology* 102, 2: 585–92.

Spillman, Lyn. 1997. *Nation and Commemoration*. Cambridge. Cambridge University Press.

Sterling, Anne-Fausto. 2000. *Sexing the Body: Gender Politics and the Construction of Sexuality*. New York. Basic Books.

Strauss, Anselm. 1956 [1934]. (ed.) *The Social Psychology of George Herbert Mead*. Chicago. University of Chicago Press.

Sullivan, Deborah. 2004. *Cosmetic Surgery: The Cutting Edge of Commercial Medicine in America*. New Brunswick. Rutgers University Press.

Sweetman, Paul. 2001. "Stop Making Sense?: The Problem of the Body in Youth/Sub/Counter-Culture," pp. 183–200 in Sarah Cunningham-Burley and Kathryn Backett-Milburn (eds.), *Exploring the Body*. New York. Palgrave Macmillan.

Swidler, Ann. 2001. *Talk of Love: How Culture Matters*. Chicago. University of Chicago Press.

Thayer, H. S. 1973. *Meaning and Action: A Study of American Pragmatism*. New York. The Bobbs-Merrill Company, Inc.

Thompson, Charis. 2005. *Making Parents: The Ontological Choreography of Reproductive Technologies*. Cambridge, MA. MIT Press.

Thompson, E. P. 1978. *The Poverty of Theory and Other Essays*. London. Merlin Press.

Thornton, Sarah and McRobbie, Angela. 1995. "Rethinking Moral Panics for Mass-Mediated Worlds," *British Journal of Sociology* 46, 4: 559–74.

Tilly, Charles. 1981. "Useless Durkheim," pp. 95–108 in *As Sociology Meets History*. New York. Academic Press.

Tiryakian, Edward. 1995. "Effervescence, Social Change and Charisma," *International Sociology* 10, 3: 269–81.

Tucker, Robert C. 1978. (ed.) *The Marx–Engels Reader*. New York. Norton.

Turkle, Sherry. 1979. *Psychoanalytic Politics*. London. Burnett Books.

Turkle, Sherry. 1995. *Life on the Screen: Identity in the Age of the Internet*. New York. Simon and Schuster.

Turner, Bryan. 1990. (ed.) *Theories of Modernity and Postmodernity*. London. Sage.

Turner, Bryan. 1992. *Regulating Bodies: Essays in Medical Sociology*. New York. Routledge.

Turner, Bryan. 1993. "Baudrillard for Sociologists," pp. 70–87 in B. Turner and C. Rojek (eds.), *Forget Baudrillard*. London. Routledge.

Turner, Bryan. 1994. *Orientalism, Postmodernism and Globalization*. London. Routledge.

Turner, Bryan. 1996 [1984]. *The Body and Society*. London. Sage.

Turner, Bryan. 2000. "Introduction – Bodily Performance: On Aura and Reproducibility," *Body & Society* 11, 4: 1–17.

Turner, Bryan. 2004. *The New Medical Sociology: Social Forms of Health and Illness*. New York. W. W. Norton & Co.

Turner, Graeme. 2002 [1996]. *British Cultural Studies*. London. Routledge.

Turner, Victor. 1974. *Dramas, Fields and Metaphors*. Ithaca. Cornell University Press.

Turner, Victor. 1977 [1969]. *The Ritual Process*. Ithaca, NY. Cornell University Press.

Turner, Victor. 1986. *The Anthropology of Performance*. New York. PAJ Publications.

Vale, V. 1989. *Modern Primitives*. San Francisco. Re/Search Publications.

van Gennep, Arnold. 1960 [1908]. *The Rites of Passage*. London. Routledge and Kegan Paul.

Venturi, Robert, Scott-Brown, Denies, and Izenour, Steven. 1977 [1972]. *Learning from Las Vegas*. Cambridge, MA. MIT Press.

Wacquant, Loïc. 2004. *Body and Soul: Notebooks of an Apprentice Boxer*. Oxford. Oxford University Press.

Wagner-Pacifici, Robin. 1986. *The Moro Morality Play*. Chicago. University of Chicago Press.

Wagner-Pacifici, Robin and Schwartz, Barry. 1992. "The Vietnam Veterans Memorial," *American Journal of Sociology* 97, 2: 376–420.

Warner, W. Lloyd. 1975 [1959]. *The Living and the Dead*. Greenwich CT. Greenwood Press.

Waskul, Dennis. 2003. *Self-Games and Body-Play: Personhood in Online Chat and Cybersex*. New York. Peter Lang.

Waters, Malcolm. 1995. *Globalization*. London. Routledge.

Weber, Max. 1958 [1904]. *The Protestant Ethic and the Spirit of Capitalism*. New York. Charles Scribner's Sons.

Weber, Max. 1968 [1922]. *Economy and Society*. New York. Bedminster Press.

West, Cornell. 1994. "The New Cultural Politics of Difference," pp. 65–81 in S. Seidman (ed.), *The Postmodern Turn*. Cambridge. Cambridge University Press.

White, Harrison and White, Cynthia. 1965. *Canvases and Careers*. New York. Wiley.

Williams, Raymond. 1961. *The Long Revolution*. London. Chatto and Windus.

Williams, Raymond. 1971 [1958]. *Culture and Society*. London. Penguin.

Williams, Raymond. 1976. *Keywords*. New York. Oxford University Press.

Williams, Raymond. 1985 [1977]. *Marxism and Literature*. Oxford. Oxford University Press.

Williams, Simon. 2003. *Medicine and the Body*. London. Sage.

Williams, Simon and Bendelow, Gillian. 1998. *The Lived Body: Sociological Themes, Embodied Issues*. London. Routledge.

Willis, Paul. 1977. *Learning to Labour*. London. Saxon House.

Wilson, William Julius. 1978. *The Declining Significance of Race: Blacks and Changing American Institutions*. Chicago. University of Chicago Press.

Winant, Howard. 2004. *The New Politics of Race: Globalism, Difference, Justice*. Minneapolis. University of Minnesota Press.

Wolff, Janet. 1993. *The Social Production of Art*. London. Macmillan.

Women's Studies Group. 1978. *Women Take Issue*. London. Hutchinson.

Wright Mills, C. 1959. *The Sociological Imagination*. New York. Oxford University Press.

Wuthnow, Robert. 1989. *Communities of Discourse*. Cambridge, MA. Harvard University Press.

Index

accounts/accountability/accounting (in ethnomethodology) 64
ad hocing 65
Adorno, Theodor 39, 41–3, 45, 145, 160, 169–70, 198
  biography 42
advertisements 106
aesthetic and authorial ideology 51
African-American social theory 154, 236–7
agency 4, 27–8, 54, 66–7, 93, 130–1, 135, 136–7, 141, 159, 173, 183, 185, 214, 227, 239
agenda setting (in media) 160–1
AGIL model 29–31, 45
Alexander, Jeffrey 192–3
Alexander, Victoria 171
alienation 7–8, 17, 34, 39, 277
allocation 28–9
Althusser, Louis 46–50, 51, 110, 125, 129, 144, 146, 147, 152, 156, 200–1
  biography 47
  critique of 49–50, 201
  influence on cultural theory 50
Americanization 224
Anatomy of Criticism (Frye) 178, 186
anchoring 148, 155
Anderson, Elijah 23, 25, 242, 250
Andrejevic, Mark 163
Année Sociologique 69
anomie 9–10
Anti-Oedipus (Deleuze and Guattari) 200, 203–4
Apollonian and Dionysian principles 250

Archaeology of Knowledge, The (Foucault) 116–17
architecture 41, 118, 208–9, 218, 221
Aristotle 178
Arnold, Matthew 2
art worlds 168, 171
arts, the 2, 101–2, 132–4, 142, 210, 220, 234, 238
Asylums (Goffman) 58–9
audience *see* reception studies
audience ethnographies *see* reception studies
audience research *see* reception studies
aura 39
authority 14–15
autoethnography 184
autonomy of culture 2–3, 47–8, 94, 99, 112, 117, 126, 144, 148, 156, 173, 179

backstage 57
Baker, Houston 237
Bakhtin, Mikhail 78, 154–5, 180–1, 187–8
  biography 180
  critique of 188
Balzac, Honoré de 75
Barbin, Herculine 256
Barthes, Roland 102–8, 114, 126, 134, 148, 154–5, 176, 182
  biography 108
  critique of 106
  influence on cultural theory 105, 108
base/superstructure model 7, 47–8
Bastille, the 86

Bataille, Georges 74–5, 90, 204
Baudelaire, Charles 40, 75
Baudrillard, Jean 212–17, 238
Bauman, Zygmunt 126, 221–2, 229–31, 233–4, 238
Beck, Ulrich 139, 226–7
Becker, Howard 62, 168, 171, 272, 274
behaviorism 27, 33
Bell, Daniel 217
Bellah, Robert 33, 80–1
Benedict XVI (Pope) 52
Benjamin, Walter 19, 39–41, 146, 218, 220
  biography 40
Bennett, Andy 151
Bennett, Tony 135–6
Berger, Peter 278
Beyond Belief (Bellah) 80
Beyond Left and Right (Giddens) 139
Bhabha, Homi 232, 236–7, 246
Bhaskar, Roy 51, 270
binary opposition/binary codes 96, 98–9, 102, 106, 176–8, 182–3, 193, 229, 233, 236
biopower 118–9
Birmingham School *see* British Cultural Studies
Birth of the Clinic, The (Foucault) 116
Birth of Tragedy out of the Spirit of Music, The (Nietzsche) 21
black underclass 23–4
Blumer, Herbert 56
body
  options 269
  pedagogics 268–9
  projects 269
  regimes 269
  techniques/technologies 271–6
Body and Society, The (Turner) 263–4, 276
Bonaventure Hotel 218
Bond, James 182–3
Bonilla-Silva, Eduardo 241
bons à penser 109
border zone 180
Bouglé, Celestin 74
boundary maintenance 87
Bourdieu, Pierre 16, 19, 50, 65, 100, 110, 128–36, 142, 248, 264–7, 276
  biography 129

critique of 134–6
  influence on cultural theory 128–9, 142
bourgeoisie 7
breaching experiments 64
bricolage/bricoleur 99
British Cultural Studies 38, 43, 88–9, 105, 144–57, 162, 164, 188
  critique of 156–7
Bryson, Bethany 166–7
Buckingham, David 163
bullet model of communication 159–60
bureaucratization 14, 45–6
Butler, Judith 236–7, 255–7, 260

Caillois, Roger 75, 89–90
Calhoun, Craig 221–2, 235, 239
Callinicos, Alex 222–3, 238
capillary nature of power 119
capitalism 7–8, 35, 39, 41–3, 45, 47–9, 104, 138–9, 197–8, 201, 203–4, 217–20, 222, 224
carnival and carnivalesque 77–8, 187–8
Cashmore, Ellis 250
Castells, Manuel 225–6
Castoriadis, Cornelius 204
celeactors and celetoids 167
celebrity culture 167
Center for Contemporary Cultural Studies (CCCS) 144, 147
center and periphery 79, 81–2
charismatic authority 14–15, 82–3
Chicago School 19, 55–6
Chodorow, Nancy 257–8
civil religion 80–1
civil society 36–8, 43–4
Civilization and its Discontents (Freud) 196–7
Civilizing Process, The (Elias) 140–1
class 7, 15, 74, 85, 133, 145–6, 150–3
class consciousness 7, 35
classical social theory, importance of 6
classification 71–2, 74, 78–80, 98–9, 103, 109, 116
Clifford, James 101–2, 191
closed texts 182
closure 114, 124
CMC (computer-mediated communication) 215–16
code of the streets 243–50
Cohen, Stanley 88–9, 152

collective conscience 9, 87
collective effervescence 10, 77
collective memory 72–3, 86–7
Collège de Sociologie 75
Collins, Randall 84–5
colonialism 236
Coming of Post-Industrial Society, The (Bell) 217
commemoration 72–3, 86–7, 173–4
commodities and commodification 35, 40–1, 70, 104, 138–9, 198, 204, 276–8
    see also consumption and consumers
commodity fetishism 35, 104, 277
common-sense knowledge 63–5
communicative reason 45
Communist Manifesto, The (Marx and Engels) 7
communitas 76–7, 85
Communities of Discourse (Wuthnow) 174–5
conjunctural, the 153
connotation 103, 105, 148
Constitution of Society, The (Giddens) 136–8
consumption and consumers 18–19, 24, 39–41, 106, 109, 138–9, 198, 204, 207–8, 212, 218, 222, 227
    see also commodities and commodification
conversation analysis (CA) 66
"cool pose" culture 250
Cooley, Charles 55
corporeal realism 270
corporeal schema 266–7
cosmopolitanism 222–3, 226–7
Course in General Linguistics (Saussure) 93–4
Crane, Diana 158, 168–71
critical realism 51
Crossley, Nick 135, 265–7, 271–2
Cultural Bias (Douglas) 78–80
cultural capital 131–3
Cultural Contradictions of Capitalism, The (Bell) 217
cultural diamond 3
cultural entrepreneurs 170
cultural imperialism 224
cultural omnivorousness 166–7
cultural policy 161, 170
cultural repertoires 243
cultural system, the 28–9
cultural trauma 244
culture industries 41–3, 160, 169

Culture and Practical Reason (Sahlins) 109
Culture and Society (Williams) 146
cybernetic model 31
cyborg 255, 259
Czarnowski, Stefan 74

Das Kapital (Marx) 7–8, 34, 47
Dayan, Daniel 85–6, 173
Daynes, Sarah 248–9
de Certeau, Michel 154–5, 188
De Sade, Marquis de 75, 114
Death and the Right Hand (Hertz) 74
death of the subject 112
decentering the subject 93, 113, 139, 200, 239
decoding 148
de-differentiation 219–20
definitions of culture 1–4
Deleuze, Gilles 200, 203–4
demystification 7
DeNora, Tia 271
denotation 103, 105, 148
Derrida, Jacques 75, 107, 111, 114, 123–7, 144, 179, 233, 236
    biography 125
    influence on cultural theory 125–6
desire 75, 119, 135, 196, 199–204
deviance 9, 62, 87–8, 116, 156
deviance amplification 88
Dewey, John 54–5, 233, 268
diachronic 94, 103
Dialectic of Enlightenment (Horkheimer and Adorno) 41–3, 45, 198
dialogic (Bakhtin on) 180–1
difference 229–31, 234–7
differentiation 219
Dilthey, Wilhelm 12, 35, 188
DiMaggio, Paul 170–1
disapora 246–7, 260
disciplinary power 118
Discipline and Punish (Foucault) 117–18
discourse 116–17, 230–2, 236–7
disenchantment 14, 15–16, 39–40, 178
Distinction (Bourdieu) 132, 135–6
Division of Labor in Society, The (Durkheim) 9, 76, 87
docile body, the 118
documentary culture 146
documentary method, the 65

dominant ideology 7
dominant reading 149
dormant body 279
double consciousness 24
Douglas, Mary 72, 78–80
  critique of 80
dramaturgical metaphor 56–7
duality 136–7
DuBois, W. E. B. 6, 23–5, 243, 250
  biography 25
Duchamp, Marcel 101–2
Dumézil, Georges 101
Durkheim, Emile 9–12, 26, 28, 45, 59,
    69–91, 96–7, 214, 224, 262, 270
  biography 9
  compared to Lévi-Strauss 96–7
  compared to Weber on religion 14
  critique of 11
  influence on cultural theory 9, 11–12,
    69–91, 96–7, 224, 262, 270
Durkheimian cultural theory 69–91
  critique of 83, 90

Eagleton, Terry 51–2
Eco, Umberto 181–3
Economic and Philosophical Manuscripts of
    1844, The (Marx) 7–8, 34–5, 47
Economy and Society (Parsons and Smelser)
    29–30
Economy and Society (Weber) 12–13
education 48
ego, the 195
Elementary Forms of Religious Life, The
    (Durkheim) 10–11, 72, 75, 76, 77, 78,
    81, 83, 87, 91, 96
Elementary Structures of Kinship, The
    (Lévi-Strauss) 97–8
Elements of Semiology (Barthes) 102–3
Elias, Norbert 140–3, 270, 278
  biography 141
  influence on cultural theory 142–3
Eliot, T. S. 145
Elliott, Anthony 204–5
Emmison, Michael 135
emotional energy (EE) 84
emotions 140–1, 143
Empire Strikes Back, The (Centre for
    Contemporary Cultural Studies) 153
encoding 148

environmentalism 139
episteme 117
epistemological break (in Marx) 47
Erikson, Kai 87–8
Essays on the Caste System (Bouglé) 74
etc. clause (in Garfinkel) 65
ethics 121, 139
ethnomethodology 63–7
  critique of 66–7, 137
Evans-Pritchard, E. E. 76
exchange 69–71, 97
exchange theory 27
expert systems 138
Eyerman, Ron 244

face work 59
facticity 253
false consciousness 7
false needs 198
Family Television (Morley) 164
fan fiction (fanfic) 165
fashion 18–19
Fausto-Sterling, Anne 256–7
Feagin, Joe 242
Featherstone, Mike 224–5
feminism/feminist cultural theory 50, 153,
    155, 163–4, 200–1, 230, 253–5, 273
Field of Cultural Production, The (Bourdieu)
    134
fields 133–4
figurational sociology 141
Fiske, John 155, 164
flâneur 40–1
flexible accumulation 219
folk devil 88
Folk Devils and Moral Panics (Cohen) 88–9
food 78, 264, 274
Fordism 219
Foucault, Michel 22, 31, 46, 50, 61, 101,
    115–23, 155, 163, 200, 204, 229,
    231–2, 236, 262–3
  biography 115
  critique of 122
  influence on cultural theory 115, 120,
    126
foundationalism 233
fragmentation of consciousness 35, 39
Frame Analysis (Goffman) 59
Frankfurt School 38–46, 197–8

Freud, Sigmund 28, 95, 195–7, 199–201,
    247, 249
  biography 196
Fromm, Erich 39, 197–8
frontstage 57
Frow, John 135, 222
Frye, Northrop 178–9, 185–7
functionalism 9, 69, 75–6
functions (in Propp) 177

Gadamer, Hans-Georg 188–9
Gainsbourg, Serge 167
game theory 27
Gans, Herbert 165–6
Garfinkel, Harold 63–6
gatekeepers 170–1
Gay Science, The (Nietzsche) 20
Geertz, Clifford 33, 189–92, 231
  critique of 191–2
Geisteswissenschaften 12
Gemeinschaft/Gesellschaft 31
Gender Advertisements (Goffman) 59
general theory 28, 231–2
generalized media of exchange 30–1
genre 178, 182
geology 95
Giddens, Anthony 136–9, 143, 269, 276,
    278
  biography 137
  critique of 138
  influence on cultural theory 143
Gift, The (Mauss) 69–71, 124–5
gift exchange 69–71, 124–5
Gilroy, Paul 153–4, 246–8, 260
Gitlin, Todd 160–1, 165
global, the 224
globalization 223–6
god trick 254
Goffman, Erving 56–61, 62, 84, 138, 262
  biography 57
  critique of 59–61, 62
Goodwin, Andrew 150–1
Gouldner, Alvin 32
governmentality 120
grammatology 123
Gramsci, Antonio 35–8, 50, 144, 146, 147,
    152–4, 244–5
  biography 36
  evaluation 37–8

grand narratives, decline of 211–12
Greimas, Algirdas-Julien 101–2
grid/group model 78–80
Griswold, Wendy 3–4, 158, 169–70, 172,
    184
Grusky, David 85
Guattari, Félix 200, 203–4
Gulf War of 1991 186

Habermas, Jürgen 43–6, 186, 238
  critique of 44, 46
habits 267–8
habitus 130–3, 135, 264–8, 276
Halbwachs, Maurice 72–3, 86, 249
  biography 72
Halkias, Alexandra 259
Hall, Stuart 50, 147–9, 152–3, 155, 163
  biography 149
Haraway, Donna 254–5
Harding, Sandra 230, 242, 253
Harlem Renaissance, the 237
Hartley, John 164–5
Harvey, David 219, 221
Hays, Sharon 258–9
Hebdige, Dick 150, 156
Hegel, G. W. F. 7, 8, 12, 34, 47, 51, 52
hegemonic bloc 37, 153
hegemony 36–7, 147, 150–1, 153
hermeneutics 12, 188–93
Herrschaft 14
Hertz, Robert 74
heteroglossia 181
heterology 75
Hill Collins, Patricia 242, 258, 260
Hirsch, Paul 170
historical changes in meaning of culture
    1–3
history 86, 114–15, 120–1, 218–20
History and Class Consciousness (Lukács) 35
History of Sexuality, The (Foucault) 118–19,
    204
Hoggart, Richard 144, 145–6, 147, 150
Holocaust, the 192–3
Homo Academicus (Bourdieu) 134
homogenization (of global culture) 224–5
horizon of interpretation 189
Horkheimer, Max 39, 41–2, 145, 160,
    169–70, 198
Hubert, Henri 74, 75, 251

Husserl, Edmund 62–3
hybridity 135, 208, 227, 237, 246, 260, 273, 277
hypersimulation 214
hyperspace 218
hypodermic model of communication 159

id, the 195
ideal types 14
identity 17–19, 23–4, 58, 234–7, 265, 268, 271–6
ideological state apparatus (ISA) 48, 152, 200–1
ideology 7, 123–4, 155–7, 159–61
    aesthetic and authorial 51
    of intensive mothering 258
imagination 204–5
immigration 246
impression management 57
indexicality 65
individualism and individuality 17–19, 32, 138–9, 141, 272
informational politics 226
Inheritors, The (Bourdieu and Passeron) 133
institutional ethnography 254
institutionalized individualism 32
integration (of society) 28
Interaction Ritual (Goffman) 59
interpellation 200–1
Interpretation of Cultures (Geertz) 189–91
interpreters (intellectuals as) 231
intersexed 256–7
intersubjectivity 63
intertextuality 210
Iranian Revolution 120–1
Iraq War of 2003 186
Irigaray, Luce 202
iron cage, the 14

Jacobs, Ronald 189–7
James, William 54
Jameson, Fredric 217–18, 238
Jencks, Charles 208–9
jouissance 108, 202
judgmental dope 33, 64

Kant, Immanuel 12
Katz, Elihu 90, 173
Kertzer, David 83

Khomeini, Ayatollah 120
kinship 97
Klinenberg, Eric 278
Kluckhohn, Clyde 1
Knowledge and Human Interests (Habermas) 44
Kristeva, Julia 201–2, 204
Kroeber, Alfred 1
Kuhn, Thomas 230
Kultur 2

labeling theory 62, 88
Lacan, Jacques 49, 105, 112, 144, 155, 199–202, 236
    biography 199
    critique of 200–2
    influence on cultural theory 200
Lamont, Michèle 136, 243–4
language-game 211–12
langue 94, 103
Laqueur, Thomas 257
Lasch, Christopher 138–9
Lash, Scott 219–20, 223
last instance 48
Law of the Father 199–200, 204
Lazarsfeld, Paul 160, 162
Le Corbusier 209
Learning to Labour (Willis) 151
Learning from Las Vegas (Venturi et al.) 209
Leavis, F. R. 2, 145, 146
Lebenswelt 63
Lee, Orville 248–9
legal-rational authority 14–15
legislators (intellectuals as) 231
Lemert, Charles 228, 235
Lemert, Edwin 62
Lennon, John 204–5
Les Lieux de mémoire (Nora) 86
Lévi-Strauss, Claude 46, 71, 74, 93, 94–100, 109, 110, 112, 113, 114, 129, 148, 176–8, 182, 200
    biography 96
    critique of 100
    influences upon 94–7
Leviticus, Book of 78
life and death drives 196–7
lifeworld
    Habermas on 45–6
    in phemonenology 63, 131

liminality 74, 76–8, 188
literary mode of production 51
local, the 224–5
Lockwood, David 11, 90
logocentrism 123, 232
Long Revolution, The (Williams) 146
looking-glass self 55
Louis XIV 124
Lowenthal, Leo 39
Lukács, Georg 19, 34–5, 146
Luker, Kristen 259
Lukes, Steven 83, 90
Lyotard, Jean-François 210–12, 222–3, 228, 231

MacCannell, Dean 216
Madness and Civilization (Foucault) 116
Maffesoli, Michel 90
Maintenon, Madame de 124
Mandel, Ernest 221
Mandela, Nelson 247
Mannheim, Karl 39, 65
Marcuse, Herbert 39, 197–9
Marx, Karl 6–8, 35–6, 47, 95, 119, 224, 244–5, 262, 270, 276–7
  biography 8
  critique of 8
  influence on cultural theory 9, 95, 244–5, 262, 270, 276–7
Marxism and Literature (Williams) 146
Marxism and neo-Marxism 6–8, 34–53, 117, 119, 144–5, 211–12, 219–20, 244–5, 276–7
mass media 39–40, 41–3, 85–6, 88, 147–9, 152–3, 156, 159–62, 208, 226
mass society and mass society hypothesis 42, 159
materialism 7, 34, 95, 109
Mauss, Marcel 69–72, 96, 101, 124–5, 251, 265, 267
  biography 71
McDonaldization 224
McRobbie, Angela 89, 153
Mead, George Herbert 55
means of production 7
means of symbolic production 192–3
mechanical solidarity 9, 31
media *see* mass media
media effects 159–62

Media Events (Dayan and Katz) 85–6, 173
media supersaturation 161
members (in ethnomethodology) 65
membership categorization device (MCD) 65
Mennell, Stephen 142
Merleau-Ponty, Maurice 265–8
metaphysics of presence 123
Metropolis and Mental Life, The (Simmel) 17–18
microphysics of power 119
micro theories 54–68
  evaluation 67–8
mimesis 178, 186
mirror stage 199
Mitchell, Juliet 201
mode of production 7
model reader, the 182
Modern Primitivism 272
modernism 208–10
modernity
  critique of, in postmodern theory 228–31
  Durkheim on 9–10
  Freud on 196–7
  Parsons on 31–2
  Simmel on 17–18
  Weber on 14–15
Modernity and Ambivalence (Bauman) 229
Modernity and Self-Identity (Giddens) 138–9
money 17, 30, 45
Monoghan, Lee 274
monoglossia 181
monologic meaning 180
moral panic 88–9, 152
  critique of 89
Morley, David 163–4
Moro Morality Play, The (Wagner-Pacifici) 185
Morphology of the Folktale, The (Propp) 177
Morris, Meaghan 156
MTV (Music Television) 150–1
Mulkay, Michael 233
multiaccentuality 181
multicultural capital 166–7
multidimensional social theory 33
myth 74, 75, 85, 98–101, 104–6
Mythologies (Barthes) 104–6
mythemes 98

narrative 72–3, 81, 176–9, 183–7, 189–93, 211–12, 216, 218
Nationwide Audience, The (Morley) 163
Natural Symbols (Douglas) 78–80
naturalization (of ideology) 104–5, 147–8
negotiated reading 149
neoclassical economics 27
network society, the 225–6
New Left, the 38, 144, 146
Nietzsche, Friedrich 19–22, 75, 114, 120, 250
  biography 22
Noelle-Neumann, Elisabeth 161
nomadicity 161
Nora, Pierre 86
normalization 118
Nuer Religion (Evans-Pritchard) 76

Oedipus complex 196, 203
Oedipus myth 98, 176, 196
Omi, Michael 244–5
On the Genealogy of Morals (Nietzsche) 20
One Dimensional Man (Marcuse) 198–9
ontological security 138
open texts 182
opinion leaders 161
oppositional reading 149
Order of Things, The (Foucault) 116–17
organic intellectuals 36
organic postmodernism 220
organic solidarity 9
Orientalism (Said) 236
Other, the 201, 226–7
Outline of a Theory of Practice (Bourdieu) 130
outsider within 242

panopticon, the 118, 122
paradigmatic, the 103, 176
paradigms 230
Paras, Eric 121
parole 94, 103
Parsons, Talcott 3, 12, 16, 26–33, 45, 75, 69, 119, 189, 263
  biography 27
  critique of 32, 33, 45, 189
  influence on cultural theory 26, 33, 263
Passeron, Jean-Claude 133
pattern variables 31–2
Patterson, Orlando 249–52

Peirce, Charles Sanders 54–5
personal influence 160
personality system 28
phallocentrism 202
phallus, the 200–2
phenomenology 62–3, 93, 135, 188–9, 267
  critique of 67–8, 93
Philadelphia Negro, The (DuBois) 23–4
Philosophy of Fashion, The (Simmel) 18–19
Philosophy of Money, The (Simmel) 17
Picard, Raymond 134
play 59, 89–90, 209
  forms of play (*agon, alea, ilinx, mimicry*) 90
pleasure principle, the 195–6
Pleasure of the Text, The (Barthes) 107–8, 154, 176
plot 177–87
Policing the Crisis (Hall et al.) 152–3
Pollner, Melvin 66
pollution (symbolic) 74, 78
polymorphous perversity 201
postcolonial melancholia 247
postcolonial theory 126, 144, 154, 155, 225, 236–7
post-Fordism 219
posthuman body 277
postindustrial society 136, 207
postmodern/postmodernism/postmodernity 19, 33, 50, 52, 87, 111–12, 139, 151, 153, 154, 156, 162, 164–5, 190–2, 203–4, 207–40
  critique of 217–23, 237–9
  definitions of 207–8
  postmodern culture and society, characteristics of 207–27
  postmodern and poststructural critical theory 228–40
  postmodernism in art and architecture 210, 217–19
poststructuralism 19, 50, 93, 107–8, 111–27, 154, 156, 162, 188–9, 191, 199–204, 228–31
  contrasted with structuralism 112–15
  core characteristics 113–15
power 20, 30–1, 36, 45, 48, 82, 100, 114, 117–20, 133–4, 200–2
pragmatism 54–5, 68, 233
Presentation of Self in Everyday Life, The (Goffman) 56–8

Primitive Classification (Durkheim and Mauss)
    71–2, 78
Prison Notebooks (Gramsci) 36–7
process sociology 141
production of culture 158, 167–75
profane, the 10, 71, 74, 78, 251
proletariat 7
Propp, Vladimir 177–8, 182
props 57
Protestant ethic, the 13–14, 19, 61
Protestant Ethic and the Spirit of Capitalism,
    The (Weber) 13–14
Proust, Marcel 135
Pruitt-Igoe housing scheme 208–9
psychoanalysis *see* psychoanalytic
    approaches
psychoanalytic approaches 195–206, 247,
    249
  critique of 205
Psychoanalysis and Feminism (Mitchell)
    201
public sphere 43–4, 185–7
punk 150
pure/impure 71, 74, 78–80
Purity and Danger (Douglas) 78

queer theory 126, 144, 236

Rabelais and his World (Bakhtin) 187–8
race 23–5, 152–4, 230, 235, 241–61
  practices 248
racial ensemble 248
racial formation 244–5
racial identity 241–8
racial inbetweenness 245
racial projects 244
Radcliffe-Brown, A. R. 69, 76
Radway, Janice 163–4, 184
rap music 90
rational actor models 27
rationalization 15, 16–17, 38, 42, 46, 48,
    50, 208–10, 212, 224, 238
readerly, the 107, 181–2
reading (of culture) 39–40, 106–8, 149,
    161–5, 173, 181–3,
reality television 159, 163, 167
reception studies 43, 126, 161–5
reciprocity of perspectives 63
reflexive body techniques 267, 271

reflexive modernization 139
reflexive sociology 130
reification 35
relations of production 7
relations of ruling 253
relative autonomy 48
relativism 122, 190–1, 223, 227, 229, 231,
    239
religion 10–11, 13–14
repression (in psychoanalysis) 196–7, 204
repressive desublimation 198
repressive state apparatus (RSA) 48
reproduction (of capitalism) 47–8
Resistance Through Rituals (Hall and Jefferson)
    150
ressentiment 20, 21
revaluation of all values 19–20
Ricoeur, Paul 188–9
Riley, Alexander 90
risk society 80, 139, 275
rite of passage 58
Rite of Passage, The (van Gennep) 58
ritual 10–11, 21, 58, 59, 70, 74–5, 77, 81,
    83–7, 89–90, 117, 251, 271
  formal 84–5
  natural 85
Ritual Process, The (Turner) 76–8
Ritzer, George 224
Roediger, David 245–6
Rojek, Chris 167
role distance 57
roles 28, 57
romance (genre of) 178–9, 187
Romanticism 1, 3
Rorty, Richard 126, 233
Rose, Nikolas 120
rules and resources (in Giddens) 137
Ruskin, John 2

Sacks, Harvey 65
sacred, the 10, 39, 52, 59, 71, 74–5, 81–3,
    90, 251
sacrifice 52, 251–2
Sahlins, Marshall 109
Said, Edward 236
Salem witch trials 87–8, 193
salvation 13–14
Sane Society, The (Fromm) 197–8
Sartre, Jean-Paul 93, 120, 129

Saussure, Ferdinand de 93–4, 96, 103, 123, 148, 176, 193, 199
   critique of 123, 181
Savage Mind, The (Lévi-Strauss) 93, 98–9
scene 151
Scheper-Hughes, Nancy 277
Schutz, Alfred 63, 131
Schwartz, Barry 86–7, 173–4
science
   postmodern critique of 229–32
   social studies of 66, 175, 229–31, 233
science of the concrete 99
Science Question in Feminism, The (Harding) 230
Seidman, Steven 223, 231
self, the 17–18, 56–9, 118, 130–1, 135, 138–9, 140–1, 196–205, 268–9, 271–9
self-stigmatization 272
semanalysis 202
semiotic square 101–2
semiotics 55, 67, 93–4, 101–5
sensitization 88
sensual sociology 268
Sewell, William 135, 138
sex and sexuality 75, 108, 118–19, 195–202, 249–50, 254–7, 259, 272–3, 276, 277–8
Shepherd, John 150
Shilling, Chris 268–70, 279
Shils, Edward 16, 33, 81–3, 90
   biography 82
Simmel, Georg 16–19, 34, 242
   biography 17
   influence on cultural theory 19
simulacrum 212, 220, 222
simulation 212–16
situated knowledge 254
Smith, Dorothy 253, 260
Smith, Philip 84, 86, 122, 135, 193
social drama (Turner) 184–5
social facts (Durkheim) 9, 10, 137
social movements 220, 235
social system, the 28–9
Social System, The (Parsons) 28–9, 31
socialization 26, 28, 137, 141
Societies: Evolutionary and Comparative Aspects (Parsons) 32
solidaristic bloc 37

solidarity 9
somatic society 263–4
Souls of Black Folk, The (DuBois) 24
sovereign power 117–18, 122
space 40–1, 71, 86, 208–9, 218, 220, 226
   of flows 226
species being 7–8
spectral postmodernism 220
Spillman, Lyn 87
spiral of silence 161
standpoint epistemology 230
state, the 35–6, 38, 43, 45, 47, 48, 258–9
status 11, 15, 16, 19, 24, 271
stranger 242
strategies of action 4
Structural Anthropology (Lévi-Strauss) 96, 98
structuralism 46, 92–110, 111–15, 176–9, 181, 191
   critique of 100, 109–10, 113–15, 130, 191–2
   influence on cultural theory 111
structuralist poetics 176–9
   critique of 179
structural linguistics 93–4, 96, 97–8, 123
structuration and structuration theory 136–8
structure of feeling (Williams) 146
Structure of Scientific Revolution, The (Kuhn) 230
Structure of Social Action, The (Parsons) 26–7, 64
Studies in Ethnomethodology (Garfinkel) 64–5, 66
subaltern 245
Subculture: The Meaning of Style (Hebdige) 150
subculture, study of 150–1, 153
subject positions 49, 200–1
Suicide (Durkheim) 10
superego, the 195
supplements 124
symbolic exchange 214
symbolic interactionism 19, 55–62
Symbolic Law 199–200
symbols/symbolic classification 29, 55, 63, 71–2, 74, 78, 98–9, 109
synchronic 94, 103
syntagm 1–3
syntagmatic 103

System of Modern Societies, The (Parsons) 32
systems of transformation 99
systems theory
    (Althusser) 46–9
    (Habermas) 45
    (Marxist) critique of 119
    (Parsons) 28–31
system world (Habermas on) 45
S/Z (Barthes) 107, 176

taken-for-granted, the 63–4
taking the role of the other 55
    generalized other 55
    significant other 55
taste
    culture 165–7
    publics 165–6
technologies of the body 271, 278
Television Culture (Fiske) 155, 164
texts 253–4
textuality 232
Thatcherism 147, 152–3
Theory of Communicative Action, The
    (Habermas) 44–6
theory, definition of 4
There Ain't No Black in the Union Jack (Gilroy)
    154
thick description 188–91
thick/hot and thin/cool societies 271–2
Thompson, Charis 259
Thompson, E. P. 49–50
Thornton, Sarah 89
Tilly, Charles 90–1
Tiryakian, Edward 84
Toennies, Ferdinand 31
total institution 58–9
totalism *see* totality
totality
    postmodernism on 229
    Western Marxism on 35, 39
tourism 216–17, 223
Toward a General Theory of Action (Parsons
    and Shils) 28–9, 31, 64, 81
trace 124
traditional authority 14
tragedy (genre of) 52, 179, 187
trifunctional hypothesis 101
Tristes Tropiques (Lévi-Strauss) 94
Turkle, Sherry 203–4, 215

Turner, Bryan 215, 263–4, 271–2, 276
Turner, Graeme 147
Turner, Victor 76–8, 85, 184–5, 188, 192,
two-step flow of communication 160
typification 63

universalism 31, 32
Uses of Literacy, The (Hoggart) 145–6
utilitarian dilemma, the 27
utilitarian model of human action 27

value generalization 32, 45
values (Parsons on) 29–30, 32, 158
van der Rohe, Mies 209
van Gennep, Arnold 58, 76–7
van Gogh, Vincent 218
Venturi, Robert 209
Verstehen 12–13, 16, 54, 56
video games 216
Vietnam Veterans Memorial 86, 173–4
voluntaristic model of action 28

Wacquant, Loïc 267–8
Wagner-Pacifici, Robin 86, 173–4, 185,
    187
waning of affect 218
Warhol, Andy 218
Warner, Lloyd 81, 83
Waskul, Dennis 215–16
Watergate 193
Wayward Puritans (Erikson) 87–8
Weber, Marianne 252
Weber, Max 12–16, 19, 26, 28, 34, 38, 81,
    82, 119, 129, 219, 224, 262–4
    biography 15
    compared to Durkheim on religion 14
    critique of 15–16
    influence on cultural theory 16, 263–4
Wertrational 13–4
West, Cornell 234–5
Western Marxism 34–53
    critique of 50, 114
    influence of 50
White, Cynthia 171
White, Harrison 171
whiteness studies 245–6, 260
Wildavsky, Aaron 79
will to power 20–1
Williams, Raymond 1, 144, 145–6

Williams, Simon 278–9
Willis, Paul 151
Wilson, William Julius 241
Winant, Howard 244–5
Wolff, Janet 167–8
Women Take Issue (Women's Studies Group) 153
Work of Art in the Age of Mechanical Reproduction (Benjamin) 39–40
working-class culture 145–6, 150–1
workout culture 273–4

Wright Mills, C. 32
writerly, the 107
Writing Culture (Clifford and Marcus) 191
Wuthnow, Robert 174–5

Yale Strong Program in cultural sociology 192–3
youth culture 150–1, 153

Zeitgeist 146
Zweckrationalität 13–14, 38, 41, 45